Gender and Politics

Series Editors
Johanna Kantola
Senior Lecturer in Gender Studies
University of Helsinki
Helsinki, Finland

Sarah Childs
Professor of Politics and Gender
University of Bristol
Bristol, UK

'This first significant book on how Muslim women participate in western civic and political life and develop their capacity for action, examines issues concerning Muslim women and what motivates or hinders their participation. It represents impressive field research which nonetheless cannot be reduced to empiricism since the authors present a theoretical frame combining Archer and Touraine's orientations with a feminist approach. There are innovative results - that Muslim women are not passive, male-dominated or alienated; they are subjects.'

—Michel Wieviorka, Director,
Maison des Sciences de l'Homme, Paris, France

'Khursheed Wadia and Danièle Joly present the results of a 4-year empirical research among Muslim women in France and Britain. The results reveal the level of political awareness and diverse forms of political participation that defy western perceptions of 'the subdued Muslim woman'. This work is a welcome addition to gender studies and political science.'

—Professor Jocelyne Cesari,
University of Birmingham, UK

'Pioneering but accessible, the authors of this excellent book bring a comparative understanding to a topic that is frequently misunderstood. *Muslim Women and Power* will prove invaluable to students, researchers and policy makers alike.'

—Professor Nasar Meer,
Strathclyde University, Glasgow, UK

The Gender and Politics series celebrates its 5th anniversary at the 4th European Conference on Politics and Gender (ECPG) in June 2015 in Uppsala, Sweden. The original idea for the book series was envisioned by the series editors Johanna Kantola and Judith Squires at the first ECPG in Belfast in 2009, and the series was officially launched at the Conference in Budapest in 2011. In 2014, Sarah Childs became the co-editor of the series, together with Johanna Kantola. Gender and Politics showcases the very best international writing. It publishes world class monographs and edited collections from scholars - junior and well established - working in politics, international relations and public policy, with specific reference to questions of gender. The 15 titles that have come out over the past five years make key contributions to debates on intersectionality and diversity, gender equality, social movements, Europeanization and institutionalism, governance and norms, policies, and political institutions. Set in European, US and Latin American contexts, these books provide rich new empirical findings and push forward boundaries of feminist and politics conceptual and theoretical research. The editors welcome the highest quality international research on these topics and beyond, and look for proposals on feminist political theory; on recent political transformations such as the economic crisis or the rise of the populist right; as well as proposals on continuing feminist dilemmas around participation and representation, specific gendered policy fields, and policy making mechanisms. The series can also include books published as a Palgrave pivot.

Editorial Advisory Board
Louise Chappell, School of Social Sciences, University of New South Wales, Australia
Joni Lovenduksi, Birkbeck College, University of London, UK
Amy Mazur, Washington State University, USA
Judith Squires, University of Bristol, UK
Jacqui True, Monash University, Australia
Mieke Verloo, Radboud University Nijmegen, The Netherlands
Laurel Weldon, Purdue University, USA

More information about this series at
http://www.springer.com/series/14998

Danièle Joly • Khursheed Wadia

Muslim Women and Power

Political and Civic Engagement in West European Societies

Danièle Joly
Emeritus Professor
University of Warwick, UK

Khursheed Wadia
University of Warwick, UK

EHESS, MSH, Paris, France

Gender and Politics
ISBN 978-1-349-69398-6   ISBN 978-1-137-48062-0   (eBook)
DOI 10.1057/978-1-137-48062-0

Library of Congress Control Number: 2016963259

© The Editor(s) (if applicable) and The Author(s) 2017
Softcover reprint of the hardcover 1st edition 2017 978-1-137-48061-3

The author(s) has/have asserted their right(s) to be identified as the author(s) of this work in accordance with the Copyright, Designs and Patents Act 1988.
This work is subject to copyright. All rights are solely and exclusively licensed by the Publisher, whether the whole or part of the material is concerned, specifically the rights of translation, reprinting, reuse of illustrations, recitation, broadcasting, reproduction on microfilms or in any other physical way, and transmission or information storage and retrieval, electronic adaptation, computer software, or by similar or dissimilar methodology now known or hereafter developed.
The use of general descriptive names, registered names, trademarks, service marks, etc. in this publication does not imply, even in the absence of a specific statement, that such names are exempt from the relevant protective laws and regulations and therefore free for general use.
The publisher, the authors and the editors are safe to assume that the advice and information in this book are believed to be true and accurate at the date of publication. Neither the publisher nor the authors or the editors give a warranty, express or implied, with respect to the material contained herein or for any errors or omissions that may have been made. The publisher remains neutral with regard to jurisdictional claims in published maps and institutional affiliations.

Cover illustration: © Ikon Images / Alamy Stock Photo

Printed on acid-free paper

This Palgrave Macmillan imprint is published by Springer Nature
The registered company is Macmillan Publishers Ltd.
The registered company address is: The Campus, 4 Crinan Street, London, N1 9XW, United Kingdom

Acknowledgements

This book is an outcome of a four-year project 'Women from Muslim communities and politics in Britain and France', funded by the Economic and Social Research Council (ESRC),[1] which ran from June 2007 to May 2011. We owe thanks to many people who contributed in so many ways to the project while it ran and to the writing of this book. First and foremost we owe a huge debt of gratitude to our respondents in Britain and France—those who very generously made time to be interviewed (sometimes more than once), those who took part in the Sociological Intervention focus groups over a period of weeks and those who responded to the survey. We are also indebted to the various community organisations and campaign groups which allowed us to join meetings and other events as observers and to Ipsos-Mori for permitting use of their survey questionnaire on political engagement. We worked with a number of wonderful people. Among them were Alexandra Poli and Giulia Fabbiano, both researchers based at the CADIS—Centre d'Analyse et d'Intervention Sociologiques (at the École des Hautes Études en Sciences Sociales Paris)—with whom we had many long and lively discussions and without whom the French part of the project could not have been achieved; they remain our close and valued colleagues. We would also like to thank Michel Wieviorka and Philippe Bataille (both directors of the CADIS while the project and writing of this book was under way) who agreed to partner us in this research and responded positively to every help that we requested. Others who made a key contribution include Angèle Malatre, Audrey Lenoël, Charlotte Cavaillé, Clothilde Giner, Alice Moscaritolo and Jaber Ferhat—thank you all for assisting so very efficiently and cheerfully with the fieldwork in both countries, by undertaking some of the interviews and observations, organising the Sociological Intervention sessions, transcribing audio recordings and translating some of the material. Georgina Collins, Nicolas Jara-Joly and Zubin Bativala deserve our gratitude for helping with the compilation of the register of community organisations, NGOs and statutory bodies dealing with Muslim women's issues and for translating some of the source material. Gill Allwood at Nottingham Trent University commented on some of the chapter drafts—thank you for your invaluable remarks and edits. Many other people have taken an interest in our research and this book on Muslim women and politics and have offered useful insights and we would like to thank them too, in particular our closest colleagues at the University of Warwick, the École des Hautes Études en Sciences Sociales and the Fondation Maison des Sciences de l'Homme, Paris. Last but not least, we are grateful to the editorial staff at Palgrave Macmillan for their encouragement and support in the writing of this book and to the anonymous reviewers who saw merit in the book proposal and at the same time offered suggestions on how to improve it. All responsibility for translations (unless otherwise stated), interpretations of colleagues' comments and remaining errors rests on us.

NOTE

1. Grant reference RES-062-23-0380.

Contents

1	**Introduction**	1
	Aims and Scope of the Research	5
	How the Study Was Carried Out	9
	Structure of the Book	15

Part I Concepts and Contexts … 21

2	**Muslim Women and Politics: Analytical Framework**	23
	Introduction	23
	Conceptual Bases	23
	Muslim Women and Politics	28
	Ethnicity and Religion	30
	Majority Society	31
	Muslim Women Within Majority Society	32
	Ethnic Group	33
	Islam, Muslim Group	36
	Conclusion	45
3	**Muslims and Women in Britain and France**	47
	Introduction	47
	Muslims and Islam in British and French Society	48

	Muslim Women Between Feminism and the State	69
	Conclusion	80
4	**Migrations, Demographics and Socio-Economic Profiles**	**85**
	Introduction	85
	Debates on Population Categorisation and Ethnic Monitoring in Britain and France	86
	Muslims in Britain and France: Migration Histories	91
	Muslims in Britain and France: Demographic Profile	95
	A Sociological Profile of Women from Muslim Communities in Britain and France	104
	Conclusion	117

Part II Muslim Women, Politics and Action   121

5	**Politics and Activisms**	**123**
	Introduction	123
	Political Participation and Civic Engagement: Literatures and Approaches	123
	Interest in Politics and Typology of Political Participation and Civic Engagement	127
	Muslims/Muslim Women as Voters	133
	Muslim Women's Activism in Community Organisations	145
	The Growing Visibility of Muslim Women's Organisations in the 9/11 Era	152
	Conclusion	159
6	**Ethnic Group and Islam**	**163**
	Introduction	163
	The Ethnic Group	164
	Islam and the Muslim Group	178
	Conclusion	193
7	**Majority Society and Women's Capacity of Action**	**197**
	Introduction	197
	Majority Society: Britain	197

Majority Society: France		204
Muslim Women and Action		212
A Typology of Strategies		225
Conclusion		228
8	**Islamic Dress, the War on Terror, Policing Muslim Women**	**231**
	Introduction	231
	Issues of Concern to Women from Muslim Communities	232
	Islamic Dress	236
	The War on Terror—Britain	250
	Policing Women's Behaviour—France	254
	Conclusion	257
9	**Conclusion**	**261**
References		**273**
Index		**305**

GLOSSARY

Arabe (French) Second (or even third) generation of French citizens of North African descent. The word also applies to Arabs in general, but in contemporary France it applies mainly to people of North African background who live in disadvantaged inner city areas.

Banlieue (French) A disadvantaged inner city area, with roughly the same meaning as *cité*. Originally, the word simply meant 'city' but now refers largely to areas with high unemployment, deprivation, crime rates, feelings of insecurity and a high density of inhabitants of North African, sub-Saharan African or South East Asian origin.

Barelvi (Urdu) Sufi movement originating in South Asia, opposed to Salafism and claiming to be the only legitimate form of Islam in that region.

Beur (French) An inverted and modified slang form of *Arabe* (see above). The word can carry a derogatory connotation resented by many people, including Arabs.

Biradari (Urdu) System of kinship networks within South Asian Muslim communities.

Burka (Arabic) A one-piece veil worn by Muslim women in public and in front of males who are not immediate family members, and which is taken to be a religious and/or cultural obligation, which covers the head,

Cité

Conseil d'État

Deobandi

Eid

Étranger

Fatwa

face and body, leaving a mesh screen, in front of the eyes, through which one may see.

(French) A poor inner city area where levels of poverty and exclusion are high. *Cités* are usually part of municipal authorities, but the word can also apply to districts of a city, such as Clichy-sous-Bois in Paris, inhabited by disadvantaged populations.

(French) France's highest administrative court which also acts as legal adviser to the executive branch of the state.

(Persian, Urdu, Pashto, Bengali, Hindi) A revivalist movement in Islam, founded in Deoband, India, in the wake of the failed revolt against British imperial rule, in 1867. It advocates the purification of Islam, tainted by Western influences as they see it, and a return to original Qur'anic models as embraced by the Prophet Muhammad.

(Arabic) Eid al-Fitr is the annual Muslim festival which marks the end of the holy month of fasting—*Ramadan*. Eid al-Adha is the annual Muslim festival of sacrifice which honours the Prophet Ibrahim's willingness to sacrifice his son, as an act of submission to God. Eid is an occasion for getting together with family and friends and exchanging gifts.

(French) Meaning 'foreigner', this constitutes a legal status which refers to anyone resident in France but who is a non-national; that is, someone who does not possess French citizenship but has another foreign nationality or no nationality. A person born in France, of non-national parents, is not automatically granted French citizenship but may acquire it through naturalisation. Neither is she/he considered an immigrant or *immigré* (see below).

(Arabic) An Islamic legal decision made by an expert in religious law (*mufti*) on a specific matter. It is usually issued at the request of an individual or judge in cases where Islamic jurisprudence is unclear. It is not a death sentence, as is commonly assumed in the West.

GLOSSARY xiii

Foulard (French) Meaning 'scarf' refers to the Muslim headscarf or *hijab*. It is often used interchangeably with *voile* as in 'l'affaire du foulard'/'l'affaire du voile' (the headscarf affair).

Francité (French) Being French or Frenchness.

Fundamentalist (English) A theological term originating in late-nineteenth-century Protestantism in the USA, but which has come to mean 'radically extreme'. Journalists use *fondamentaliste* interchangeably with '*intégriste*' (see below) in French. Muslims often take exception to being called 'fundamentalist', since it implies that one should not follow the fundamentals, which would then lead to heresy.

Hadith (Arabic) Meaning 'report', in Muslim terminology it usually refers to a report of what the Prophet Muhammad said.

Halal (Arabic) 'Licit' or 'permissible'; that is, in accordance with Muslim jurisprudence. It often refers to food, which would mean food which is licit or permissible to eat, since certain types of foods are not permissible under Muslim jurisprudence.

Haram (Arabic) That which is 'illicit' or 'forbidden', according to Muslim jurisprudence.

Harkis (Arabic) North African troops who remained loyal to France during the struggle for Algerian independence.

Haut Conseil à l'Intégration (French) The High Council on Integration is an agency of the state, overseeing the integration of minorities into French society.

Hijab (Arabic) A 'concealment' or 'barrier'; in Muslim terminology, it refers to a garment covering the head, but not the face, which many Muslim women wear in public and in front of males who are not immediate family members; it is taken to be a religious and/or cultural obligation.

Hizb ut-Tahrir (Arabic) 'Party of Liberation'; a political movement which originated in Jerusalem in the 1950s, dedicated to creating an Islamic revolutionary state in the Arab world.

Ijtihad (Arabic) An Islamic legal term meaning independent reasoning, it can be applied to the reinterpreting of sacred Qur'anic texts and *hadiths* in order to challenge established interpretations, including dominant male interpretations of Islam, and to generate new thinking and action, independent of existing schools of Islamic jurisprudence.

Imam (Arabic) Muslim religious leader.

Immigré (French) An immigrant is legally defined as someone born a 'foreigner', outside France but who is ordinarily resident in France. Those born abroad but with French nationality (i.e. of parents who are French nationals) and who ordinarily reside in France are not counted as immigrants. Immigrants can become French through naturalisation. However, the attribute and label 'immigrant' is permanent even when one acquires French nationality through naturalisation. Over and above the legal definition of the term, French children of non-White immigrant background are often referred to as 'issus de l'immigration' whether they are of 'second', 'third' or subsequent generations.

Intégriste (French) A person whose religious outlook is not compatible with the French expectation that religious feelings should not be expressed in public and who is suspected of being mildly intolerant. The term is ambiguous enough to be used sometimes to include all outlooks which call *laïcité* into question. See also fundamentalist.

Intifada (Arabic) 'Uprising' referring to the Palestinian revolt against Israeli occupation of the West Bank and Gaza which lasted from 1987 to 1991 (the First Intifada) and that against Israel which occurred repeatedly between 2000 and 2005 (the Al-Aqsa Intifada).

Izzat (Urdu) Honour or reputation—generally of the family or household.

Jamaat-e-Islami (Urdu) A follower or member of the Jamaat-e-Islami (JI) Party founded in Pakistan in 1941. JI is a highly conservative Islamic party whose objective is to transform Pakistan from its current state as a liberal

	parliamentary democracy to a fully fledged Sharia-governed state.
Jeunes	(French) Often used to refer to young men who live in the *banlieues*. It is a vague term, including men as old as 30, and can refer specifically to young Frenchmen of Arab descent. It can be a euphemistic way of avoiding direct talk of ethnicity.
Jihad	(Arabic) Meaning 'struggle' or 'striving', it can take a number of different forms, whether a militaristic form in defence of Islam, or the eradication of poverty and so on. It is commonly and misleadingly translated as 'holy war'.
Jilbab	(Arabic) Refers to any long and loose-fitting coat or floor-length over-garment worn by some Muslim women in public and in front of males who are not immediate family members; it is taken to be a religious and/or cultural obligation.
Khalifa	(Arabic) Political and military leader or successor of Prophet Muhammad.
Laïcité	(French) A legal, moral and political principle of state neutrality in matters of religion which excludes the latter from the public sphere.
Maghrebi	(English) An English translation of *maghrébin*; see below.
Maghrébin	(French) A person from the former French colonies of Algeria, Morocco or Tunisia, or a descendant of immigrants from North Africa to France; also referred to as North African in this book.
Markazi Jamiat-al-e-Hadith	(Urdu) Salafist Islam found largely in India and Pakistan which teaches what are considered to be the original or fundamental tenets of Islam.
Niqab	(Arabic) Also referred to as the 'face veil' or 'full-face veil', the niqab is a piece of cloth covering the face, but not the eyes, which is worn by some Muslim women in public and in front of males who are not immediate family members. It is taken to be a religious and/or cultural obligation.

Salafi (Arabic) An adjective derived from *salaf*, meaning 'predecessor'. Today, it refers to the first three generations of Muslims starting with the Companions of the Prophet and is a movement amongst Sunni Muslims who claim to follow what they see as the original ways of Islam. The assertion, implicitly and explicitly, is that Muslims not of this movement have strayed from that original practice, something which the majority of the Muslim world community does not accept.

Tariqa (Arabic) A school or order of Sufism which seeks ultimate truth through a set of spiritual practices.

Ulema (Arabic) Generally a scholar or learned person; more specifically, a scholar of Muslim religious law.

Ummah (Arabic) A community of people comprising all Muslims across the world regardless of their nationality. Ummah should not be confused with 'nation', a political concept describing a community of people(s) within a legal territorial entity, with its own government, where citizenship is accessed regardless of religious belonging.

Veil (English) The term veil is often used generically in public and political discourses to refer to various forms of Islamic dress.

Voile (French) A generic term used widely at the time of the *affaire du foulard* (1989) and since then to describe all forms of head and face covering worn by Muslim women.

Wahhabi (Arabic) A member of a strict orthodox sect of Sunni Islam, Wahhabism (founded in the eighteenth century), who would advocate a return to early Islamic models and practices. Wahhabis constitute the dominant religious force in Saudi Arabia.

List of Tables

Table 4.1	Muslims in the UK	96
Table 4.2	Age profile of Muslims	97
Table 4.3	Muslims and country of birth	98
Table 4.4	Muslims and ethnicity	99
Table 4.5	Estimates of Muslims in France 1998–1999	102
Table 4.6	Muslims in France: a young population (percentage)	103
Table 4.7	Unemployment according to country of birth: 25–64 age group (percentage)	108
Table 4.8	Unemployment of descendants of immigrants according to sex and parents'/grandparents' country of birth (percentage)	109
Table 4.9	Unemployment rates by religion and sex (16–64 years) (percentage)	110
Table 4.10	Highest level of qualification by religion 16+ years (percentage) 2001–2011	112
Table 4.11	UK-resident, first degree undergraduate qualifiers receiving a First or 2/1 degree by ethnicity: 2003/4–2011/12 (percentage)	113
Table 4.12	Qualifications obtained by immigrants aged 18 to 60 according to period of migration (percentage)	115
Table 4.13	Qualifications obtained by descendants of immigrants, aged 18 to 50 (percentage), according to parents' country of birth	116
Table 5.1	Knowledge and interest	128
Table 5.2	Muslim women's political participation and civic engagement	131
Table 5.3	Registration and turnout percentage rates—1997, 2005 and 2010 general elections	136

Table 5.4	The participation of young people aged 19 to 25 in the 1995 presidential elections (second round)	142
Table 8.1	Majority society	233
Table 8.2	Ethnic culture and communities	234
Table 8.3	Islam and Muslims	234

CHAPTER 1

Introduction

Since the 1970s, a number of events in international politics have placed the spotlight on Islam and Muslim communities as never before. The list runs from the Iranian Revolution of 1979 and the Rushdie affair of the 1980s, the establishment of Afghanistan's Taliban regime in the 1990s, the events of 9/11, the Gulf War of 2003–2004, the Madrid train bombing of March 2004, the Beslan school siege of September 2004, the 7/7 (2005) London transport bombings and the Mumbai November 2008 terror attacks to the Peshawar army school massacre in December 2014 and more recently the Charlie Hebdo shootings (January) and the multi-site terror attacks (November) in Paris, in 2015.[1] In Europe, these events have provoked a backlash against Muslim communities and led to repeated debates on Islam's compatibility with Western life and values and the desire and ability of Muslims to engage legally and effectively with the political structures and cultures of liberal democratic states. Such debate has featured strongly in British and French political, academic and media circles and has generated a number of studies related to the political participation and civic action of Muslims in these two countries and elsewhere in Europe.[2]

However, taking the Muslim male as the standard model of individual and collective action within and outside Muslim communities, most studies disregard the situation of women from Muslim communities.[3] Although women (and girls) constitute a half of Muslim communities in Britain and France (see Chap. 4 for precise figures), historically they barely figure in public and political discourses on the place of Muslims in public life. Where women are mentioned, it is almost always in relation to questions of sexual and gender relations (wearing Islamic dress, forced marriage, honour crimes, female genital mutilation) so that ultimately Western discourses end up reinforcing the view that Muslim women are hidden from the public eye, that they are submissive and subjugated, apathetic and uninformed beings, unable or unwilling to act as subjects in their own right and hence not entirely worthy of the many rights accruing from social, economic and political participation. Moreover, while feminist political scientists (Bourque and Grossholtz 1974; Lovenduski and Hills 1981; Randall 1987; Pateman 1988; Lovenduski and Norris 1996) have succeeded in placing the question of gender firmly within the theoretical and empirical study of political participation in the West, certain categories of women continue to be overlooked. Hence the literature on gender, ethnicity and political participation is small but gradually expanding.[4] And while there now exists a body of work on women, Islam, politics and society in Muslim-majority countries and a number of works on Muslim women in Western societies, these tend to cover the history and evolution of Muslim women's participation in education and the labour market, the historical and current position of Muslim women in gendered relations in specific types of society and women in Islamic religious and cultural life.[5] With the exception of one or two publications (Werbner 1996; Mélis 2003), it is only recently that scholars have turned to the question of Muslim women, politics and civic life (see Akhtar 2015; Ali 2012; Belli 2013; Fournier 2008; Joly and Wadia 2012; Manier 2007; Massoumi 2015; Rashid 2013; Sanghera and Thapar-Björkert 2007; Takhar 2013a; Wadia 2015).

The increasing salience of Islam in the public space means that it is not only appropriate to gain insights into the behaviour and thinking of Muslims generally (particularly at a time when the focus on them is of an intense and negative nature), it is all the more necessary to focus on Muslim women's participation which is too often ignored where politics is concerned. The research on which this book is based is thus dedicated to the political participation and civic engagement of women from Muslim communities through a comparative study of France and Britain. It is important to specify that the term 'women from Muslim communities' refers to women whose family origins are situated in countries where Islam is the majority religion. Moreover, the use of this term also reflects this study's recognition of the diversity of practice, customs and interpretation of faith across Muslim societies and communities and our concern with not just devout/practising Muslim women but also with women who may not practise or adhere to the principles of Islam. Our decision to include the latter (sometimes termed 'cultural Muslims'—see Akbarzadeh and Roose 2011) is based on a number of reasons. First, in conversations with women from Muslim communities before the start of this research project, during fieldwork and after its completion, we found that many non-practising (or religiously 'apolitical') women, nevertheless, retained a strong attachment to their Muslim families, communities and elements of Islamic cultural practice (e.g. concerning marriage and birth celebrations, death rituals, dietary customs and Eid festivals) and because of this referred to themselves (with qualification) as Muslim. Second, among those who did not practise or believe because they were either disenchanted with institutional Islam or 'westernised'/secularised, the desire to be included in the Muslim fold was expressed for fear of otherwise being left out and unheard. Third, in the post-9/11 climate of anti-Muslim feeling, many 'westernised', secularised, religiously sceptical or atheist women from Muslim communities chose to group themselves with their Muslim families and communities in order to place a clear distance between themselves and Islamophobic discourses and action in the public and political arenas.

Thus, while religion may be the main driver behind the worldview of a large number of Muslim women, many others would not attribute their agency solely or in part to Islam, and factors other than religion may shape their political beliefs and activism. However, it is worth mentioning that in Britain the overwhelming majority of the women we spoke to identified strongly as Muslim and saw Islam as one of the drivers behind their politics whereas in France a larger proportion of our respondents were secularised (e.g. Naïma who described herself as 'musulmane laïque'), were religiously sceptical (Lutfiyah who said she was not practising but subscribed to a 'culture musulmane') or rejected Islam altogether (for instance, women such as Lina and Hayat who were atheist because their personal experiences of radical Islam—in the form of the Front Islamique du Salut—in Algeria had led them to this position) but who, nevertheless, in their majority, wished to identify with their Muslim families and communities in an environment where hostility against Muslims was widespread. Finally, it should be noted that because the term 'women from Muslim communities' can be cumbersome, as indicated in Note 3, it is used interchangeably throughout this book with 'Muslim women' or 'women of Muslim background' to mean the same.

The notion of 'political participation' also calls for clarification. In lieu of a traditional acceptation of what constitutes political participation, it is employed here in the broadest sense to cover not only conventional and accepted unconventional modes of participation but also what Chowdhury and Nelson refer to as '…the politics of everyday life…the terrain between state and family that is usually ignored in conventional investigations of politics' (1994: 18).

Danièle Joly and Khursheed Wadia, whose work is grounded in sociology and political science, respectively, have pursued enquiries over many years in the field of immigration and ethnic relations. Joly has published extensively on immigrants and Muslims in Europe (Joly 1989, 1995, 2001, 2007, 2012; Joly and Imtiaz 2002; Beckford, Joly and Khosrokhavar 2005; Beckford and Joly 2006) while Wadia's research has resulted in numerous publications on gender, ethnicity, migration, politics and policy in Britain and France (Wadia 1999, 2004, 2015; Allwood and Wadia 2000, 2001, 2002, 2004, 2009, 2010; Lazaridis and Wadia 2015; Wadia and Allwood 2012). We have both wide and in-depth knowledge of these areas of investigation and realised very quickly that the question of political participation and civic engagement among women from Muslim communities was being largely neglected by social scientists despite the fact that the latter population was becoming increasingly visible, particularly in the post-9/11 context. We also have a long collaborative history with the Paris-based Centre d'Analyse et d'Intervention Sociologiques, at the École des Hautes Études en Sciences Sociales with whom the French part of this project was implemented, in particular with Alexandra Poli and Giulia Fabbiano who have long-standing research experience in the areas of immigration and race discrimination. An important aspect of this research is that we accord pride of place to the social actors constituting the subject of this study in their interaction with their societal and political environment. Our research focuses on Muslim women's capacity of action, and the processes through which this action is developed, which, in addition, takes on particular importance in view of the assumptions and prejudices to which this population of women is subjected in Western societies. This has led us to use a framework which draws on three main sources: Archer's realist sociology (1995), Touraine's methodology of Sociological Intervention (SI) (1978) and a feminist approach to the study of women, politics and civic activism.

AIMS AND SCOPE OF THE RESEARCH

Aims

Our research pursues a number of objectives. It documents Muslim women's participation in political processes and structures. It challenges prevalent stereotypes in public and political discourses which portray this group of women as 'subjugated', 'passive', 'uninterested', 'uninformed'. It examines how women from Muslim communities (re)gain the capacity to constitute themselves as social actors in their interaction with the structural and cultural frameworks of majority society. It offers data to policy and decision makers about the concerns, views and political comportment of this group. Public policy can then be better equipped to take account of the specific problems, achievements and aspirations of women from Muslim communities in areas such as political and civil rights, immigration and nationality, health and welfare or education.

Experiences of living and being raised in the West has meant that women from Muslim communities have had to tread an uneasy path between Western ideas and ideals of modernity, on the one hand, and Islamic values and traditions, on the other hand, in ways that both non-Muslim women in the West and women in Muslim-majority countries find difficult to grasp. If, as Deniz Kandiyoti (1991) argues, Muslim women have come to represent an 'inner sanctum' of Islamic identity and a visible cultural marker against Western imperialism, then nowhere is this more sharply displayed than in the 'imperialist heartlands' themselves. Muslim women in Britain, France and elsewhere in Europe have had to identify both obstacles and facilitators within Islam combined with their specific ethnic culture in order to negotiate a means of living in the private sphere of family and close community and within the public spaces of Western society. Moreover, the public spaces of Western societies are not welcoming, marked as they are by racism and since 9/11 by a sharpened hostility towards Muslims. The fact that some Muslim women wear Islamic dress, thus publicly affirming their faith, has made all Muslim women the targets not only of outright racists but also of certain secular groups, liberals and feminists who fear that the values of personal freedom, secularity, Western democracy and women's advancement may be undermined. Given this context, it is important to counter negative beliefs and attitudes surrounding women from Muslim communities.

The Context of Muslim Women's Participation

Muslim women's modes of participation derive from experiences at the confluence of diverse societal contexts, that is, in Western society and in their countries of origin and/or Muslim-majority countries. In the first instance, women long settled or born in Britain and France, and originating from ex-colonies, may draw directly or indirectly on histories of national independence struggles waged alongside men. Women's participation in independence movements was deeply gendered and unequal, but promises of equal citizenship reinforced their commitment. This generation of women continued to work alongside men after decolonisation despite the fact that women's presence in the state and political structures of newly independent countries remained insignificant. Secondly, growing numbers of Muslim women have arrived in Western Europe as asylum seekers and refugees over the past 25 years, bringing vastly different experiences from those of labour and marriage migrant women and their descendants. Experience of direct or indirect political and ethno-cultural persecution may generate political views and behaviour that are uncommon among labour and marriage migrant women. This means that a history and tradition of political struggle alongside men in male-dominated organisations and movements has developed.[6] Moreover, this tradition has continued in difficult settlement conditions, in the endeavour to create a space for their particular community. However, increased political activity and activism independent from that of men is becoming a more common feature. More recently, as Muslim communities have come under heavier surveillance and policing after 9/11, women have been compelled to play roles previously eschewed. In many cases, wives, mothers, sisters of men suspected of and/or imprisoned due to 'terrorist' activity have had to take on traditionally male family responsibilities. They have also helped establish and/or supported campaigns for the fair treatment and release of male relatives and friends. Some women have been directly subjected to heavy surveillance, questioning and arrest by the police. In such a context, Muslim women have become rapidly politicised and this has been evidenced through their increased visibility in political spaces. In twenty-first-century France, many Muslim women have become the target of increasingly restrictive legislation related to Islamic dress which was operationalised for ideological and electoral purposes, coalescing around the theme of national identity. Nevertheless, despite evidence of political action and activism on their part, the negative image of Muslim women in

Western society and the fact that they have traditionally mobilised under male leadership means that they have not been seen as political subjects in their own right. Their diverse, sometimes particular, modes of activism have therefore gone largely unreported.

Comparing France and Britain

France and Britain offer good comparative sites for this investigation because they share a number of similarities but equally display fundamental differences in their respective political histories, cultures and institutions. Britain and France, along with the USA, have traditionally featured as subjects of comparison in the field of political science. A number of general reasons are given for this comparability; for example, that both countries have a long history of parliamentary democracy and that they are broadly marked by a liberal ideology. It is pointed out that change in French politics and society is marked by revolutionary upheaval based on sharp ideological oppositions while British political and social institutions have evolved as a result of pragmatism and compromise. Nonetheless, both countries are currently in the grip of a neo-liberal economic agenda. A number of sociologists have also lent their attention to a comparison of the two countries. There are specific reasons why these two countries may be considered for the study of Muslim women's political participation. Both have extended histories of immigration linked to their colonial past which have given rise to the settlement of large Muslim populations although each country's approach to issues of immigration and race relations differs. Britain has, since the late 1960s, favoured a multiculturalist approach while republican universalism shapes French public policy towards the integration of migrants and their descendants; including those from Muslim communities. Moreover, the French state is based on secularist principles which have gained renewed importance since 1989 and provided justification for the law of March 2004 banning Muslim girls from wearing the headscarf (deemed a conspicuous religious symbol) in state schools and that of 2010, prohibiting the wearing of clothing concealing one's face in public spaces, which was aimed at the full Islamic face veil or burka. In Britain, the Established Church is evidence of the non-separation of state and church. As a consequence, public expression of religious faith is accepted in state and state-supported organisations thus facilitating Muslims' endeavours to gain certain rights or concessions related to their faith and practice. It has been argued that Muslims and

Islam have undergone a measure of institutionalisation in Britain (Joly 2012). Furthermore, in a study of Muslim women, one must take into account differentiated attitudes to the question of women and gender, legislation as well as differences in the feminist movements which characterise France and Britain, and particularly in the way that they have reacted to the situation of Muslim women in the West.

In addition, these differences raise issues of terminology and concepts related to the populations which are the subject of this study. For instance, the term 'ethnic minority' which, in Britain, refers to long-established immigrants and their descendants is not recognised in France while the term 'Muslim' invites a number of comments. In Britain, populations originating in countries where Islam is the majority religion were not immediately conceptualised as Muslims. Initially, they were subsumed under a general race relations paradigm and subsequently became part of ethnic categories such as Pakistanis, Bangladeshis and so on. However, Muslims have now acquired a sociological reality in terms of their categorisation by majority society and their self-identification. This was confirmed by the inclusion of a religion question in the 2001 national census. In France, the use of 'Muslim' (*musulman*) as a label to identify a social category remains ambivalent and ambiguous. It is worth reiterating that French political culture does not accord a place to religion in the public sphere while constitutional rules do not allow any religious or ethnic identification of citizens. Yet, the term 'Muslim' has been present in official discourse but along a fragmented path. In French Algeria, at the time of the colonial empire, 'Muslim' was the term used for Arabs and Berbers who had retained their 'personal status' (*statut personnel*)—that is, the right to be judged by Muslim courts in matters pertaining to the person, namely, where family and inheritance law was concerned.[7] The label 'Muslim' was employed to distinguish local inhabitants who were Arab-Berbers from European Algerians and Algerian Jews, establishing legal discrimination against Arab-Berbers. This colonial discrimination reached a peak during the Algerian War, when 'Muslims' were considered a national threat (Joly 1991).[8] However, the designation 'Muslim' was not maintained for those who immigrated to mainland France before or after independence. Since the 1990s, Islam has gained prominence and the term 'Muslim' has gradually reappeared in the public sphere but its use as a sociological category is not generally accepted in France and invariably poses problems while a kind of demonisation of Muslims has taken place in public, media and political discourses. Altogether, this had an impact on our treatment of the fieldwork. In Britain the presentation of the project was readily accepted by all respondents without question or challenge and we were welcomed. It was more problematic in France where the description of a project on women of Muslim background almost invariably necessitated a great deal of explanation as many of the women questioned the notion of 'Muslim' and its meaning. In some cases it initially attracted suspicion. Furthermore, differences between French and British political systems and cultures gave rise to methodological difficulties such as in accessing comparative gender/ethnicity/faith disaggregated data regarding the populations concerned. So, while the UK national census yields detailed data owing to the introduction of the question on ethnicity since 1991 and religion since 2001, such data is absent from official statistics in France. Scholars themselves have to deal with the ethical watchdog, the Commission Nationale de l'Informatique et des Libertés (CNIL), before they can conduct large quantitative studies which include ethnicity and/or religion questions. Nonetheless, we were able to derive French supporting data from secondary literature and surveys carried out by scholars and polling organisations.

How the Study Was Carried Out

In order to gain breadth and depth, our methodological approach combined several methods. Archival work entailed the examination of media reports and dossiers; statutory and voluntary agency reports; government policy statements, consultation papers and statistical accounts; parliamentary debates and legislative commission/committee documents. We drew up a register of over a 100 third sector organisations involving women from Muslim communities or dealing with issues of concern to this population from primary material, Internet sites, telephone calls and visits to already known organisations. Our empirical research was undertaken mostly in Birmingham and Paris with secondary sites in Coventry, Cardiff, Manchester, Bradford, Rotherham, Glasgow and Lyon. Birmingham was chosen because it is home to the largest Muslim population in a unitary local authority in Britain and the Midlands area is a major pole of Muslim concentration. Cardiff and Glasgow are major cities of Wales and Scotland, respectively, and inhabited by significant Muslim communities while a few interviews were carried out in Rotherham, Manchester and Bradford. In France, Paris and the Île-de-France conurbation stand out as a centre of large Muslim populations. In addition, Lyon constitutes a significant second site in terms of the size of its Muslim population and of the political mobilisation of Muslims living there. Our fieldwork included a survey questionnaire on political participation and was run in each country. It was adapted from the first annual *Audit of political engagement* (2005) undertaken by IPSOS-MORI who granted us permission for the use of their questionnaire. We aimed to gather 120 questionnaires in each country in order to gain indicators of Muslim women's political participation and civic engagement. Over 500 questionnaires were distributed and 119 completed responses were obtained in Britain and 107 in France. The survey reported on the core indicators of political engagement categories of 'knowledge and interest'; 'action and participation' and 'efficacy and satisfaction'. The results (reliable rather than statistically valid due to the small sample size) were useful in triangulation with interview and focus group findings.[9]

The major part of our empirical research focused on qualitative data gathered in diverse ways. We carried out semi-structured interviews with 40 key informants (20 in each country) in Birmingham, Bradford, Cardiff, Coventry, Glasgow, London, Manchester, Rotherham, Paris/Île-de-France and Lyon. These interview samples comprised women from Muslim communities in leadership positions in local and national politics, in the third sector and in media and cultural organisations. These interviews yielded useful information about the informants' personal and political journeys, the interplay of power and influence between Muslim and other communities including majority society, how power is distributed and decisions are made within these communities and on the social, political, economic and cultural factors which impact on Muslim women's capacity to act as political subjects in their own right. A more general selection of 40 women (20 in each country) from Muslim communities (and not known beyond their own family and friendship circles) was interviewed in Britain and France. They were chosen according to age, ethnicity and branch of Islam (Sunni and Shi'a) to compose a sample that was as representative as possible of the female Muslim populations in both countries. In addition, we carried out 20 instances of direct observation at selected events (meetings within organisations, workshops, public rallies, demonstrations etc.) in Britain (Birmingham, London, Glasgow, Rotherham) and France (Paris/Île-de-France region). The ten events in each country involved Muslim women and permitted a focused observation of behaviour, activity and decision-making processes related to specific issues and events important to this population of women.

A significant segment of our empirical work relied on focus group meetings which took place in Birmingham, Coventry and Paris using an SI approach. As a methodology, SI derives from a specific theory of social action developed by Alain Touraine (1973) within a Weberian framework: in Touraine's view social action is meaningful and subjectively oriented by responses to a situation because it is defined by the social actors' commitment to values, principles and rules. Moreover, social action cannot be separated from the social relations within which it is produced (Dubet 1994, 1999).[10] Thus:

> Sociological intervention starts from the idea that the nature of a collective behaviour can be best known by interpreting the work performed by a group of actors as the group analyses its own actions under conditions created by researchers and managed by both parties. (Touraine 1978: 296)

This method presupposes that actors can know what they are doing and see through ideologies and the spontaneous categories of practices (Dubet and Wieviorka 1996) and it also encourages the subjects' self-reflexivity. It is grounded in the notion that a debate between actors and researchers within set conditions can produce knowledge, working on what is said, the group's history and the analyses developed during discussions. This enables its subjects to gain greater understanding about themselves and to acquire knowledge over the course of this transformative process (Dubet 1994). Dubet and Wieviorka stress the need to shift 'towards the conditions for increasing the capacity of individuals for autonomous actions' (1996: 73). This accounts for our choice of this methodology since one main objective of our research was to examine Muslim women's autonomisation and capacity of action and participation. The term 'autonomisation' refers to the process by which the women increase their capacity to take decisions and engage in action as autonomous subjects in the realisation of their life journey or project in the public and private spheres. In French the term *autonomisation* has been used by Zahra Ali (2012) in her work on Muslim women in France and new forms of religious action within Islamic feminism. She uses the term to describe Muslim women's simultaneous reappropriation of Islamic discourses and their politicisation as exemplified in the emergence of Muslim women's community organisations since the mid-1990s (Ali 2012: 2, 8).[11]

In Britain, two SI focus groups were formed for the purpose of this research. While Muslim women in Britain constitute a diverse population, we did not attempt to gather a representative sample as it was not possible to match the national population profile of Muslim women; the group size was too small and in any case the methodology of SI does not aspire to achieve such representativity. However, we aimed to bring together as diverse a group as possible which reflected the characteristics of the majority of Muslim women in Britain. Two SIs took place, one each in Birmingham and Coventry. Participants were recruited through contacts established in previous research projects on Muslims and ethnic minorities and through community and student organisations.

Although the groups were not a statistically representative sample, we took into account Muslim women's ethnicity, country of origin, nationality, branch of Islam, residence status, civil status and age. In terms of ethnicity/nationality the groups included women from Pakistan (Punjab and Azad Kashmir), Bangladesh, India, Tanzania, Nigeria, Algeria, Bosnia, Turkey, and Iraqi Kurdistan. Most were British-born but some were born in the country of origin. The largest proportion originated from the Indian subcontinent, reflecting the majority component of Muslims in Britain. Regarding the branches of Islam, the groups included both Sunnis and Shi'as, most of whom were practising Muslims (except for three), although with varying levels of religious intensity. About one-third of them wore a headscarf (*hijab*) but none wore the *niqab* or full-face veil. All but three were British citizens and several were born and brought up in Britain. Two of the women were refugees. In Birmingham, the group included mostly married women and women who were or had been in employment but subsequently became mothers/homemakers. The Coventry SI group included mostly young women aged between 20 and 35. Of the students and young women in Coventry, only one had been married and divorced; the rest were unmarried. The groups met weekly with the researchers over several weeks. The Birmingham group met over 13 weeks while the Coventry group met over 5 weeks. This included sessions with invited interlocutors and closed sessions during which analysis took place. A variety of interlocutors were invited to the focus group meetings; for example, politicians from the two main parties and the Greens, the Chair of the Stop the War Coalition, a radio journalist, educationalists, a trade unionist, leaders of community organisations and NGOs, an imam and the head of a Muslim women's Islamic study group. Following the end of the SI in Birmingham, the group requested further catch-ups and so we continued to meet a couple of times a year. This continued over four years and provided an opportunity to gain updates on developments in the women's life and on their views of topical political issues, thus enriching our knowledge of their engagement.

In Birmingham, the setting up of an SI group which met weekly, over 13 weeks, presented a number of issues. The greatest difficulty rested with securing such a long-term commitment while the participants knew little of the process and the benefits they might draw from it. Two elements were paramount: the intrinsic interest of the research proposed and the relationship built up during the long recruitment process between the researchers and the involved participants. The timing of the sessions also constituted a challenge as it was problematic for women working full time to attend while those with family responsibilities had to fit in attendance during the school day or find someone to care for children under school age or ailing elderly relatives. Of the 13 women recruited to the Birmingham group, 9 rarely missed meetings while the rest attended less consistently. All the Birmingham group participants had a basic to high level of education (end of secondary education/GCSE to first degree) and were in work, had previously worked in a paid or voluntary capacity or were students. The respondents' varying levels of interest and participation in civic and political life reflected the systematic findings in studies of political participation that those with the highest level of education and employment are most likely to participate in public life. The Coventry group brought together students from different regions of Britain and other young local women. Some worked and studied part-time. The group was diverse in terms of nationality (two respondents did not hold British nationality) and family origins which included Turkey, Nigeria, Pakistan and India. In addition, only one woman in this group wore the hijab at all times while one wore it when she 'felt like it', mostly to subvert the expectations that fellow students, her lecturers and others had of her. This group proved less difficult to organise in terms of their availability and meeting time except during the exam period which is why the number of meetings was limited to five as we came up against participants' varying revision timetables. However, the attendance of all eight participants was unfailing over the five weeks. The aim of the Coventry sessions, in common with the Birmingham ones, was to elicit knowledge of the participants' personal histories and to investigate—through their interaction with each other, the invited interlocutors and the researchers—their political interests and views about issues of concern to Muslim communities and Muslim women, their involvement in the political and civic arenas and the factors influencing their participation or absence in these arenas. The participants of both groups were involved in agenda setting and decisions about which interlocutors to invite. In the closed sessions they were invited to analyse their own interventions and those of the interlocutors.

The logistical difficulties of establishing longitudinal focus groups based on the SI method were fully revealed during our fieldwork in France. Undertaking fieldwork abroad means relying on paid research assistance locally which is strictly bound by time and although we spent significant chunks of time in France it proved unfeasible to set up groups which would meet repeatedly over a number of weeks, comprising the same participants. The difficulties encountered were compounded by suspicion, on the part of some women, about the research topic. Therefore, in France, four focus groups (of 6, 12, 5 and 7 participants) met separately, each comprising a different group of women but which, nevertheless, reflected the variety of national origins, generations, social occupations and key branches of Islam found among Muslim communities in France. They included women from Algeria, Morocco, Tunisia, Mali, Guinea-Conakry and Turkey who ranged in age between 20 and 50 plus. Some were first generation migrants who had acquired French nationality or permanent residence in France whilst the majority were born or brought up in France since a young age. They adhered to different branches of Islam although some did not practise their religion and a couple even claimed to be agnostic and atheist. The groups comprised women from labour and family migration backgrounds as well as those from refugee families. Although each of the Paris focus groups met once, the sessions lasted four to five hours while the last group acted as a 'plenary' group bringing together participants from the first three. Hence, this allowed participants to get to know each other and to intervene with a certain amount of confidence in group discussions. The length of the sessions also gave participants the opportunity to set the agenda in accordance with the discussion themes suggested by the researchers and to offer analysis at the end of the discussion. In the Paris groups, participants were most interested in discussing the tensions of being Muslim in France, their relationship with majority French society and politics and how one's commitment to Islam might shape political beliefs, choices and behaviour. The groups' organisation and activity therefore ensured the involvement of the women in discussions of issues based upon their lived experiences and understanding, and hence in the very analysis of their situation, in keeping with the SI approach and the aim of feminist research to break down hierarchies between researchers and researched subjects and involve the latter in achieving research objectives and the production of knowledge.

Much to our regret, one category of women which was not represented among the focus groups participants, in both Britain and France, was that of women (particularly older or recently arrived women) from the most socio-economically deprived sections of Muslim communities whose origins generally lay in poor rural areas of their country of origin. Such women often belong to traditional families and communities and were unable to participate due to their lack of autonomy and also because their English/French language proficiency was insufficient.[12]

STRUCTURE OF THE BOOK

This book is organised in two distinct parts where Part I introduces the reader to key concepts and contexts informing and situating the analyses of Muslim women's political participation and civic engagement. Part II, on the other hand, based on our empirical research, comprises chapters which provide a sociological portrait of the subjects of this research and which also examine and make sense of the politics and action of Muslim women through an explanation and analysis of the motivating factors and obstacles which affect them in their quest to act as autonomous political subjects.

In Part I, Chapter 2 on the conceptual framework considers Muslim women's relationship to politics within the context of gender and politics in general. It draws on a broadly feminist approach to the study of women as political and civic actors, Archer's realist approach (1995) and Touraine's SI methodology (1978, Dubet 1999; Dubet and Wieviorka 1996) which lends itself well to the use of the two aforementioned approaches. It situates the women's action within a particular approach regarding the interaction between the individual, the collective and society. It proposes the parameters of an analysis based on intra-group and inter-group relations. It is structured on the basis of the key reference groups to which the women relate, identifying the three major arenas which constitute the theatre of their action: majority society, the ethnic group, the Muslim group, all three being traversed by contradictions within and across each of them. The chapter draws on a literature review pertaining to those themes and on the research experience of the authors.

A contextual chapter examines the relationship of Muslims with British and French society. It provides a brief profile of the populations involved and examines the positioning of Muslims within the framework of institutional logics and political culture in British and French societies. In the case of Britain, it delineates the successive paradigms which have articulated the integration of immigrants in Britain: race relations, multiculturalism and finally the rise of Islam onto the public agenda. It takes on board the particular role played by the existence of an established church. It also pays attention to the modes of organisation and mobilisation among Muslim populations. It traces the contours of the War on Terror and its impact on British Muslim populations. Where France is concerned it looks at the evolution of policies and debates regarding a large population of immigrant origin, most of whom are of Muslim background. In mainland France they were initially categorised on the basis of their former colonial but 'foreign' status as 'immigrants' and subsequently as 'Arabs', the question of Islam having reached the public agenda only recently. The themes developed include the young Muslims' initial campaign for citizen rights, the controversy over ethnicity and communalism, the whole issue of *laïcité* and more recent state policies targeting Islam in the public sphere. Also taken into account is the reaction of feminists in Britain and France to the question of Muslim women and Islam.

Chapter 4 presents a historical, demographic and socio-economic profile of the population of women under study, in Britain and France. It maps out the main migration histories of those from Muslim-majority countries (both former colonies and, more recently, countries in the Middle East, North Africa and sub-Saharan Africa regions which have undergone political and socio-economic upheavals) to Britain and France and the establishment of Muslim ethnic communities. Second, it presents some of the key demographic features of Muslim populations and records their geographical distribution. Third, it puts forward a general socio-economic profile of Muslim populations in both countries, spotlighting women. Hence the areas of employment and education are examined. Also included in this chapter is a discussion of the emergence of ethnicity and religion as categories in the UK census and other social surveys which allow for the disaggregation of demographic and social data along lines of ethnicity and religious attachment and how this contrasts with the situation in France where the state (supported by French social sciences) prohibits public, private and third sector organisations from gathering data based on ethnicity or religion for the reason that such a practice, attributing certain markers of identity to groups of citizens, runs counter to French republican ideals. This discussion explains why the data presented on Muslims, and Muslim women more specifically, is more complete in Britain than that in France and hence why this chapter cannot provide a thorough statistical account of these matters but instead presents an indicative demographic and socio-economic profile of the population of women under study, within the broader context of the intersecting religious, migrant and ethnic communities of which they form part.

The fifth chapter examines and explains the political participation and civic engagement of women from Muslim communities in Britain and France through the establishment of a typology of participation and activism. It identifies the structures and processes through which Muslim women's action and activism takes place, for example, formal processes such as voting and institutional structures such as political parties and elected assemblies, as well as alternative forms such as street protest, political consumerism, public service and community politics and civicism. The above constitutes the landscape of political participation and civic engagement in which two types of participation in particular are highlighted: voting and activism through organisations and groups in the third sector. As revealed by our research, these are among the most common types of participation among women from Muslim communities in the countries under study here.

Chapter 6 examines the relationship between women from Muslim communities in France and Britain and two key collectives which constitute the theatres of their action: the ethnic group and the Muslim group. It aims to elucidate what factors contribute to the formation of barriers against and facilitators of action in the collectives involved. First, with regard to the ethnic group, the women point to central factors impacting on their capacity of action such as the immediate and extended family, the family-in-law and the community, with an emphasis on the role of men. Second, we examine the relationship of Muslim women to Islam and the Muslim group. Although in terms of population the ethnic and Muslim groups broadly overlap, Islam is understood by the women as constituting a distinct entity. The chapter looks at the positioning of the women vis-à-vis Islam and the various areas of dispute, wherein the women develop their challenge against or within Islam in the quest for greater autonomy. It provides an account of many women's utilisation of Islam as a moral compass and a potential tool for emancipation.

Chapter 7 comprises two components. First, it focuses on the women's relationship to British and French society which display a differentiated kaleidoscope of features affecting the women's action: prejudice related to colour, ethnicity, religion, gender; the evolution of policies and perception in majority society's approach to immigrants/ethnic minorities and Muslims; the significance of multiculturalism in Britain, of *laïcité* in France. The second part of the chapter is dedicated to the parameters which make it possible for women to engage in action in the public sphere, and the repertoire of strategies they summon to negotiate the winding path of obstacles and facilitating factors encountered amidst the ethnic group, the Muslim group and majority society.

The eighth chapter considers key issues of concern to women from Muslim communities. Foremost among the key issues is that of women's Islamic dress, focusing on the headscarf (*hijab*) given that all our respondents who wore Islamic dress wore the *hijab*. The other issue is that of control, whether by the state through the War on Terror or within Muslim communities by men. These issues were selected on the basis of the data gathered by the authors, through their fieldwork, archival surveys and contemporary testimonies published in the media. While these questions are of importance to women in both Britain and France, the emphasis placed on them varies in accordance with the political context in which they have emerged in each country and the extent to which the women have been impacted by them. So, for instance, the male policing of individual women within the family and community affects women in both countries but was emphasised more by Muslim respondents in France than in Britain. The issue of Islamic dress for women is far more controversial in France where Muslim women have not only faced stresses within their own families and communities over this question but have also been subject to pressure by the state, through laws aimed at banning the headscarf in state schools and the face veil in public places. Finally, the consequences of the War on Terror were raised by Muslim women in Britain more so than in France. Arguably, until recently, the impacts of the War on Terror were felt more keenly by Muslim women in Britain given Britain's role as the USA's closest Western ally in the wars in Afghanistan and Iraq over the past 12 years and in fighting 'Islamic terrorism' generally; and also because British policies on fighting 'home-grown terrorism' has led the state to invite Muslim women to join in this fight through programmes such as Prevent (Prevention of Violent Extremism—PVE). Nevertheless, the events of 2015 (the *Charlie Hebdo* shootings of January and the Paris terror attacks of November) will undoubtedly place greater surveillance and control on Muslim communities as France has initiated its own war against terror within its borders and this will impact on Muslim women. All these issues are central to public and political debate in both countries and feed into discussion about the compatibility of Islam with Western liberal democratic values and that of the integration of Muslims in Europe.

NOTES

1. The January and November 2015 terror attacks in Paris occurred when the writing of this book neared completion. Therefore, we have not had the opportunity to include an analysis of their early impact on Muslim communities, particularly women, in France. This will be the subject of a forthcoming journal article.
2. See, for example, Abbas 2005; Amiraux 2003b; Bowen 2009; Boyer 1998; Bouyarden 2013; Fredette 2014; Gémie 2010; Joly 1995; Laurence and Vaïsse 2006; Koşulu 2013; Lewis 1997, 2002; Modood 2003; Mustafa 2015; Parvez 2013; Peace 2013, 2015a, b; Peach and Vertovec 1997; Shadid and van Koningsveld 1996.
3. The term 'women from Muslim communities' refers to women whose family origins lie in one or more countries where Islam is the majority religion. The terms 'Muslim women' and 'women of Muslim background' are used to mean the same.
4. For example, see Andall 2003; Ba 2014; Châabane 2008; Davis and Cooke 2002; Kofman et al. 2000; Lesselier 2000; Lloyd 1997, 2003; Mirza 1992; Parmar 1982; Patel 1997; Phillips 1993; Quiminal 2000; Siddiqui 2000; Sudbury 1998, 2001; Takhar 2003, 2007, 2011, 2013b; Thiara 2003a, b; Wadia 2004.
5. See, for example, Afshar et al. (2005); Ahmad (2001); Andezian (1983); Bhimji (2012); Brah (2001); Cheruvallil-Contractor (2012); Dyke and James (2009); Gaspard and Khosrokhavar (1994); Guénif-Souilamas (2000); Haw (1998); Jawad and Benn 2003; Killian (2006); Knott and Khokher (1993); Kocturk (1992); Mounir (2003); Peach (2006); Pottier (1993); Roald (2001); Tersigni (2008); Timera (2004); Tyrer and Ahmad (2006) among others. For the interested reader, Yvonne Haddad (2005) presents a more ample bibliography of the study of Muslim women in the West rather than on women in the political and civic arenas.
6. This is a situation common among migrant and ethnic minority women of other faith backgrounds.
7. The French colonial state in Algeria maintained a 'quasi-apartheid regime' (Bell 2000: 36) where Arab and Berber Algerians could only apply for French citizenship (in order to acquire full political,

social and economic–fiscal rights) if they renounced their 'personal status' as Muslims and eschewed local customs based on Islam. The French colonial state's so-called respect for Muslims' personal status (seen to be incompatible with the French Civil Code) was used as justification for their exclusion from French citizenship.
8. Today 'Muslim French' is officially employed to designate a particular category, the *harkis*, that is, native Arab-Berbers who served in the French Army during the Algerian War of Independence, their families and descendants.
9. The survey was conducted with women aged over 18, either face-to-face (in colleges, mosques, community gatherings) or via email exchange. The final country samples subjected to data analysis were as representative as possible in terms of age, ethnicity, branch of Islam (Shi'a/Sunni) of the female Muslim population in both countries.
10. For a more detailed account of the Sociological Intervention method in relation to this research, see Joly (2016).
11. The concept of autonomisation has previously appeared in the literature on women and human development (Kabeer 2001) and is defined by Moghadam and Senftova as 'the complex process of women gaining access to and participating fully in civil, political, social and economic life and exercising associated rights' (2005: 426).
12. Our funding did not cover the employment of interpreters.

PART I

Concepts and Contexts

CHAPTER 2

Muslim Women and Politics: Analytical Framework

Introduction

This research investigates the participation of Muslim women in politics and the development of their capacity of action in environments in which obstacles and facilitating factors intertwine. This chapter introduces the conceptual frameworks which inform our study: a broad feminist approach to the study of Muslim women's participation; Archer's realist approach and Touraine's methodology of sociological intervention (SI). It then presents the references groups which constitute the theatres of action for Muslim women: majority society, the ethnic group and the Muslim group.

Conceptual Bases

Feminist Approach

This study of Muslim women's political participation and civic engagement combines a number of frames of feminist thinking. It takes as its starting point the view that women have been and continue to be largely excluded from instances of public and political power and are also marginalised within written history; that this exclusion cannot be attributed solely to factors ('supply side') which motivate individuals to participate in public life and politics, such as time, material and financial resources, support networks, political knowledge and skills and so on, but that other factors ('demand side') which block or restrict women's access to sites of power play a key role in their exclusion—such factors would include the male-dominated nature of social, economic, cultural and political institutions and political and legal–historical cultures which see women as inferior citizens and therefore not admissible to spheres of influence and power. The supply and demand model has been used by feminist political scientists to explain women's (under)/representation in political structures (e.g. Norris 1993: 308–330; Norris and Lovenduski 1995; Randall 1987; and more recently Franceschet 2005) but it can also be used to understand women's participation generally in the political and civic arenas. By considering demand side factors, as many feminist scholars do in response to the tendency in traditional political science to emphasise supply side factors, women are relieved of the blame for their historical under-participation or lack of participation which is put down to their apparent lack of knowledge, interest and competence. Moreover, it also places a responsibility on scholars to examine the barriers that women face in their quest to act politically in the public domain and to highlight the facilitators of their action in order to show that change to the status quo must consider the nature and role of public institutions and cultures. Both supply side (facilitators) and demand side (barriers) factors are examined in Chapters 5, 6, and 7.

As feminist scholars we also recognise that Muslim women in Britain and France have varying histories depending on which part of the world they or their families and communities originate from and that these histories may include individual, family or collective political struggles in favour of women's rights whether in anti-colonial movements, as in India and Algeria, or postcolonial liberation and pro-democracy movements such as in Bangladesh (1971 Liberation War), Palestine (Intifadas emerging in 1987 and 2002) or other Middle Eastern and North African countries (movements for increased political representation in the early to mid-2000s). In line with feminist approaches which value the link between women's history and contemporary women's political and civic activism (Rowbotham 1977; Githens et al. 1994; Springer 1999), we believe it is imperative to hear and acknowledge these histories, to visibilise Muslim women and build up-to-date knowledge about them in Western society, to understand their role as political and civic actors in Britain and France today and how their interrogation and views of their past inform their politics today. Such knowledge forms an essential part of the historiography of women's participation and that of ethnic minorities in Western society. Aspects of the history underpinning Muslim women's presence and situation in Britain and France are presented in Chapters 3 and 4. Moreover, their personal testimonies in Chapters 5, 6, 7and 8 also give the reader an insight into the links they make between their situation as Muslim women in Britain and their family/community ethno-national origins.

In our study of Muslim women's political participation and civic engagement, we understand that experiences of oppression and exclusion cannot be universal and that women do not constitute a single category with shared characteristics. Because women live a plurality of different experiences, it is important to acknowledge that Muslim women's exclusion is constructed through a number of intersecting inequalities based not only on their gender but also 'race'/ethnicity, faith and class. Thus not only do Muslim women find themselves in an exclusionary position within their own communities because of prescribed gender roles, they are also 'outsiders within' Western majority society (Collins 1990: 11) who, aware of their marginalised position as ethnic minority women of Muslim faith/background, are constantly obliged to navigate majority society rules to become autonomous social and political actors. This study explores the intersecting effects of gender, 'race'/ethnicity and faith on Muslim women.[1] Thus in Chapters 6 and 7, we develop an analysis of how Muslim women experience barriers to their participation in civic and political life by looking beyond just the category of gender or of 'race'/ethnicity or faith. In addition, by considering Muslim women's capacities of self-definition, self-determination and self-appraisal at locations where gender, 'race'/ethnicity and faith intersect, we demonstrate how they resist various discriminations in order to achieve their autonomisation.

Archer's Realist Approach

We draw upon Archer's study of the relationship between structure and agency to capture Muslim women's interaction with the societal framework presiding over their action. In the first instance, she establishes an analytical difference between structure and agency, whereby those are discrete arenas separated on a temporal basis 'with their own autonomous, irreducible emergent properties' (Archer 1995: 159). The notions of emergence and emergent properties are instrumental in analysing Muslim women's social action. The specific features of emergent properties are stipulated by Archer as relative endurance, natural necessity and possession of causal powers (1995: 167) so that they are neither haphazard nor contingent; they are not reducible but are characterised by their homogeneity, their durability, their necessity and their capacity to bring about consequences. Emergent properties pertain to the different strata of the social world so that they apply to both structure and agency (1995: 176). Archer differentiates between structural emergent properties (SEPs) and cultural emergent properties (CEPs), the former belonging to the domain of material resources (both physical and human) and the latter lying in the realm of ideas. There is a paramount differentiation between structural emergent properties and cultural emergent properties which, despite being interrelated, are not identical or necessarily congruent; in fact, it is more often the case that one outlives the other, creating a tension which impacts choice and change. The notion of emergence is also applied to agency as people emergent properties (PEPs).

SEPs and CEPs shape people's situation and generate conditions more or less favourable to certain courses of action, thus providing a situational logic which proposes strategic directional guidance without determining action (1995: 196). Indeed, Archer warns against a deterministic interpretation (1995: 153) which is prevented by 'one of the most important differentiating powers proper to people [...], their intentionality' (1995: 198). People have projects, hopes and aspirations subject to constraints and enablements which render certain courses of action more attractive to a group or an individual (1995: 253). Notwithstanding, freedom of interpretation is available to them (1995: 208), as values, affects and subjective weighting may intervene in the equation of choice, on the basis of discretionary judgements.

Touraine's SI

Touraine developed his theoretical approach, within a Weberian framework, against prevalent functionalism and structural materialism, both of which stressed the system and systemic features of society. He argued that the study of society and its production should centre around social action authored by the actor within social relations and through the prism of social conflict (Touraine 1965). He also challenged resource mobilisation and social role theories (Vaillancourt 1991) since the meaning of action and the values actors invest in their action constitute a central tenet of his approach. According to Touraine (1978) social action is constructed through the integration of three principles:

- Identity: how the actor defines herself/himself.
- Opposition: how the actor defines her/his opponent.
- Totality: what is at stake in this relationship (Touraine 1978).

Furthermore, Touraine developed a novel methodology for the study of action and social movements in the shape of SI. As a methodology, SI thus derives from a specific theory of social action which, according to Touraine, is meaningful and subjectively oriented by responses to a situation, because it is defined by social actors' commitment to values, principles and rules (Touraine 1973). Moreover, social action cannot be separated from the social relations within which it is produced (Dubet 1999; Dubet and Wieviorka 1996).

SI was also applied to the study of experience, exploring the tensions between 'belonging to a culture or having a sense of identity and [...] participating in the world of rationality' (Dubet and Wieviorka 1996: 70). SI was thus elaborated to investigate experience as well as individual and collective action, through a notion developed by Touraine himself, the capacity of 'subjectivation' (Touraine 2013). His key concept of subjectivation is designated as 'the process through which an individual turns into a social actor, that is an agent actively promoting and defending fundamental and universal human rights' (Touraine 2015: 16). We shall see in the following chapters that this is particularly pertinent for Muslim women.

Since our research focuses on social actors and their capacity of action, Touraine's approach proved particularly valuable as it throws light on the agency of Muslim women, giving pride of place to social actors and drawing on their reflexivity; which meets our epistemological position. We deployed this methodology to understand how the women developed their action amidst allies and adversaries, what were the modes and sites of action, what were the meanings and the values which guided the projects they individually and collectively pursued.

What are the implications of those concepts for research on Muslim women in France and Britain? The Muslim women in this study find their origin in other countries and societies, because they themselves, their parents or their grandparents have migrated. There is a situational logic to their action whereby SEPs, CEPs and PEPs in both societies (of origin and settlement) and groups of reference provide strategic guidance, without determining their mode of organisation and action. Indeed, the women's self-reflexivity and the meaning of their action lie at the heart of the analysis.

Muslim women's collective and individual participation is formulated within the context of the groups and societies to which they belong: in Britain and France, the population under study is characterised by its national/ethnic origin and its religion, differentiated according to the branches of Islam embraced. It is also divided on a socio-economic/class basis. We have identified three major entities which are the theatres of Muslim women's action: the ethnic group, the religious group and majority society. All three are traversed with contradictions within each and between them. The interface between majority society on the one hand and both ethnic minorities and Muslims on the other hand is steeped in unequal relations of power. But this does not signify that the relationship between ethnicity and Islam is free from tensions. Unequal relations of power also affect the women with regard to the men. Muslim women have to situate themselves and their action within this complex web of interactions. The relations of power within and between the groups assume special significance since we are examining political participation. We take into account the distinction between inter-group and intra-group relationships in the light of McAndrew's proposition (McAndrew 2006). In her study of Muslims and education, McAndrew warns against the pitfalls of unilateral paradigms regarding ethnicity: either focusing on external boundaries which singles out 'the central role played by the dominant group in the maintenance of ethnic boundaries' (2006: 154) and implies that ethnicity is imposed from without solely as the result of categorisation and discrimination or adopting essentialism which constructs a monolithic in-group without allowing a space for inner contradictions. The first option leaves out the role of internal boundaries such as historical memory and affect, thus underestimating the capacity of social actors to define themselves and act accordingly. The second one ignores power relations between minority and majority but also among the minority group itself. Drawing on those parameters, our conceptualisation of Muslim women's action as collectives and individuals situates it within the web of contradictions framing the underpinnings of interactions between groups and within each group.

Muslim Women and Politics

The specific question of Muslim women's participation in politics necessarily has to be related to the relationship between politics and women in general. It is widely assumed that women are less interested than men in politics, as recounted by Duverger: 'they think that politics is mainly a man's thing, because everything encourages them to think this: tradition, family life, education, religion, literature' (cited in Allwood and Wadia 2000: 140). Considerable debate has taken place on women's political participation where their higher involvement in political life has been found to be commensurate with educational level and employment outside home, while economic dependence and low employment status has been associated with minimal political engagement (2000: 141).

Allwood and Wadia identify three categories of explanation in their study of women's political participation in France: legal–historical, environmental and political–institutional (2000: 33). In her scrutiny of surveys on women's participation in electoral and party politics, Christy submits four types of answers to account for women's lesser participation: 'they can't' (1994: 34), this pertains to structural resources which include education, socio-economic status and income, employment/work status, marital status, family and children, age and generation, religiosity, race and ethnicity (1994: 36); 'they won't', this corresponds to cultural attitudes, the more significant aspects of which are political interest and sense of civic duty (1994: 41); 'nobody asks them', if they do not partake of mobilising agencies such as networks, trade unions, churches and so on (1994: 44); finally, 'the rules and context deter them' (1994: 47). This permits a more refined analysis of women's participation, which begins to challenge on several grounds assumptions that they participate less *per se*.

It has been argued that this situation has been changing with the alteration of women's circumstances (socialisation, education, employment) and with women acquiring a clearer stake in politics as the welfare state is taking over some of their traditional functions (Christy 1994: 27). Another major criticism is methodological as both terminology and definitions are said to warp surveys on women's participation. The term 'political' is posited as 'off-putting' while formulation of a similar content under 'important social issues' prompts much greater interest (Christy 1994: 139). In addition, it has been put forward that the classical definition of politics, that is, political parties and electoral politics, has excluded other forms of participation which are precisely the ones that tend to attract women's participation: 'women do not participate less than men; instead, they participate differently [...], more ad hoc and unstructured community associations, voluntary organisations and protests groups' (Githens et al. 1994: 5–26). In some circumstances, the politicisation of the private domain has drawn out dense political activism among women: this was the case in Chile under the dictatorship where women had mobilised into the public sphere, on the basis of their role as mothers and household providers (Waylen 1998: 148). A politics of ethics was also developed by women in extreme conditions of repression (Waylen 1998: 161).

There is still a dearth of research carried out on the participation of Muslim women. When this question is examined, their presence is noticeable in actions on the ground in their neighbourhood, but remains sparse in sites of decision-making (Amiraux 2003a: 90). This has to be situated within the wider areas of participation in collective activities. Muslim women have to steer their action within a complex social fabric astride the three spheres of ethnic group, Muslim group and majority society. The inner workings of each of those arenas provide them with opportunities and paths of action but also throw up contradictions which spur them to act. A kind of syncretism of action arises from the interaction between ethnic, religious and majority society domains.

ETHNICITY AND RELIGION

Before turning to an examination of the three arenas of Muslim women's action, it is necessary to clarify the interconnection between ethnicity and religion for the groups under study. Ethnic groups and ethnicity have been the object of much debate and literature while religious groups have also motivated many writings. Whereas religion and ethnicity are two key references for the subjects of our study, they should not be confused with each other. Unlike ethnicity, religion is highly formalised and mediated through a complex apparatus of texts, rituals, codes, organisations, personnel, and it is governed according to specific international and national laws (Beckford, Joly and Khosrokhavar 2005: 61); naturally, religious interpretation and practice may introduce many nuances to those prescriptions. Nevertheless, religion and ethnicity can to a certain extent overlap, particularly where minorities of migrant origin are concerned. Ball and Beckford use the compound adjective 'ethno-religious' communities to 'underline the fact that local political activity sometimes follows the contours of communities which *define themselves* in terms of religion *and* ethnicity, usually in subtle and shifting combinations' (authors' emphasis, Ball and Beckford 1997: 194). Kivisto (2007) offers the term 'religio-ethnic' groups in his thorough review of writings exploring the relationship between ethnicity and religion. According to Adamson, there are four types of relationships involving religion and ethnicity: (1) religion is the major foundation of ethnicity, (2) an ethnic group is grounded in religion but has a more marked association with a territory, (3) distinct ethnic groups share a common religion, (4) a loose relationship leads religion to play a small insignificant part in the definition of an ethnic identity (quoted in Kivisto 2007: 1210, 1211). Types two and three are the most relevant to the populations we are studying, since it includes groups which are united and divided along the lines of territorial origin and theological differences. Meanwhile, a Muslim paradigm has developed in France and Britain whereby Muslims are categorised as such by majority society and sometimes mobilise to defend their interests qua Muslims (Joly 2012). The women will thus negotiate their action within a triangular relationship vis-à-vis the ethnic group, the Muslim group and majority society.

Majority Society[2]

Although we do not lose sight of regional, class, generational and gender differentiations which penetrate British and French society, it is not our purpose to examine all these internal cleavages and the potential conflicts involved. It is noteworthy, however, that those societies display persisting inequalities between men and women despite laws, policies and women's mobilisation to achieve a greater degree of equity. In addition, the relationship between the state and religion plays a significant role in those two societies. All those traits inevitably impact on the positioning of Muslim women and their capacity of action, but one must be careful not to make hasty assumptions. For instance, Muslim women will not automatically perceive the feminist movement as a champion of their interests. In the same vein, the agenda of laïcité in France and the Established Church in Britain may be perceived as allies by some while others consider them an impediment (Beckford and Gilliat: 1998).

Ethnic groups in Britain have been recognised and broadly written into a multicultural policy despite controversies over this model (examined in the following chapter). This means that anti-discrimination laws and policies address ethnic minorities' right to maintain and pursue their culture in public institutions. Islam has also achieved a good measure of recognition in British institutions, where its practice and symbols are in the main accepted.[3] In France, the situation is quite different since ethnic groups are not allowed any official recognition, while religion is confined within the private domain on account of the separation between the state and the church. Nonetheless, Islam has been awarded some measure of official recognition through the state's support for the creation of a Council of Muslims, the Conseil français du culte musulman (CFCM). Meanwhile, both countries display racism and categorisation vis-à-vis minorities of immigrant origin and Muslims. While prejudices and stereotypes initially focused on ethnic/racial characteristics rather than religious aspects, Islam has now become a prime target. International events and the emergence of

Islam worldwide have turned Muslims into potential suspects of terrorism or threats to 'European' culture. In Britain, in particular, Islamophobia has much increased since the 11 September 2001 events in New York (9/11), the war in Iraq and the London 7 July 2005 terrorist attacks (7/7). In France, the 2004 law prohibiting the wearing of conspicuous religious symbols in schools was clearly aimed at Muslim girls while a law directed at the full-face veil in public spaces came into effect in April 2011. As a consequence, these groups suffer from a double disadvantage linked to 'race'/ethnicity, 'colour' and religion. Where Muslim women are concerned, a third kind of stereotype may be exercised: the image of the passive, subdued, subordinated woman, incapable of autonomous thinking or action and, more recently, that of the radicalised Islamist.

Another significant feature of British and French society is that they promote political and philosophical liberalism, insisting on the individual's right to autonomy vis-à-vis the community and/or the family. At the same time, majority society in both countries extols the values of justice and democracy and has established certain standards of rights for women, protected by legislation and policies.

Muslim Women Within Majority Society

According to the literature, the interaction of Muslim women with wider society in Britain seems to be fraught with contradictory findings. On the one hand, a number of stereotypes are evidenced, portraying them as bearers of family and culture, oppressed subjects of patriarchal 'Asian-ness' and symbols of non-integration because of their assumed limited knowledge of the English language (Ray 2003: 860). Public policies were formulated accordingly which, at best, would be inappropriate for some. According to Yuval-Davis, this is the direct result of the ideology of multiculturalism which constructs 'cultures as static, ahistoric, in their "essence" mutually exclusive of other cultures', especially from the host society culture (1998: 172). Those prejudices are also manifest at school and occasionally in employment, as noted by the Pakistani Forum which quotes discrimination on the grounds of racism, sexism and class; for instance, the educational level of Pakistani girls brought up in Britain was still lower than that of natives in the 1990s (Akhtar 1996: 98). Discrimination linked to the *hijab* is corroborated by Afshar (1998: 123). On the other hand, research brings to light a number of ambiguities. According to one study, while discrimination was exercised on the basis of language (Anwar and Shah

2000: 236) and prejudices pertained to Asian-ness in general rather than Islam (although Muslims were singled out more definitely after 9/11), none of the women interviewed for this piece of research felt that they had to compromise their faith or background to achieve success.

Studies in France reveal sharper dilemmas facing Muslim women. While being confronted with similar prejudices and discrimination as in Britain, they also face legal constraints about dress codes linked to Islam in institutions and the public space. Additionally, the social imaginary surrounding Muslim women entrap them in a closed choice predicated on their relation to integration whose contours are traced by Guénif-Souilamas. Three types are posited, one of which Muslim women must match: (1) they demonstrate cultural and social integration which carries an emotional and social cost, in addition to the alienation caused by assimilation; (2) they fail at school and marry within the Muslim community, which attests that their origins prevents their integration; (3) they embrace cultural particularism, which signifies that they reject the dominant culture (Guénif-Souilamas 2000: 60).

A plethora of arenas and issues are potential domains of action in majority society. Women could, in principle, take part in the numerous associations set up to defend ethnic minorities against discrimination and disadvantage suffered by the whole group. Some are mainly based among the ethnic or religious group, while others constitutes transversal alliances. Beyond their ethnic/Muslim communities, young women educated in Europe are the ones most likely to take part in majority-wide associations and actions such as demonstrations and campaigns (movements against racism, immigration laws and deportation exercises). Another possibility is that Muslim women become involved in local initiatives and collectivities or may volunteer in humanitarian organisations and charities. Furthermore, increasing levels of Islamophobia have brought about diverse responses from the women: on the one hand, protests and representation against anti-Muslim prejudice and behaviour; on the other hand, symbolic declarations of intent through the wearing of religious artefacts and demands for those to be allowed in the public space.

Ethnic Group

The ethnic groups that are relevant for our study are those formed from immigrant populations settled in France and Britain. There is a plethora of literature on the nature of ethnic groups and ethnicity which cannot be surveyed here (see Fenton 2003; Rex and Tomlinson 1979; Reitz et al. 2008). The ethnic group has been considered *inter alia* as an intermediary group between the individual/family and society in the Durkheimian sense (Rex 1995; Kivisto 2007). It has been well-documented through numerous pieces of research that it could provide protection and comfort within an unknown or hostile wider society, through offering a familiar environment, cultural markers and some forms of solidarity. In such an environment, the individual who belongs and does not transgress the norms is not left to fend on his/her own, which can be of great benefit for the women in an alien society wherein they have been transplanted through migration. For example, ethnic associations are identified as instrumental to settlement in their functions identified by Rex and Tomlinson (1979): overcoming social isolation, helping the individual in the solution of personal and material problems, combining to defend the group's interest in conflict, providing shared patterns of meaning. Within the context of conflicts with majority society, the ethnic group can act as a pressure group to protect and defend members' interests, a welcome benefit for those who are more vulnerable such as women. In both France and Britain, groups of immigrant origin have deployed great efforts to improve their situation. In Britain, in particular, where they enjoyed political rights from the initial stages of their settlement, they have successfully used them to pressurise for anti-discrimination legislation and policies, to promote a multicultural policy and to ameliorate their material situation.

However, women may suffer from the fact that the ethnic groups concerned are steeped in a traditional patriarchal culture, wherein the extended family is paramount. Indeed, within their ethnic group, women are encased in a largely disadvantageous relation of power typified by an assignation to well-defined roles according to the group's conception of the family: as a daughter, a sister, a daughter-in-law, a wife, a mother and a mother-in-law. Their relationships are well-defined vis-à-vis the men of the family, to whom they are bound by a specific range of duties. Furthermore, women are the receptacle of family 'honour', the moral community regulating and deciding on what is allowed or taboo. In most situations, women are subordinated to men according to traditional patterns, but at least one of those roles places one woman under the control of another: the daughter-in-law vis-à-vis the mother-in-law. In addition, elder men in the extended family and the community assume responsibility and control over the whole group. Consequently, several potential sources of tensions can be found within the ethnic group: the individual versus the community, women versus men and occasionally woman versus woman. Supplementary dimensions need to be mentioned, such as *biradari* and caste cleavages, which confine the women furthermore.

Criticisms have been levelled at essentialism when, in conceptualisation and policies, ethnic groups are considered as monoliths within which individual or subgroup interests are subsumed. For instance, the 2001 riots in Bradford revealed that young Muslim men were not only frustrated by unemployment, police harassment and lack of positive perspective for the future, but were equally disenfranchised by older male community leaders, who monopolised power in their dealing with the city council (Burlet and Reid 1998: 275). Proposals responding to the young men's demands for a share in the mechanisms of recognition and representation were countered by women who called instead for the representation of diverse strands within the community, including women (Burlet and Reid 1998: 284). The masking of internal differentiation in a group submitted to discrimination does not come as a surprise since it has been well-documented that processes of oppression cause 'more attention [to be...] placed on "community" needs rather than on the needs of individuals or subgroups' (Burlet and Reid 1998: 273; Gilroy 1993; Hall and Du Gay 1996; Benyon and Solomos 1987). Multicultural policies unreservedly extolling the community have come under severe criticisms. Yuval-Davis argues that the ideology of the community, which portrays the latter as a '"natural" social unit [...] assumes an unproblematic transition from individual to collective power' (1998: 174), and thus induces notions of internal differences to be subsumed. In the same vein, Macey (1999: 861) launches an indictment of multiculturalism which she construes as a bartering exercise, exchanging votes against an unwritten licence bestowed on community leaders to govern their community, concluding that it awards such leaders 'most control over the family, women and children. Together with the state, community leaders define the needs of the minority communities' (Macey 1999: 861). This is a recurrent theme; women studies analysts in particular have denounced the marginalisation of women's issues within communities (Yuval-Davis 1998; Maynard 1994).

Muslim Women Within the Ethnic Group

Within the ethnic arena, women play a role in strictly in-group activities such as weddings, birth celebrations and mourning rituals together with other extended family gatherings and cultural festivals. They may take part in ethnic association's activities such as burial societies, ethnic language classes and old people clubs but their leadership roles are frequently curtailed, because of male supremacy in those arenas. Moreover, multiculturalist policies as applied in Britain have not made it easier for women, since those have consolidated the control of first generation males through recognising the latter as the sole or main representatives of the group. Contradictions within the ethnic group, as explored above, give rise to a whole new canopy of activity domains and issues, especially when the women's aspirations and projects encounter obstacles due to ethnic norms and practices. For example, individual and collective action may be motivated by their desire to promote access to education and employment against the potential disapproval of the community, and by their opposition to arranged marriages, which may become forced if the woman disagrees. Domestic violence and genital mutilation have also motivated the creation of associations and mobilisation to oppose them. Finally, the whole implementation of the 'honour' issue which can impose a great number of constraints on women may be challenged. However, although those are in-group questions, they often bring into play interaction with majority society in terms of legislation, ideas and resources. For instance, women are protected by the law against genital mutilation and honour killings. Alliances are struck with individuals and collectives from majority society and/or other groups on common causes, such as domestic violence which affects women's rights across ethnic boundaries and within majority society. Some Muslim women have set up and taken part in groups to oppose domestic violence, or to support refuges for women threatened with violence or subjected to abuse, while others have set up organisations to challenge young men's prescriptions on modesty.

Islam, Muslim Group

Although the ethnic and Muslim groups most often cover the same population and overlap, it is useful to separate the two reference groups for the purpose of our analysis. Research has shown that transplanting their religion plays a role in the efforts of immigrants to claim a place in the land of settlement (Warner, quoted in Kivisto 2007: 1220; Joly 1995), in so far as it helps them to counter the alienating and uprooting character of the migration experience (Hirschman, quoted in Kivisto 2007: 1225). Analysing the Muslim group is a tall order because it is fragmented on the basis of ethnicity and/or nationality but also along theological lines;

it is in reality composed of several communities and groups. This accounts for the proliferation of mosques side by side in the same neighbourhood, as in the UK where there is currently little restriction on the creation of Muslim places of worship. Nevertheless, federations of mosques also exist for mosques and Muslim associations of the same branch of Islam, in addition to a few large mosques which gather the faithful from diverse backgrounds (Joly 1995). Finally, different Muslim organisations liaise on particular issues on a national (British/French) or local basis. This gives rise to tensions in the relations of power within Muslim communities, which provide the context for Muslim women.

In Britain the largest national populations of Muslims come from the South Asian subcontinent; they are also those who settled first and were able to make a place for Islam in British society, thanks to their status as Commonwealth citizens (see Chapter 4 for a more detailed examination of Muslim migration to Britain). They have achieved a kind of hegemony over the other Muslim groups, even after the latter increased in numbers, in the same way as Hirschman sees the Irish and other Catholics in the USA (quoted in Kivisto 2007: 1225). As a consequence, British Islam is strongly marked by a South Asian subcontinental agenda. In France, North African Islam prevails but is fraught with rivalries between Algerian-, Tunisian- and Moroccan-based factions, complemented by Turkish and sub-Saharan African strands of Islam. All vie for influence.

Ethnic and nationally based divisions are augmented with theological cleavages. The Shi'a/Sunni division, conflict-ridden in other parts of the world, is not so salient in France and Britain, where Shi'as remain a small minority and tend to exist alongside Sunnis. One significant discrepancy occurs between the Sufi branches of Islam and political reformist movements: in Britain, for instance, on the one side there are *Barelvis* and on the other side the UK Islamic Mission (*Jamaat-e-Islami*), *Deobandis* and the *Markazi Jamiat-al-e-Hadith*; in France, there are spiritualist/maraboutist branches versus adepts of the Muslim brotherhood. Reformist movements propose a criticism of what they consider the interference of cultural practices through a return to the sacred texts, Qur'an and *Hadith*; they also aim to re-Islamise Muslims they deem have drifted away because of living in a non-Muslim country. This does not mean, however, that they constitute one and the same branch of Islam; they are further divided according to the texts they prioritise, their interpretation of those and the *Khalifa* they follow. Most reformist movements can be included in what may be called political Islam and they demand a place for the public manifestation of their religion. They are often labelled 'fundamentalist'. Altogether, against a society which they judge corrupt, sexually promiscuous and too materialistic, they propagate their interpretation of Islamic standards to emphasise, *inter alia*, family values and well-ordered relationships between the sexes. Others have claims to represent universalist currents in Islam which assume many hues. Yang and Ebaugh identify two trends among immigrant-based religions: (1) a return to theological foundations in response to the pervasive influence of majority society, which can take two different forms, either an affirmation of an insular conservatism, akin to fundamentalism, or the more reflexive purging of various historically grounded cultural practices; (2) a shift from ethnically exclusive religions to more universalistic ones (quoted in Kivisto 2007: 1221, 1222). Nonetheless, most of those branches of Islam correspond to what was described above as 'ethno-religious', including those who claim to adhere to a 'purer' form of Islam. In addition, some branches have led to the development of offshoots into radicalism. Consequently, in-group tensions and contradictions penetrate Muslim populations. Finally, *ijtihad* makes it possible to reinterpret the sacred texts and innovate.

Within the scope of majority society, Muslims face increasing prejudices. As an extreme example, Huntington's vision of the world and his clash of civilisation (1993) accuse not only radical Islam but Islam *per se* of incompatibility with individual liberties in Western civilisation. Likewise, in majority society's social imaginary, the presumed oppression of Muslim women bears the mark of an anti-modern and archaic religion, symbolising the antagonism between Islam and values of individual liberty. In their relationship with majority society, Muslims have come together to promote their interests *qua* Muslims, in an atmosphere of growing suspicion and hostility. In Britain, their early mobilisation against Salman's Rushdie's *Satanic Verses* and the Education Reform Act 1988 was followed by challenges to deprivation and Islamophobia. Muslims have joined ranks with other sectors of the opposition against the war in Iraq and protested at the suspicions cast on Muslims since the 9/11 and 7/7 events. They have made a number of gains, so that the practice of Islam and adjustments to make it possible were accepted in most public institutions. In France the whole controversy regarding the wearing of *hijab* in schools and public institutions has witnessed the mobilisation of Muslims from different national origins and branches of Islam. Other issues include racism, discrimination and exclusion.

Muslim Women and the Muslim Group

The relations of power within Muslim groups display potential conflicts of interest between the women and the men: as a case in point, Muslim organisations and places of worship tend to be dominated by men, largely to the exclusion of women in any position of influence. Moreover, some studies have depicted how Islam could be harnessed for the control of women. Macey demonstrates how young Pakistani men in Bradford have marshalled a particular Islamic code as a power resource against both women and the white establishment (1999: 857). Rather than correlating it with regression into tradition, she uncovers elements of rational choice and a manipulation of cultural and religious resources, supplemented with modern North American 'gangsta' styles (1999: 852). In this case political ideology under the guise of religious orthodoxy is mobilised to recruit young men into the perpetration of violence, illustrated by leaflets advocating the rape of Sikh women, a kind of violence that comprises male aggression, both in public and in private domains, some of which focuses on the honour of women and the community on 'religious' grounds (1999: 855). Macey also notes the class component of such a situation which predominantly impacts the poor, illiterate, non-English-speaking women who are unable to access alternative meanings to those imposed within patriarchal community structures. Macey concludes that they are almost totally disempowered on account of their socialisation into traditional gender roles, the pressure to uphold family honour and their financial dependence on abusive men (1999: 859).

Although Macey's comments pertain mainly to highly disadvantaged strata, Islamic interpretations most commonly signify limitations in the sphere of all women's action. Women's participation in Muslim endeavours is generally confined to women's circles since the mixing of sexes is often frowned upon. Many aspects of life are strictly regulated with an emphasis on duties towards family members, codes of modesty and the preservation of women's reputation. Women are generally attached to one variety of Islam according to their early socialisation through the family and the community they are born into. Nonetheless, educated women can take advantage of diversity in Islamic options, which permit a certain amount of choice since moderate and/or progressive versions of Islam stand in contrast to more fundamentalist or traditional ones.

Islam, a Resource for Women?

The salience of Islam lies at the nexus of contradictions between traditional culture and majority society. Muslim women are facing multiple demands and aspirations: the norms of British society, those of the community and family, their own individual and collective projects. However tempting the perceived absence of constraints may seem in majority society, severing links with ethnic cultures and Islamic norms to embrace unreservedly French or British ones remains the exception. Many women endeavour to find a way of reconciling both, and much of the existing research points to Islam as a significant vector permitting negotiation between diverse influences. In contrast with Macey above, some scholars like Jacobson focus on young women who make a point of disaggregating ethnicity and religion. The latter define ethnicity as loyalty to the traditions or customs of the minority group and attachment to a country or region of origin 'generally perceived to be a more peripheral aspect of their sense of identity' (Jacobson 1997: 239, 240). Those young women believe that religious teachings are, on the contrary, universally applicable and a testimony to belonging to a global community (1997: 245), so that they herald in Islam 'a set of doctrines which asserts the intrinsic equality of humans across all boundaries of "race" and nationality' (1997: 240). They also attribute to tradition and culture, rather than religion, features which they reject such as caste, dowries, arranged marriages and the inequality between men and women. They even appeal to Islamic teachings to resist parental and community restrictions on behaviour (1997: 241). One major trend seems to be the differentiation between ethnicity and religion which, according to Jacobson, revolves around the nature of the boundaries involved. Ethnic boundaries are assessed as pervasive and open to change, so that they fail to propose solid grounding in governing one's life through British society; they are deemed semi-permeable and too easy to cross in most social situations (1997: 247). The women surveyed appreciate religious boundaries for their universalism and clarity, which 'provides a means of dealing with the ambiguities and contradictions contained within their social environment' (1997: 254).

Zubaida in his research on patterns of religious orientation and associational life also finds that a good number of women make a distinction between religion and culture (Zubaida 2003). He establishes four main orientations among Muslims: the communal ethnic orientation, orientation to countries of origin, the secularist orientation and the universalist orientation. He establishes that women are noticeable among the accommodationist universalists, who favour a claim for recognition and an accommodation with wider society. Born and educated in Europe, women judge the traditional culture and religion of their parents as 'backwards' and restrictive, arguing that the oppression of women is alien to original Islam (2003: 91, 92); they uphold a universal and original Islam based on scriptures, law and theology, subject to rationalisation and adaptation to modern life. Knott and Khokher also list a number of studies which bear out the distinction between religion and culture outlined by Muslim women. Knott and Khokher delineate three types of approaches adopted by young Asians, including Muslim women in Britain—cultural synthesis, anti-religious feminism and religious identity (1993: 597)—and signal women opposed to fundamentalism, who attempt to forge the integration of Western and non-Western elements in a point of balance. But the women mostly dwell on the religious identity strategy which they clearly describe as a modern approach, forging a satisfying way forward through Islam: 'this strategy does depend for its existence to some degree on the influence of [...] Western education, including the use of English language materials, the technique of textual analysis [...] speculative reasoning and current debates about the role of women' (Knott and Khokher 1993: 596).

For Khosrokhavar, religion enhances Muslim women's response to conflictive expectations: it plays a plurality of roles comprising a provider of identity, a principle of distinction with others, a tool of affirmation of self in the family and a sociability mechanism (2000: 97); symbolically the *hijab* is not a display of radical Islamism or submission to patriarchal authority but an answer to the tensions between demands from the family (upholding family honour) and those of society (emancipation) (2000: 94). The *hijab* may take on different meanings which Gaspard and Khosrokhavar (1995) associate with first generation immigrants, compromise and revindication. Tietze (2001) also sees in Islam a mode of subjective construction of modernity; she identifies four types of Muslim religiosity: ethicisation (morals and dogma), belief in rules as a way of guiding one's behaviour; communitarianism (social memory, history, politics; belonging to Islam is more important than beliefs); emotionalisation (perfecting oneself, theological knowledge entirely directs one's life); culturalisation (habit and custom without subjective meaning). This classification applies to all Muslims. Tietze also concludes that Muslim religiosity 'no longer reflects a lack of integration or a problem of cultural adaptation. Identification with Islam becomes an ordinary tool [...] for the construction of subjectivity and the capacity to act in society' (2001: 7).

It cannot be presumed that this apparent return to Islam is related to an acceptance of traditional roles. New formulations of religious affiliation appear to emerge from settlement in Europe, purging Islam from its national traditions. For Amiraux, 'practices are not inherited but reinvented' (2003: 89). According to Afshar, Islam has something to offer women (1998: 107), in the shape of control over their own resources, absolute rights and entitlements, an idealised version of marriage and motherhood, a haven of support, honour and dignity, which are acceptable to both devout and enlightened women (1998: 109). Afshar explains those developments against the backdrop of racism at school, reduced opportunities, privatisation policies and the decrease of social services. Islam thus offers a refuge and a site of empowerment. However, the women interviewed by Afshar are aware of the moral policing deriving from Islamist interpretations in the community which are used as a means of control over women. To challenge the latter, they have organised their own Islamic classes in order to use the Qur'an as a tool in bargaining with patriarchs but also matriarchs in the family. In Afshar's words, Islamic classes are not envisaged as 'a badge of identity' but as a means of negotiation and 'a pathway towards an "Islamic" liberation' (1998: 118). Zubaida outlines a similar trend towards 'a kind of Muslim feminism' (2003: 92) among educated women within his typology of orientations among Muslims. Through their reading of the Qur'an and sacred sources, they arrive at their own interpretations which are said to be empowering to women and the family in society (2003: 92). This seems to correspond to a global tendency examined by Maumoon (1999) who writes about Muslim women beyond Europe. In the first place, she takes note of an increasing feminisation of Islam concomitant with women's claims for positions in the running of religious institutions. This is accompanied with the 'growth of a "feminist" consciousness among Muslim women' (1999: 270). The latter accuse the West and Western style feminism of having failed them because they were an instrument of colonialism and caused family breakdown; at variance with Western feminists, they call for an honoured and recognised space for marriage and motherhood (1999: 275). Maumoon asks whether such views could be an internalisation of patriarchal thinking but she decides that their kind of feminism is written within the context of 'Third World Feminism' and cultural feminism (1999: 280), on the grounds advanced by those women that the norms and values of

Western feminism are unworkable for their communities. Zubaida in his article on Islam in Europe also reaches the conclusion that Muslim women 'confront Western feminism with an "authentic" Islamic feminism, distinct from that of the West, but empowering to women' (2003: 92).

Undoubtedly, feminist struggles among ethnic minority women have had to contend with the dilemma presented by the ambivalent role of the family, simultaneously a site of patriarchal oppression and of resistance against racism as pointed out by Gemma Tang Nain in her study of black women in the USA (1994: 216). Alma Garcia notes that this conundrum led Chicano women to call for the autonomous organisation of all women of colour (1994: 192). Lending her voice to Muslim women, Maumoon warns against the homogenising tendency of Western feminist discourse and stresses that 'the integration of other voices is necessary to prevent the Muslim woman from taking the place of the irrational and inferior Oriental unable to represent herself' (1999: 281). In her view, Muslim women reclaim religion to arm themselves with a liberation theory and are creating a gender activist strand within Islam (1999: 274, 277). They defy Islamists such as Sayyid Abdul A'la Maududi, who reject the mingling of the sexes, and they defend the right to mix at work as long as the woman is suitably attired (1999: 273); they find in religious movements a legitimate space for them to study, work and be politically and publicly active, while preserving their virtue and modesty. The gender activist discourse challenges the notion of permanent economic dependency of wives on husbands through paid employment outside the home; they promote the inclusion of a right to divorce in marriage contracts and of separate property entitlement (1999: 276). Maumoon finds a degree of similarity between Islamic and non-Islamic gender activists; in her opinion 'be it in the Middle-East or in Muslim communities in the West, there is pursuit of the goals of female autonomy and subjectivity either under the idiom of "feminism" and "Western dress" or that of "Islam" and "the veil"' (1999: 277): both kinds of feminism support women's rights to education, work and equality in public life and their full entitlements to political rights. The majority of young Muslim women assert the equal humanity of all rather than the gender hierarchy ingrained in technical, legal and doctrinal Islam (1999: 277). When Maumoon quotes Badran who defines feminism 'broadly as being an awareness of constraints placed on women because of their gender compiled with attempts to remove those constraints', she makes a convincing case for the acceptance of Muslim women to be quoted as feminists (1999: 270). They combine aspects from feminist movements in the West: close to the egalitarian variant in their campaign for equality of rights but partial to a differentialist form, as they opt for complementarity of the sexes, although they differ from Western feminists in their adherence to strictly defined gender roles (1999: 270). Notwithstanding, this positive assessment of feminism steeped in Islam is interrogated by Zia's research on secular and Islamic feminism in Pakistan, which voices concern over the framing of debates on women's rights solely within Islamic discourse by Islamic revivalist feminists. Zia warns of the danger that it may engender notions of a 'polarized "good" vs "bad" Muslim woman' and produce a 'new, radicalized, religio-political discourse' (2009: 29).

The women's engagement in established Muslim associations and mosques generally faces the same hurdles as were presented by ethnic associations on account of prevalent male control. The women will take part in religious festivals, in important rites of passages that involve a religious component and in some activities which mosques deliver as community centres. A few will have real opportunities to be involved in running events or activities in some Muslim associations, but more often they will set up separate Muslim women's study groups. The political involvement of Muslim women in wider society has not been well-documented. One possible typology proposed includes three main strands: those who address their politics to a universal Muslim community, those active in the politics of the host society, either on Muslim or on non-Muslim issues, and those who pursue activism related to the country of origin (Zubaida 2003: 95–96). Zubaida notes that middle-class Muslim women tend to partake in what he calls the accommodationist universalist group who consider Islam to be part of a plural, multicultural society, and seek recognition within it; they constitute pressure groups and associations campaigning for recognition and inclusion as, Muslims, in the media, education and politics (2003: 91). Their cause is helped by a renewed tendency to pay heed to religious rights in democratic societies (Beckford 2003). Moreover, Muslim women's religious stance awards them 'respectability', 'a source of status claim' within and outside of the ethnic community, a font of moral worthiness in wider society (Kivisto 2007: 1231). Within an adverse context where ethnic communities are the target of racism and discrimination while anti-Islamic trends have reached disproportionate degrees, nationally and internationally reasserting Islam enables the expression of solidarity towards the group. For instance, in their interaction with the feminist movement, Muslim women can adopt a position which challenges the colour blindness of those movements in Europe and develop their own form of feminism based on Islamic guidelines.[4]

Conclusion

Muslim women's action is situated at the nexus of multiple tensions and contradictions within and between their various reference groups. There are both objective and subjective factors which may lead the women to act upon a particular issue, in a particular way. Moreover, one contradiction may be the principal one at some point, motivating one particular kind of action, while it could transform itself into a secondary contradiction at another point, so that a different contradiction supersedes the previous one and thus triggers a new path of action. For instance, the disadvantageous relations of power between minorities and majority society may cause the women to support mobilisation as an ethnic minority group. However, this is not static. As ethnic minorities become more established and gain more rights, other contradictions can come to the fore such as the one between men and women within the group, all the more so when the nature of the relationship between majority society and minority groups becomes stabilised through the positioning of men as interlocutors, granting them greater control over the whole. Furthermore, women's claims within the group are likely to be enhanced by their experience of Western society wherein the relations between men and women are not as cemented as in traditional societies. In this conjuncture, Muslim women may come together to defend their interests *qua* women. However, this does not signify that the women necessarily find a place in mainstream feminist movements; on the contrary, many prefer to build separate organisations and forms of action, which can take on board their disadvantage as an ethnic minority, as Muslims and as women. The prominence of Islam has introduced further variables in this equation. On the one hand, majority society's increased hostility to Islam sometimes means that Muslim women will make a stance in defence of their religious group. Nonetheless, contradictions between men and women within Muslim groups can also produce women's challenges to the latter or lead them to discard religious issues altogether. The latter is more noticeable in France than in Britain, as a result of the differentiated relationship between the state and religion in both countries. A third possibility is the action of Muslim women as Muslims but independently of Muslim men. Contradictions between and within groups is supplemented by contradictions in the realm of ideas, whereby some ideals are posited as opposed and/or superior to others. This is the case when women call upon Islam to challenge tradition. Paths and forms of action are thrown up by the enmeshment of multifarious factors deriving from the changing nature of contradictions between and within the different reference groups. In all cases, subjective factors also play a role according to the women's awareness of and sensitivity to particular issues.

Notes

1. The idea of the simultaneous experiences and impacts of multiple oppressions based on sex/gender, 'race'/ethnicity, class and so on was discussed by Black American feminists from the 1970s onwards (Combahee River Collective 1979; Smith 1983). However, it was Kimberle Crenshaw (1989) who coined the term 'intersectionality' to acknowledge not just the simultaneity of oppressions but also that multiple oppressions are each endured as one single, synthesised experience.
2. The parameters pertaining to majority society are fully developed in Chapter 3.
3. Although this is challenged it remains prevalent.
4. It is important, however, to take note that these possibilities are not open to all Muslim women: they mostly apply to those who have the resources to pursue them, such as a certain degree of education, a distance from rural, traditional life and time not taken up by the burden of caring for family and the home.

CHAPTER 3

Muslims and Women in Britain and France

INTRODUCTION

This chapter delineates the societal and institutional context in which women from Muslim communities participate in Britain and France. Two aspects of this context have a bearing on their action in the public domain; one central aspect is that of Islam and Muslims and the other relates to their relation with majority society women's movements and politics. With respect to the former, the evolution of policies and the conceptualisation of populations of Muslim background in their interaction with majority societies are examined. The populations concerned emigrated from former colonies to arrive in Britain and France broadly after the Second World War (see Chapter 4). In Britain, the status of Commonwealth subjects awarded them, on arrival, all the social and political rights on a par with native British citizens while in France they had no such rights on account of their non-national or foreigner (*étranger*) status. It is worth noting that in both countries Muslims were not identified as such in the early stages of settlement as Islam did not constitute a marker of (self)-identification or categorisation. In Britain, immigrants of Muslim background were initially subsumed under a race relations paradigm and an ethnic identification as Asians, Pakistanis and Bangladeshis. In France, for several decades they were mostly categorised as Arabs or *Maghrebins* (North Africans). Islam and 'Muslim' emerged in the European public sphere only in the 1990s as a result of Islamist actions on the national and international levels. In Britain, the 9/11 events and London 7/7 bombings brought Islam and

Muslims into the glare of publicity with changed modes of interaction between them and British society. In France, the Islam/Muslim question was first raised in public debates in the 1990s by headscarf issues and, in the 2000s, Islam became entangled in controversies around ethnicity and communalism, *laïcité* and gender equality, the whole thing being surrounded by the spectre of terrorism. As far as the second aspect is concerned this chapter looks at the relationship between Muslim women and women's movements in Britain and France, exploring to what extent they, and issues with which they are concerned, are integrated within women's movements and the demands which feminists have made of the state in order to improve women's lives. A greater part of this chapter is dedicated to the question of Muslims and Islam than to women's movements and their relation with Muslim women as our research establishes that the former has impacted to a greater extent on the political participation and civic engagement of Muslim women.

MUSLIMS AND ISLAM IN BRITISH AND FRENCH SOCIETY

Conceptual Tools: The State and Society

Since this study addresses Muslim women's participation in the public arena, Jepperson's typology (2002) has provided a useful tool for the presentation of societal and political contexts for Muslims in France and Britain. Jepperson defines two constitutive dimensions for European societies: the organisation of *society* which can follow either a 'corporatist' or an 'associational' model and the organisation of *collective agency,* itself subdivided into a 'statist' versus a 'societal' model. In his opinion, France and Britain belong to the 'associational' type whereby collective action and actors have replaced corporations, taking the form of a 'society of individuals organised into classes or other associations rather than a society of orders' (2002: 65); in sociological terms, one could say that *Gemeinschaft* has long given way to *Gesellschaft*. With respect to the organisation of collective authority, he locates France in the 'statist model', characterised by its highly centralised structure whereby the state and society are two antagonistic forces, while in Britain's 'societal' model, state and society both have a place and do not stand in opposition to each other (2002: 67). Moreover, in Britain, the state/society distinction does not reflect as strong a private/public division as in the statist model. One can look at Muslim populations' integration in their respective majority societies in the light of this typology.

Populations of Muslim background arrived as labour migrants to meet the needs of post-Second World War economies in France and Britain where they occupied the lower echelons of the socio-economic pyramid characterised by lower wages, poor working conditions, run-down housing and other indices of poverty. They suffered from both social and racial disadvantage and constituted what sociologists have sometimes labelled 'an underclass' (Rex 1988). Although their structural position, on arrival, was comparable in France and Britain, their modalities of integration reveal marked differences a few decades later. This can be explained by several variables which have played a central role in the development of their interaction with majority societies: their legal status, the history of links between country of origin and country of settlement, the structure of the state, the latter's relationship with the church and the very characteristics of immigrant populations in the respective countries. Moreover, their modalities of action and mobilisation constituted a key factor in the construction of their interaction with their country of settlement.

Britain

Immigrants of Muslim background were first subsumed, with all other labour migrants, under racial and ethnic labels. They were not identified as 'Muslims' until well into the 1990s, when they began to claim a collective Muslim identity and when the categorisation of 'Muslim' emerged in public policy and discourse. The Nationality and Commonwealth Act of 1948 undoubtedly had a pivotal influence on the policies towards those immigrants and on their modes of social organisation. It is vitally significant that the legal status of post-Second World War immigrants who came to Britain from the New Commonwealth is unequalled in other European countries. As Commonwealth subjects, they did not need a visa to enter Britain (although this was progressively restricted from the 1960s onwards) but, more importantly, they enjoyed all social and political rights, on a par with British citizens, soon after their arrival. Unrestricted *jus soli* until 1983 reinforced this trend towards a solid acquisition of citizenship rights (Joly 1995). Moreover, immigrants' collective organisation could take place unhindered by any legal restrictions on the establishment and running of associations by citizens and foreigners (*étrangers*) alike. Commonwealth immigrants seized upon those opportunities to organise and mobilise with great efficiency in the defence of their interests.

Race Relations
The question of immigration rapidly surfaced onto the British political agenda. Post-war Britain was the theatre of contending trends so that the inner tensions traversing different political interests and pressure groups led to a trade-off. The domain of immigration policy staged an increasingly restrictive approach on racial bases towards limiting the arrival of New Commonwealth subjects[1] (Miles and Phizacklea 1984) through successive Immigration Acts, while an integration policy introduced anti-discrimination laws. In this context, immigrants did not remain passive recipients but positioned themselves as major instigators of policies through their agency. Roy Jenkins' 1966 speech is often quoted as the launching pad of a race relations paradigm subsequently leading to an ethnic relations approach and a multicultural policy (Lapping 1970; Patterson 1968). In reality, those policies were largely driven by social action emanating from grass-roots actors at the local level. Immigrant workers constituted the backbone of action in response to a series of events which evidenced the rise of racism in Britain.[2] They broadly organised to defend their collective interests on the basis of class combined with 'race' (Joly 2012). On the one hand, they undertook concerted initiatives to fight for trade union recognition on the shop floor through a series of strikes. On the other hand, they mobilised against racist discrimination in the public sphere through a variety of actions (Josephides 1992). Immigrants from Muslim background were subsumed under this race relations paradigm.

The mass mobilisation of the 1960s and 1970s scored obvious success. On the social level policies were formulated to address the 'social disadvantage' and 'urban deprivation' of immigrants from the New Commonwealth (Candappa and Joly 1994).[3] Anti-discrimination legislation prohibited racial discrimination in the public sphere in 1965, in housing and employment in 1968 and culminated in the wide-ranging Race Relations Act of 1976 (RRA 1976), which was the most developed legislation of its kind in Europe, and from which European Union directives and the RRA (Amendment) Act 2000 have derived.[4] Racial discrimination was explicitly prohibited along the following criteria: 'colour, race, nationality or ethnic or national origin' (RRA 1976, Chapter 74, 2). The RRA 1976 also introduced the concept of indirect discrimination and established the Commission for Racial Equality (CRE), an independent, (relatively) well-funded institution with extensive prerogatives (Layton-Henry 1984).[5] However, the law did not include religion as a criterion of discrimination although this was debated.

Ethnic Communities

In Britain the public recognition of community associations was facilitated by characteristics of the UK state cohabited by several national communities and colonial traditions accustomed to ruling through local structures and leaders. The recognition of new types of communities such as ethnic communities (Parekh 1990) did not present the political structure and culture with the same dilemmas as in France. In addition, a high degree of decentralisation occurred in Britain as far as the management of ethnic relations was concerned despite PM Thatcher's measures to curb the powers of local authorities in general in the 1980s. These factors facilitated interaction between government institutions and community associations, a dialogue assisted by the associational model of British society.

The 1980s witnessed the start of momentous changes in British society at the hands of Thatcher's government which pursued two key objectives: imposing a neo-liberal project marked by privatisations which undermined the welfare state and breaking the back of the working-class movement. The dominant agenda changed, attesting the ebb of working-class-based action and left-oriented ideology. The RRA 1976 had an important symbolic significance but its limited success in practice failed to meet the raised hopes of immigrants and their descendants, especially among the youth, born and brought up in Britain, who felt entitled to equal treatment on a par with their White peers. Moreover, neo-liberal policy which radically undermined any potential amelioration of their situation was compounded by recurrent racial harassment and insulting by police of youth of immigrant backgrounds. Consequently, British cities erupted in riots staged by young people, beginning with Bristol in 1980 and followed by riots in several large industrial towns and cities in 1981 and 1985 (Solomos 1986; Joly 2007). Although those riots were a spontaneous upsurge devoid of planning and organisation, they conveyed a clear message of anger and frustration against racial and social discrimination. They constituted a wake-up call in a country whose self-image was one of 'civilised' negotiations and compromise between civil society and the government. This triggered the beginning of a policy subsequently called the British model of multiculturalism.

The government was prompted to adopt a medium favoured as a legacy of the empire, accustomed to ruling through indirect rule (in India); in Britain this meant that community leaders became significant interlocutors and transmission belts of policies designed to manage the immigrant population. The government made available a considerable amount of funding to be awarded and administered by local authorities enlisting the collaboration of ethnic community associations and leaders. A clear benefit was consequently awarded to this form of social organisation, which had already been promoted by components related to these populations' process of settlement. Indeed, the 1970s ending of new immigration (barring family reunification) had reinforced chain migration and achieved the completion of demographically balanced communities, that is, women and/or children as well as other relatives joining specific neighbourhoods in industrial conurbations in the UK. Moreover, the granting of funds on the basis of ethnic identification meant that mobilising ethnic communities had become the best course of action for immigrants in the defence of their interests, under the new situational guidance (Archer 1995). As a result, populations of Muslim background self-identified through their community associations as Pakistanis and Bangladeshis with additional cleavages along regional lines (in the country of origin).

Social movements among people of immigrant origin pursued two main objectives: the improvement of their living conditions and the securing and transmission of their culture. The policy introduced in the 1980s strengthened the process of ethnic mobilisation, with Muslims adopting the dominant ethnic pattern. Local authorities, under obligation to consult with ethnic associations (Cross et al. 1988), became the main agents of implementation of multicultural policies which broadly rested on three axes: equal opportunity, the recognition of difference and anti-racism. However, the conceptualisation and implementation of multiculturalism were fraught with tensions and conflicts so that a differentiated emphasis was placed on each of the three axes in line with competing interpretations according to the forces at play, the various institutional and social actors and the period examined; the controversies involved have fed an abundant literature which cannot be developed here (Barry 2001; Candappa and Joly 1994; Kundnani 2002; Modood 2007; Runnymede Trust 2000; Sivanandan 2006; Wadia and Allwood 2012). This created a mosaic at the local level which at a later stage came to represent the British model (Joly 2012). Furthermore, a large measure of power was devolved to local government, local institutions and interest groups.

Prior to the early 1980s riots, immigrants had begun to participate in British politics through two main channels: elections and grass-roots associations. A large number actively took part in mainstream British politics, voted, joined the Labour Party and began to stand for elections at least at the local level. The potential access to resources gave a boost to the already flourishing network of associations, but modified the orientation and meaning of their action. The dominant mode of organisation which had derived from a class/race approach thereafter drew mostly on ethnic bases. The change of paradigm was sealed by the inclusion of the ethnic question in the 1991 census; long-settled post-war 'immigrants' became 'ethnic minorities'. A complex set of reasons led to the subsequent differentiation of populations based on Islam. Those include factors related to the international conjuncture, the British national context and the specificity of British Muslim communities. When Islam and Muslims were projected to the fore, mobilisation was based on a Muslim rather than ethnic basis and interaction with public institutions drew out community leaders who self-identified as Muslims. Nonetheless, the recognition and acceptance of Islam were not taken for granted in British society, on account of its prevalent Christian character. Furthermore, this process was slowed down because populations of Muslim background were traversed by cleavages based on ethnic and national origins and along theological lines.

Church, State and Muslim Mobilisation
The existence of an established church, the Church of England, played a significant role in the institutionalisation of Islam in Britain. The Church of England's influence in major domains of state control must not be underestimated (Beckford, Joly and Khosrokhavar 2005), and the fact that the Queen remains the official head of both the state and the church carries great symbolic significance. Notwithstanding, the presence of two long-standing minority religions had led to adjustments for the benefit of Catholicism and Judaism. As a consequence, a window of opportunity was open to potential claims emanating from Islam, a newly established religion (Beckford and Gilliat 1998). Furthermore, Muslims have seen their endeavours boosted by a process of 'deprivatisation' of religion in Europe as pointed out by José Casanova (cited in Beckford 2003: 60), who shows how transnational religious traditions can seek to replace failed secular ideologies by new normative values in the public sphere. This is to be found in religious mobilisation pitted against the domination of markets and through the vision of a common good to offset the individualism of prevalent neo-liberalism. Various tactics are adopted by religious organisations in the pursuit of these goals: lobbying the state apparatus, linking up with political parties, taking up legal actions, striking alliances with groups holding similar views, mobilising sympathisers for protests, sensitising public opinion through the media (Haynes 1998: 8). While Haynes'

proposition was developed from a scrutiny of churches in Europe, it is noticeable that Muslims pursue similar goals through comparable methods. This is the context which guides the self-identification of Muslims, *qua* Muslims, the development of a Muslim paradigm resting on three major factors: Muslim mobilisation, world events projecting Islam to the centre-stage and the London suicide bombings.

Muslims played a central part in the emergence of Islam and Muslims onto the public agenda, through their collective action. The structure of housing and employment and concomitant geographical concentration had favoured the reconstitution of extended family networks together with community and religious institutions which were the main mode of social organisation. The first Muslim requests in the public sphere dealt with planning permission for mosques, Muslim spaces in cemeteries and religious prescriptions in schools, advanced through negotiations on a local level (Nielsen 1992). Education became an important arena of contestation for Muslims and prompted them to overcome their differences. For instance, this concern motivated the creation of the Muslim Liaison Committee in Birmingham to negotiate with the Local Education Authority (LEA) and achieved a *modus vivendi* for Islam in the school environment through the publication of LEA *Guidelines on Meeting the Religious and Cultural Needs of Muslim Pupils* in schools (Joly 1995, 2007). Similar appropriate provisions were negotiated for hospitals and city council services.

At a later stage, two major issues generated a process of mobilisation on a national level in the late 1980s: new education legislation and the publication of Salman Rushdie's *Satanic Verses*. The Education Reform Act 1988 that reaffirmed the Christian character of compulsory collective worship in schools attracted a clamour of protests from Muslim associations which regrouped nationwide and, in alliance with their Jewish counterparts, obtained the introduction of amendments taking their needs into consideration. The Rushdie Affair provoked a massive national mobilisation among Muslims in Britain, much before Ayatollah Khomeini launched his 1989 *Fatwa* against Rushdie's *Satanic Verses*. A heated public debate ensued, which saw the main Christian and Jewish leaders as well as the then Labour Party Deputy Leader, Roy Hattersley, expressing their sympathy for Muslims (Joly 1995, 2007).

The affirmation of a Muslim identity ensued from a combination of social and religious factors. Muslims had failed to benefit from the ethnic agenda and remained greatly disadvantaged compared to other Asians.

Moreover, they suffered from ever-growing Islamophobia. Muslim self-identification in Britain was undeniably the cultural expression of frustration resulting from exclusion, discrimination and deprivation, at the same time as it was underpinned by aspirations to dignity, respect and equality. The emergence of Islam worldwide lent strength to it and the British government reinforced this trend as it instrumentalised Muslim associations in the management of communities. Muslims succeeded in pushing forward their claims for accommodating Islam throughout British society and institutions. They have undoubtedly made a place for themselves in British society (Nielsen 1992; Joly 1995) but remain under-represented in formal political institutions as evidenced by their presence in the House of Commons (13 out of 650 MPs or 2 per cent) compared with the proportion of Muslims in Britain (4.8 per cent—see Muslim Council of Britain 2015: 16). At the local council level, Muslims have done better in recent years and in 2014 Muslim councillors in England constituted 6.5 per cent of newly elected councillors (Buaras 2014). Overall, Muslims have proved to be among the strongest ethno-religious minorities to take part in elections (further detail is provided in Chapter 5).

British Islam in the Twenty-First Century
Islam was projected into the limelight as a consequence of events abroad, beginning with the Iranian revolution in 1979 and followed by the rise of Muslim political movements in other Muslim-majority countries. The collapse of communist regimes gave more salience to Islamic movements, then perceived as the chief challengers to Western powers, in particular the USA whose undisputed hegemony was exporting their model of democracy and economic neo-liberalism. Muslims came to be considered as a potential threat, especially in Britain because of its close identification with the US agenda. This position is clearly expressed in Tony Blair's speech of 5 August 2005, attributing 'some of the same characteristics as revolutionary communism' to radical Islam (*The Guardian* 2005a). Britain's intervention in Iraq alongside the USA reinforced the negative image of Islam which was further exacerbated by the London 7/7 events.

The British model of multiculturalism had held sway for about two decades. However, in the twenty-first century, a new policy orientation was triggered by riots which involved young Muslims in the north of England. The Home Secretary's response was to set up a Ministerial Group on Public Order and Community Cohesion and to commission two government reports which blamed multiculturalism for those riots

(Cantle 2001; Denham 2001). Deploring the community segregation and even the self-segregation which they attributed to Muslim populations in those areas, the reports promoted social/community cohesion.[6]

Multiculturalism also became the target of criticisms from various other sources. Although community cohesion was adopted as a policy substitute to multiculturalism, it can be argued that the latter underwent modifications, taking on the shape of a Muslim paradigm. Indeed, it is noticeable that the strategy developed by the government in response to the 7/7 events focused on Muslim communities in a similar way to when they had responded to the 1980s riots, with ethnic minority interlocutors and associations being replaced by Muslim ones. Although a Commission on Integration and Cohesion was set up following the 7/7 events (DCLG 2010), the general plan mooted in response was implemented through the Preventing Violent Extremism programme (Prevent) which made available a relatively large amount of funding: 70 councils in the UK were awarded £6,000,000 in 2006 and £45,000,000 between 2008 and 2011. Prevent emphasised that it was 'vital that faith leaders and community leaders are involved', and that Prevent initiatives implemented and managed by local authorities must be 'owned by communities and voluntary groups' (Audit Commission 2008: 5). Funding was thus awarded to a large number of Muslim associations, many of which were women's and youth associations. Notwithstanding, the Prevent programme remained highly controversial and gave rise to much criticism. It was accused of dividing different communities, of targeting Muslim extremism while ignoring the extreme right and of failing to address deprivation and marginalisation. Nonetheless, Prevent increased the capacity of Muslim associations as a vector for marshalling resources, just as Black and ethnic minority associations had previously. Finally, the relevance of Islam in British society was evidenced by the inclusion of the religion question in the 2001 census (see Chapter 4).

Muslim Associations and the State
The first Muslim national committee was set up to campaign against the *Satanic Verses* and laid the basis for a more long-term national organisation encouraged by the Labour government elected in 1997. This led to the creation of the Muslim Council of Britain (MCB) in November 1997, bringing together 380 affiliated associations. An interaction between the government and the MCB was established and intensified following the 9/11 events and again after the 7/7 events in 2005. The MCB stressed Muslims' duty to vote (Joly and Imtiaz 2002) and called for Muslim sup-

port of the Labour Party in the 2001 and 2005 elections despite Britain's intervention in Iraq.[7]

Muslims have been at the receiving end of increasingly hostile attacks from the media and public opinion. Although the 9/11 and 7/7 events did not create anti-Muslim prejudice, they considerably strengthened it, generating a 'moral panic' comparable to the anti-Black prejudice depicted by Stuart Hall and others (Hall et al. 1978), and verbal and physical aggressions against Asians and Muslims despite the fact that all the major Muslim organisations had categorically denounced the terrorist attacks. These developments spawned a new type of racism in Britain based on cultural/religious rather than biological criteria. In 1997 the Commission on British Muslims and Islamophobia recorded the specific characteristics of Islamophobia (Commission on British Muslims and Islamophobia 1997: 4). The government two-pronged strategy forged in the wake of the 9/11 events which was designed to appease Muslims in Britain while unconditionally supporting US initiatives in the War on Terror was replicated in 2005 with a reinforced internal security approach. In 2005, Tony Blair vouched that a firm stance was to be adopted: 'the rules of the game are changing' (*The Guardian* 2005a) and tougher anti-terrorist measures were introduced. The 2001 Anti-Terrorism Crime and Security Act was strengthened in 2005 by new legislation. The Prevention of Terrorism Act 2005 and the Terrorism Act 2006 comprised around 200 new anti-terrorist provisions including the extension of the detention period to 28 days, with proposals for further extensions being periodically raised. Numerous raids and arrests in Muslim neighbourhoods also took place.

Britain's military intervention in Afghanistan and Iraq brought about unintended outcomes. The Stop the War Coalition campaigning against British intervention was founded by a left opposition to the Labour government but released new channels of participation for Muslims, who accounted for around 20 per cent of campaign participants (Yaqoob 2005). This alliance between the Far Left and Muslims was rendered possible by a social and political culture, whereby the acceptance of Islam was written into an engagement against discrimination and for the defence of human rights. When Britain entered the war, traditional community male leaders cautiously stood back: it appears that they were alarmed by the intense Islamophobia resulting from the 9/11 events and Britain's unconditional support for the War on Terror (Yaqoob 2005). This opened up a window of opportunity for Muslim women's participation, which erupted onto the public scene.

The anti-multicultural, anti-Islam rhetoric further increased in 2011. Prime Minister Cameron emphatically condemned Islam and Muslims at a European Summit on Security (Wintour 2011). He announced that his government would 'no longer fund or share platforms' with 'organisations that while non-violent are certainly in some cases part of the problem' and accused 'these segregated communities [of] behaving in ways that run counter to our values' (Ibid.). This rhetoric was matched by massive cuts in public spending and a partial dismantling of the Prevent programme whose funding, although highly controversial, had supported many Muslim associations. The most lethal feature of Cameron's policy in this respect might simply have been its drastic reduction of funding to all associations, a measure which disproportionately hit Black and minority ethnic and Muslim communities.

Although the *hijab* does not raise any controversies in current public debates, the *niqab* has been the object of challenges and discussions (see below). Meanwhile, Muslims are at the receiving end of growing prejudice and hostility that have been evidenced by opinion poll data between 2008 and 2010 (Heath and Martin 2013: 1006), despite the enactment of the 2010 Equality Act which covers discrimination on religious grounds. Anti-terrorist measures were accumulated through five pieces of anti-terrorist legislation in eight years between 2000 and 2008 (Kapoor 2013: 1030). Raids in Muslim neighbourhoods and arrests of young people multiplied, as testified by a Ministry of Justice report which took note of the increase in searches under the Terrorism Act 2001: 37,000 in 2006–2007, 117,000 in 2007–2008, and 148,000 in 2009 (Kapoor 2013: 1041). Also, if deemed an unquestionable threat, individuals could be extradited and their citizenship removed (Ibid.). At the same time, the English Defence League (EDL), a far right nationalist and anti-Islamic group, emerged with fresh vigour, demonstrating against the 'threat of terrorism' but also alleging that Islam posed a danger to English culture.

Muslims and Islam in France

The majority of post-Second World War immigrant workers initially came to France from former French colonies in North Africa where Islam was the main religion,[8] while immigrants from Turkey and sub-Saharan Africa arrived at a later stage. In its first phase, French immigration policy followed a laissez-faire approach, which allowed entry whether or not immigrants held work and residence permits. Determining the conditions of entry and settlement was supposed to be the responsibility of the Office National d'Immigration (ONI) under the auspices of the Ministries of Employment and that of Population. In reality, anarchy prevailed as companies organised parallel recruitment circuits, with immigrant workers obtaining regularised status *a posteriori*. Notwithstanding this, discrete administrative practices attempted to prioritise Europeans over North Africans. In 1974, the oil crisis and economic recession brought about the closure of French doors to immigration. As in Britain, it engendered important changes in the demographic profile of immigrant populations so that family reunification turned temporary labour migration into a long-term, subsequently definitive settlement (Leveau 2002).

Legal Status, Perception, Participation
According to Jepperson's typology, France constitutes an 'associational' society characterised by channels of participation. However, this only applies to French citizens, thus excluding post-Second World War immigrants, who, in their vast majority, were attributed the legal status of foreigners and were thus deprived of political, civic and social rights. The legal position of Algerians was more complex but only a minority gained French nationality. Furthermore, a waiting period withheld eligibility to vote or to stand for local and national elections, once naturalised French (Bertossi 2004: 111). This was a major obstacle standing in the way of immigrants' participation in French society and presented a critical difference with Britain since, in France, immigrants most of whom were not French citizens could not take part in the political process or public institutions, being consequently deprived of the political clout enjoyed by their counterparts in Britain.

In France, immigration remained for a long time an economic issue but was projected onto the political agenda by the Front National (FN) whose influence grew with its electoral successes from 1983 onwards, gaining 35 deputies in the National Assembly in 1986. The main plank of its campaign was anti-immigration, vilipending those it called the *Français de papier* (French on paper). A right-wing government elected in 1986 set in train reforms limiting access to French nationality for populations from former colonies and their children. The initially resisted White Paper was pushed through Parliament in 1993 by the Minister of the Interior, Charles Pasqua, so that the 1993 Reform of the Nationality Code denied many immigrants access to French nationality and raised obstacles for all of them. The new Code was undeniably designed to exclude people from former colonies (most of whom at the time were of Muslim background) and their children. Although certain clauses were withdrawn at a later stage to reinstate the status quo ante, this stop and start policy constantly pushed back real possibilities of participation for immigrants and their offspring. It also encouraged a long-lasting exclusionary attitude on the part of majority French society.

The legal status discrepancy between the two countries under study has many implications. In Britain, immigrants/ethnic minorities were entitled to all the social and political rights even if they suffered a social and racial disadvantage in practice. In France, they were victims of the same disadvantages not only *de facto* but also *de jure*. At the height of the welfare state and economic expansion, most North African immigrants were excluded from its benefits and found themselves relegated to the margins of society. In addition, discrimination and overt racism prevailed in the absence of legal instruments capable of curbing them. Furthermore, the Algerian War exacerbated negative perceptions of all North Africans (Joly 1991), through its war propaganda which portrayed them as traitors and enemies of the nation, and being part of a culture/religion which was alien to the French one. Islam was clearly intertwined as a component of this stigmatisation since the Algerian population had waged a national liberation war and was designated as *Français musulmans* in the three French departments of Algeria. In mainland France, where the term 'Muslim' was not in use, their marginalisation and exclusion multiplied.

Associations
In contrast with Britain, French law did not allow foreigners to organise associations (until 1981), which further hindered most immigrants' ability to pursue collective action. Moreover, they missed out on all the resources deriving from associative life in the country of settlement (Rex et al. 1987). Finally, a political culture came to prevail, which fixed a conceptualisation of these populations as everlasting 'immigrants', evidenced by the terminology in use; that is, their children and grandchildren born and brought up in France were being called *issus de l'immigration* ('stemming from immigration'), although they were French nationals. The dominant political culture also conveyed the notion that their political participation was out of place or unwelcome, a perception illustrated by the National Assembly's 2 per cent of Black and ethnic minority deputies (Keslassy 2012)[9] which remains disproportionately low compared with

the corresponding 12 per cent (estimated by the Conseil représentatif des associations noires, CRAN 2012) of the same population in France.

In 1981, the newly elected Socialist government granted foreigners the right to form associations, supported by public funding, which then flourished among immigrants. However, the subsequent change of government in 1986 reduced institutional support, dealing a lethal blow to many associations (Lapeyronnie 1993; Cesari 1998). The early 1980s had also witnessed the mobilisation of young people, the descendants of immigrants, who protested against racist crimes through mini riots in the Minguettes, a high-rise housing estate located in Venissieux, in the greater Lyon area, followed by a mass demonstration, the *Marche pour l'égalité et contre le racisme* (the March for equality and against racism) or *Marche des Beurs*. The march left Marseille on 15 October with 32 young people and was 100,000-strong when it reached Paris. The demonstrators demanded the creation of a ten-year residence permit for settled immigrants and the right to vote in local elections, with the motto 'Living together, with our differences, in a society of solidarity', a testament of their aspirations for citizenship and equality, against racism and discrimination. The ten-year residence permit was accorded but not the right to vote.

Twenty-four years after the *Marche pour l'égalité*, the ten-year residence permit was called into question by Nicolas Sarkozy's government, while the criticism that those populations do not want 'citizen's integration' keeps peppering media and politicians' discourse. It seems that the 'associational' character of French society remained largely null and void for immigrants from former colonies who were for the most part Muslims. The immigrants' foreigner status, the alternating policy between an integration and a non-integration approach, the traumatic baggage of the Algerian War led to the perception that these populations do not belong to the national community, with Islam being subsequently put forward as the ultimate marker of Otherness.

Ethnicity and Communalism
One key parameter established through the Jacobin heritage of the 1789 Revolution is that the Republic is 'one and indivisible'; hence it excludes recognition of any particular cultural identity in the public institutional domain. In effect, the national community imposes the cultural traits of the majority on minority and regional groups. The doctrine of assimilationism implemented in the colonies was applied to immigrants and the very concept of 'community' has become anathema in France.

Moreover, in the 2000s, Islam has been intermittently mobilised by politicians and media to discredit the populations concerned (Van Reekum et al. 2012). The supposed cultural incompatibility of immigrants with French society had already been posited during the 1984–1986 major strikes in the metals industry (Noiriel 2007: 613). North African populations, in particular, were quoted as a cause for concern by the authorities on account of their cultural identity and their social organisation. For those who extol the integrity of the Republic and social stability and who claim that any kind of communalism threatens French identity, Muslim populations in the 2000s embody this danger on two levels: in deprived neighbourhoods where young people's frustrations spill over and on the international front because the youth in the *banlieues*[10] are deemed susceptible to the attraction of the Muslim *ummah* and its radical offshoots (Roy 2005: 143). Muslims have been pilloried by prominent politicians and members of the government for 'communalism' whilst the latter has never been defined. Communities and 'communalism'[11] were purported to be anti-republican by politicians, President Chirac himself warning against the danger it represented for France: 'The danger lies in the unleashing of centrifugal forces, the glorification of particularisms which divide. [...] Communalism cannot be France's choice [...]. She would lose her soul' (Chirac 2003). The fact is that these declarations primarily addressed Muslims and Islam, as illustrated by the following discussion on *laïcité*.

Laïcité and National Identity
The emergence of a religious/Muslim paradigm in France was predicated upon highly centralised relations between the state and religion which are encapsulated in the concept of *laïcité*, covering a cluster of values and institutions. *Laïcité* was fully developed under the Third Republic, with the 1905 law separating the state and the church and which continues to govern the relations between the two even today (see Poulat 1987; Boepflug et al. 1996; Baubérot 1997, 2000; Willaime 2004).

Throughout its history, *laïcité* has evolved and continues to lends itself to various interpretations, comprising at least three operative meanings: first, setting religion and the state in an antagonistic and mutually exclusive relationship; second, making no concession to religion in institutional terms although in practice showing flexibility towards religious rights; third, interpreting *laïcité* as a neutral attitude of the powers that be towards religion. *Laïcité* broadly implies that all faiths are to be treated on par, and that the state recognises them if they respect public order, pluralism and the exclusion of religion from the institutions of the Republic—especially state-run schools (Beckford, Joly and Khosrokhavar 2005). On the other hand, as Willaime (2004: 296, 330–333) emphasises, the degree of actual—as distinct from ideological or legal—separation of church and state is open to nuance. For example, the public culture of France has remained predominantly Catholic; the Republic still finances extensive religious activities in the Alsace-Moselle region and in some overseas territories; state funds contribute to the maintenance of church buildings forming part of the national heritage. Historically, the Catholic Church, which was radically opposed to *laïcité*, progressively (and particularly since Vatican II) came to make compromises. The concept of *laïcité* is more complex than could appear. For instance, Roy (2005) defines *laïcité* as a philosophy, a political principle and a legislative apparatus while Baubérot identifies three dimensions of *laïcité*: 'liberty of conscience and liberty of cult', the 'non-recognition of cults' and 'the freedom of organisation for churches' (2004: 8, 9). *Laïcité* is sometimes deemed an ideology, humorously described as a typically French religion, France's 'fourth religion' (Pinto 2004: 78). It is sometimes accused of *laïcisme*, an ideological tool in the hands of politicians: it would appear that this increasingly hardened interpretation of *laïcité* is currently prevalent.

The appeased tension between state and religion was rekindled with the establishment of Islam in France, a newcomer which faces numerous problems in the public domain. As minorities of Algerian background still constitute a significant proportion of Muslims in France, this means that Islam in the *banlieues* continues to suffer the painful stigmas of the traumatic decolonisation process which threw France and Algeria into the throes of a murderous war (Joly 1991). Generalised atrocities committed by the French army have remained unacknowledged by French governments (although briefly mentioned by President Hollande in Algeria during his 2012 official visit). Consequently, latent memories of this war endure in French society and among Muslims in France, sometimes two or three generations after their settlement (Amiraux 2002). The populations involved were long conceptualised as Arabs and/or *Maghrebins* until the end of the 1980s when Islam was placed under the spotlight. In 1989, the wearing of headscarves by two schoolgirls at a school in Creil generated a politico-media storm (see Chapter 8). Islam was posed as a societal problem with a gender dimension for the first time and placed onto the public agenda; an interrogation on North Africans' capacity to integrate applied to all generations. Moreover, conflicts taking place in Algeria between the state and the Front islamique du salut (FIS) also affected the image of Muslims, as bombs were exploded in Paris in the 1990s. On 11 September 2001, these issues were compounded by the Al Qaeda attacks on the Twin Towers in New York and Pentagon in Arlington, Virginia. Although France did not espouse Bush's War on Terror unconditionally as did Britain, Islam and Muslims in France, nonetheless, suffered the brunt of heightened hostility and suspicion. New terrorist attacks in Paris on 7 and 9 January (the *Charlie Hebdo* killings) and on 13 November 2015 have exacerbated this process. However, these events did not alter the results of our empirical research since they took place after the completion of our fieldwork. Moreover, they are too recent to permit a valid assessment.

A negative image of Islam prevails in France, an image which equates it with communalism, with an anti-republican/anti-democratic political project and with terrorism (Khosrokhavar 1996). In the 1990s, the dispute over the wearing of the Islamic headscarf at school was resolved by a decision of the Conseil d'État which permitted it as long as it was not accompanied by proselytism. However, the further feminisation of the question of Islam was engineered through revived controversies in the early 2000s with Muslim women becoming a renewed object of contention between majority society and the North African/Muslim minority.[12] The Stasi Commission, appointed by President Chirac, published the *Rapport de la Commission de réflexion sur l'application du principe de laïcité dans la République* on 11 December 2003, which resulted in the law of 15 March 2004, prohibiting the wearing of 'conspicuous' religious symbols at school. Officially, this law concerns all religious symbols but it was aimed specifically at Muslim pupils wearing a headscarf. As a consequence, general hostility and discrimination against headscarfed women increased significantly and gradually spread throughout French society. Although such legislation only applies to the public sector, the Collectif contre l'islamophobie en France points out the abusive use of the law in the private sector where many companies prohibit headscarves in their dress regulations or in practice. For instance, a court case was brought in 2008 against a private nursery (the Baby Loup affair) by an employee dismissed for wearing a headscarf. After lengthy legislative wrangling, a second appeal court hearing, in 2013, found against the plaintiff while on 28 March 2013 President François Hollande declared that he was in favour of a law on respect for *laïcité* in all establishments looking after children, including private ones (Gorce 2013). The gender dimension was pursued in 2010 by a discussion on the wearing of the full-face veil in public spaces, a debate purportedly designed to defend women's rights and dignity. Although an infinitely small number of women were wearing it,[13] this motivated the enactment of a law voted in the National Assembly, on 13 July 2010, to prohibit the concealment of one's face in public spaces.[14] This took place concurrently with a debate launched by the French government on national identity, which evidently targeted Islam and Muslims as antonymic to French identity. The close link between the full-face veil and national identity had already been substantiated by the refusal to naturalise a Moroccan woman who wore the full-face veil because the 'practice of her religion [is] incompatible with essential values of the French community and in particular the principle of the equality between sexes' (Conseil d'Etat 2008). Likewise, an Ipsos-*Le Monde* 2013 opinion poll delivered sombre results of French people's views of Islam: 74 per cent considered Islam as 'intolerant' and incompatible with French values, 80 per cent thought that Islam tried to impose its way of life on everyone and more than 50 per cent judged that the majority of Muslims were totally or partly 'fundamentalist', a term heavily loaded with extremist connotations in France (Le Bars 2013). Incidents and declarations involving women's dress code and *laïcité* have multiplied which confirm the tension node surrounding this issue. A few examples illustrate this situation. In April 2013, President Hollande declared that agencies which delivered a public service or received public funding needed to follow the same rules (*inter alia* about dress code) as public institutions (Camus 2013). In Trappes, an adolescent was insulted and attacked violently by White men who beat her up and tore off her headscarf (Ibid.). She subsequently attempted suicide, jumping out of the window of her family apartment. In May 2015, one pupil was suspended from a secondary school on the grounds that she wore a long skirt deemed to infringe the law on *laïcité*. The Observatoire de la laïcité was commissioned by the government to provide a report on the question of banning the headscarf in universities (Interview 24 June 2015 Paris).

The increasing salience of *laïcité* is symptomatic of a hardening French identity, symbolically excluding Muslims from the national community, as explicated by scholars (Wieviorka 2015). Bowen identified French identity as a close 'association between *laïcité* and *francité*', prevalent among intellectuals and politicians (Bowen 2004: 328). *Laïcité* is often quoted as the mark of France's unique character described as 'the French exception'

(Baubérot 2004: 6). According to Baubérot and Roy, France is experiencing the development of an '*laïcité* identity' (Baubérot 2004: 6; Roy 2005: 33). This analysis is further supported in the political domain by the Stasi Report which states that '*laïcité* is also related to national identity' (Stasi 2003: 18) and equates *laïcité* with a founding myth (Stasi 2003: 3). Indeed, according to this Report, *laïcité* underpins both national unity and the Republic, 'a value on which national unity is grounded', 'a corner stone of the republican pact' (Stasi 2003: 4). President Chirac himself upheld the glorification of *laïcité*: '*laïcité* is written in our traditions. It is at the heart of our republican identity' (17 December 2003). It can be argued that *laïcité* constitutes a vessel, the content of which changes according to the electoral needs of particular politicians and governments. One serious consequence of the founding myth discourse around *laïcité*, reinforced and legitimised by legislation, is that it has been subsequently embraced by large sections of French society. What is overlooked is that the campaign for the separation of the state and the church in the nineteenth century opposed the full might of the Catholic Church and its invasive influence over state institutions such as government, the army and schools, coupled with its pervasive cultural and moral domination. In contrast, the offensive against Islam and Muslims targets a discriminated, disadvantaged group that wields little influence in majority society.

The Conseil Français du Culte Musulman
Nevertheless, Muslims in France are the largest Muslim population in a Western European country. This has brought about initiatives to regulate the interaction between the state and Islam. Quite unexpectedly the methodology of *laïcité* provided a formula which sought to turn Islam from being a problem into Islam as a solution (Pinto 2004: 84). This strategy was unwittingly revealed by the Stasi Report which promoted *laïcité* as a means 'to conciliate living together with pluralism and diversity' (Stasi 2003: 19). On the strength of the 1905 law, the state in the 2000s has taken upon itself the novel duty to intervene, purportedly to correct the historical lacuna which had not accounted for Islam alongside Catholicism, Protestantism and Judaism.[15] According to the Haut conseil à l' intégration, the legitimacy of state intervention was grounded on the following three principles: the principle of equality, the liberty of conscience and the respect of order and public health (Haut conseil à l' intégration 2000: 56, 57, 58). The principle of equality was the weightiest since it justified the claim that *de jure* and *de facto* inequalities between religions existing on

French territory ought to be redressed. Liberty of conscience and practice coincided with the question of order and public health, since Islam remained hampered by obstacles to the organisation of its practice, such as obtaining planning permission for mosques and the ritual slaughter of animals. The decision to act to create a representative Muslim organisation, the Conseil français du culte musulman (CFCM), was approved by the two political parties (the Socialists and the Gaullist Rassemblement pour la République) which had alternated in government after an early initiative from Pierre Joxe who, in 1989, had convened a Conseil de réflexion sur l'Islam en France (CORIF) (Boyer 1998). The French government stated that it aimed to counteract foreign influences (from countries of origin or from international Islamic movements) to replace 'l'islam en France' with 'l'islam de France' (*Europe* 1–2 May 2012) and to invite Islam to the 'table de la République' (Mas 2003). Additionally, unofficial government objectives included the domestication or taming of Islam and controlling young people in the *banlieues*, who were considered a threat to law and order or potential recruits for radical Islam. The latter objective was certainly not achieved as seen below, while the creation of the CFCM has in no way alleviated discrimination and prejudice against Muslims.

The Riots
Autumn 2005 witnessed an epidemic of riots throughout France for about a month. A state of emergency was declared on 15–16 November on the strength of a law passed during the Algerian War in 1955. Politicians from the governing Union pour un Mouvement Populaire (UMP) conjured up the danger of 'extremism', blamed drug traffickers, indicted polygamy and Islam. They implied that the rioters' actions were planned and organised even though a police intelligence service (Renseignements généraux) report, in December 2005, rejected the notion of planned riots and that Islamists were responsible. However, the report failed to dispel the suspicions projected onto Islam despite the fact that it emphasised the young people's 'condition of social exclusion from French society' as the chief cause of the riots (*Le Monde* 2005). Social disadvantage was demonstrated by various pieces of research much before the 2005 riots, documenting the precarious living conditions of these populations which formed ghettoes of poverty marked by unemployment, derelict living conditions and failure at school. For instance, a 2005 study and a more recent report in 2015 demonstrated how middle-class Whites had created segregation akin to *de facto* apartheid for pupils of those neighbourhoods (Felouzis et al. 2005; Son and Riegert 2015).

This catalogue of negative factors does not suffice, however, to explain the 2005 riots. It is impossible to understand them without taking into account recurrent racism and discrimination, which are omnipresent fellow travellers in all spheres of French society and public life. The 1972 law on racism and more recent laws adopted in conformity with European directives have failed to curb racism and discrimination which continue unabated. The influence of the FN has suppressed any discourse and proposals which may have advocated effective legislation and policies against discrimination and racism. Official reports reveal a bleak balance sheet in this respect. For example, the Observatoire des discriminations demonstrated that a job applicant of North African origin is likely to receive five times fewer positive responses to job applications lodged. The conclusions of the Groupe d'études et de luttes contre les discriminations (GELD) criticised the operation of the 114 telephone helpline and of the Commissions départementales d'accès à la citoyenneté (CODAC)[16]: of the 120 daily calls to the 114 helpline, 82 per cent were not followed up; and most cases were shelved *sine die*, particularly when complaints against police or schools were involved (CNCDH 1993). The GELD records the passivity of the judiciary regarding racism and the climate of impunity resulting from it (Poli 2005). Institutional barriers are compounded by the distrust expressed by victims of racism (Poli 2005: 218, 406). In the 2000s, discrimination against Muslims has been further exacerbated by legislation (the 2010 law against the face veil in public spaces) which excludes many Muslim women from participation in the public sphere. Social, racial and religious disadvantage are made worse by the fact that Muslims are not well-represented or heeded in the political sphere. Young people rebel against what they perceive as a democratic deficit, illustrated by the National Assembly which includes the smallest number of deputies of Maghrebi or Middle Eastern, and by association Muslim, immigrant background.

The tensions surrounding Islam were exacerbated when *Charlie Hebdo* journalists and hostages taken in a Kosher supermarket were killed by radical Islamists on 7 and 9 January 2015, respectively. The President and Prime Minister were careful to differentiate Muslims from radical Islamists in their declarations but attacks against mosques and Muslims, nonetheless, increased considerably. In February 2015, the Interior Minister, Bernard Caseneuve, announced the creation of a new body whose purpose was to provide a better representation of Muslims. This body would comprise the CFCM, Muslim regional committees, imams, Muslim intellectuals, theologians and other relevant persons and would meet twice a year with government representatives (*Le Monde* 26 February 2015).

Muslim Women Between Feminism and the State

Western feminism[17] is seen by Black and ethnic minority feminists in Europe and North America and by those in the developing world to address the concerns and aspirations of affluent White women only and to consider sexism and misogyny as the principal axis of women's oppression in human societies. Western feminism has long been accused of ignoring the intersecting oppressions of 'race'/ethnicity, faith and class endured by women worldwide and women's struggles structured by colonialism and racism and hence of excluding equality demands based on grounds other than sex/gender. The neglect of experiences of women who are not White, middle-class and of a Judeo-Christian background is considered by many Black and ethnic minority feminists in Britain and France to have undermined their struggles and contributed to their misrecognition[18] by the state. It also led Black and ethnic minority women, Muslims among them, to organise separately. The section below does two things: it examines relations between mainstream women's movements in France and Britain and women from Muslim communities; and, second, considers how these relations triangulate with the state's approach to Muslim women where relevant. Because Muslims have only been seen and spoken about as a category relatively recently, parts of the discussion below refer to women from Black and ethnic minority communities rather than Muslim women *per se*. It should be understood that Muslim women were involved in Black and ethnic minority women's organisations and struggles (see Chapter 5).

France

The MLF and 'Race'/Ethnicity
The second wave feminist movement in France (Mouvement de libération des femmes, MLF) emerged later than its British counterpart, emerging from the New Left and student militancy of the May 1968 events (see Allwood and Wadia 2000: 173–190; Wadia 1993: 148–169; Allwood 1998: 25–44). Although a heterogeneous movement in terms of the jostling liberal, traditional Left, New Left and radical feminist ideologies it contained, it was overwhelmingly White and middle-class. The idea that

immigrant or Black and ethnic minority women could have different experiences, problems and claims from White women was largely non-existent. Feminist grass-roots activists and public intellectuals who were starting to build alternative narratives of French society, culture and politics in order to place women centre-stage worked on a model of White, middle-class women, thus ignoring not just immigrant women settling in France from the 1970s onwards, but also Black and ethnic minority women from France's overseas departments and poor White working-class women. The Senegalese author Awa Thiam, whose work *La parole aux negresses* was published in France in 1978, was an early critic of French/Western feminism. She pointed out that by believing that sexism happened to women and racism to (Black) men, French feminists were invisibilising Black women whose experiences and position in society were different to those of White women. This disregard meant that issues affecting migrant and ethnic minority women (whether related to their legal status in France as immigrants, their exclusionary position in education or the labour market or their under-representation in elected decision-making bodies) were not taken up by the MLF in its campaigns and, consequently, little or no pressure was placed on politicians and public to acknowledge such issues. Indeed, the lack of support for this category of women, by French feminism, meant that the republican state's refusal to recognise sex/gender, ethnicity/'race' went unchallenged most of the time. However, it is possible to locate some voices within the MLF which accepted that ignoring differences of 'race'/ethnicity among women could lead to inequalities in policy outcomes. For example, feminists in the Mouvement pour la liberté de l'avortement et de la contraception—MLAC—called on MLF activists to denounce what it called racist and Malthusian government policy which produced inequalities between young women due to the banning of contraception for young (White) French women under 18 in mainland France while it was imposed on poor, young Black women in France's overseas departments. By and large, however, calls to recognise that systems of sexism and racism intersected to produce certain inequalities and to campaign against both these systems of oppression went unheeded in 1970s France. And certainly the French state did not engage with migrant and ethnic minority women *qua* women on the basis that the state's relationship was with individual citizens characterised by 'oneness' or 'sameness' (Scott 2007: 11) rather than any specific social, ethnic or religious identity.

The 1980s saw the demobilisation of the MLF and the entry of many feminists into state structures such as the Socialist Ministry of Women's

Rights (MWR) established in 1981 and third sector organisations. Although visible feminism and street politics had declined, the advent of Socialist government in 1981 and increased funding, through the MWR, for women's community organisations, gave rise to new autonomous groups, campaigning around single or linked issues, among migrant and ethnic minority women. The decline of the MLF as a mass movement appeared to create a space in which smaller groups often pooled meagre resources and organised on both an anti-sexist and an anti-racist basis. Thus the early to mid-1980s saw the formation of small alliances between certain mainstream feminists and migrant and ethnic minority women's groups around issues of racism and discrimination in public services and housing, the workplace and the question of immigration and nationality. However, as small organisations their influence on local and national policy formulation was minimal.

Feminists and the Veil
However, it is the headscarf debate and the 2004 law banning conspicuous religious symbols in state schools which brought relations between French feminists, the state and Muslim women into sharp focus. The controversy over wearing the Islamic headscarf/*hijab* in state schools dates back to 1989 when three Muslim girls were excluded from school, in the town of Creil, for not removing their headscarf while at school.[19] The school's failure to reach a compromise with the girls meant that the state assumed responsibility for the issue, thus sparking off a national debate which split French society into camps for and against the headscarf. Although the debate subsided following a compromise ruling of the Conseil d'État (see above), its seeds were sown and similar debates would resurface after the 9/11 events eventually resulting in the 2004 law. The divisions cut across social groups, party politics and religious affiliations. They also split French feminism and led to the accusation by many Muslim women that feminism's support for the state whether intended or not let them down, that an anti-Islamic feminism paved the way for the adoption of a law against women from disadvantaged minority communities.

The overwhelming majority of French feminists declared themselves against the wearing of the headscarf or veil (*voile*) in school on the basis that it undermined gender equality. Some also opposed it because, they argued, it would weaken French republican principles (among which *laïcité*) deemed the best protection for women's equal rights. Those opposing the headscarf may be placed in two distinct categories as identified by Dot-Pouillard (2007): that of second wave 'legacy feminism', concerned with protecting the gains made by women since the 1960s; that of neo-republican feminism. The first category comprised mainly ex-MLF activists in third sector women's organisations which formed part of large federative networks such as Collectif national pour les droits des femmes, the Mouvement pour le planning familial and the Collectif d'associations pour le droit à l'avortement et à la contraception. These feminists were resolute in their opposition to Muslim schoolgirls wearing the headscarf but at the same time refused to side with the (right-wing) government in favour of a ban because they doubted the latter's newfound zeal for women's rights. In taking a line against the government and the headscarf law, legacy feminists were preserving a feminism which was anti-establishment in its roots and wary about engagement with the state. On the other hand, by positioning themselves against the wearing of the headscarf by Muslim schoolgirls, legacy feminists saw themselves continuing MLF traditions of opposing conservative, reactionary forces as represented by religion.

However, what was striking about their *ni loi, ni voile* position was that the voices of a socially deprived, minority population of women were entirely erased by those whose claims historically had rested on the defence of women's independent interests. Moreover, Islam was essentialised—presented as a homogeneous creed, incapable of being interpreted and expressed by anyone other than radical Islamists and certainly not by Muslim women. While this represents the majority position of legacy feminism, there were voices of dissent including that of Christine Delphy who argued that it was neither possible nor helpful to draw parallels between feminist opposition to a historically powerful French Catholic Church and opposition to institutional Islam in France and to essentialise Islam as a unitary religious force (represented by fundamentalists) which manipulated Muslim girls and women (Delphy 2004, 2005).

The category of neo-republican feminists who opposed the wearing of the headscarf in schools was represented by a younger, more ethnically diverse generation of women activists belonging to or following groups such as Fadela Amara's Ni putes ni soumises and its satellite groupings[20] and the *Prochoix* journal collective established by Fiametta Venner and Caroline Fourest. It also enjoyed wider support from Socialist Party women and less substantial backing from feminists in the Communist Party and the far Left. While the starting point for these feminists was also the protection of gains made by women over four decades, their strategy was to link issues of equality between women and men with *laïcité* and the reinforcement of French republicanism which for them constituted the front line against anti-feminist and anti-democratic forces. For these feminists, the explanation for young Muslim girls wearing the headscarf (whether willingly or through pressure) was not to be found in any crisis of identity brought about by social exclusion (as argued by legacy feminists), but in the rise of a macho Islamism and communitarianism in the inner city areas of Paris and other French cities. And while legacy feminists believed that the only way to draw young Muslim women away from retrograde ethno-religious practices was by improving their social conditions and giving them a stake in French society, neo-republican feminists saw the defence of *laïcité* and state republicanism as the only way to defeat aggressively masculine Islam which forced girls and women to cover up. Hence their critique of the veil became the main element of their women's rights campaigns; they were fervent promoters of the law, supporting the state in banning the headscarf and excluding girls who flouted the law from school.

In opposition to the two components of French feminism discussed above, a third strand supported girls who wore the headscarf at school without promoting the wearing of the headscarf. This strand of feminism comprised groups such as the Collectif une école pour tout-e-s (CEPT), supported by women from far Left groups and Muslim organisations such as the Collectif des musulmans de France and the Collectif féministes pour l'égalité (CFPE) whose members included legacy feminists such as Christine Delphy and Monique Crignon and which also enjoyed the support of some academics and groups such as the Collectif des féministes indigènes led by Houria Bouteldja of Les indigènes de la république. This assembly of feminists included both Muslim and non-Muslim women who called for a repeal of the 2004 law on the grounds that it was racist (its main target being Muslims from Black and ethnic minority background and their religion), sexist (it impacted disproportionately on Muslim girls) and essentialist (it implied the headscarf was universally a symbol of oppression despite the various interpretations attached to it by wearers and non-wearers). Many also saw the law as part of the French colonial imaginary which represented Muslims and their religion as the exceptional Other. Hence, the reaction of mainstream French feminism to the headscarf and Muslim women and girls was seen as an outcome of the same colonial legacy. Adopting the strapline 'Against a single model of women's liberation', these feminists challenged the view that feminism was universal as in the dominant French/Western model and that only one meaning (the oppression of women in Islam) was ascribable to the Islamic headscarf.

The relationship between French feminists and Muslim women continues to be troubled (Delphy 2015), with tensions heightening each time reports of Muslim women abused in their family or community come to light, with the eruption of every urban rebellion involving young Muslims, with every act of terrorist violence committed by Muslims and every law passed which targets Muslim women or Muslims generally. French feminism is accused by Muslim women of not just siding with the state but of accepting the state's redefinition of feminism. In accepting the state's view that Muslim women's dress signifies their oppression by Muslim men and that *laïcité* protects women's rights, French feminists are indicted for forgetting two fundamental principles: a woman's right to choose, 'We do not promote the wearing of the veil yet we defend the right for each woman to choose' (Ismahane Chouder CFPE, cited by Naili 2014); and upholding the right of girls to education after years spent fighting to earn that right (Marie Laure Bousquet CFPE, cited by Naili Ibid.). The French sociologist Saïd Bouamama, a supporter of the CEPT, sees the collusion (whether intended or not) between French feminism and the state in its attitude towards Muslim women and girls as rooted in France's colonial history:

> In the end, it comes down to playing the [French] 'values' card, calling on the state school to liberate these girls, in spite of themselves, as they are trapped by parental authority and the weight of traditions (…) It is for their own good that one should not take their opinion into account. They must be constrained in order to be freed. [France's] civilising mission which claimed to free the natives in spite of themselves will have been at work here. (Bouamama 2004b: 41–42)

The collusion between feminism and the state in France and the conflation of French values and women's rights has meant that the struggle for Muslim women's rights takes place outside mainstream women's organisations. However, without the support of the large women's rights networks such as the Collectif national pour les droits des femmes and given that Muslim women's organisations, where they exist, are small and poorly resourced means that their concerns and interests remain blocked.

Britain

The Women's Movement and Black Feminism[21]
In Britain, as in France, the women's liberation movement (WLM), which emerged and developed in the 1960s and 1970s, was White and middle-

class. Although it comprised various ideologies (liberal, radical, socialist, Marxist), the starting point for the majority of WLM feminists was that women's subordinate position in the family, reproductive controls, their historical exclusion from the labour market and politics and so on were primarily features of patriarchy (see, among others, Bouchier 1983; Coote and Campbell 1987; Gelb 1986, 1989; Randall and Lovenduski 1993). The WLM's understanding of Britain and the international order was shaped by Britain's colonial past and informed by a profound eurocentricity where women from Black and ethnic minority communities were viewed as victims if they were at all visible. Such feminist analyses of British society came under fire, from the late 1970s, by Black women's organisations, activist journalists, writers and academics (Amos and Parmar 1984; Bryan et al. 1985; Carby 1997; Ramzanoglu 1989). Together they constituted a Black British feminism whose roots lay in the postcolonial struggles of Caribbean and South Asian women who had come to Britain as part of labour migration flows between the 1950s and mid-1970s. They contested the notion that women were bound by common sisterhood, stressing that in a society marked by differences and inequalities of 'race'/ethnicity, White women were among the oppressors and that racism existed within the WLM. Black feminists made the experiences and standpoint of Black and ethnic minority women central to their understanding of British society and highlighted their concerns: the interlocking struggles against colonialism, racism, sexism and oppression based on class; the idea that family and community was often a place of safety and strength in a hostile White world rather than one of oppression and that theory could be built from everyday lived experiences (Thomlinson 2016).

Tensions Between White Feminism[22] and Black Women's Struggles
The call to White feminism to understand the impact of racism in society and within the women's movement, on Black and ethnic minority women, was noted by many grass-roots activists and publicly known figures in the WLM. Some effort was made, therefore, to diversify feminist collectives, campaigns and written output whether academic or activist. For example, the writer-activist Jenny Bourne admitted that Western feminists appeared to believe they had nothing to learn from the history and postcolonial struggles of women in the Third World and Britain and called on them to integrate anti-racism into feminist practice (Bourne 1983). The *Spare Rib* magazine collective invited more Black and ethnic minority journalists and writers to guest editorials, contribute articles and accepted that a debate about racism and sexism in the women's movement was

necessary (*Spare Rib* 1983: 3). Various mainstream feminist organisations expressed support for existing and new Black and Asian women's projects and organisations set up in the 1970s and 1980s (Southall Black Sisters, the Organisation for Women of Asian and African descent, Sheba Press, Shakti Women's Aid and so on) as a result of increased government funding being made available, through local authorities, to Black and ethnic minority communities.

Nevertheless, several points of tension persisted. First, while White feminism acknowledged that racism within wider society and the women's movement intersected with sexism to oppress Black and ethnic minority women they failed to move beyond such recognition. In an unambiguous message to White feminists, the activist-writer Amrit Wilson had spelled out how White feminists could support Black and ethnic minority women:

> What White women could do more effectively to help in the liberation of their Black sisters is to support already existing struggles of Black women—to support their strikes, make political issues of their at-present-ignored battles with immigration officers, to take a stand on racist education methods if you are a parent, to refuse to implement them if you are a teacher; in other words, to attack the racism which defines the position of Black women in British society. (1975: 8)

Black feminists noted that few if any White feminists took part in industrial disputes and campaigns involving Black and ethnic minority women, citing long-running strikes in the 1970s waged by South Asian women—for example, at the Grunwicks film processing plant in London (1977) or the Mansfield hosiery factory (1972). Nor did they join campaigns against repressive immigration rules such as the 'virginity testing' of women from Pakistan and India, carried out in the late 1970s by immigration officers at Heathrow airport, ostensibly to expose sham marriages; or the many anti-deportation campaigns organised by the Southall Black Sisters, the Asian Youth Movement and the Black Parents Movement in support of Indian, Pakistani and Caribbean women in the 1970s and 1980s.

Second, to many Black and ethnic minority activists, it appeared that their inclusion in the mainstream women's movement (whether in feminist academic journals and magazines or campaigns against domestic violence) depended on the largesse of White feminists who occupied central positions in the women's movement and decided whose contributions were valuable enough to improve the movement in terms of diversity and its capacity to speak for all women. The debates about who to include and who could speak on behalf of whom which took place in feminist meetings across the country were reflected in feminist publications such as *Spare Rib* (Boyd n.d.), *Women's Report*, *Shrew* and *Wires* over many years.

Third, a set of tensions was related to the unwillingness of many White feminists to recognise Black feminism as a political response to racism, sexism and other oppressions rather than mere resistance, based on colour, to White feminism. For example, Knowles and Mercer (1992) dismissed Black feminism as essentialist, arguing that in setting itself apart from White feminism, it ignored differences between Black women, for example, African women and Black Caribbean women. Citing the case of Nigerian women's groups who apparently did not attach the same importance to racism as Caribbean women, they called for an analytical separation of sexist and racist oppression, failing which, they claimed, feminism could not defeat the effects of various oppressions on women. Such tensions have persisted within the women's movement over time and some are not uncommon within current British feminisms which have seen an upsurge since 2008 (Budgeon 2011; Charles and Wadia 2014; Cochrane 2013; Evans 2015; Long 2012; Mackay 2015). Such tensions continue to trouble the relationship between White and Black feminists and more recently Muslim women and feminists.

Muslim Women, Feminism and the State

In Britain, Muslim women became the focus of public and political attention in the 9/11 era. As in France, Islamic dress, particularly the face veil—because by then the headscarf was mostly accepted—symbolised the rejection of Western values and women's equal rights. Investing women's Islamic dress with such attributes has led to long-running controversies over the meaning and purpose of the *hijab/niqab/burka*. In addition, Muslim women were solicited as allies of the state, in the latter's War on Terror, through an array of instruments including the Prevent programme.

The French bans on the headscarf in schools and face veil in public spaces undoubtedly influenced British public opinion, lining up on one side politicians and others who applauded the French state for mounting an apparently righteous defence of French/Western values and who argued that similar bans in Britain would protect Muslim women from the pressure to dress in a prescribed way and uphold women's rights. In opposition, supporting Muslim women's right to wear Islamic dress, were a number of standpoints, not necessarily aligned with the Left or Right, Muslims or non-Muslims: that such bans undermined the right of religious expression;

that it was reprehensible to side with an all-powerful state with all the legitimate means of force at its disposal against a small, powerless group; that the face veil or other Islamic dress was not the cause but outcome of inequality and subjugation; that banning the face veil was no different from imposing some form of Islamic dress on women, as in countries such as Saudi Arabia or Iran. There were also so-called pragmatists who asserted that banning the face veil would prevent terrorists from evading security checks, make it easier for certain professionals (teachers, health and social work professionals, lawyers/judges) to do their job better.

Debates about the veil have surfaced periodically, triggered not only by controversies in France but also by domestic events. For example, clamorous arguments ensued when the incumbent Labour Foreign Secretary and MP, Jack Straw, told the press in 2006 that he preferred Muslim women in his constituency who wore the face veil or *niqab* to remove it before consulting him. He added that while he did not favour a legal face veil ban, he intended opening a public debate on the subject because of the face veil's 'implications of separateness' (BBC News 2006). Straw's intervention is blamed by many for the rise in Islamophobia at that time but had limited political and policy impact and in 2010 Straw offered an apology over his comments, stating, 'If I had realised the scale of publicity that they [his comments] received in October 2006, I wouldn't have made them and I am sorry that it has caused problems…' (MEND 2010). Such debates have surfaced periodically and will undoubtedly re-emerge[23] but given the place accorded to religion in state and civil society institutions, within a tradition of multiculturalism among other factors, it is unlikely that a British government, in the foreseeable future at least, would support coercive legal measures over a 'soft' issue when it can afford to appear liberal and democratic. This is reflected in the fact that private members' 'face-coverings' bills introduced to Parliament, in 2010 and 2014, failed to progress past the House of Commons first and second reading stages, respectively, and barely attracted media attention.

Mainstream feminists and women's organisations have largely taken a back seat in Britain's unfinished veil debates. Therefore, it becomes difficult to identify clear-cut feminist positions. Nevertheless, a line separates the few feminists (often with a history of activism in the WLM and other 1960s/1970s social movements) who have chosen to be vocal from a silent majority of activists. If the former group has chosen to speak out, it is partly because its constituents—mainly journalists, writers, politicians—have access to public attention. It includes figures such as Joan Smith (journalist and writer), Suzanne Moore (journalist), Julie Bindel (writer-activist), Yasmin Alibhai-Brown (journalist and writer), Harriet Harman (Labour politician and MP) among others. The majority of these feminists have taken an anti-veil position, arguing that the veil—understood generically to include all forms of Islamic dress—is a physical manifestation of a minority patriarchal culture which subjugates women. Hence, some would approve a ban:

> At best, the more extreme forms of Islamic dress are ideological garments, expressing the puritan notion that women's features are too disturbing for public display; at worst, they've been used as cover by Islamist suicide-bombers and escaping terrorists. They are discomforting on both counts, but most of us are too polite to suggest that they be banned here. (Smith 2006)

Others have opposed the veil without supporting a legal ban, for example, Bindel for whom 'casual acceptance' of the veil as a normal part of British society has been deeply aggravating (Bindel 2013) and Alibhai-Brown for whom 'The hijab, jilbab, burqa and niqab are visible signs of this retreat from progressive values' (Alibhai-Brown 2015). A few publicly known feminists of the 1960s/1970s generation, among them Lindsey German (left-wing activist and Marxist feminist), have called for solidarity with Muslim women and their right to wear the face veil in public (2007: 136–137). Other journalists and writers, such as Laurie Penny or Kira Cochrane, who have expressed support for or given voice to Muslim women who wear Islamic dress belong to a younger generation of feminists.

In a mixed meeting of White, Black and ethnic minority feminists debating the question of 'The veil, feminism and Muslim women' (organised by the Fawcett Society in December 2006), three main positions on the face veil were identified within White feminism: solidarity with veiled Muslim women, opposition to the face veil as an instrument of male oppression and a position of 'false division' where Muslim and Black feminism generally is seen as a divisive force which ultimately threatens the wider feminist project (Fawcett Society 2006). The latter is certainly a minority position; however, it is unclear whether White feminism's general silence over the face veil indicates majority support for Muslim women's right to dress as they please or otherwise. Given that younger generations of White feminists have grown up and participated in an increasingly multicultural and multifaith society, it is likely that within the new feminisms of the 2000s, there is a real desire to reflect British society's multiple differences through theory and practice which honour 'contradictory experiences and deconstruct categorical thinking' (Krolokke and Sorensen 2006: 16). This is evidenced by the increased presence and contribution of Black and ethnic minority women, including those from Muslim communities, on the boards of organisations such as UK Feminista and Object and on panels and workshops of major feminist conferences, and by the growth of transversal actions across cultural boundaries, for example, events such as the annual Million Women March and the UK part of the 1Billion Rising worldwide campaign. It is probable therefore that a large proportion of White British feminists support Muslim women's right to wear what they want and that the majority oppose any legally imposed face veil ban, particularly in opposition to governments and male politicians claiming to protect women's rights.

Nevertheless, the message of Muslim women, especially the feminists among them, is that White feminists are still not aware enough of ethno-religious differences and that there is a tendency to tell Muslim women how to behave. In addition, they demand of mainstream feminism not to be complacent in its acceptance of difference but to visibly demonstrate solidarity with Muslim women, whether it is over the right to wear Islamic dress or in support of Muslim women and their families in the state's War on Terror against them (Fawcett Society 2009: 6; Janmohamed 2013; Yaqoob 2006). But until such solidarity becomes real Muslim women continue to defend their interests by organising and participating in politics outside mainstream women's organisations. Although they have not been able to count on their White sisters, they have managed to bypass mainstream women's organisations and gain some access to policymakers at the local if not the national level. Between the 1970s and 2000s this was achieved as part of a Black and ethnic minority women's movement which had expanded in relative size and influence as local authority funding for community organisations increased. Over the past decade, many Muslim women have used resources made available by the state, through programmes such as Prevent, to set up organisations and campaigns which advance the concerns and needs of Muslim women.

Conclusion

In both France and Britain, the emergence of Islam on the national and international stage has placed Muslims at the heart of political and societal controversies. In both countries, racism and discrimination have followed a similar paradigm shift, concentrating on biological criteria in the early decades of immigrant settlement to subsequently focusing on cultural and religious dimensions from the late 1990s onwards. North African Arabs in France and Pakistanis and Bangladeshis in Britain became Muslims in public discourse and policies, the religious marker crystallising Otherness.

In Britain, the political and social rights accorded to Muslims (as Commonwealth subjects) in the early stages of settlement eased the institutionalisation of Islam. Muslims have undoubtedly made a place for themselves in British society through their mobilisation and participation in the public sphere. However, Islam has stood at the nexus of contradictory trends. While British Muslims enjoy a recognition unparalleled in Western Europe, they are also among the most socio-economically disadvantaged. Moreover, they have become the target of increased hostility and prejudice, generated by a moral panic which conflates Islam and terrorism. The War on Terror is pitted against the integration of Muslims, as it exacerbates Islamophobia and the marginalisation of Muslim populations which are the object of ever-reinforced anti-terrorism legislation and policies. Paradoxically, these developments have also constituted a vector of participation for young Muslims and women who have emerged onto the public scene through expanding community organisations and their contribution to the anti-war campaign (see Chapter 5 and Joly 2007; Joly and Wadia 2012).

In France, Muslims' participation in the public arena was initially hampered by their legal status as foreigners. Additionally, French political culture—the 'indivisible' character of the Republic and *laïcité*—fomented constraints which further hindered the creation of a space for Islam and Muslims in France. In the twenty-first century, the public arena has been fraught with debates about communalism, *laïcité* and gender equality, under the shadow of perceived terrorist threats. An ideological and political offensive has been sustained against Islam on issues surrounding the headscarf and full-face veil. The way in which *laïcité* has been pursued politically has turned many women from Muslim communities into hostages of an ideological tug of war. Moreover, legislation on religious dress and accessories, applying solely to the public sector, is increasingly being taken up in the private sector. A kind of state discrimination thus positions Muslim women at the centre of an offensive against Islam. In other words, the legislative and cultural counterparts of the War on Terror, which targets all Muslims in Britain, has been the onslaught against Muslim women's religious dress in France.

Besides the above contextual factors, an exploration of Muslim women's relations with majority feminism and their triangulation with the state's approach to Muslim women shows that the latter's concerns are left out of mainstream gender equality campaigns and demands because little attention is paid to race/ethnicity/faith, even in Britain where White feminism widely accepts the concept of intersecting oppressions. This means that women from ethnic Muslim communities in France and Britain most commonly wage struggles against the effects of sexism and racism/Islamophobia with other Black and ethnic minority women or on their own. Although women from Muslim communities have established their own organisations over the last decade, the lack of scope for building feminist alliances with majority women's organisations means they have limited influence on policy formulation and political decision-making. In Britain, younger generations of White feminists have taken some steps to include Black, ethnic minority and Muslim feminisms in various political formations and actions but have yet to go out and join Muslim women in their battles against sexism and racism/Islamophobia. In France, although many younger White feminists have joined with Muslim women in organisations such as CFPE, the majority have chosen to 'protect' either the Republic or the legacy of WLM feminism against Islam and in doing so have created a chasm between themselves and Muslim women with little possibility of waging a common fight against sexism and racism/Islamophobia. These are the contextual factors which provide the framework for the participation of women from Muslim communities in political and civic life.

Notes

1. After 1968, following the principle of 'patriality', only Commonwealth subjects who had a British-born parent or grandparent were exempted from immigration regulations. An obvious discrimination against 'non-Whites', this was incorporated into the 1971 Immigration Act.
2. This included the 1958 Notting Hill (London) and Nottingham riots involving White racists against immigrants; the emergence of racist discourse in electoral politics; the creation of neo-fascist organisations such as the National Socialist Movement in 1962 and the promulgation of racially based immigration legislation.
3. Section 11 of the 1966 Local Government Act, the 1968 Urban Programme and the 1977 Policy for the Inner Cities targeted areas with a certain percentage of New Commonwealth populations.

4. The RRA 1976 was repealed by the Equality Act 2010 which supersedes and consolidates all previous (116) UK discrimination laws.
5. The CRE's mission included combatting discrimination, promoting equal opportunity and good community relations, monitoring the application of the law and proposing amendments. It was authorised to investigate cases of racial discrimination in private and public companies and government departments; serve legally enforceable non-discrimination notices; support individual victims of discrimination in court; prepare good practice guides with legal value and reports on discrimination in different sectors.
6. While various definitions of social and community cohesion were discussed within the Cantle report, the terms were used almost interchangeably at the time. Following publication of the report, the two concepts became separated so that community cohesion came to focus entirely on ethnic minorities, particularly Muslims of South Asian background, and hence on culture and religion without reference to social class (see Wadia and Allwood 2012).
7. Muslim scholars Ala'aud Deen Siddiqui, Abdur Razzaq Shahid and Jafar Bilal Barkati wrote to *The Guardian* asking 'Why Muslims should vote for a Labour government' (*The Guardian* 2005b).
8. There were also Spanish and Portuguese immigrants.
9. Keslassy uses the term *minorités visibles* which he defines as 'all those who come from a non-European immigrant background (mainly of African and Asian origin) and those who are from [France's] overseas department and territories'. Keslassy explains that this definition does not include the *pieds noirs* and their descendants whose (migration) history is very different (Keslassy 2010). We use the English term Black and ethnic minority here as it corresponds most closely to *minorités visibles*.
10. Disadvantaged urban neighbourhoods largely populated by ethnic minorities, equivalent to British inner city areas.
11. These concepts feed an abundant literature which cannot be examined here.
12. During the Algerian War, the 13 May military putsch of 1958 compelled Muslim women to remove and burn their veil in public.
13. At the time, the Renseignements généraux (police intelligence service) counted 367 face veil wearers, half of whom were non-Muslim French women who had converted to Islam (*Le Monde* 2009).

14. The term 'public space' was interpreted in the broadest sense to include spaces such as streets, public buildings, shops, state administrative offices, public transport and so on.
15. Islam had existed within the territory of the French Republic in 1905, in Algeria, but had been ignored.
16. The CODAC provides an information service, monitors incidents of discrimination based on 'race'/ethnicity at the departmental level and is supposed to ensure that organisations follow equal opportunity practices in employment and so on.
17. Western feminism covers West European, North American, Australian feminisms. It is defined in relation to Second (Central/East European) and Third World feminism(s), and feminism(s) of migrant, ethnic minority and Muslim women (Islamic feminism) in Western countries. It is also used in place of White feminism. Feminism here encompasses women's movements from the 1960s to the present.
18. 'Misrecognition' is used here to mean the denial of recognition (in the Bourdieusian sense; see Taylor 1994).
19. A significant literature exists, in French and English, on the French headscarf controversies, for example, Allwood and Wadia 2009: 152–183; Bowen 2008; Gaspard & Khosrokhavar 1995; Nordmann 2004; Rochefort 2002; Scott 2007; Winter, 2008.
20. Many Algerian women in France who considered themselves cultural Muslims were in favour of the 2004 law. They had fled Algeria in the 1990s when the Salafist Front islamique du salut gained 55 per cent of the vote in the 1990 local elections (Martinez 2000: 20). FIS-controlled municipalities introduced numerous discriminatory measures against women locally.
21. In Britain 'Black' feminism has been used as a political concept to include women from all racialised minorities who fight against racial, sexual, heterosexual, class and other oppressions.
22. 'White feminism' has been widely used by Black feminists in Britain to refer to 'any feminism which comes from a White perspective, and universalizes it' (Aziz 1992: 296). It is not understood as an essentially fixed category comprising White women only. White feminism is seen as an expression of the failure to recognise 'the wider social and political context of power in which feminist utterances and actions take place, and the ability of feminism to influence the context' (Ibid.).
23. For key events (2006–2013) instigating and surrounding the face veil debate in Britain, see Claystone (2014: 15–28).

CHAPTER 4

Migrations, Demographics and Socio-Economic Profiles

INTRODUCTION

This chapter presents a historical, demographic and socio-economic profile of the population of women under study, in Britain and France. It maps the main migration histories of those from Muslim-majority countries, including former colonies, to Britain and France and the establishment of Muslim ethnic communities. Second, it presents the main demographic features of Muslim populations and records their geographical distribution. Third, it puts forward a general socio-economic profile of Muslim populations in both countries while spotlighting women, especially in the areas of employment and education. First, however, it is important to trace the emergence of ethnicity and religion as categories in the UK census and other social surveys which allow for the disaggregation of demographic and social data along lines of ethnicity and religious attachment. This contrasts with the situation in France where the state, supported by the French social sciences, prohibits public, private and third sector organisations from gathering data based on ethnicity or religion for the reason that such a practice which attributes certain markers of identity to groups of citizens runs counter to French republican ideals. This discussion explains why the data presented on Muslims, and Muslim women more specifically, is more complete in Britain than in France and why, therefore, the aim of this chapter is not to provide a thorough statistical account of these matters but an indicative demographic and socio-economic profile of the population concerned, within the broader context of the overlapping religious, migrant and ethnic communities of which they are a part.

Debates on Population Categorisation and Ethnic Monitoring in Britain and France

The 'Ethnic Question' in Britain: 1975–1991

Questions about ethnicity and religion are a given feature of the UK census[1] today. Hence, it is easy to forget that proposals to incorporate the 'ethnic' and 'religion' questions gave rise to heated debates among social scientists, politicians and media commentators in the 1970s/1980s and 1990s, respectively (Ballard 1996). The desire to include an ethnic question in the 1991 census goes back to the mid-1970s when initial field trials were undertaken to establish the feasibility of a question on ethnicity/'race'. Two opposite concerns were at play. Ranged on one side were those who had become increasingly alarmed at the rate of social change taking place in Britain since the late 1950s as a result of immigration from the New Commonwealth countries and the tensions created by these changes. Post-war, large-scale immigration differed from previous waves which had brought visibly indifferentiable populations from Europe and the Old Commonwealth and which practised familiar Judeo-Christian cultures. The arguments in favour of knowing the size of New Commonwealth immigration rested on the aim of ultimately controlling or stopping it.

The other side argued that Black and ethnic minority populations in Britain were too often subject to racism and discrimination and that accurate statistics were required to assess the extent of racial discrimination and to be able to address it. Many local authorities believed such evidence would back up claims to central government for an increase in their rate support grant in order to respond to the different needs of immigrant and ethnic minority populations in their area.

Objections to the inclusion of the ethnic question in census questionnaires were articulated across the political spectrum and by immigrant and minority communities also. For example, objectors on the Left argued that asking questions on ethnicity/'race' was morally and politically wrong because it reified the socially constructed concept of 'race' and its proxy 'ethnicity' and that data on ethnicity could be used by the state or institutions to disadvantage Black and ethnic minority populations further.

On the Right, objectors saw the ethnic question as a violation of personal freedom and privacy. Many Black and ethnic minority groups opposed the ethnic question and proposed responses because the conception of diversity on which they were based implied a setting apart of Black and ethnic minority groups from British society. In addition, academics and other experts had criticised the uncertain definition of 'ethnicity' and hence the validity of the ethnic question which arguably lent itself to varying interpretations and therefore yielded questionable raw data (Ballard 1996: 4; Booth 1985). Despite strong objections to it the ethnic question was included in the 1991 census. Moreover, it achieved a high response rate across different ethnic populations. The acceptance of the ethnic question in census questionnaires paved the way for the inclusion of a question on religion in 2001.

The Religion Question: 1996–2001

The campaign in favour of including a religion question in the 2001 census emerged in 1996 when a number of faith groups formed the census 2001 Religious Affiliation Sub-Group (RAG). Lobbying political parties and government on the inclusion of a religion question in the census questionnaire was not new and had historically been debated in Parliament since the mid-nineteenth century each time a census bill was presented to MPs. Successive governments had fought off attempts to include a religion question, reluctant to be drawn into intra-faith disputes which had underpinned lobbying. By March 1997, a united RAG had persuaded the Office for National Statistics (ONS) about the usefulness of the religion question and had gained enough political support by 1999 for a Private Member's Bill on the religion question to be introduced and approved, albeit with the trade-off that responding to the question would be optional. In June 2000, the bill on the religion question was finally passed in the House of Commons and the question included in the 2001 census (Sherif 2011; Hussain 2008).

Many of the arguments in favour of the religion question echoed those which had been made vis-à-vis the ethnic question. For example, many local authorities and the RAG claimed that data on religion would help monitor discrimination; plan religiously sensitive services in health, education and community care and help third sector and religious organisations to extend the provision of many essential services. They convinced the government that data on religion would usefully complement that on ethnicity. Objections to the religion question were voiced by groups such as the Union of Muslim Organisations on the grounds that religion was a private matter and that information about people's beliefs should not enter the public domain and that a question on religion could lead to state surveillance and control of particular populations if the 'wrong' kind of government came to power. The British Humanist Association (BHA) had also objected to the framing of the religion question which asked about religious belonging rather than belief. The BHA argued that the wording would lead to an inflation of the number of people recorded as religious because the question would encourage respondents to answer in terms of whatever loose religious affiliation they may feel rather than their actual beliefs. However, discussion about the religion question was not as protracted or intense as that on the ethnic question. There is little doubt that those in favour of it were helped by the ethnic question debate which had been aired in the 1970s and 1980s.

'Les Statistiques Ethniques': France

The last 20 years has seen flare-ups of polemical debate over whether or not ethnic and religion statistics should be gathered through the national census and other surveys undertaken in France, and hence whether or not the 1978 Information Technology and Civil Liberties Act which prohibits the collection and recording of any data on the ethnic/'racial' origin or religious belonging of people should be amended.[2] Historically French censuses and other population surveys have gathered information relating to people's place of birth and nationality.

The debate on collecting ethnic statistics was initiated in 1998 in an argument between two well-known demographers, Hervé Le Bras (at the École des Hautes Études en Sciences Sociales, Paris) and Michèle Tribalat (at the Institut National d'Études Démographiques [INED], Paris). Le Bras and other social scientists were against Tribalat's use of ethnic categorisation in her work on the grounds that it played into the hands of the far Right Front National which had an interest in counting immigrants and those of immigrant descent in order to argue against their presence in France.[3] Tribalat's distinction between those of (pure) French ethnicity, *français de souche*, and those who were French nationals of other ethnic origins, *français issus d'autres origines*, was considered by Le Bras as an example of dangerous and 'repulsive' categorisation (Le Bras 1998). Tribalat responded that such statistics were essential in obtaining a true picture of social life and, in this case, of immigrant populations and their experiences. She contended that the most important consideration in the use of ethnic statistics was that they served a purpose and that the use of ethnic categories was a question of vocabulary rather than ideology (Tribalat 1998; Bernard and Weill 1998).

By and large academics and others opposed to ethnic statistics have argued along lines of principle. The arguments put forward most repeatedly are, first, that attributing an identity based on ethnicity/'race' runs counter to French republican principles where the individual, citizen or not, is not seen in terms of immutable characteristics which are a fact of birth; second, that the imposition of an ethnic identity on a population by researchers or other agents would be tolerated rather than claimed and hence could become a factor of discrimination against those to whom the identity is ascribed (the example of population statistics disaggregated by 'race' and kept by the Vichy regime as a tool of repression is often cited)—Le Bras and others have often argued that it is not the ethnic data *per se* which is problematic but the ends to which such data may be used; third, that while the European Commission against Racism and Intolerance among other EU agencies has encouraged EU member states to collect ethnic data (ECRI 2011), there is no accepted definition of the concept of ethnicity.

Conversely, those in favour of ethnic statistics tend to base their arguments on pragmatic grounds while principles are a secondary factor. Thus, the most important reasons put forward in support of ethnic statistics are, first, that it is important to know the real extent of inequalities and discrimination in order to find solutions to end them; second, that 'choosing not to use ethnic and racial categories in statistics…prevents the accumulation of discrimination data and contributes to euphemizing the social impacts of racism'; that in 'wishing to avoid the hardening of ethnic and racial divisions, statistical invisibility contradicts the experience of the dominated and functions as a normative imposition' (Amiraux and Simon 2006: 204).

By the turn of the millennium the debate was placed on the back burner but erupted again in 2007 when Nicolas Sarkozy, a candidate in the French Presidential elections of that year, declared that he was in favour of affirmative action for France's visible minorities which meant taking into account their ethnicity in any research and analysis undertaken. In making this declaration, Sarkozy had wanted to counter criticism that his response, as Interior Minister, to the 2005 urban riots involving mainly young people of Maghrebi origin had reflected a fundamentally racist attitude. At the time he had linked delinquency with ethnicity and claimed that ethnic monitoring would have provided a useful tool for determining exactly who the delinquents were, to analyse the impact of their actions and suggest future integration strategies. Sarkozy was also responding to European agencies pressurising countries such as France to produce ethnic statistics as a means of combating discrimination based on grounds of 'race'/ethnicity.[4]

In 2008, as President, Sarkozy appointed a Commissioner for Equal Opportunities in the person of the French-Algerian businessman Yazid Sebag who supported the use of ethnic and religion questions in surveys carried out by the national statistics agency Institut National de la Statistique et des Études Économiques (INSEE) and other bodies. Sebag set up a committee for the evaluation of diversity (Comité pour la mesure et l'évaluation de la diversité—Comedd) whose remit was to conduct an enquiry into the use of ethnic statistics and report to the President. The establishment of Comedd provoked anger among academics and public figures who, under Le Bras, formed a counter committee named Carsed (Commission alternative de réflexion sur les statistiques ethniques et les discriminations). In a 2009 book, the members of Carsed launched a withering condemnation of the Comedd's thinking (Carsed 2009), accusing the latter of promoting an ethnically fragmented society where each community would compete for resources with other communities while the state looked on complacently (Roucaute 2015). Despite support from trade unionists and minority activist organisations such as the Conseil Représentatif des Associations Noires (CRAN), the long-awaited report of the Comedd, on ethnic statistics, was a much compromised version of what had been expected (Comedd 2010).[5] The Comedd report confirmed the Commission National de l'Informatique et des Liberté's (CNIL) position that large-scale population surveys undertaken by the INSEE and other public bodies to measure inequalities and discrimination should continue to use data on nationality and country of birth, including respondents' parents' country of birth, but that some ethnic data could be gathered and used in smaller studies under the strict control of the CNIL. An example of such research is the *Trajectoires et origines géographiques* (TeO) study undertaken in 2008–2009 by a team of researchers from the INSEE and the INED (Beauchemin et al. 2010). In addition, the Comedd recommended that companies with 250 employees or more should be encouraged to undertake 'diversity surveys' and collect ethnic data to develop anti-discrimination policies and practices. This approach has since prevailed. The Socialists' accession to power in 2012 did not change policy in respect of ethnic statistics. If anything, François Hollande attempted to shut down the debate in February 2015, stating that it was sufficient to identify areas where high levels of educational under-achievement and unemployment existed, in order to analyse the causes and find solutions in such zones (Baumard 2015).[6] The fact that population surveys in France, in particular the census, do not collect data on ethnicity or religion means that it is difficult to make direct comparisons of the socio-demographic situations of Muslim populations in Britain and France.

MUSLIMS IN BRITAIN AND FRANCE: MIGRATION HISTORIES

Migration of Populations from Muslim-Majority Countries to Britain

The majority of Muslims in Britain are of South Asian origin and their roots can be traced back to the migrations of the late 1950s and in the 1960s from Pakistan, India and later Bangladesh. These post-Second World War migrations are linked to British imperial rule in South Asia; Britain called on workers in its ex-colonies to contribute to its economic reconstruction. Muslim migration to Britain was not new after 1945 and went back to the start of the nineteenth century, first, when sailors from South Asia working on British ships settled in London and Liverpool and, second, when Yemeni sailors, working on the shipping route between Britain and the Far East, settled in Cardiff, Liverpool, South Shields, Hull and London. However, what was markedly different about post-war immigration was its scale, type and patterns. The immigration of New Commonwealth citizens, including Muslims from South Asia, in the 1950s and 1960s was unmatched by previous non-European migrations in terms of the numbers of people who came to Britain.[7] Moreover, those who arrived during this period were mainly semi or unskilled labour migrants, young men who came to work not only in the growing public sector represented by transport and the NHS for example but also in the metalwork foundries of the West Midlands and the Lancashire cloth mills where they replaced White British workers who were leaving because of paltry wages and poor working conditions.

Young South Asians of Muslim background formed part of migration chains which saw the movement of people from particular parts of the South

Asian subcontinent to towns and cities in Britain where employment and accommodation was found through previous cohorts of migrants. Along with migrants from other parts of the New Commonwealth, these mainly male, Muslim migrants constituted what may be termed the first wave of post-war migration. It reached its peak in 1961–1962[8] when emigration from Pakistan brought over 50,000 Muslim workers to Britain whereas the average annual figure for the period 1955 to 1959 had been just 2930 (House of Commons 1976).[9] By 1971, those of Pakistani origin, and, by association, of Muslim faith numbered 136,000 (ONS 2013). This wave of large-scale migration came to an end in the mid-1970s as the oil crisis of 1973–1974 signalled the end of 30 years of economic growth and led to protectionist policies including a halt on inward labour migration

The conceptualisation here of post-war migration in terms of 'waves' encompasses periodicity, migration motives and socio-demographics. Thus, the first wave occurring in the 1950s and 1960s was motivated by economic factors and comprised mainly young, male migrants. While this approach could over-simplify migration processes (e.g. glossing over long-established migrations from Ireland and the Old Commonwealth), it provides a convenient way of characterising migratory inflows which have become the focus of public attention and generated political controversy.

A second wave of post-war migration started in the mid-1970s and was marked by the feminisation of Muslim migration to the UK, bringing the wives and children of labour migrants to Britain. The majority of Muslim men who came to the UK in the 1950s and 1960s had not envisaged long-term settlement. They had often worked on a rotational basis where one man would work for a period of time, return to Pakistan/India and be replaced by another male family or clan member, often in the same job. This rotation declined after the introduction of entry restrictions in 1962 in favour of permanent settlement with families and was accelerated in the mid-1970s as entry of primary labour migrants was halted. Moreover, family reunification was being encouraged during this period by international human rights and labour organisations (ILO 1974: 27). Hence, the number of Muslim women who entered Britain as marriage or family migrants after the mid-1970s increased significantly.

The third and most recent migratory wave from Muslim-majority countries, comprising 'new migrants', has occurred since the late 1980s and has continued into the 2000s. A significant number of new migrants have fled political conflict and repression in their country of origin. Therefore, the last 25 years have seen a large increase in those seeking asylum, including political figures, student activists and people who have faced repression on grounds of their ethnicity, faith, gender and sexuality. In addition to refugee flows from countries such as Iran, Iraq, Afghanistan, Egypt, Algeria, Somalia and Syria among others, some labour and family reunification migration has continued to bring Muslims to the UK. This last wave represents the greatest diversity in the composition of the large migratory flows to Britain since 1945, not just in terms of migrant categories but also in terms of nationalities and the fact that the proportion of Muslim women migrants as principal asylum claimants, dependents of asylum claimants or as part of family reunification processes has continued to increase.

While figures relating to immigration are provided by UK census and other data sources, it is not possible to gather accurate data on Muslims for the period covered above. The lack of an ethnic group question before the 1991 census (with the attendant inconsistency of definitions used for ethnic groups between different data sources) and of the religion question before 2001 makes it difficult to trace the development of Muslim communities in a reliable way. Moreover, the ethnic diversity of Muslims in Britain is often overlooked as smaller ethnic Muslim groups are often subsumed in the category 'other'.

Muslim Migrations to France

In common with the UK, large-scale immigration to France in the post-war period may also be conceptualised as three distinct waves occurring between 1945 and the mid-1970s; between 1975 and the late 1980s and from the late 1980s to the present. Although Muslims had settled in France since the early years of the twentieth century,[10] large-scale immigration from Muslim-majority countries began only after 1945 in response to France's call to its colonies, Algeria particularly, to become part of the economic reconstruction effort. Thousands of Algerian workers, called *français musulmans d'Algérie*, emigrated to France after 1946 and by 1954 numbered 211,000 (CNHI n.d.).[11] During the early post-war years, the state-established Office National d'Immigration recruited Algerian workers to the construction industry. Some found employment in the metal industries and car manufacturing. These Muslim migrant populations lived and worked in France's most urbanised and industrialised regions: Île-de-France (Paris region), the Rhône (Lyon especially) and Provence-Alpes-Côte d'Azur, Marseille in particular. Young Algerian men immigrated to France in large numbers until Algerian independence in 1962 when their status as French subjects ended and France began to look for sources of labour elsewhere in the Maghreb and sub-Saharan African regions. In common with young men who immigrated to Britain from South Asia in the 1950s and 1960s, Algerian men had also become part of migration chains, working in rotation with family and friends from their village or town. From 1962, Algerian labour immigrants to France, numbering 350,000, were joined by Muslims from Tunisia and Morocco and French (ex)-colonies in sub-Saharan Africa (CNHI n.d.). This first migratory wave ended in the mid-1970s as France, like Britain, closed its doors to labour migrants in the face of the economic downturn. One specific group of Muslims from Algeria which formed part of this first wave of migration and which should not be ignored are *harkis*. The *harkis*, Algerian troops who fought for France in the Algerian War, sought refuge in France after 1962. Fear of reprisals by the new Front de Libération National (FLN) administration pushed thousands of *harkis* and their families to settle in France. Initially placed in internment camps along the south coast of France, they eventually settled in Marseille and other towns in the South. Different from other Algerian migrant groups, in terms of not only their political allegiances and their migration motives but also their demographic profile, the *harkis* and their families formed a significant part of France's Muslim population after 1962 and contributed to its feminisation.[12]

The end of labour migration in the 1970s marked the arrival of wives and children of Muslim male migrants from the Maghreb and sub-Saharan African countries who decided to make France their permanent home. This feminised migratory wave contributed to balancing out the sex profile within Muslim immigrant populations in France; for example, the proportion of women within the Algerian population increased from 32 per cent in 1975 to 41.4 per cent in 1990.

Finally, third wave migration to France introduced greater heterogeneity in terms of the Muslim-majority countries from which immigrants originated. Muslims arrived as asylum seekers and family migrants from the Middle East and Asia (Turkey, Iraq, Afghanistan) and from Mali and Algeria. This wave brought increased numbers of women migrants so that by 2005 a balance between male and female migrants, especially in the age group 20 to 52 years, was reached across migrant populations including those from Muslim-majority countries (INSEE 2005). The number of women migrants continued to increase; family migration was given a boost by the 1997 immigration amnesty which led to legalised status for 68,000 undocumented migrants and also by the Chevènement Act of May 1998 which introduced the private and family life (*Vie Privée et Familiale*—VPF) residence card for dependents of asylum seekers given subsidiary protection. Thousands of women from Muslim-majority countries took advantage of the 1997 amnesty and the VPF residence card scheme.

The development of marriage and family migration of Muslims to both France and Britain after 1975 resulted in the establishment of populations of ethnic Muslims born and brought up in the two countries under study. Together with overseas-born Muslims who have immigrated to both countries and with those who convert to Islam from other religions, they form part of the Muslim populations of France and Britain. Moreover, British- and French-born ethnic Muslims account for the fastest-growing component of the Muslim populations of each country. For example, British-born Muslims account for almost half of the Muslim population in Britain (NOMIS 2015a). In France, figures pertaining to those of 'immigrant descent' (*descendants d'immigrés*) show that the latter have far overtaken those born abroad (Bouvier 2012: 19).

Muslims in Britain and France: Demographic Profile

Britain

This section presents a demographic profile of Muslims, highlighting data related to Muslim women based on the 2011 census results. According to the 2011 census, there were just over 2.7 million Muslims in the UK. Women account for 48 per cent of this population, numbering almost 1.3 million. This represents an increase of about 70 per cent on the number recorded in 2001 (767,507) and makes Muslims the fastest-growing and second largest religious group after Christianity (Table 4.1). Several reasons explain the expansion in Muslim numbers of which the most salient are the age profile of the Muslim population is skewed towards a concentration of women in the most fertile, childbearing age ranges combined with the tradition of having large families; continuing immigration from Muslim-majority countries. That women make up just under half of all Muslims in the UK contrasts with the dominant pattern where women outnumber or equal men in other religious categories and reflects the age

Table 4.1 Muslims in the UK

	2001		2011	
	Number	Per cent	Number	Per cent
Muslims total population	1,546,626	100	2,706,066	100
Women (of total Muslim population)	767,507	48.3	1,296,776	48
Men (of total Muslim population)	821,383	51.7	1,409,290	52

Source: ONS (2004); NOMIS (2015c); all census data is ONS Crown copyright reserved

structure of Pakistani and Bangladeshi populations which have more men than women as a result of their immigration histories.

Sex and Age Profile
Since the 2001 census, Muslims have remained the youngest of all religious populations in the UK; 48.4 per cent is under 25 years old while only 3.95 per cent falls in the over-65 age group. This compares with 24 per cent Christians aged under 25 and 22 per cent over 65 years of age. Within the Muslim population, women and girls have a similar age profile to men and boys; 49 per cent of Muslim females are aged under 25 compared with 48 per cent of males (NOMIS 2015c). At the upper end of the age scale also, female and male profiles are similar although women slightly outnumber men in the 60 to 69 age range and the over-85 age group (Table 4.2). The youthfulness of the Muslim population is explained by its roots in post-war immigration and particularly the wave of family migration which materialised in the 1970s when immigrant women arrived at a life stage when they were bearing or bringing up young children. A consequence of this family immigration was the emergence of a British-born second generation which largely adopted the patterns set by their parents of having children while young and in larger numbers than the British average per family. Further family migration in the 1990s and 2000s which brought women of childbearing age and of young, dependent children to Britain means that the trend towards youthfulness in this population continues.

Country of Birth
In 2011, 87 per cent of the UK population was born in England and Wales. Christians were most likely to be born in the UK (89 per cent)

Table 4.2 Age profile of Muslims

Age	All persons	Males	Females
All categories	2,706,066	1,409,290	1,296,776
Age 0 to 4	317,952	162,491	155,461
Age 5 to 7	177,119	89,982	87,137
Age 8 to 9	108,112	55,227	52,885
Age 10 to 14	245,480	126,290	119,190
Age 15	46,474	24,173	22,301
Age 16 to 17	88,982	46,793	42,189
Age 18 to 19	87,222	46,526	40,696
Age 20 to 24	238,041	124,031	114,010
Age 25 to 29	273,505	138,826	134,679
Age 30 to 34	270,278	141,767	128,511
Age 35 to 39	227,166	122,453	104,713
Age 40 to 44	179,128	96,902	82,226
Age 45 to 49	119,992	64,874	55,118
Age 50 to 54	97,899	52,656	45,243
Age 55 to 59	75,000	39,631	35,369
Age 60 to 64	46,890	22,272	24,618
Age 65 to 69	33,457	16,172	17,285
Age 70 to 74	33,742	17,871	15,871
Age 75 to 79	22,758	11,911	10,847
Age 80 to 84	11,356	5805	5551
Age 85 and over	5513	2637	2876

Source: NOMIS (2015c)

although the number of those born abroad was growing due to migration from Europe. Where Muslims are concerned, 53 per cent were born outside the UK in 2011 (ONS 2013: 10). Although the number of Muslims born overseas has almost doubled between 2001 and 2011, from 828,000 to 1.4 million, there has been a corresponding rise in the number of Muslims born in the UK, from 718,000 to 1.2 million in the ten-year period preceding the 2011 census (Ibid.). Thus 47 per cent of Muslims are UK-born. A higher proportion of Muslim women and girls are UK-born (49 per cent) compared with men and boys (46 per cent) (Table 4.3).

The majority of non-UK-born Muslims are from Asia and Africa although more recently from countries in the Middle East and Europe (Table 4.3). It is worth noting that more Muslim women than men born in EU countries have settled in the UK. The reasons for this are unclear but may be related to the fact that free movement within the EU has

Table 4.3 Muslims and country of birth

Country of birth	All Muslims	Men	Women
All categories	2,706,066	1,409,290	1296776
UK total	1,278,283	646,084	632,199
Ireland	3677	1987	1690
EU countries total	65,658	31,983	33,675
Rest of Europe total	96,634	52,257	44,377
Africa total	275,812	141,788	134,024
Middle East	174,461	106,806	67,655
East Asia	3034	1583	1451
South Asia	772,877	410,469	362,408
South East Asia	23,224	10,360	12,864
Central Asia	3441	1667	1774
The Americas and Caribbean total	7991	3814	4177
Antarctica/Oceania (including Australasia)	966	487	479
Other	8	5	3

Source: NOMIS (2015a)

encouraged women, especially those with sufficient social and cultural capital, to seek work in the UK as care work has proliferated within a largely deregulated labour market. Conversely, there is a large gap between men and women born in Middle Eastern countries choosing to settle in the UK. Again, the reason is unknown but one can speculate that the dangerous land and sea routes used to flee political instability and war in countries such as Iraq, Yemen and Syria deter women especially those with young children and dependent elders.

Ethnicity and Geographical Distribution

In 2011, the majority (86 per cent) of the UK population identified with the category 'White', all subcategories included. However, the UK has become an increasingly diverse country since 2001 with greater numbers of people identifying themselves as members of ethnic minority communities. In keeping with this trend, Muslims in the UK identified themselves with more ethnic categories than in 2001, including 'gypsy or Irish traveller' although Pakistanis continued to comprise the largest Muslim ethnic group in 2011, representing 38 per cent of the Muslim population (Table 4.4).

Where the geographical distribution of populations is concerned, over three-quarters of Muslims live in four English regions, namely, London, the West Midlands, the North-West and Yorkshire and Humber and are

Table 4.4 Muslims and ethnicity

Ethnic group	All categories	Muslims
All categories: Ethnic group	56,075,912	2,706,066
White: English/Welsh/Scottish/Northern Irish/British	45,134,686	77,272
White: Irish	531,087	1914
White: Gypsy or Irish Traveller	57,680	378
White: Other White	2,485,942	131,056
Mixed/multiple ethnic group: White and Black Caribbean	426,715	5384
Mixed/multiple ethnic group: White and Black African	165,974	15,681
Mixed/multiple ethnic group: White and Asian	341,727	49,689
Mixed/multiple ethnic group: Other Mixed	289,984	31,828
Asian/Asian British: Indian	1,412,958	197,161
Asian/Asian British: Pakistani	1,124,511	1,028,459
Asian/Asian British: Bangladeshi	447,201	402,428
Asian/Asian British: Chinese	393,141	8027
Asian/Asian British: Other Asian	835,720	194,485
Black/African/Caribbean/Black British: African	989,628	207,201
Black/African/Caribbean/Black British: Caribbean	594,825	7345
Black/African/Caribbean/Black British: Other Black	280,437	57,469
Other ethnic group: Arab	230,600	178,195
Other ethnic group: Any other ethnic group	333,096	112,094

Source: NOMIS (2015b)

concentrated in four English cities: London, Birmingham, Manchester and Bradford. While the clustering of Muslims in these areas may suggest a process of self-segregation since the settlement of immigrants from the late 1950s onwards, recent research shows that as the UK's Muslim population has grown, processes of 'spreading out' have increased and that the index of dissimilarity has decreased for Muslims as for other ethnic minority faith groups (CoDE 2012; Simpson et al. 2008). In 2011, Muslims communities were present in all the nine regions of England and in Wales. Census surveys do not provide a differentiated breakdown by sex where ethnicity and the geographical distribution of populations is concerned and it can be assumed that the difference is numerically insignificant.

The demographic data presented above reveals that Muslim women constitute a young population when compared with the national average for women in the UK where 30 per cent of women are under 25 and 18 per cent are over 65 (NOMIS 2015c). Just under half of Muslim women are UK-born and belong to diverse ethnic groups while those born overseas are mainly from South Asia. Finally, Muslim women form part of communities which are spread across the UK while the main clusters are in large metropolitan areas.

France

Counting Muslims: Producing a Credible Estimate

As the French census and other official surveys do not collect religion-based data, it is difficult to evaluate the size and demographic characteristics of France's Muslim population let alone determine the profile of population subsets based on sex, age and ethnicity. Much reliance is placed on studies and analyses of surveys carried out by academics (e.g. Boyer 1998; Tribalat 2004, 2011), public intellectuals (such as Couvreur 1998) and polling organisations (such as IFOP 2011 for the Catholic daily newspaper *La Croix*) to provide data on Muslim populations. Such studies and surveys are to be approached with caution as significant variation is found between the results obtained. Tribalat and others have critiqued polling organisations and individual studies mainly on issues of definition and methodology (Tribalat 2007; Brouard and Tiberj 2005). The most enduring critiques of such studies and polls are to do with definitional flaws relating to the term 'Muslim'; to the immutability attributed by researchers, journalists and pollsters to the state of being Muslim and to extrapolative methods used to estimate numbers of Muslims in France and how these will evolve in future. For example, on the issue of defining Muslims, one of the flaws lies in assuming that those born or whose family origins lie in a Muslim-majority country will necessarily believe and practise Islam. Such assumptions can be further compounded if fixity is ascribed to being Muslim—that is, one remains Muslim from cradle to grave. In the case of polling organisations, it is argued that the methodology of counting Muslims in France is entirely undermined by the idea that surveys can be undertaken of so-called representative samples of a population about which nothing is known; and because the national census does not count religious groups then nothing can be known about Muslims as a population. Finally, private studies which aim to uncover the socio-demographic characteristics of Muslim populations are critiqued on the grounds that they survey very small numbers of people.

Because of the varying results obtained by polling organisations and other academic studies, France's Muslim population is estimated anywhere between three and five million. However, the proportion of Muslims has been wildly overestimated in the French public imagination—31 per cent of the total population according to one recent poll (Ipsos-Mori 2014). Politicians and journalists have cited figures ranging from five to six million (Menegaux 2011; AFP 2010). Separate counts undertaken in the 1990s by Boyer and Couvreur estimated the Muslim population at 3.59 (Boyer 1998: 18) and 3.45 million (Couvreur 1998: 10–13), respectively. However, both Boyer's and Couvreur's methodologies, involving use of census data on country of birth information to calculate numbers of Muslim immigrants in France and of other not so reliable sources for counting French-born Muslims, have been criticised by demographers.

Additionally, on the basis of an INSEE/INED survey of 1999 on family history (*Étude de l'histoire familiale*—EHF), Tribalat (2004) provided more reliable estimates of France's Muslim population than previously. The study was exceptionally large—surveying 380,481 people of immigrant origin—and for the first time gathered information on respondents' parents' country of birth so that when combined with data on the respondents' country of birth and that of their children a demographic profile of three generations was produced. Although this study is considered to have produced the closest estimate of Muslims in France up to that point, Tribalat admitted that the survey did not account for smaller immigrant origin groups containing Muslims nor did it count converts; thus the estimated number of Muslims at 3.65 million was most likely an underestimate of real numbers (Ibid.: 29). None of these surveys include sex-differentiated data (Table 4.5).

The most recent study in which demographers have tried to evaluate the size of the Muslim population is *Trajectoires et origines*, undertaken jointly in 2008–2009 by the INED and INSEE (Beauchemin et al. 2010). The study, which aimed to describe and analyse the life of individuals set against their social background and links with immigration, surveyed about 21,000 people aged 18 to 60 in Metropolitan France although the established age range of the French-born descendants of immigrants who took part in the survey was 18 to 50. A question on religious affiliation was put to respondents although questions about specific religious practices intended to give a firmer indication of affiliation were rejected by the CNIL.

The TeO study found that whereas 45 per cent of the French population aged between 18 and 50 declared itself atheist or agnostic, over 75 per cent of immigrants and their descendants declared a religious affiliation.

Table 4.5 Estimates of Muslims in France 1998–1999

Population group	Boyer (1998 Study)	Couvreur (1998 Study)	Tribalat (EHF 1999 Study)
Algerian	1,500,000	1,500,000	1,577,000
Moroccan	1,000,000	1,000,000	1,004,000
Tunisian	350,000	350,000	417,000
Middle Eastern including all Turkish Muslims		350,000	
Middle Eastern including Turkish Arab Muslims	100,000		
Middle Eastern including Turkish non-Arab Muslims	315,000		
Turkish			313,000
Sub-Saharan Africans	250,000	250,000	
Harkis (and French-born descendants)	450,000		
Converts	40,000		
Total number of Muslims (Per cent of total population)	3,590,000 (6)	3,450,000 (6)	3,650,000 (6.0)

Figures adapted from Boyer (1998: 18); Couvreur (1998: 10–13); Tribalat (2004: 30); Beauchemin, Hamel and Simon (2010)

Moreover, there was a clear gap between those who declared a religion and were from Muslim-majority countries and other categories. Not only was the proportion of those without a religion from Muslim-majority countries very small but even among those born in France, of Muslim immigrant descent, references to Islam were frequent—for example, 87 per cent of Algerians and their French-born descendants declared themselves Muslim (Beauchemin et al. 2010: 115). On the basis of their sample, TeO researchers estimated there were 2.1 million Muslims in France aged between 18 and 50 in 2008 (Beauchemin et al. 2010: 124). Analysing the TeO data on religious affiliation, Tribalat extrapolates from the figure of 2.1 million Muslims (accounting both for children under 18 and for adults over 50 years old) and arrives at a total of 4.2 million Muslims representing 6.7 per cent of the population of Metropolitan France in 2009 (Tribalat 2013). Of this 4.2 million, Tribalat estimates that 70 per cent are French-born Muslims while the rest is constituted by immigrant populations (Ibid.).

Sex and Age Profile of Muslims in France
Analysis of the TeO data on Muslims was not disaggregated in relation to sex but, based on available data, it is reasonable to state that the

proportion of Muslim women and girls in the overall Muslim population mirrors the sex balance in the general population in France which in January 2015 was 51.5 per cent female and 48.5 per cent male (INSEE 2015). This statement is based not just on the fact that the proportion of French-born Muslims far outweighs that of Muslim immigrants (Ibid.) where, traditionally, the male component was greater due to the dominance of labour migration until the mid-1970s, but also that in recent years women have formed the greater part of migratory flows to France (INED 2013). The similarity between the sex profile of the Muslim population and that of the general population is supported by a 2011 survey, carried out by IFOP for *La Croix*. This survey compares the 48–52 per cent split of the general population in favour of women and girls with a 49–51 per cent divide among Muslims, also in favour of women and girls (IFOP 2011: 5).

However, where the age profile of Muslims is concerned, clear differences emerge between this group and the general population. Muslims in France, as in the case of their counterparts in Britain, form a young population (Table 4.6) and for similar reasons—for instance, the youthful age of immigrants on arrival in France; the divergent fertility rates of the immigrant and general populations; the adoption by French-born generations of their parents' preference to have children early and form larger families.

Geographical Spread
Historically, as Muslim migrants came to France in search of work, it follows that Muslims are clustered in urban and industrial regions where there are jobs on offer. These include the Île-de-France, Rhône-Alpes and

Table 4.6 Muslims in France: a young population (percentage)

Age group	General population[a]	Muslims
18–24	12	31
25–34	17	31
35–44	18	18
45–54	15	8
55–64	17	6
65+	21	3

Source: IFOP (2011: 5)

[a]It is assumed that IFOP's undefined use of the term 'population' is the same as general population

Provence-Alpes-Côte d'Azur regions which have been the three richest economies in France due to the density of manufacturing industries and more recently the hi-tech and financial sectors. There are also significant Muslim populations in the Nord-Pas-de-Calais, especially Lille and Roubaix and Alsace, where there were jobs in the textile, wool and metal industries before these declined after the late 1970s. Hence, 60 per cent of immigrants are settled in the richest regions: 40 per cent in Île-de-France, 11 per cent in Rhône-Alpes and 9 per cent in Provence-Alpes-Côte d'Azur (INSEE 2005). Considering Muslims specifically, IFOP's survey for *La Croix* indicates that they comprise over 10 per cent of the population of Île-de-France, and between 5 and 9 per cent of the populations of the Rhône-Alpes, Provence-Alpes-Côte d'Azur and Nord-Pas-De-Calais regions (2011: 4). It is worth reiterating that the above data comprise estimated figures which should be treated cautiously. However, the data offers a useful indication of Muslim population numbers, disaggregation by sex and age where available, and provides valuable information about settlement patterns. Moreover, the TeO statistics on the Muslim population in France provide the basis for the most reliable estimates to date.

A Sociological Profile of Women from Muslim Communities in Britain and France

Compared with research undertaken on the socio-economic position of women in relation to their ethnic or migration background, little has been written about the impact of religious affiliation on women's employment, education outcomes, living conditions and so on. In the UK and France, research undertaken over many years on the relation between ethnic minority and/or migration status and socio-economic position has shown that people of ethnic minority and migrant backgrounds most often have lower rates of educational attainment, economic activity and higher rates of unemployment which in turn have a negative and enduring effect on their living conditions and quality of life. Studies in the UK have examined and analysed the link between religion, ethnic minority and socio-economic status with a good proportion of these focusing on employment and education (Heath and Martin 2013; Khattab 2009; Khattab et al. 2011; Khattab et al. 2015). Such studies have been boosted since the introduction of the religion question in the 2001 UK census. In France, there appear to have been no studies on the link between religious affiliation and socio-economic status, largely due to the lack of reliable data on religion as discussed above.

Where gender, religion and socio-economic status is concerned, quantitative studies are negligible in both France and Britain. However, a number of works, based on the secondary analysis of quantitative and/or qualitative data, cover aspects of this subject, referring to South Asian (Pakistani and Bangladeshi) women in the UK and North African (Maghrebi) and/or Turkish immigrant women in France, although the majority of these focus on women's position in the labour market as an area of enquiry. For example, in the 2000s, UK studies were carried out by the Equal Opportunities Commission (EOC) (2007) and the Fawcett Society (2009) on Black and ethnic minority women, including those of Pakistani and Bangladeshi background, and their participation, pay and progression in the labour market. The London Development Agency (LDA) also carried out a study of Muslim women in the labour market in 2009 (LDA 2010). Using data from existing surveys and, in the case of the EOC, data from a small indicative survey it had commissioned, all these studies concluded that Black and ethnic minority women, particularly Pakistani and Bangladeshi or largely Muslim women, faced various forms of discrimination and disadvantage in employment, on gender and race grounds, and that they were concentrated in the most precarious sectors of work. While the EOC and Fawcett studies do not highlight religion, they acknowledge that Muslim women face stereotyping and discrimination on religious grounds. A number of academic works (Ahmad et al. 2012; Peach 2006; Salway 2007) echo the EOC and Fawcett findings. In addition, new work on Muslim women and employment, undertaken by Nabil Khattab, at the University of Bristol, uses existing data from well-established national surveys between 2002 and 2013 in order to analyse the labour market participation of Muslim women and provide explanations for their low economic activity and high unemployment rates (University of Bristol 2015). While there are some works which specifically examine Muslim women, religion and education (Ahmad 2001; Pickerden 2010), more consider Pakistani and Bangladeshi women in this respect (e.g. Bagguley and Hussain 2007; Dwyer and Shah 2009).

Despite the existence of a respectable body of work on immigrants and their socio-economic status, and some recognition by successive French governments that women from migrant and ethnic minority communities constitute an important vector of integration and hence social stability, the case of women immigrants from Muslim-majority countries and their daughters remains understudied in France. A handful of academic works, most notably by Merckling (2002, 2011, 2012), Chaïb (2004, 2006),

Meurs and Pailhé (2008), focus on immigrant women, particularly those of Maghrebi and Turkish origin. These works synthesise secondary analysis of statistical data produced by the INSEE and other agencies with the analysis of their own qualitative data gathered through interviews with migrant women. These studies have been supplemented by one-off works on migrant women workers and discrimination, supported by public agencies such as the Fonds d'action et de soutien pour l'intégration et la lutte contre les discriminations (FASILD) (2004) and research groups such as the now defunct Groupement de recherches, d'échanges et de communication (1990). The common findings of these studies are that immigrant women from the Maghreb and other Muslim-majority countries are highly disadvantaged in the labour market; that their lack of employment, poor working conditions, pay and the sectors of employment in which they work compound the difficulties they face in other areas of social and private life.

The following section presents a socio-economic profile of Muslim women not only in relation to Muslim men but also in relation to women from other ethno-religious groups where data is available. It covers Muslim women's participation in the labour market and in education. In the French case, data on immigrant women and their descendants, particularly those of Maghrebi and Turkish origin (although posing a tricky proxy for Muslim women for reasons already discussed),[13] is used to provide an indicative socio-economic profile of Muslim women. For the UK, census data on religion is used to construct a socio-economic profile of Muslim women while data on ethnicity (Pakistani and Bangladeshi as a proxy) is also examined to report on Muslim women in education.

Muslim Women and Employment in Britain and France

France
Immigrant women in France comprise 51 per cent of the total immigrant population although this is not the case of women from the Maghreb and Turkey whose numbers are proportionately smaller than those of their male counterparts due to different migration histories (INSEE 2012: 106–107). Nationally, 47 per cent of immigrant women aged 15 to 64 are in employment.[14] Two-thirds of them, compared with 54 per cent of non-immigrant women, work in low-paid, manual or service sector jobs which require no skills or where the skills they use are unrecognised

as such, for example, in care work. A further 14 per cent of immigrant women, in contrast with 27 per cent of non-immigrant women, work in intermediary occupations and 11 per cent in supervisory and managerial jobs. It is only in this last category where the gap is closed between Algerian, Moroccan and Tunisian-born immigrant women and non-immigrant women (INSEE 2012: 193). In addition, a high proportion of jobs undertaken by immigrant women—for example, in the domestic and care sector, hotel and catering, public sector cleaning and maintenance—are governed by part-time or zero-hour terms. Thus, immigrant women are frequently employed on a part-time or casual basis. Over one-third of immigrant women are employed part-time and for women from Muslim-majority countries this rate increases sharply—42 per cent of Algerian-born women work part-time compared with 24 per cent of women born in Spain (INSEE 2012: 202). Short-term jobs are also more commonly held by immigrant rather than non-immigrant workers.

While immigrant women in employment endure poor conditions of work and low pay, they also face a greater threat of being unemployed because of the nature of the casualised jobs they do in sectors less able to withstand the effects of economic crises. Additionally, many young women leaving school and college and older women seeking work, having raised children to school age, find it difficult to access employment as labour market starters. As a result immigrant women experience high levels of unemployment in relation to immigrant men but also compared with their female, non-immigrant counterparts. While the rate of unemployment among immigrant women born outside the EU was 22 per cent in 2010, that among men in their communities was 18 per cent and that among non-immigrant women was nine per cent (INSEE 2012: 185).

A clearer picture of how all Muslim immigrants fare emerges when the rates are compared on a country of origin basis (see Table 4.7). The unemployment rate of immigrants from Muslim-majority countries varies between 19 and 25 per cent whereas that of (mainly White non-Muslim) immigrants from the EU averages out at 8 per cent. Gender-disaggregated unemployment rates, based on country of origin, are unavailable but these vary and women are not always in a worse position than men; for example, the unemployment rate of Turkish-born immigrant women is twice as high as that of their male counterparts but the rates are more or less even for women and men from sub-Saharan countries, many of which include significant Muslim populations (Ibid.: 184).

Table 4.7 Unemployment[a] according to country of birth: 25–64 age group (percentage)

EU (27) immigrants		Non-EU immigrants		French nationals[b]
Country	Per cent	Country	Per cent	Per cent
Spain	9	Other Europe	11	8
Italy	7.5	Algeria	22	
Portugal	5	Morocco	21.5	
EU other	10.5	Tunisia	19	
		Africa other	22	
		Turkey	25	
		South East Asia	8	
		Asia other	12.5	
		Americas	11.5	

Figures adapted from INSEE (2012: 185)

[a] The unemployment rate of any category is calculated by the INSEE as a proportion of the total economically active population in that category

[b] French nationals include the French-born descendants of immigrants

The French-born children of immigrants are not better off than their immigrant parents/grandparents. In 2010, the unemployment rate of descendants of immigrants was 15 per cent compared with 8 per cent for White French nationals. Moreover, those whose immigrant parents were born in Muslim-majority countries experienced far more difficulty in finding and retaining employment than those whose parents were from other European countries; so, for instance, a large variation exists between the unemployment rate of descendants of Moroccan immigrants and that of descendants of Italian or Spanish immigrants. The situation of young people (women and men) aged 15 to 24 years is even more aggravated (see Table 4.8).

Britain

In 2011, as in the census of 2001, Muslims were found to have the lowest employment rates of all religious and non-religious populations in Britain. Among them, women were particularly affected across all ethnic groups although there was some variation; for example, White British Muslim women experienced the highest employment rates among Muslims while Pakistani and Bangladeshi women had the lowest employment rates of all ethnic and sex categories among Muslims. In 2011, of the Muslim women

Table 4.8 Unemployment of descendants of immigrants according to sex and parents'/grandparents' country of birth (percentage)

	Descendants of EU-born immigrants			Descendants of immigrants born outside the EU			White French nationals		
	Men	Women	All	Men	Women	All	Men	Women	All
							8	8	8
15–24 years	21	25	23	44	34	40	19	22	21
25–64	7	9	8	19	18	19	6	7	7
Spain	9	9	9						
Italy	7	10	8						
Portugal	9	12	11						
EU other	9	8	9						
Europe other				11	14	12			
Algeria				27	23	25			
Morocco				28	28	28			
Tunisia				27	25	26			
Africa other				32	19	26			
Turkey				21	27	24			
East Asia				19	12	16			
Other countries				13	15	10			

Figures adapted from INSEE (2012: 187)

who were economically active, 79 per cent were in employment compared with an employment rate of 95 per cent for economically active Christian women.[15] Moreover, Muslim women's employment rate must be placed in the context of Muslim women's high economic inactivity rate of 61 per cent—the highest of all religion and sex categories (NOMIS 2015d).

Muslim women in employment tend to be concentrated in certain sectors of the economy. In the 1970s and 1980s, many Muslim women from South Asia became home-based workers taking in piece work from the garment industry; however, home-based work of this type is no longer an option favoured by their daughters and granddaughters. Muslim women continue to work in the light manufacturing, catering and retail sectors and have more recently entered employment in banking, finance and insurance and also in public and third sector health and education, mainly in clerical, administrative, training and care roles. Whether Muslim women work in the private, public or third sector, many experience job insecurity. The fear of losing employment has been more acute since the start of the economic crisis in 2008.[16] In addition, a high proportion of them—almost 49 per cent of employees and 55 per cent of self-employed women—work part-time (NOMIS 2015d) on low pay and face lack of progression in the workplace. As a result, and along with Muslim men, they form the least likely religious group able to establish themselves in managerial and professional positions. Finally, in common with their counterparts in France, Muslim women in Britain face multiple barriers in accessing employment and in 2011 their unemployment rate was higher than that of Muslim men and four times as high as that of women of Christian background (Table 4.9).

A number of reasons are put forward to explain the low economic activity and high unemployment rates of Muslim women in both France and Britain. It is argued that traditional Muslim family cultures among immigrants and ethnic minorities from North Africa, South Asia and the Middle East require that Muslim women bear even more of the responsibility of looking after home and family than women from other religious groups; UK census 2011 figures appear to lend support to that view. For example, of the various reasons cited for economic inactivity, that relating to home and family accounts for 44 per cent of Muslim women not actively seeking work compared with 10 per cent who are retired, 9 per cent who cannot work due to long-term illness or disability or 21 per cent who are studying. Also, the proportion of Muslim women who are inactive because of family responsibility exceeds the average of 16.5 per cent of women from all religious groups who cite family responsibilities (NOMIS 2015d). In France also, the economic inactivity rate among immigrant women

Table 4.9 Unemployment rates by religion and sex (16–64 years) (percentage)

Religion	Women	Men
Muslim	21	15
Christian	5	7
Buddhist	9	9
Hindu	9	7
Jewish	4	5
Sikh	8	9
Other	8	11
No religion	8	7
Religion not stated	6	8
All	7	8

Source: NOMIS (2015d)

increases the more children they have, with women born outside the EU experiencing the lowest economic activity rate for this reason. The gap between the economic activity rates of non-European immigrant women with at least one child under six months and French nationals in the same situation is 35 percentage points (INSEE 2012: 180). Another reason put forward is the lack of qualifications. However, recent research in the UK by Nabil Khattab reveals that Muslim women were 71 per cent more likely than White Christian women to be unemployed, even when they had the same educational level and language skills. Khattab's figures, based on the analysis of a sample of 2643 Muslim women, were also adjusted to take into account Muslim women's marital status, whether or not they had children and their religiosity (University of Bristol 2015). In France, a 2007 study supports the view that despite increasing levels of educational attainment by immigrants, male and female, the latter suffer higher rates of unemployment even when they have the same qualifications as French nationals. For example, the unemployment rate among Algerian- and Turkish-born immigrants who possess the equivalent of a Bachelor's degree, is three times that experienced by French nationals with the same qualification (INSEE 2008). Hence, many recent studies conclude that Muslim women are victims of discrimination in the labour market and that greater unemployment among them is due to recruitment and retention practices among employers which arise from processes of racialisation of religious attachment (Amnesty International 2012: 40–46; APPG on Race and Community 2012; EOC 2007; Fawcett Society 2009; LDA 2010: 63–68; Dyke and James 2009). However, it is also important to acknowledge that differences exist within religious groupings where labour market participation is concerned, and that such variation will be a consequence of the distinct behaviours and strategies of religious groupings based on ethnicity or gender for example (see Modood and Khattab 2015).

Muslim Women and Education

Britain
As Muslim communities in the UK and France experience high levels of economic deprivation and social exclusion, it is predictable that children from these communities have not been as successful in education as their White counterparts of Christian backgrounds. In Britain researchers found that ethnic background was not a factor in preventing educational

success and that the upward mobility of Black and ethnic minority children, except in the case of Pakistani and Bangladeshi young people, eclipsed class background as a factor shaping their future (Platt 2005). Historically, Muslim (Pakistani and Bangladeshi) children and students in post-16 education have fallen short of the national average of results achieved at key stages of educational testing between the ages of 11 and 16. Table 4.10 which is not disaggregated by sex shows the levels of qualification attained by Muslims in 2001 and 2011 in comparison with the average for all religions. In 2001, 39 per cent of Muslim pupils left school without any qualification compared with 29 per cent for the general population. This was attributed to the fact that, in addition to the disadvantages they faced in common with other groups from deprived communities, Muslim pupils had little opportunity to speak English at home and therefore lacked fluency when they started school. However, they often did better than their White counterparts in terms of their rate of progress during their school years as their fluency in English increased and parents became more ambitious over time about their children going on to higher education in order to secure a better future (Modood 2004).

Table 4.10 Highest level of qualification[a] by religion 16+ years (percentage) 2001–2011

	2001				2011			
	Muslims		*All*		*Muslims*		*All*	
	Number	*Per cent*	*Number*	*Per cent*	*Number*	*Per cent*	*Number*	*Per cent*
All age 16+	1,010,114	100	37,607,438	100	1,810,929	100	45,496,780	100
No qualifications	390,164	39	10,937,042	29	464,434	26	10,307,327	23
Level 1	122,509	12	6,230,033	17	245,043	13	6,047,384	13
Level 2	149,652	15	7,288,074	19	206,940	11	6,938,433	15
Level 3	94,630	9	3,110,135	8	179,253	10	5,617,802	12
Level 4 and above	208,241	21	7,432,962	20	434,742	24	12,383,477	27
Apprenticeships and other	44,918	4	7,432,962	7	280,517	16	4,202,357	10

Source: NOMIS (2015c); MCB (2015: 60)

[a]For an explanation of the qualifications included at each level, see MCB (2015: 61)

By 2011, the gap between Muslim pupils and those from other religious groups had decreased significantly. Not only were children of British-born Muslims speaking English from an early age but their parents, many born and educated in Britain, were familiar with British schooling and able to support their children at school and at home. In addition, in line with the national picture, Muslim girls were performing significantly better in relation to Muslim boys but their measurable attainment was only slightly lower than the national average for girls (Wilkinson 2015: 121). However, this story of progress is not the same for pupils who have recently arrived in Britain from Muslim-majority countries in the Middle East and Africa and while attainment gaps are decreasing between Muslim students and those from other religious groups, the former do not enter higher education on an equal footing with many other groups, in particular White students of Christian background.

In a report for the Department for Business Innovation and Skills, Gilby et al. (2011: 5) estimate that there are 167,763 Muslim students (including overseas students) at UK universities, making up 6 per cent of the total university student population. Women make up 44 per cent of this Muslim university student population although they outnumber men when it comes to all South Asian Muslim ethnic groups (Equality Challenge Unit (ECU) 2013: 177). Muslim students generally and women more specifically are disadvantaged where admission to Russell Group universities[17] is concerned and a significant proportion of them study in the new universities/old polytechnics sector (Noden et al. 2014). Although, proportionately, a larger number of students from Black and ethnic minority groups stay on in post-16 years education and attend university, their rates of attainment are lower than that of White British students. There has been a persistent degree attainment gap between the latter and students from Muslim ethnic groups who leave university with a first class or 2/1 honours degree (see Table 4.11).

Table 4.11 UK-resident, first degree undergraduate qualifiers receiving a First or 2/1 degree by ethnicity: 2003/4–2011/12 (percentage)

	White	Pakistani	Bangladeshi	All
2003/4	63	40	41	61
2008/9	67	44	46	64
2011/12	72	49	52	68

Source: ECU (2013: 83)

Moreover, an examination of graduate destinations confirms what has already been observed in the section on employment above: that even degree-level qualifications do not always translate into employment for Muslims. For example, 57 per cent of White UK-resident degree-level leavers found full-time employment compared with 43 per cent of Pakistanis and 42 per cent of Bangladeshis and within this category 45 per cent of White graduate leavers entered professional full-time employment as opposed to 34 per cent of Pakistanis and 30 per cent of Bangladeshis. In addition, the unemployment rates for Pakistani and Bangladeshi graduate leavers average out at 15 per cent—more than double that for White graduates which is 6 per cent. ECU figures do not include sex-disaggregated figures but the LDA study (2010: 51) findings suggest that 38 per cent of British-born Muslim women leave school with Level 2 qualifications (Advanced Level and equivalent) and that 36 per cent leave university with a first degree and 8 per cent with a postgraduate qualification. However, the LDA data also reveal that almost one-third of Muslim women with a university degree are out of work (Ibid.).

France
Successive studies on immigrants in France have shown that their level of education and qualifications has increased with the entry of each new cohort into schools and higher education. However, some variation exists in the level of education reached depending on immigrants' country of origin, the structures of formal education within the country of origin, their migration histories and modes of entry to France. For example, among immigrants who arrived before 1974, aged between 18 and 60 years, 76 per cent had very basic school leavers' qualifications or none at all and only 11 per cent were graduates (Table 4.12). By contrast, 34 per cent of those who arrived in France after 1998 were educated to graduate or postgraduate level while only a quarter came without qualifications or with a school leavers' certificate. Although these figures are not broken down by sex, the periods of immigration and the primary modes of migration related to them will give some indication of breakdown by sex of educational levels reached. For example, immigrants who arrived during the 1974 to 1983 period, under family reunification rules, were mainly women from the Maghreb countries; therefore it can be said that Muslim women from Algeria, Tunisia and Morocco accounted for a good proportion of the 66 per cent of immigrants who had no qualifications or who were poorly qualified.

Table 4.12 Qualifications obtained by immigrants aged 18 to 60 according to period of migration (percentage)

Period of immigration	No qualification	School leaving certificate	Baccalaureate	University first degree/postgraduate qualification	Total
Before 1974	44	38	7	11	100
1975–1983	42	24	12	22	100
1984–1997	29	24	16	31	100
1998 onwards	25	22	19	34	100
All periods	31	25	16	29	100

Figures adapted from TEO study (Beauchemin et al. 2010: 42)

Differences in education levels and qualifications are also marked according to immigrants' country of origin, its level of development and traditional gender roles; so, for example, 78 per cent of women from the Muslim-majority countries of the Sahel, one of the poorest regions of Africa, arrive in France without any qualifications at all. Men from the Sahel are far better qualified which suggests that economic under-development of immigrants' country of origin combined with traditional family roles ascribed to women explain the exceptionally low educational attainment of women from this region. While the levels of education among Muslim Maghrebi women are higher than those of women from the Sahel, similar factors explain their lack of qualifications at higher levels. On the other hand, European migrants, both female and male, enjoy easier access to education at all levels compared with their counterparts from developing countries; thus, for instance, 27 per cent of women from Spain and Italy arrive in France without qualifications while 39 per cent are graduates and outnumber Spanish and Italian male migrants in this category (Beauchemin et al. 2010: 41). Even where immigrant women from developing Muslim-majority countries hold graduate qualifications, as 22 per cent of them from the Maghreb countries do, they are unable to translate their academic success into employment in the way that women from the French majority population do.

The differences between French-born descendants of immigrants and White French children narrowed in the 1990s, particularly in the case of daughters and granddaughters of immigrants and this is supported by various studies (e.g. Gaspard 1996). Schoolgirls of Maghrebi background have consistently outperformed schoolboys from their communities over the past 25 years. Despite this success, on average, French-born descendants of immigrants are less likely to hold a university degree than White French students as school careers advisors tend to direct them away from the study of academic subjects and study at university towards shorter, more vocational courses of study. However, the French-born daughters/granddaughters of immigrants have created a considerable performance gap at the university level between themselves and the sons/grandsons of immigrants which means that 33 per cent of young women of immigrant parents leave university with a degree compared with 25 per cent of their male counterparts (Beauchemin et al. 2010: 44). This advantage runs through all immigrant communities of Muslim background with the exception of the Turkish community where young men and boys outperform girls and young women at school and in higher education and where it appears that the French-born children of Turkish immigrants have continued gendered patterns of educational attainment set by their parents' generation (Table 4.13).

That the daughters of immigrants from Muslim backgrounds continue at a disadvantage in education is due to a number of factors both external and internal to their communities, including discrimination on the grounds of race, sex and religion in majority society and constraints placed on them by family because of ethno-religious gender norms and expectations. However, a principal reason is rooted in social class. The majority,

Table 4.13 Qualifications obtained by descendants of immigrants, aged 18 to 50 (percentage), according to parents' country of birth

Country	No qualifications		First degree level+	
	Women	Men	Women	Men
Algeria	19	25	22	18
Morocco and Tunisia	12	20	34	27
Sub-Saharan Africa	20	11	35	25
South East Asia	7	13	49	47
Turkey	26	25	14	17
Portugal	9	16	37	20
Spain and Italy	11	16	30	23
All descendants of immigrants	13	17	33	25
Majority White French	9	10	37	32

Figures adapted from Beauchemin et al. (2010: 44)

65 per cent, of descendants of immigrants belong to working-class families by virtue of immigration histories which brought their fathers and grandfathers to work in manual industrial jobs. In the case of descendants of Maghrebi parents, the proportion of working-class fathers/grandfathers rises to 70 per cent, compared with 41 per cent of their White French counterparts who are working-class (Beauchemin et al. 2010: 49). The weight of class disadvantage will therefore have contributed significantly to their historical under-achievement in the French education system.

Conclusion

Britain and France are home to a combined population of just over 7 million Muslims (4 to 4.5 million in France and 2.7 million in Britain) and women, who form the focus of this book, account for almost half. An understanding of who is being studied is therefore crucial. This chapter provides that understanding through an examination of the two countries' migration histories, explaining the arrival of the first large groupings of Muslim women and the emergence of subsequent generations of their daughters in France and Britain. Both countries conform to similar models of immigration although the inward flows of Muslims, particularly between the 1950s and the late 1980s, have originated from the different countries forming part of the former British and French colonial empires. From the late 1980s onwards, both countries have seen a diversification of migratory flows in terms of the countries from which they emanate, their gender composition and in relation to the type of migration involved—family reunification and forced migrations becoming the dominant forms. An understanding of the main actors in this study is also derived from knowing their demographic characteristics and socio-economic position. The demographic portrait which emerges from the study of Muslim women in both countries is one of a predominantly young and multi-ethnic population concentrated in the two capital cities and other major British and French urban centres. Further, the majority are positioned at the bottom of the socio-economic pyramid of Western society. Knowledge of this positioning provides an important context for the understanding which develops in later chapters of not only how Muslim women live and move between different areas of social and political life and activity but also of the barriers and facilitators they encounter in making a place for themselves in British and French society. Finally, this chapter provides an account of how Muslim women and the different ethnic populations to which they belong are constructed as a category and counted. This account explains the problems of counting Muslims and importantly also throws light on the French universalist and British multiculturalist frameworks which determine whether and how they should be counted and understood. In both countries, counting in relation to gender is a relatively recent development although gender-disaggregated data is more widely available in Britain and therefore allows one to develop a more accurate account of the demographic and socio-economic characteristics of women from Muslim communities.

Notes

1. The UK census refers to population counts in England and Wales only. Hence information on Muslims in this chapter relates to England and Wales only. Besides, Muslims form a small part—1.4 per cent—of Scotland's population (Scotland's Census 2012). In Northern Ireland they are subsumed under 'other religions' accounting for 0.8 per cent of the total population (NISRA 2015).
2. The 1978 Loi informatique et libertés exempts research organisations which collect and process ethnic/religion data for good medical reasons or the protection of human life. However, all data are scrutinised by the Commission National de l'Informatique et des Libertés (CNIL—France's data protection commission) which gives final approval for the publication of such research. The law also exempts polling organisations which can ask respondents, forming a representative sample of the French population, questions about ethnicity and religion.
3. Tribalat is seen as a republican of the Left, but the Front National has cited her work. Using certain statistical data, Tribalat has recently concluded that immigration does not contribute to France's economic growth or demographic deficit (Journet 2011).
4. In 2005 the European Monitoring Centre on Racism and Xenophobia (EUMC) signalled to France that the battle against race discrimination in the EU was being undermined by member states refusing to develop ethnic monitoring systems.
5. The campaign for ethnic statistics was also undermined by a 2007 ruling of the French Constitutional Council which judged that Article 63 of the 2007 Immigration, Integration and Asylum Act, authorising the use of ethnic statistics, was anti-constitutional as it

contradicted Article 1 of the French Constitution which holds all citizens equal regardless of race or religion.
6. The right-wing Republican Party has recently argued that ethnic statistics are an important tool in controlling immigration and integrating non-nationals living in France (*Le Monde* 2015).
7. Movement from New Commonwealth countries to Britain was boosted by the 1948 British Nationality Act which gave all Crown subjects the right to live, work and exercise political rights without restrictions.
8. The highest numbers of immigrants from South Asia to Britain were recorded in 1961 and 1962, before the 1962 Commonwealth Immigrants Act placed restrictions on entry. The Act required Commonwealth citizens to apply for an entry which was granted according to the individual's skill and qualification. It denied the principle of equal citizenship for all British subjects regardless of country of birth.
9. The only way of identifying changes in the religious composition of the UK population prior to 2001 is by associating religion with country of origin information until 1991 and to ethnicity after that. While not all Pakistanis are Muslim, 98 per cent of those claiming Pakistani ethnicity also profess Islam as their faith (DCLG 2009: 7).
10. Munitions workers and soldiers from the Maghreb and sub-Saharan Africa were deployed by France in the First World War. Many Algerians who could move freely between Algeria and France until Algerian independence in 1962 emigrated to France for economic reasons.
11. Algeria was administered as three French *départements* and formed an integral part of France. Native Algerians, considered neither French nor 'foreigners' or immigrants because Algeria was part of France, were referred to as *indigènes, sujets français* (native, French subjects) or *français musulmans d'Algérie*. However, in the French psyche they were immigrants.
12. There are an estimated 400,000 *harkis* and their descendants in France (LDH Toulon 2003).
13. Most of the data here is derived from INSEE's thematic dossier *Immigrés et descendants d'immigrés en France* (2012), in which the statistics relate to 2010.
14. The INSEE calculates the rate of employment within a population category as a proportion of the total working age population of that category.

15. Employment and unemployment percentage rates are calculated here as a proportion of the total economically active population according to the standard Labour Force Survey method, and are rounded up to the nearest whole number.
16. A large proportion of South Asian women including Muslims work in the public and third sectors. Given that these sectors have experienced brutal cuts, this group of women will have been disproportionately affected (APPG 2012: 9).
17. This group consists of 24 self-selected universities deemed the most prestigious in the UK.

PART II

Muslim Women, Politics and Action

CHAPTER 5

Politics and Activisms

INTRODUCTION

This chapter examines and explains the political participation and civic engagement of women from Muslim communities in Britain and France, establishing a typology of participation and activism. It identifies the structures and processes through which Muslim women's action and activism takes place; for example, formal processes such as voting and institutional structures such as political parties and elected assemblies, as well as alternative forms such as street protest, political consumerism, public service and community politics and civicism. The above constitutes the landscape of political participation and civic engagement in which two types are highlighted: voting and activism through organisations and groups in the third sector. As revealed by our research, these are among the most common types of participation among women from Muslim communities in the countries under study here.

POLITICAL PARTICIPATION AND CIVIC ENGAGEMENT: LITERATURES AND APPROACHES

There exists a significant body of literature on women, political participation and civic engagement in Britain and France although women from immigrant, Black, ethnic minority and faith communities form a very small part of it. While public and academic interest in Muslim women has increased in both countries, thus far it has translated into a slim body of work. It is reasonable to state that little has been published on Muslim women and their involvement in French political and civic life[1] (Ali 2012; Fournier 2008) although a huge number of publications has built up, in French and English, on the issue of the headscarf/veil in France and its political, legal, socio-cultural and philosophical repercussions. A limited amount of work has been done on the political and civic activism of Maghrebi women within third sector organisations (Manier 2007; Mélis 2003) and the situation of these women and girls in education (Hassini 1997; Keaton 2006), employment (Belhadj 1998; Touati 2012) and related questions of discrimination (Amar 2001) and integration in French society (Nigaud and Ripoll 2004; Vassberg 1997). Finally, there is considerably more written on Muslim and Maghrebi women, identity and gender relations in Islam and Arab cultures (Andezian 1983; Gaspard and Khosrokhavar 1994; Killian 2006; Mounir 2003; Pottier 1993; Tersigni 2008; Timera 2004 among others).

Much of the literature in Britain covers Muslim women's participation in areas of public life other than the polity: education, employment, organised religion and culture (Ahmad 2001; Bhimji 2012; Brah 2001; Cheruvallil-Contractor 2012; Dyke and James 2009; Haw 1998; Jawad and Benn 2003; Peach 2006; Tyrer and Ahmad 2006). Some work focuses on particular issues, for example, Muslim women and feminism (Afshar et al. 2005; Cheruvallil-Contractor 2012, Chapter 6; Takhar 2013b); Islamic dress and identity (Cheruvallil-Contractor 2012, Chapter 5; Dwyer 1999; Hopkins and Greenwood 2013) or Islamic dress and the law (Malik 2008; Ward 2006); marriage/family legal codes and practices (Bano 2012); Muslim women, Islamophobia and racism (Allen et al. 2013; Williamson and Khiabany 2010; Ryan 2011; Takhar 2013a); and Muslim women, counter-terrorism and social cohesion (Brown 2008; Jones et al. 2014; Rashid 2014). There are also a small number of works which deal more explicitly with the question of Muslim women and politics (e.g. Akhtar (2015); Allen and Guru 2012; Belli 2013; Joly and Wadia 2012; Massoumi 2015; Sanghera and Thapar-Björkert 2007; Wadia 2015; Werbner 1996).

A Political Participation and Civic Engagement Approach

The involvement of citizens in public life has been approached and categorised in several ways. Traditional political science has focused on the polity and conventional political activity aimed at influencing government thinking, policy and action either directly or indirectly (Verba et al. 1995: 38). Activity aimed at directly influencing government includes lobbying MPs or demonstrating against specific government policies, while indirect influence, through selecting legislators, would include voting. Women's movements in the 1970s challenged these narrow definitions of what 'doing politics' involved. Their claim—'the personal is political'—brought new issues onto the political agenda and expanded the definition of the political to include activities in which women were involved.

In the 1980s, feminist scholars, explaining the absence of women in politics through reasons other than 'political apathy' and/or a 'lack of political knowledge' as defined by traditional political science (Goot and Reid 1984), or arguing that women were differently active from men (Hernes 1984: 21–31; Lovenduski 1986: 126–127), de-emphasised methods of study of mass and elite political behaviour and instead placed value on the combined searches of historical archives and primary materials, interviews with activists and studies of the law and policymaking processes in order to reveal a rich history of women's political participation. An important finding of early feminist studies was that while a gender gap (in men's favour) concerning participation in political institutions and elections existed (Randall 1987: 57), it was explainable by examining the structural barriers women faced in entering the political arena. Such studies also found that women participated at the grass-roots level in social movements, protest politics, informal community groups, voluntary organisations and so on and that they often addressed issues of social and political importance through the legal system and by targeting specific policies. Thus feminist scholars expanded the definition of the political to include not just electoral and institutional (elite) politics but also alternative political activity such as direct action and protest at the grass-roots level, in favour of social and political transformation. In this chapter, Muslim women's activism will be examined and understood through this expanded definition of politics. However, within this broader conceptualisation of 'doing politics', we use the term and concept 'civic engagement' to refer to involvement which takes place in civic arenas as opposed to within explicitly political structures and processes. While civic engagement has been variously defined (Adler and Goggin 2005), we use the definition provided by Zukin et al. (2006: 7) which sees it as an organised voluntary activity, undertaken by citizens individually or collectively, which is aimed at helping others in a community find solutions to social and other problems and eventually bring about societal change.

Whether civic engagement can be considered political has been the subject of lengthy debate. For instance, scholars such as Burns, Schlozman and Verba concede that 'voluntary activity in both the religious and secular domains outside of politics intersects with politics in many ways' (2001: 58), but they conclude that political activity is that which 'seek[s] to influence either directly or indirectly what the government does' (Ibid.). Hence, they argue that serving in a community soup kitchen may be a precursor to political activity through the development of transferable skills but that it is not a political activity in itself. However, it can be argued that the context in which serving in a soup kitchen occurs must be considered, that the act of volunteering in a soup kitchen is not necessarily apolitical but may express disapproval of a government's economic and welfare policies and also constitute an attempt to shame politicians and influence public policy. In the UK, those volunteering at food banks since the economic downturn in 2008 have become increasingly vocal in their criticism of government austerity policy and its impact on disadvantaged groups. Supporting an expanded definition of politics to include activities undertaken in the civic sphere, by voluntary organisations and unstructured community groups, Pippa Norris argues:

> While these groups are not conventionally seen as political, their status should be redefined since as part of their work they can engage in activity which is designed to influence public policy, understood in broad terms. In response, traditionalists might argue that these activities…should not all be considered instances of political participation…Participants in these activities may not necessarily see themselves as engaging in 'politics' since their actions are not directed, in the first instance, towards influencing the state. Nor are they using the conventional political mechanisms of parties and elections. The level of involvement may be relatively trivial and undemanding. Nor may they necessarily see themselves as formal members of an organized group or voluntary association…Nevertheless in a broader conception, participation in these groups can be seen as political since, as part of their functions, they address policy issues of public concern. These organizations can have a significant indirect impact on conventional politics. (Norris 1991: 60)

Here the term and concept civic engagement is introduced within a broad conceptualisation of 'doing politics' for a number of reasons. First, because both explicitly political and civic activity/activism are equally important forms of public involvement and, on their own, neither can tackle the innumerable problems and issues arising in our society nor produce the solutions and decisions which must be formulated in response to them; second, it provides a detailed picture of changing citizen involvement in public life over time as groups or individuals stick to one form, move from one to another or are both politically and civically involved. Such an understanding may be useful in assessing the legitimacy accorded to democratic systems by citizens and also the impact of different forms of public involvement on policy. Most importantly, in terms of the population under study here, it allows the inclusion, within the ambit of citizen participation, of populations which have historically been excluded from the polity and because often those very social actors may see themselves as non-political or even anti-politics. However, the fact that their involvement occurs in the public arena and that they engage with community organisations and indirectly with political institutions and thereby influence public policy means that they are acting politically and thus neither the intentionality of individual actors nor the explicit expression of political commitment is a crucial element in the definition of 'doing politics'.

Interest in Politics and Typology of Political Participation and Civic Engagement

Women from Muslim communities have become increasingly visible political actors in twenty-first-century Europe. The 9/11 attacks, the London transport bombings of 2005 and attacks carried out elsewhere by radical Islamic groups have undoubtedly shaped their political awareness, opinion and action. The majority of the respondents in this study had previously voted in parliamentary, French presidential and subnational elections if eligible while some also had experience of political and civic activism, most commonly including forms of public service and community activism which ranged from active involvement via paid or voluntary work in community organisations to a looser affiliation with such organisations. Below, we consider the extent to which women from Muslim communities are interested in and knowledgeable about politics and construct a typology of their action and activity in the political and civic spheres. This typology is based on data from our survey of Muslim women and individual interviews whereas information about their interest in politics and knowledge of current affairs is drawn from interviews with women with a public profile in their communities and beyond as well as with 'ordinary' Muslim women; that is, women not known beyond their everyday circles of family, friends and neighbours.

Politics: Knowledge and Interest

Although many of the 'ordinary' Muslim women interviewed prefaced their response to the question 'how much do you feel you know about politics?' with the opinion that they were not 'politically minded', their individual narratives and the survey responses revealed that they were far more interested in and knowledgeable about political and civic life than they believed. Thus, only 6 per cent of survey respondents in Britain and 1 per cent of respondents in France felt they knew 'a great deal' about politics although, more positively, 47 per cent of UK Muslim women and 44 per cent of the women surveyed in France said that they knew 'a fair amount' (see Table 5.1).

As far as interest in political life was concerned, the majority of women in both countries—62 per cent in Britain and 70 per cent in France—claimed a high or fairly high level of interest. These indications contradict the prevalent public view in Western society that women from Muslim communities are closed off from the world and are consequently uninformed about and/or uninterested in public and political life. The readings of our survey suggest that proportionately Muslim women in Britain and France are more willing to state their interest in and knowledge about politics than the general electorate in both countries. For example, over the last 12 years, according to the annual *Audit of political engagement*

Table 5.1 Knowledge and interest

Knowledge of politics	Muslim women—Britain (per cent)	Muslim women—France (per cent)
A great deal	6	1
A fair amount	47	44
Not very much	37	48
Nothing at all	5	7
Don't know	5	0

Interest in politics	Muslim women—Britain (per cent)	Muslim women—France (per cent)
Very interested	11	15
Fairly interested	51	55
Not very interested	28	24
Not at all interested	10	7
Don't know	0	0

undertaken in Britain, an average 51 per cent of voters claimed to have a fair to high level of interest in politics (Hansard Society 2015: 24) while an average of 46 per cent believed they had a great deal or fair amount of political knowledge (Ibid.: 26). In France, according to presidential election surveys carried out in 2007 (post-election) and 2012 (pre-election), the self-declared level of interest in politics (ranging from a fair to high level of interest) among voters was 62 per cent (CEVIPOF-Ministère de l'Intérieur 2007: 24) and 56 per cent (Denni 2011), respectively.[2] Muslim women's reported interest in and knowledge of politics also seems to buck other trends noted in the aforementioned UK audits of political engagement and French presidential election surveys, which are that women and Black and ethnic minorities are amongst groups reported to be disproportionately less interested in and knowledgeable about politics. However, the fact that Muslim women have been cast into the glare of politics in the 2000s, across the Western world, will have increased their interest in politics and knowledge of current affairs and in turn expanded their repertoire of action in political and civic spaces.

Typology of Action and Activity

The forms of political participation and civic activism in which Muslim women take part may be categorised under four main headings: formal institutional politics; street politics; everyday politics; public service and community politics. This non-exhaustive typology is developed through the triangulation of data from the survey questionnaire (based on the political participation and civic engagement questions asked in the *Audit of political engagement 5*, 2008), qualitative interview data and researcher observations. Table 5.2 provides a representation of the forms of participation undertaken by respondents. The popularity and frequency of each form is indicated by a four-level tick code where four ticks represent a dominant activity or form of activism (undertaken by over 50 per cent of survey respondents); three ticks indicate a fairly frequent form of activism (carried out by 25 to 49 per cent of respondents); two ticks denote an infrequent form of activism (performed by 11 to 24 per cent of respondents); and one tick represents an occasional form (i.e. undertaken by 1 to 10 per cent of survey respondents). For example, voting in national elections (parliamentary and presidential) is a dominant form of participation given that 52 per cent of Muslim women in Britain and 60 per cent in France said they had voted at the last national election to have taken place. Among

Muslim women in Britain this was the only dominant form of participation whereas in France, other dominant forms of participation included having political discussions with others, urging others to vote and signing petitions. Contrasts between the two countries are worth noting where street politics are concerned—for instance, 49 per cent of respondents in France said they had participated in demonstrations, marches and pickets (against the Iraq and Afghanistan wars, the Israeli blockade of Gaza and education policy including the 2004 'headscarf law'), compared with 18 per cent in Britain (in the Stop-the-War Campaign against the Afghanistan and Iraq wars and Israeli attacks on Palestinians). Additionally, 47 per cent of respondents in France had taken part in strike action compared with 7 per cent in Britain. These patterns conform with the different cultures of street politics and direct action in the countries concerned. On the other hand where community politics and activism are concerned, 35 per cent of Muslim women in Britain claimed to have helped organise charity events compared with 13 per cent in France, and 29 per cent of respondents in Britain had participated in fundraising sponsored events compared with 11 per cent in France. Muslim women in Britain were also more likely to have donated money or been a member of a charitable or community organisation or campaign (49 per cent) than Muslim women in France (36 per cent). The difference in the level of Muslim women's involvement in community politics between the two countries can be ascribed to two factors: first, the historical dominance of *non-dirigiste* state policy in Britain which encouraged citizens to 'look after themselves' compared with a history of French state interventionism in economic and social affairs accounting for a weaker third sector and community action; second, the accordance of full political rights to New Commonwealth immigrants since their arrival in the 1950s which has led to the establishment of a strong associative culture among migrants and ethnic minorities in Britain compared with a weak associative culture and sector among their counterparts in France, due to laws restricting non-nationals from establishing organisations until 1981.

Finally, where party political activism (party membership, involvement in election campaigns, standing as a candidate on behalf of a party and so on) is concerned, Muslim women in both France and Britain tend to be occasional participants. This is reflected in their low presence in formal political institutions including elected assemblies at national and sub-national levels. While a small number of women of Muslim background (among them Rachida Dati, Rama Yade, Fadela Amara, Najat Vallaud-Belkacem)[3] have held significant posts in French government, these have been in the gift of incumbent presidents (Sarkozy and Hollande) wishing to be lauded as promoters of ethnic diversity. These women have also run for and won elections at the municipal and regional level but it is noteworthy that none, apart from Rama Yade (for the right-wing Union pour un Mouvement Populaire in 2012), were selected as candidates by their respective party to run in a parliamentary election. In the 2012 parliamentary elections, the number of French deputies of Black and ethnic minority background rose (from 3 in the previous parliament) to 12, representing 2 per cent of deputies in the French National Assembly (Keslassy 2012; Observatoire des inégalités 2012). This figure reveals the massive under-representation of Black and ethnic minorities in France which constitute 12 per cent of the population (CRAN 2012).[4] Of these, six were women and two of Algerian family background although, observing republican universalist principles, none of the parliamentary candidates referred to religion or ethnicity during or after their campaigns. All but one of these deputies represent the Socialist Party. In Britain, Black and ethnic minorities are under-represented in the House of Commons at 6.6 per cent of all MPs (Bengtsson et al. 2015) while Black and ethnic minority populations (including those of mixed ethnic groups) make up 14 per cent of the UK population (ONS 2012: 1). This under-representation also operates in the case of Muslim women MPs who make up 1.2 per cent of all MPs as opposed to their part in the UK population of over 2 per cent.[5] The representation of Black and ethnic minorities including Muslim women in subnational legislatures and executives in both countries is also very weak relative to their presence in the respective population of each country (Wood and Cracknell 2015: 9; CRAN 2014).

Table 5.2 Muslim women's political participation and civic engagement[a]

Type of politics	Britain	France
Formal institutional politics		
Voted in parliamentary and/or presidential elections	✓✓✓✓	✓✓✓✓
Voted in municipal elections	✓✓✓	✓✓✓
Stood for public office/elected to a national/subnational assembly	✓	✓
Taken active part in a party's parliamentary/presidential election campaign	✓	✓
Taken active part in a party's local election campaign	✓✓	✓
Taken active part in a political campaign	✓✓	✓

(*continued*)

Table 5.2 (continued)

Type of politics	Britain	France
Presented views to a local councillor	✓✓✓	✓✓
Contacted local council	✓✓✓	✓✓
Donated money/paid membership fee to political party	✓	✓
Signed petitions	✓✓✓	✓✓✓✓
Street politics		
Taken part in demonstrations, marches, pickets	✓✓	✓✓✓
Taken part in a strike	✓	✓✓✓
Made a speech before an organised group	✓✓	✓
Taken part in a political meeting	✓✓	✓
Everyday politics		
Written letter to a newspaper, radio, TV editor	✓	✓
Discussed politics with others	✓✓	✓✓✓✓
Urged others to vote	✓✓✓	✓✓✓✓
Urged others to contact a local councillor		
Boycotted products for ethical and political reasons	✓✓✓	✓✓✓
Public service and community politics		
Been an officer of an organisation/club	✓✓	✓✓
Donated money/paid membership fee to a charity or campaign	✓✓✓	✓✓✓
Helped with fundraising	✓✓✓	✓✓
Helped organise a charity event	✓✓✓	✓✓
Taken part in sponsored event	✓✓✓	✓✓
Done voluntary work	✓✓✓	✓✓✓
Served as school/hospital etc. governor	✓	✓

[a]Respondents were asked about their political participation and civic engagement over the previous two to three years

The above typology of participation excludes two notable forms: digital or Internet politics and cultural politics. Questions about participation in these categories did not form part of our survey. However, the qualitative interviews and researcher observations revealed that women from Muslim communities are engaged in both cultural and digital politics.

Cultural forms of participation in which respondents in the British study participated include community art events (film screenings, poetry readings and theatre with a social or political message), lectures and seminars (at community centres and mosques) on themes of relevance to Muslims in Britain—women mentioned meetings on the Afghanistan and Iraq wars or issues such as forced marriage. Such meetings sometimes doubled up as socio-cultural events with food and other activities. Interviews and observation undertaken in France showed that women from Muslim communities took part in various forms of cultural politics including reading circles, 'cook-ins' (bringing people together to share a meal and political discussion), anti-racism and political party festivals (such as the Communist Party's *Fête de l'Humanité*), Muslim women's/girls' sports clubs, community radio shows disseminating political and social messages, and creative writing as a means of expressing political ideas and the annual Muslim fair at Le Bourget. Cultural politics can be said to constitute an infrequent form of participation in the repertoire of Muslim women in Britain although a larger proportion of respondents in France were involved in cultural politics. Muslim women were also found to be active in digital politics although there was a clear divide concerning Internet access and usage between those who worked or were students and those whose main focus was home and family, with the latter being less involved in Internet activism. The most common form of digital activism included online petitioning and the mobilisation of family, friends and workplace colleagues through social media to support Internet campaigns and causes (against Islamophobic and anti-immigration discourses or the West's policy in the Middle East and Central Asia) or oppose certain government policies (e.g. domestic security policies targeting Muslims or the ban on religious symbols and dress in public places). Students and women who were in paid or voluntary work in third and public sector organisations were most active in digital politics and for some women (whether studying, employed or at home) digital activism served as a first step towards politics outside the home. Our interviews and observation suggest that digital politics was a fairly frequent form of participation among respondents in both countries. However, as Internet activism has increased significantly among the general publics of both countries, over the last five years (Howard 2014; France Inter 2014), it would be fair to say that this growing trend is also reflected in the political repertoire of women from Muslim communities. The sections below examine two of the dominant forms of political participation and civic engagement found among women from Muslim communities in France and Britain: voting and community activism through third sector organisations.

Muslims/Muslim Women as Voters

The participation of immigrants and ethnic minorities, including Muslims, in elections has a longer and more successful history in Britain than in France. In contrast with the situation of immigrants in France, post-war immigrants to Britain arrived as British subjects (from former colonies which became part of the Commonwealth) with full political rights. Not only were they entitled to vote in local and national elections but they also had the right to stand for election. In France, immigrants (barring those who acquire French citizenship) are not entitled to vote despite long-standing campaigns for voting rights.

Britain

Muslim Voters

Religion does not figure systematically in the analysis of voter registration and turnout. Therefore, indications about Muslim voters' electoral participation are provided through reference to ethnic minority voters, particularly those of Pakistani and Bangladeshi background given that Muslim voters in other aggregate ethnic groups (Black, White, mixed and other) and more recently settled migrant groups who are eligible to vote[6] remain largely unknown. Moreover, the analysis of voting data by ethnic group seldom spotlights or comments on women voters and gendered voting patterns.

It is difficult to judge differences in voter registration and turnout according to ethnicity (for example, between Pakistanis, Bangladeshis and Indians) for elections which took place from the 1970s and the late 1990s as analyses and commentary during this period normally referred to the electoral participation of four aggregated identity categories only: White, Black, Asian and Other (Le Lohe 1975; Layton-Henry and Studlar 1985; Anwar 2012). However, some studies carried out in constituencies densely populated by particular immigrant and ethnic minority groups gave a better indication of how those groups voted; for example, studies undertaken in Bradford by Le Lohe, over 30 years, from the 1960s onwards (1984, 1990), drew attention to the participation of Pakistani voters.

From the findings of the above-mentioned studies, it can be asserted that Muslims have voted consistently and conspicuously even though their early years of settlement in Britain were marked by non-registration rates of over 50 per cent, low turnout (Deakin 1965 cited by Anwar 2012: 47) and indifference on the part of the main political parties towards them. Few efforts were made by political parties to engage ethnic minority voters because most were concentrated in Labour's traditional industrial heartlands where their vote was deemed unimportant compared with that of the White working class in terms of eventual election outcomes. However, the general election of 1970 proved to be a watershed where the participation of immigrant and ethnic minority voters was concerned. The aggressive anti-immigration campaign waged by Enoch Powell and others spurred a great many of them to register and vote against the Conservatives. In 1972, a parliamentary by-election in Rochdale demonstrated the impact that an upsurge of ethnic minority voting could have on electoral results. In this case a decisive role was played by Pakistanis in mobilising against both the British Campaign to Stop Immigration and Conservative candidates in favour of the Liberal candidate who emerged the winner. The expansion of the Black and ethnic minority electorate in the 1970s, particularly of Muslim background, coincided with the permanent settlement of labour migrants and the arrival of wives and children after 1974 and with larger migratory flows from the newly independent Bangladesh. Le Lohe's local study (1975) of Bradford's immigrant and ethnic minority voters showed that although Bradford's South Asians had started from a low baseline (turnout-wise) in the mid-1960s, this had changed dramatically by the 1974 general election when South Asian turnout rates exceeded those of non-Asians. This upward trend continued in the 1980s and 1990s in towns where South Asians were concentrated and was further boosted by the emergence of parliamentary and local election candidates from those communities (Anwar 2012: 82; Le Lohe 1984, 1990). In the 1997 general election, registration rates for South Asian communities reached exceptional levels at 90.2 per cent of Pakistanis and 91.3 per cent of Bangladeshis (Fieldhouse and Cutts 2007: 9). These compared with rates achieved by African Caribbean populations but were lower than the registration rates of Indians and Whites. Higher turnout at the 1997 general election among Pakistanis and Bangladeshis reflected the increased voter registration. Numerous factors (both structural and conjunctural) account for differential participation rates between ethnic minority groups and are well-documented elsewhere (e.g. Purdham et al. 2002: 18–29).

In the 2000s, the registration and turnout rates of Black and ethnic minority voters were frequently reported to be lagging behind those of White voters. However, when differences between groups are examined, the overall picture appears more optimistic in the case of South Asian Muslims. Although voter registration slipped after 1997, the turnout rate of all minority groups had improved by 2010 with Bangladeshis and Pakistanis surpassing Indians and Black African and Caribbean groups and closing the gap with the majority White population (see Table 5.3).[7]

The drop in voter participation after 1997 in most ethnic groups was put down to the lack of party competition and Labour's unassailable position as top party in the early to mid-2000s. Where Muslim voters were

Table 5.3 Registration and turnout percentage rates—1997, 2005 and 2010 general elections

Ethnic group	1997		2005		2010	
	Registration	Turnout	Registration	Turnout	Registration	Turnout
Pakistani	90	75	93	70	83	78
Bangladeshi	91	74	94	76	78	78
Indian	97	82	88	67	80	75
Black Caribbean and Black African	92	67	83	58	73	75
White	97	79	Not available	68	91	78

Figures adapted from Fieldhouse and Cutts (2007: 9, 29 for 1997 figures); Mortimore and Kaur-Ballaghan (2006: 6–7 for 2005 figures); Sanders et al. (2005 for 2005 figures); Heath et al. (2013: 140, 143 for 2010 figures)

concerned, other reasons can be cited—for example, disillusionment with government policies in the wake of the 'northern riots' of summer 2001; the launch of the War on Terror following the events of 9/11 and the wars in Afghanistan and Iraq; the rise in Islamophobia. However, the closing of the participation gap between White voters and those of South Asian Muslim background, achieved by 2010, was predicted to endure in future elections (OBV 2013).

Muslim Women Emerge from the Shadows
As far as women were concerned, although those newly arrived in the 1970s and 1980s, in largely working-class Muslim communities, had little education and knowledge of British political structures and processes, they quickly became an important sub-bloc of voters within a system of clan-based or *biradari* politics, influenced in their voting choice by family and community. This system of bloc voting persists today although it is being challenged by young Muslims (Akhtar 2012, 2015; Qureshi 2012). This idea surfaced strongly in 2012, following a parliamentary by-election in Bradford West won by the Respect Party candidate George Galloway. Moreover, those who argued that *biradari* politics were on the wane saw younger, British-born Muslims, especially women, as its key un-doers (Akhtar 2012, 2015; Baston 2012; Gibbon 2012; Pidd 2012). However, the old system of household electoral registration (replaced by individual electoral registration in June 2014) where heads of household were

responsible for returning registration forms had tended to reinforce male authority in voting matters and there is considerable anecdotal evidence that in the majority of Muslim households it was the male authority—husband or father—who completed voter registration for all family members, strongly urged the family's women and young adults to turn out and vote and directed their choice of candidate.

Thus, women from Muslim communities have a history of participation in UK elections at the national and local level spanning 40 years. However, they remain a largely unnoticed group of voters and beyond the few references to them in the odd media or research report, not much is known about their electoral behaviour and motivation to participate. So, for example, analysing the above-mentioned 2012 Bradford West by-election result, *The Guardian's* Helen Pidd (2012) focused on Muslim women voters inspired, for the first time in their voting experience, and then successfully mobilised to autonomously cast their vote for a candidate who not only talked about local, national and international issues which caused them concern but also broke with the idea that they should be reached via their *biradari*. Galloway's women campaign workers went into the heart of Muslim communities, in search of eligible women voters (by accessing voter registration lists among other methods) to talk to them directly in their homes, at the school gates, in shops, at specially convened women-only meetings. Social media was also used to reach young women. The importance of reaching people in communities, beyond traditional male leaders, was stressed by one of our respondents who worked for the Labour Party and criticised the party's failure to make contact with women:

> Politicians don't want to upset male community leaders. The Labour Party relies hugely on the Asian vote, and most importantly Asian vote in groups—an entire family will vote the same. And to retain the Asian vote, they need to please the men, they have to keep them happy...I think to view any particular group as representative of the wider community is a bit premature I think. They [politicians] need to really go into the heart of communities because what you have to see is that a lot of these people have a certain client basis...what communities do they actually represent? (Walada, London)

The Bradford West by-election demonstrated two things: first, that when addressed directly, Muslim women voters were mobilised effectively and, second, that they could constitute a decisive bloc of voters in constituencies where Muslims are present in large numbers. This argument had previously been put forward by Salma Yaqoob following her election to Birmingham City Council in 2006. She attributed a large part of her electoral success to being able to reach substantial numbers of Muslim women directly:

> The unprecedented sight of teams of Muslim women, canvassing door to door during daytime in order to specifically speak to Muslim women who were at home, played an important role in persuading women to resist family pressures to support the usual suspects. It was a common refrain as I went door-to-door canvassing to have Muslim women come out to me and say, 'Our Dad is with Labour, but we are with you!' On election day, female turnout at the polling booth was noticeably up from previous elections. (Yaqoob 2008: 156–157)

Muslim women voters are also considered in Fieldhouse and Cutts' (2007) research report on the 2001 general election. In contrast with previous findings on voter turnout between men and women from Black and ethnic minority groups (Norris et al. 2004: 8),[8] Fieldhouse and Cutts' examination of the gender voting gap suggests that men and women from South Asian communities voted in more or less equal proportions in 2001. Moreover, they found that Muslim women's turnout rate exceeded that of their male counterparts by 7 per cent (Fieldhouse and Cutts 2007: 33). Their turnout also contrasted with the national picture where women were concerned. For example, a 2010 House of Commons Library study revealed that nationally the number of women voters had fallen by 18 per cent between the 1992 general election and that of 2005 as a result of non-registration (Cohen 2015). As Fieldhouse and Cutts' research was based on the study of marked electoral lists there was no scope for gathering data which may have explained Muslim women's turnout rate and why this contrasted with falling turnout among Muslim men and women nationally. Among the reasons which may be offered are, first, that in 2001, proportionately more younger Muslim women than men in the 18 to 35 age group were turning out to vote—that young men's levels of mistrust and suspicion of the system and politicians ran deeper than that of young women following police handling of the (April to July) 2001 northern riots and government responses; second, the emergence of Muslim women as election candidates at both the local and the national level after 2005 encouraged Muslim female voters to participate in larger numbers; third, as expressed by a number of our respondents, voting was seen as 'a duty, even as a Muslim' (Sultana, Birmingham). As they became more assertive voters, some spoke of encountering pressure from male family and community members who had tried to put them off voting, seen as an un-Islamic exercise. Their condemnation of individuals and Islamic groups who characterised voting as the worship of human laws above those of Allah was almost unanimous and for many voting represented resistance against such ideas.

Our study of Muslim women and their involvement in politics revealed that voting was the most common form of participation undertaken by the women interviewed and those who took part in the survey. A number of voting-related questions featured in the survey. One asked women to rate, on a scale of one to ten, the likelihood of them voting in an immediate general election. The majority (60 per cent) said they would be certain to vote while a further 20 per cent said they were likely or very likely to vote. These figures are higher than those presented by the national *Audit of political engagement* where 50 per cent of women in 2008 and 56 per cent in 2009 (the period during which our survey was undertaken) said they were absolutely certain to vote in an immediate election (Hansard Society 2009: 20; 2010: 73). Only 5 per cent of our sample of Muslim women said they would be certain not to vote while another 15 per cent thought it was unlikely they would vote, did not know or refused to answer. While the percentage of those who said they were certain or likely to vote is relatively high (80 per cent), it expressed a desire which may not be borne out in reality as demonstrated by their responses to another question on voting, which asked if they had voted at the last general election to have taken place (in 2005). In response to that question, 52 per cent said they had voted—a much lower percentage than that related to voting intention—although this lower figure would have excluded a good proportion of the respondents who were under voting age in 2005. However, that Muslim women in Britain are committed voters is confirmed by the findings presented above.

France

In France, questions about the 'Muslim vote' (whether or not it exists, the extent of voter registration and turnout among those of Muslim background and where their political allegiances lie) have only recently emerged in public discussion and debate (Brouard and Tiberj 2007; Dargent 2011; Fourquet 2012; Wakim and Le Cœur 2007). As Muslim voters are not officially counted, most scholars and commentators rely on evidence drawn from voting studies of the main ethnic groups based on data relating to nationality/national origins, hence of Maghrebis, Turks and certain sub-Saharan Africans. Moreover, there is scant gender-disaggregated data related to voting among minority groups—only one study (Richard 1999) included voter registration and turnout rates for women and men. The discussion below about Muslim women voters is mainly based on data available on immigrants and their descendants and on knowledge that the voting gap between women and men among immigrant and ethnic minority groups in France, as in the UK, has closed. This data is complemented by findings from our interviews and indicative survey on political participation. However, before examining the electoral participation of immigrants and their descendants, including Muslims, it is relevant and instructive to examine the context of long-running debates and campaigns over the lack of voting rights of resident non-French nationals from non-EU countries.

The Question of Voting Rights
In France, only those born or naturalised French possess full political rights. Therefore, non-naturalised immigrants or foreigners (*étrangers*), especially those of non-European origin, have been denied the right to participate in elections as voters and electoral candidates. Campaigners for the right of non-nationals to vote consider voting not only an important means of becoming a part of French society but also as a way of bridging divisions within migrant and ethnic minority communities between those who are integrated and those who are marginalised. There have been ebbs and flows in the campaign for immigrants' voting rights since the 1970s but the first really active campaigns surfaced in the early 1980s when a government of the Left came to power raising hopes among immigrant communities of gaining political rights. Although one of the Left's campaign promises in 1981 was to separate citizenship from nationality through limited voting rights for immigrants (in local elections for example), once in power and faced with a growing challenge from the Front National and its anti-immigration platform, the government's line changed and by 1985 the issue of voting rights was off the Left's agenda. In the 1990s, attempts to resurrect the campaign failed. Voting rights for non-EU citizens became anathema to the government of the Right (returned in the 1993 legislative elections) amidst its obligation, under EU rules, to include large numbers of European immigrants into local electorates and manage the impact of their inclusion on municipal electoral results. In

addition, divisions had emerged within the campaign for political rights. The main divide occurred between those who believed that the attainment of voting rights for immigrants at local elections should be a goal in itself which would eventually lead to an increase in social and economic rights and those who regarded voting rights as part of full, equal citizenship including the right to vote at national elections. The latter argued that focusing on the right of immigrants to vote in local elections amounted to promoting a two-tier citizenship where a privileged tier was composed of French nationals and a second tier of non-nationals.

These arguments rumbled on into the 2000s while the French-born descendants of immigrants, despite having the right to vote, became increasingly frustrated by the failure of successive governments to tackle economic and social exclusion, racial discrimination and Islamophobia and to offer them, their families and friends a stake in French society, including full political rights for non-nationals. The riots of 2005, across the urban neighbourhoods of France, involving the children of immigrants, expressed this frustration. They also reflected the fact that a sizeable section of French citizens, taught the principles of *liberté, égalité, fraternité*, felt that those principles were not being applied to them and their communities and that the state had breached the terms of its social contract with them. Voting rights for non-nationals re-emerged during the presidential election campaign of 2012 as one of François Hollande's manifesto pledges. While the latter has maintained his presidential election manifesto position, the incumbent Socialist government appears deeply divided on the issue and has repeatedly postponed taking measures to introduce voting rights for non-nationals. This issue appears to have been on the back burner for the foreseeable future.

Muslims and Muslim Women Voters
Given a context in which large numbers of immigrants from Muslim-majority countries are denied political rights and where those who possess them feel largely ignored by political powers, it is unsurprising that France's immigrant and ethnic minority communities, including Muslims, mistrust the state and disengage from political institutions and processes. Studies undertaken in the 1980s and 1990s showed that Maghrebi immigrants and their descendants were less likely to register and vote than their White French counterparts (Muxel 1988; Tribalat 1995). However, more recent work provides a more nuanced reading of the participation of young people of immigrant origin who are eligible to vote. For example,

an analysis of the participation of the latter in the 1995 presidential elections by Richard (1999) found that although voter registration rates were lower among this population than those of White French voters in the same age group (19 to 25), the turnout of young people of immigrant background was similar to that of White French voters (see Table 5.4). Richard's findings also showed that in 1995 young women's participation in both groups outstripped that of men: among voters of immigrant background, the gender participation gap, in favour of young women, was 8 per cent where voter registration was concerned and 12 per cent in terms of turnout, representing statistically significant results. Richard's analysis does not include an explanation for the higher registration and turnout rates among women from immigrant family backgrounds when compared with men from their communities although possible reasons, drawn from our respondent data, are explored below.

Richard's explanation for the differential rates of voter registration among young people generally pointed to socio-economic factors including employment status, level of education, housing conditions and so on; for example, labour market exclusion goes hand in hand with low registration rates. He argued that, by contrast, ethnic origin played a negligible part. This is supported by other scholars such as Brouard and Tiberj (2005) whose study on 'the new French' (young French nationals of Maghrebi descent) showed that while ethnicity does not appear to influence voter registration rates, the fact of being Muslim does. This is partly because a disproportionate number of Muslims find themselves in a disadvantaged socio-economic situation but also because a significant proportion of Muslims are not eligible to vote. Research carried out by the Open Society Foundation between 2008 and 2010, on Muslims in Paris,

Table 5.4 The participation of young people aged 19 to 25 in the 1995 presidential elections (second round)

	Eligible voters immigrant background		Eligible voters—White majority	
	Women	Men	Women	Men
Registration rate (per cent)	68	60	84	79
Turnout rate (as per cent of registration rate)	85	77	82	79

Figures adapted from Richard (1999: 126)

found that only 41 per cent of Muslim respondents were eligible to vote in national elections compared with 70 per cent of non-Muslims (Amiraux 2012: 221). Although this figure most likely underestimates the percentage of Muslims eligible to vote given the limited scale of the survey[9] and bearing in mind Tribalat's estimate that 70 per cent of Muslims in France are French-born (see Chapter 4, p. 102), it, nevertheless, reveals that the lack of voting rights for non-nationals impacts strongly on the political participation of Muslims generally.

Richard's findings on levels of electoral participation are also confirmed by a study undertaken just over ten years later by the Institut National de la Statistique et des Études Économiques (INSEE) and Institut National d'Études Démographiques (INED). The TeO (*Trajectoires et origines géographiques*) study which examined the electoral participation of immigrants and their French-born descendants in the 2007 presidential elections added to Richard's findings: that their turnout rates (regardless of ethnicity) matched those of White French citizens and that voter registration rates had actually increased, varying between 80 and 90 per cent for all ethnicities except those of Turkish origin. Moreover, once variables such as age, educational achievement, place and length of residence in France were taken into account, the gap in registration rates between those of Turkish origin and other ethnic groups closed and the French-born descendants of immigrants were often more likely to register and vote than the White French majority (Beauchemin et al. 2010: 113).

Richard's study indicates that Muslim women are an active part of the electorate and, on evidence of the limited gender-disaggregated data available from the 1995 presidential elections, they vote in higher proportions than Muslim men and also White majority voters. In our survey of Muslim women (of whom the overwhelming majority were eligible to vote), to the question on their intention to vote in an immediate parliamentary or presidential election, the percentage of those who said they were certain to do so was 90 per cent—a far higher figure than the one obtained from asking the same question in the British part of the survey. One explanation for this high percentage is that our survey took place in February–March 2008, not long after closely fought presidential and parliamentary elections in 2007 which saw the accession to the presidency of Nicolas Sarkozy whose record of alienating France's immigrant, ethnic minority and Muslim communities had made him an unpopular figure among younger generations particularly. The widespread street protests and strikes of November 2007 in which young people from all communities took part against public sector cuts, university and pension reform expressed this sentiment. Hence, partly, what was being reflected in response to the question about the likelihood of voting in an immediate election was a desire to turn the clock back and mobilise many more people to vote against Sarkozy and the government, a feeling of 'if only I had known this was going to be the outcome [the election of Sarkozy]…' as expressed by a rueful respondent (Sadika, Paris).

However, other reasons also explain the intended and actual electoral participation of our respondents which was 60 per cent in the parliamentary election of 2007. As in the British case, some women said they would vote because it was the duty of Muslims to vote and contribute to the improvement of society. Others felt that by voting they would be making up for the lack of political rights suffered by their immigrant parents and grandparents and previous generations of women the world over. There were those who wanted to vote because it was an opportunity to be of use: 'to give yourself a sense of what can be done, to feel useful' (Emani, Paris). When it came to actually voting in the 2007 parliamentary elections, many women did not bother because they felt a government of the Right was bound to be elected anyway following Sarkozy's success in the preceding presidential elections. It is also the case that there is normally a gap between voting intentions and actual turnout and that this gap is greater the younger the voters.

Why Muslim women have felt compelled to turn out and vote once registered, more so than their male Muslim or white female counterparts, can be explained largely by the development of immigrant and Muslim women's organisations in the 1990s and 2000s which saw civic and political education as one of their functions, thus stressing the importance of political participation and mobilising women to use their right to vote. Among organisations formed in the 1990s were Voix d'elles rebelles, the Ligue française de la femme musulmane (LFFM) and Femmes françaises et musulmanes engagées (FFME) while the 2000s saw the birth of groups such as the Collectif féministes pour l'égalité (CFPE) and the Collectif une école pour tou-te-s (CEPT). Although many of the immigrant and Muslim women's organisations are short-lived due to lack of funds, significant numbers of Muslim women voters in France have been influenced by them and associated media rather than by male figures of authority in their family or community.

In our survey, only 7 per cent of women said they were certain not to vote. Among these featured women who were ineligible to vote but equally there were women who saw voting as something which was not for them; and some strong sentiments were expressed in this respect. For example, one young woman explained that she had been persuaded to vote for the first time at the 2007 presidential elections but would not do so ever again:

> I queued for ages, there was a huge number of people—all for nothing—they told us he [Sarkozy] wouldn't get in and now he's in and people voted [against him] so what's the use of that? In any case it's one vote and that won't change things. (Diana, Paris)

Another young Parisian, Soundous, who said she was 'not a politically-minded person' had a negative view of voting. She felt that votes were sometimes traded between Muslim organisations or Muslim elected representatives and ordinary Muslim voters. She implied that organisations such as the Union des Organisations Islamiques de France (UOIF) or a local mayor, for example, expected support for their preferred candidates in return for the services they provided to Muslims. However, the latter view was not widespread among our respondents. Unlike the British case, male-dominated clan voting is not a feature of French Muslim communities because immigrants arriving in the post-1945 period did not have the right to vote and were ignored by French politicians. Generally, Muslim women in France who register to vote have proved to be committed voters and the indications are that this pattern will continue although voter registration among eligible Muslim voters, including women, remains an issue of democratic deficit but one which is common to other electorates in France.

Muslim Women's Activism in Community Organisations

An increasing number of women have participated in community activism over the past decade and a half. The major part of this engagement has taken place through community organisations of which some have attained a national profile while others have made an impact at the local level through their contribution to local services, campaigns for social justice and change and the integration of Muslim women in public life. Muslim women's organisations have a recent history and small presence in Britain and France. While men from Muslim communities have not had a significantly longer history of participation in political or civic life, their engagement with politicians and public administrators has been more dense and they have been the favoured interlocutors of public authorities and media in both countries. Presented below is an account of the development of migrant and Black and ethnic minority women's organisations from the 1970s to the beginning of the 2000s, of which women from Muslim communities have formed an important part as organisers, members or recipients of services provided by such organisations. It is worth pointing out that migrant, Black and ethnic minority women's organisations have constituted a small part of the life of community organisations in both countries and therefore the number of women of Muslim background participating in these organisations was not high especially in the early years. Organisations were most present and active in areas densely populated by migrants and Black and ethnic minorities. However, very little if any material verifying the existence and work of these organisations has been archived; hence only partial histories are captured, by researchers, of the women involved in them (Châabane 2008; Davis and Cooke 2002; Lesselier 2006; Mélis 2003; Sudbury 1998; Wilson 2006). These incomplete histories throw little light on the number of organisations which emerged and closed down over time or on the scale of women's involvement. This section provides an overview of Muslim women's organisations in Britain and France and also explains why Muslim women enter organisations in their community. It is not possible to provide an analysis of the role of Muslim women's organisations in a chapter on political participation and civic engagement; this must be left for another time and place.

Muslim Women and Participation in Community Organisations: 1970s–1990s

During the 1970s, very few organisations of women from Muslim communities existed. Those which did barely engaged with the state, locally or nationally, and relied entirely on donors, fundraising and volunteers' time in order to survive. A number of reasons explain the paucity of these organisations. First, Muslim women only began to constitute a significant population in Britain and France after the mid-1970s, following the freeze on labour migration and introduction of family reunification which allowed spouses and children to join male migrant workers. Second, while it is possible to pinpoint the few organisations established in the 1970s which convened women whose origins were in Muslim-majority countries the organisations self-identified in terms of their members' country of origin and pursued largely secular aims. Thus, the All Pakistan Women's Association, the Bangladesh Women's Association in the UK, the Femmes marocaines de France and the Groupe femmes algériennes are examples of postcolonial women's organisations which campaigned in favour of women's rights in their country of origin while joining struggles against racism and discrimination and/or providing newly arrived migrant women with information and advice to help them settle. They constituted a bridge between communities 'back home' and communities settled in Europe. Third, in the 1970s, many of the politically active women of Muslim family background were involved in mixed campaigns and organisations—that is, with men from their own ethnic Muslim communities, or with women from other ethnic groups or with men and women across all ethnic groups and majority society. These women were often university students or young workers with a family history of activism in the independence movement of their country of origin or related to men newly active in trade union movements and left-wing politics in the UK and France. Among such mixed organisations in France in which women were active were the Association des travailleurs marocains en France, the Mouvement contre le racisme et pour l'amitié entre les peuples (MRAP), the Fédération des associations de solidarité avec les travailleurs immigrés (FASTI) and the Groupe d'information et de soutien aux travailleurs immigrés (GISTI) (Verbrunt 1980; Withol de Wenden 1988). In Britain, activist women from Muslim communities were involved in progressive, feminist and women-only organisations such as Avaz, the Organisation of Women of African and Asian Descent (OWAAD) or Southall Black Sisters or worked alongside men in organisations such as the Pakistan Welfare Association, AFFOR (All Faiths for One Race) or in progressive faith-based and Black and ethnic minority housing associations which fought against racism in the housing sector and for the housing rights of South Asian (and African Caribbean) populations (Flint 2010).[10] Finally, because women from Muslim communities were less likely than their counterparts from White and other Black and ethnic minority populations to be economically active, they encountered limited opportunities for participation in civic and political organisations. Organisations involving Muslim women, in the 1970s in France and Britain, shared certain features; for example, they were often located at the intersection of struggles for women's rights in the activists' country of origin, the fight for migrant rights in their country of settlement and working-class/Left politics. Moreover, themes of international solidarity were quite dominant and very few engaged with the British/French state especially at the national level.

The 1980s saw an evolution in local structures working towards the autonomisation of women. Thus, women from Muslim communities, particularly those born or brought up from a young age in Britain and France, began to participate in greater numbers than before in local community organisations whose aim was to advance women's rights through civic education, campaigning and so on. The increase in the number of Black and ethnic minority organisations provided greater opportunities for their participation in civic and political life. In Britain this occurred following riots in several cities, involving young Blacks[11]; recommendations to the Government, by the 1981 Scarman enquiry into the Brixton riots, to tackle racial disadvantage; and the release of funds, through local government, for community initiatives aimed at breaking down barriers faced by Black and ethnic minorities in education, housing, welfare and the labour market. A proportion of these funds went towards the establishment of new community organisations or the revival or continuation of existing ones. Hence, it was in the 1980s that organisations involving and serving women of Muslim background began to develop relations with local government and be part of consultations by local authorities wishing to develop culturally sensitive services for women from Black and ethnic minority communities. Local structures to emerge during this period included a movement of Asian women's resource centres (e.g. the Newham Asian Women's Project and the Saheli Women's Group in Birmingham) and refuges for abused women (see Wilson 2006: 163–165). This new wave of organisations subscribed to a feminist worldview though not all declare themselves feminist. The odd women's organisation self-identifying as Muslim created during this period included the small network of local An-Nisa societies and the Southwark Muslim Women's Association. These emerged to fight for Muslim women's housing and health needs at the local level.

In France, the accession of the Left to power in 1981 and the reform of the 1901 association law which allowed the acquirement of formal association status by migrant groups boosted the number of organisations formally constituted by migrant women from Muslim-majority countries. The return of the Left to government after a period of 23 years also unleashed the activism of progressive social movements amongst which was the *mouvement beur* (composed of young, French-born descendants of North

African immigrants) which waged a political and cultural struggle against racism. In addition, the new Ministry of Women's Rights, which took its place in the Socialist–Communist government, reserved substantial funding, for the first time, for women's community organisations and gave rise to numerous organisations led by French-born women of Maghrebi background, including, for example, the Femmes maghrébines en action (established 1981) and Les nanas beurs (founded in 1985). The latter was one of the first groups to draw attention to the discrimination and marginalisation of Maghrebi and other minority ethnic and migrant communities from a gendered, feminist perspective while calling into question France's republican model of citizenship which produced so-called gender-neutral equality policy which ignored the intersecting impacts of racism, sexism and poverty on women from migrant and ethnic minority communities. Les nanas beurs and similar groups saw anti-racism and anti-sexism as part of one struggle which meant not just challenging the French state on issues of gender, race and economic/class equality but also their own communities over the subjugation of women. This position led Les nanas beurs to support the headscarf ban in the 2000s although it criticised the exclusion of headscarfed girls from school. It also led to campaigns around forced marriage and other violent practices carried out in the name of culture. The Turkish women's group Elele (which espoused what may be called a Kemalist—hence secular—feminism), founded in 1984, also focused on freeing women of Turkish descent from the prescribed gendered roles of traditional family culture.

The 1990s marked an increased diversification of women's organisations along ethno-national lines as larger numbers of women arrived from Muslim-majority countries as dependents of forced migrants or as primary asylum seekers and refugees in their own right. Not possessing the same economic, social and political rights as those born in France and Britain or who had acquired British/French nationality, new migrant women from Muslim-majority countries remained outside mainstream political and civic structures and processes. Many therefore became active in informal networks, organisations and campaigns organised around their country of origin (thus re/introducing a transnational dimension to women's participation in political and civic life) or around issues in which migrant women had a stake (Allwood and Wadia 2010: 137–143). These new networks and organisations were given a boost in the 2000s following the establishment of EU funding programmes (e.g. the European Refugee Fund) with grants funnelled through member state governments and national programmes aimed at integrating new migrants (e.g. the UK government's Time Bank programme and the Fonds d'action et de soutien pour l'intégration et la lutte contre la discrimination—FASILD—programme in France). Thus, Algerian, Kurdish, Somali, Sudanese and Turkish women's organisations, among others, were set up or consolidated in towns and cities in Britain and France although the most notable groups were clustered in and around the Paris and London regions. Some achieved visibility at the national level and have continued into the 2000s, for example, the Association de solidarité avec les femmes algériennes démocratiques (ASFAD) in France and the Iranian and Kurdish Women's Rights Organisation (IKRWO) in the UK. Both these organisations have developed transnational solidarity actions with women in their country of origin and focused on breaking down barriers created by traditional culture in communities settled in Britain and France, which keep women trapped in the private sphere. Thus they have drawn attention to issues of violence against women and built up social, psychological, educational and legal services for women in the country of settlement, helping them to break out of abusive family and community relations and become active agents in the public domain.

In France, alongside the migrant women's organisations there emerged another generation of organisations convening French-born women of Maghrebi descent. These organisations, for example, Ni putes, ni soumises (created 2002), Voix d'elles rebelles (established 1995) and Voix de femmes (set up in 1998), took over the reins from Les nanas beurs and similar 1980s organisations which had benefitted from Socialist integration policy but had folded due to loss of public funding when the Right returned to power in 1993. These new organisations of the 1990s/2000s responded to the Right's integration agenda, their discourse and actions against racism and discrimination firmly anchored within a feminist and republican universalist framework. Their ideological position and campaigns against violence against women, aimed at migrant and Muslim communities in France's deprived, urban housing estates, gained them approval from government and mainstream third sector organisations concerned about the perceived rise of communitarianism and the growth of Muslim organisations.

In Britain, the 1990s saw the emergence of a small set of organisations referring to Islam as a guide. These organisations have dealt with the usual long-standing issues of discrimination against Muslim women in the social and economic sphere but have also made issues of violence against women (violence in the home, in relation to trafficking and prostitution, forced marriage, etc.) and sexuality the focus of their work. They include, for example, Apna Haq (in Rotherham) whose founder and director has always articulated a Muslim feminist stand and Amina Muslim Women's Resource Centre in Glasgow which claims a woman-centred approach without explicitly stating transformative feminist goals. By contrast, only a few new Black and ethnic minority women's organisations or movements have come to prominence in the 1990s. Those such as Imkaan which have taken a secular feminist stand have, nevertheless, drawn upon a wide audience of Black and ethnic minority women regardless of faith. In common with Muslim-inspired organisations such as Apna Haq, Black and ethnic minority women's organisations in Britain have made violence against women and women's human rights the core of their action in the 1990s.

While migrant, Black and ethnic minority, and Islam-inspired organisations in Britain and France have enjoyed the participation of Muslim women as organisers, members and users throughout their development in the 1990s, and while many of their campaigns have included issues relevant to Muslim women, most have addressed a wider female base. Very few spoke on behalf of a particular religion. Hence, migrant women's organisations have tended to identify with their country of origin, the migrant communities from which they arise and a human rights approach, while many Black and ethnic minority women's organisations have asserted a feminist identity, challenging patriarchy in their communities and majority society and seeking to empower women economically, socially and politically. Some have presented themselves as strictly non-ideological, providing specialist, women-only services in their community. However, by the late 1990s, Islam as a form of self-identification had started to take on increased social importance (Modood et al. 1994; Klausen 2005).

Globalisation and migration had given rise to transnational Muslim communities in Britain and France, in which Islam provided individuals and groups with a sense of identity and belonging, allowing them to connect with Muslims in Palestine, Bosnia and other places. This prefigured the consolidation of religious identity within Muslim communities in the 2000s and contributed to the rise of new women's organisations or the strengthening and expansion of existing ones self-identifying as Muslim and seeking to represent women from Muslim communities first and foremost.

The Growing Visibility of Muslim Women's Organisations in the 9/11 Era

Britain

In the 2000s, and especially after 9/11, Muslim women's organisations started to discuss problems faced by Muslim women in a public manner, whether these problems stemmed from ethno-cultural beliefs and practices, the status of women in Islam as established by male experts in Islamic law and principles or discrimination, racism and Islamophobia in majority society. Many of these organisations started from scratch while others evolved from organisations formed in the 1980s and 1990s, informal groups or local campaigns. A number of reasons explain the increased entry of women into community spaces and the creation and expansion of organisations. First, the increased negative attention imposed after 9/11 on Muslims and particularly women, seen by sections of majority society as a visible symbol of Islam's apparent opposition to Western values and ambitions, led many Muslim women to speak out and counter increasingly Islamophobic discourses and actions. Much of this speaking out has taken place through third sector organisations as indicated by many of our respondents. Among the women who told their stories was Bilkis, a head teacher in a girls' school, who used her position in the community and the several organisations (including the Muslim Teachers' Association which she helped to set up) of which she was a member, to present positive accounts of Muslim pupils and teachers. Even women seen as outsiders, because they were deemed in some way to have subverted Islamic laws, expressed solidarity and felt it was important to show they were part of their community's struggle against prejudice and discrimination. This position was summed up by Indameera, who led a Muslim LGBT support organisation:

> We felt that we had to reach out to the Muslim community and had to defend Muslim people who were being attacked. In some ways, it was also a way to show to the Muslim communities 'Look, we're fair, we stand for you, we respect our culture and religion'. (Indameera, London)

Indameera also felt that, paradoxically, the events of 9/11 gave her and other women in an outsider situation the resolve to bridge the gap between themselves and their community in addition to speaking out against rising Islamophobia. Other ways in which Muslim women spoke out in public was through arts and sports-based projects. Thus a number of organisations such as Ulfah Arts (a mixed project in Birmingham, run mainly by Muslim women) and the Muslim Women's Sports Foundation, both launched in the 9/11 era, used various art forms and sports to encourage Muslim women to engage with their local communities and political institutions.

A second factor accounting for the growth of Muslim women's organisations relates to the question 'to which Muslim voices should political decision makers pay heed?' Historically, men had been the main if not only interlocutors in conversations with local and central government. In the aftermath of the 9/11 and London 7/7 attacks, women began to question ongoing, male-dominated exchanges about Muslims, democracy and extremism which entirely ignored women's views. This questioning fuelled their desire to speak up collectively and individually. Some went on to create new organisations or networks of local groups. Among these were the Muslim Women's Network, established in 2003 with the support of the Women's National Commission; the Safra Project, a lesbian, bisexual and trans women's organisation formed in 2001 which aims to promote the normalcy of sexual difference within Islam; the Muslim Women's Association, set up in Edinburgh in 2005; the Leicester-based Fatima Women's Network, established in 2003; the Barnet Muslim Women's Network, created in 2007; the Muslim Women's Council, launched in Bradford, in 2009; the Muslim Women's Advisory Council, in Redbridge, London; Inspire, a women's counter-terrorism organisation set up in 2009; Wingz, established in Worcester, in 2010.[12] In other cases, individual women, frustrated by what they deemed were poor responses from male Muslim leaders, decided to shout out loud while avoiding malestream Muslim organisations. One respondent's story is illustrative. Afiya became highly frustrated with politicians' reliance on opinion and intelligence gathered entirely from male community leaders in the wake of the London transport attacks of 7/7. She had joined the Islamic Society of Britain (ISB), hoping to have a say in issues relating to Muslims and Islam but found herself questioning almost everything put forward by so-called male experts at ISB meetings while realising that none of her views was ever given consideration. She left ISB:

> I noticed it was always old men representing the Muslim community in Britain. They said nothing different from what they had always said before. I thought where are the women? So I began thinking that I could as easily give my opinion on issues over which these men were always commenting.

I decided to get informed and bought myself newspapers everyday which I read, especially on Muslim issues. That's when I had the idea of [name of online polling organisation she set up in 2005] and of polling a range of Muslim views and getting them to government. (Afiya, Birmingham)

Afiya's experience was far from unique. Many respondents explained why working with men was deeply wearisome: women were rarely seen as leadership contenders; they gained little from events where male-only line-ups parroted interpretations of Islam established by so-called experts without inquiry or analysis; when women challenged what they deemed conservative male opinion on male/female rights and duties in Islam, they got perfunctory answers or were dismissed as ignorant or sacrilegious; malestream Muslim organisations seeking to influence politicians, media and wider publics were uninterested in fresh ideas or sometimes hijacked such ideas, presenting them as their own; Britain's Muslim women (and communities) were being mis/represented by out-of-touch men. Unlike previous generations of women, Afiya and other women refused to organise under Muslim men or allow them to speak on their behalf. They wanted informed and articulate women to represent them; they wanted to become such women in order to represent the concerns and needs common to ordinary women and present an alternative Muslim voice to political decision makers, media and the public.

Third, the emergence and visibility of Muslim women's organisations in the 9/11 era may also be attributed to the co-optation, by the British state, of Muslim women in the war against extremism as concern over 'home-grown terrorism' increased after the 7/7 London transport bombings. Government urged Muslim women to combat Islamic radicalism through the Preventing Violent Extremism (or Prevent) programme launched in 2007 and help promote social cohesion in their communities. The logic was that young Muslim men, considered susceptible to radical Islam, were the product of failed integration and that mothers, wives, sisters could stop sons, husbands, brothers from subscribing to extremist thought and action; the women would constitute a bridge between alienated Muslim communities and potential terrorists and majority British society.

The Prevent programme brought a significant number of Muslim women into civic and political life through the creation of new women's organisations and projects at the local level or the reinforcement of existing ones. Between 2007 and 2011, an estimated £80 million was allocated by government to Prevent with almost 80 per cent of funds passing through local authorities towards grass-roots organisations (Kundnani 2009: 11). The Tax Payers' Alliance (a Conservative Party-affiliated critic of the Prevent programme) listed organisations/projects receiving Prevent funding in 2007/2008 and 2008/2009 which included over 90 groups and projects specifically involving Muslim women (TPA 2009). While the Prevent programme was seen as a snooper's charter by many in Muslim communities because women were asked to monitor male relatives, it was welcomed, initially at least, by a number of Muslim women who saw an opportunity to engage independently with government and policy influencers and participate in the development and delivery of policy affecting Muslim women and their communities.

Among the organisations established in the 9/11 era, the majority saw themselves as providers or signposters of support and public services related to health and welfare, the law and education, where such support and services were sensitive to Islamic beliefs and practice. Few organisations—Muslim Women's Network UK among them—espoused a feminist agenda, adding awareness raising of gender and sexual politics to their work. Those articulating a feminist vision were inspired by Islamic feminism in its broadest sense: that is, locating gender equality and social justice at the heart of Qur'anic values. However, rather than contributing to the development of Islamic feminism as an ideology (as a critique either of dominant masculine Islamic thinking or of Western feminism), Muslim women's organisations in the UK have tended to use Islamic feminism as a tool to show people that the Qur'an can be read differently to afford women and men equal rights and to remind them of what those rights are.

France

The number of formally constituted, independent Muslim women's organisations to emerge or become consolidated in France, in the 9/11 era, is smaller than in Britain. In large part this has been due to the lack of funding. The 1905 law on the separation between Church and State forbids state financing of religious groups or those whose work includes a religious dimension. As the French state provides 51 per cent of the funding of associations (GHK 2010a: 24) compared with 36 per cent in Britain (GHK 2010b: 28), not to have access to state funding is highly disadvantageous. Moreover, because private income is normally derived from donors, membership fees and fundraising activities, Muslim women's community organisations find themselves in a double bind. They have too low a visibility to attract donors, too meagre resources in terms of volunteer time and skills to fundraise and a constituency which largely cannot afford membership fees. However, there has been an increase in the number of smaller, more informal local groups (*groupes de quartier*) which bring Muslim women together around specific issues and activities. Two broad categories of Muslim women's organisations may be identified in France. In the first category are formally constituted, independent organisations which have grown organically, in response to the needs and problems of ordinary women from Muslim communities. Like the majority of Muslim women's organisations in the UK they act as providers and signposters of support, social welfare, legal and other services. The second category comprises organisations and groups which may be formally constituted and fulfil a public service function but which, importantly, are also engaged in the production of Islamic feminist thought as a rejection of the Islam transmitted through family and community, and as a critique of established Islamic thinking and Western feminist responses to racism, Islamophobia and sexism. These organisations tended to be affiliated to larger networks of Muslim (and sympathetic non-Muslim) intellectuals and scholars.

Among formally constituted women's organisations which self-identified as Muslim in the 9/11 era and in which some of our respondents have participated were the Al Houda association of Rennes, the LFFM, Ndimbeul (an organisation of women performing the *Hajj*), Jeunes musulmanes sportives de France. Some of these organisations were established in the 1990s but gained greater support and visibility after 9/11. A number of organisations (e.g. Au bonheur des femmes, En avant les filles, Orientation) did not refer to Islam in their constitution but catered almost exclusively to young Muslim women whose Islamic beliefs and practice were accommodated in the organisations' activities. The decision to omit reference to Islam in an organisation's constitution was sometimes deliberate and a means of gaining state support. One respondent explained that her organisation had two arms, a secular arm which engaged young Muslim women in civic activity and a religious arm which worked with a local mosque to provide religious education and services to members. This enabled them to obtain material support (premises, office equipment, etc.) from the local council.

In the second category and among Muslim women's organisations affiliated to larger entities were the FFME of Lyon and Femmes d'aujourd'hui in Montpellier, both offshoots of the network Presence

Musulmane founded by the Muslim scholar Tariq Ramadan. Additionally, a small number of groups were part of the network Une école pour tout-e-s, established in 2003 to contest the legislation banning conspicuous religious symbols in schools. Many of these closed down once the legislation was passed in 2004. Finally, in a subcategory of its own was the mixed Muslim/non-Muslim group of women personalities (academics, politicians and human rights activists), Collectif féministe pour l'égalité, which emerged from a petition published in *Le Monde* on 9 December 2003, against the headscarf law.

Factors accounting for the rise in Muslim women's organisations in Britain either were absent or did not operate in the same way in France. Thus, although the events of 9/11 shocked both France's majority and minority communities, spurring the then Socialist government to introduce the November 2001 *Loi de securité quotidienne* (Daily Security Act), packaged as anti-terror legislation,[13] there was a prevailing sentiment among French authorities that France, unlike Britain, was not in Al Qaeda's first line of fire given its historically critical approach to American foreign policy, decades-long support for an independent Palestinian state and opposition to the first Gulf War. France's slightly more impassive reaction to the 9/11 events meant that they did not mark a turning point in French–Muslim relations as did, for example, the attacks before and after the end of the Algerian War in the early 1960s, or the more recent *Charlie Hebdo* attacks of January 2015 and the Paris multisite attacks of November 2015. They did not constitute a primary factor in the emergence of new or the expansion of existing Muslim women's organisations in the 9/11 era.

Among more French-specific reasons for the emergence of Muslim women's organisations was the resistance against growing moves to ban the headscarf in schools. Disputes between school authorities and Muslim schoolgirls and their families had started in 1989 and resurfaced periodically throughout the 1990s (see Allwood and Wadia 2009: 152–183). Thus one of the main aims of organisations such as the FFME and the Collectif féministe pour l'égalité was to provide legal and educational support to schoolgirls banned for wearing the headscarf. Many small *groupes de quartier* also helped banned schoolgirls with individual tutoring while they were excluded from school. FFME claimed to have helped three to four girls each year, from 1995 onwards, to fight their exclusion from school. This and many other organisations set up specifically to fight the ban folded soon after the law of 2004 against the wearing of conspicuous religious symbols in school came into force.

Another factor which motivated Muslim women in France to act collectively and create new organisations or expand existing ones was the specific French socio-economic and political context of the early 2000s which saw an unprecedented rise in public hostility towards migrant and Muslim communities, combined with intense socio-economic deprivation in the outlying districts of major French cities which impacted harshly on young people from those communities. So, the 2002 presidential elections, which saw the far Right Front National candidate, Jean Marie Le Pen, take second place and garner an unprecedented 17 per cent of the vote, reflected anti-immigrant and anti-Muslim feelings among voters. In addition, aggressive policing which had led to the deaths of several young Muslim men (while being stopped and searched, chased by police or in police custody) between 2000 and 2005, combined with repressive legislation (the 2003 *Loi pour la securité intérieure*—Internal Security Act), educational failure, high unemployment and scant future prospects led to a massive explosion of discontent and the riots of November–December 2005. As well as bearing the brunt of these intersecting political, social and economic disadvantages along with their male counterparts, Muslim women also had to deal with sexism and misogyny in their own communities. Thus they organised to overcome barriers imposed not only by majority French society but also by ethnic Muslim communities. Another factor accounting for the emergence of the small number of Muslim women's organisations in France, in common with their UK counterparts, was the wish to organise autonomously from men and create spaces in local communities free of masculine domination. However, even when the wish for autonomy was expressed, the obligation, in some cases, to work within or alongside mixed organisations was strong because the pooling of resources meant ensuring an organisation's continuation. Finally, a reason for working together in community organisations, cited by women in both Britain and France, was the desire to make a difference and leave the world a better place—to do so was seen as an Islamic duty and repeated many times by a large number of respondents in both countries. One respondent echoed the view of her counterparts:

> In Islam, time goes in a circle, we come from God...from paradise and the question is how to return to it having done the best we can in a humble way...by arming ourselves with all the knowledge possible in order to help ourselves and others. Each person should question her journey and ask what are the positive marks she wishes to leave on earth? (Maya, Cergy-Pontoise)

The organisations and informal neighbourhood groups in which our respondents participated performed an important social, civic and educational role among mainly socio-economically disadvantaged populations, whether in educating Muslim women and their families about how public authorities and political institutions worked, helping them to deal with their local health centre, school or immigration authorities, providing training to women to act as jurors, or school or hospital governors or organising educational or leisure trips. The motivation to participate in the community and help others, more so than other types of political participation or civic engagement, was linked with being a good Muslim. The belief that volunteerism and service for the advancement of social care and justice was an integral part of Islam was strongly held by many respondents in Britain and France. Therefore it is unsurprising that participation in community organisations proved to be one of the most common forms of political expression. On the flip side, the social care and social work role of these organisations also included denouncing inequalities and injustices, challenging the status quo and government policy and demanding social and political transformation. This encouraged many women from Muslim communities to face outwards, to engage, beyond the local, with majority society and transnational agents, to get involved in other types of civic and political actions and thereby practise an independent citizenship not entirely defined by faith. The possibility and importance of delinking religion, seen as a private matter, from their political and civic action was stated by several respondents, more so in France than in Britain. For example, one respondent, Naïma (Paris), described herself as a 'secular Muslim' (*musulmane laïque*): 'I'm a practising Muslim but I have a secular vision.' It is also worth noting that among the respondents in France (through rarely in Britain) were women who claimed a 'Muslim culture' but not Islam and worked through community organisations to make a difference.

Conclusion

In this chapter, the political participation and civic engagement of women from Muslim communities is examined within a broad feminist conceptualisation of 'doing politics'. Integrating the idea of civic engagement within this conceptualisation, our approach produces a multifaceted typology of the activity and activism undertaken by Muslim women in the two countries concerned. While certain types of participation attract very small numbers of Muslim women—for example, that related to party politics—others are highly favoured and voting and activism in community organisations are found to be the most popular forms among Muslim women in Britain and France. The reasons as to why certain participation forms are favoured over others are myriad and are related to each country's political culture (e.g. conflictual *versus* consensual), the accommodation of diverse populations within a universalist (France) *versus* multiculturalist (Britain) framework, the political opportunities available to nationals and migrants (such as voting rights or the right to form organisations) and the political and economic conjuncture at any given time—thus women from Muslim communities have become increasingly visible in civic and political arenas following the events of 9/11. On the other hand, the socio-economic situation of Muslim women collectively and individually also determines their political behaviour, how they choose to 'do politics' and the level of frequency. Finally, in the case of Muslim women, their belief and practice of Islam or their belonging to a Muslim culture or simply being part of a Muslim family and community, in combination with the aforementioned factors, also shapes their political expression. For example, in both Britain and France, Muslim men have been the favoured interlocutors of political authorities and women have had to challenge this model of state–community relations and organise autonomously in order to gain a hearing. In Britain, the clan-based (*biradari*) system of doing politics, particularly where voting and electoral representation are concerned, constitutes a further block to women's involvement in political and civic life. Despite the obstacles faced by Muslim women, and, these are discussed in greater detail in Chapters 6 and 7, our study reveals that Muslim women in Britain and France are active voters and that voter registration and turnout levels among this group may be compared favourably with those of men in their community and those of the general voting populations in both countries. Muslim women are also keen participants in legally constituted community organisations and neighbourhood groups and networks and use these as instruments of social and political change.

Notes

1. This excludes the auto/biographies of the few female politicians of Muslim background to have emerged in the 2000s, for example, Rachida Dati (of Moroccan–Algerian parentage and formerly Keeper of the Seals in the Ministry of Justice and Member of

European Parliament since 2009), Rama Yade (of Senegalese family background and former minister of human rights from 2007 to 2010; Île-de-France regional councillor since 2010), Fadela Amara (of Algerian parentage; a founder of the feminist movement Ni putes ni soumises and minister for urban policies from 2007 to 2010) and Najat Vallaud-Belkacem (French Socialist politician of Moroccan background; minister for women's rights from 2012 to 2014 and minister of education since 2014).
2. Figures for voters' perception of their political knowledge are unavailable as the French surveys did not ask this question in the same way.
3. None of these women (even if they wished to do so) will have referred to themselves as Muslim candidates or representatives of Muslims due to republican principles of engagement in political life. It is known that some of them practise Islam; for example, Fadela Amara has admitted she is a privately practising Muslim but is probably the most republican of them all and in 2004 and 2010 fully backed the banning of headscarves in schools and the face veil in public places.
4. This is an approximate figure (probably based on data on nationality/national origins) given that self-declared ethnic origin does not feature as a variable in counting the French population. It will most likely be an underestimate of real numbers.
5. Our calculations, based on ONS data (1,296,776 Muslim women out of a total UK population of 63.2 million) and UK Parliament figures (8 Muslim women MPs out of a total of 650).
6. Ford and Grove-White's study on the 2015 general election confirms that those from Pakistan and Bangladesh constitute the most significant group of Muslim voters (2015: 7).
7. Figures in Table 4.3 should not be used to make direct comparisons between one election and another as they are not based on a single calculation method. Instead, they indicate the rise and fall in voter registration and turnout over time and the narrowing participation gap between Black and ethnic minority voters and their White counterparts.
8. According to Norris et al.'s findings in the 2001 general election, Black and ethnic minority women were less likely to vote than men from their communities.

9. The survey questioned 100 Muslims and 100 non-Muslims resident in the Goutte d'Or neighbourhood of the 18th *arrondissement* in Paris (Amiraux 2012: 34).
10. Not only were the tenants of such housing associations of South Asian Muslim background but many Muslim women worked for these associations on a paid or voluntary basis, acting as a link between local authorities and tenants and developing services (English language and culture classes, family health education programmes, etc.) aimed at integrating tenants into British society.
11. Riots occurred in Bristol (St Pauls) in 1980, Liverpool (Toxteth) and London (Brixton) in 1981 and in London (Brixton) and Birmingham (Handsworth/Lozells) in 1985.
12. Some of these organisations have closed due to lack of funding following the reduction and reorientation of the Prevent programme after May 2010 and wider austerity measures which reduced third sector funding.
13. This law aimed to control young people of migrant origin, particularly young Muslims, living in urban housing estates, portrayed as a threat to social cohesion.

CHAPTER 6

Ethnic Group and Islam

INTRODUCTION

This chapter examines two of the key sites of Muslim women's participation in civic and political life. The data which substantiates it derives from the qualitative interviews and the sociological intervention (SI) group sessions. This makes it possible to investigate the barriers and enablers which Muslim women encounter and to highlight the factors which enhance or reduce participation. The findings in this chapter are structured on the basis of a double interaction between Muslim women and the ethnic group on the one hand and Islam and the Muslim group on the other hand. Within the scope of the ethnic group, Muslim women have to abide by norms governing their role and position framed by traditional patriarchal culture which tends to strengthen the limitations imposed on women's activities in the public sphere. However, this is only one dimension of the ethnic group's impact on women's lives. It can also contribute to an environment where they may find support and protection against wider society. This dichotomy was formulated as 'internal restrictions' and 'external protection' by Kymlicka (1999: 31). 'Internal restrictions' are aimed at restricting the ability of individuals within the group, while 'external protection' refers to the rights the minority group has claimed and gained from wider society, in order to reduce its vulnerability vis-à-vis the ruling economic and political power. The interaction of the women with wider society complicates matters furthermore but this is examined in the following chapter. It is also worth noting that the ethnic group is not homogeneous but is traversed by a variety of differentiations based on class, level of education, caste, generation, gender and region/village in the country of origin, in addition to the multiple theological cleavages within Islam. The second part of this chapter examines the women's relationship to Islam and the Muslim group. Not only does Islam occupy front of stage in much of the world but it has also surged up onto the social and political agenda in Britain and France; this is evidenced by both public policies and Muslim mobilisation. Within this context, Muslim women have developed a specific interest in Islam which assumes a variety of dimensions and is linked to their autonomisation. Undoubtedly, as noted in Chapter 2, it is not straightforward to differentiate culture from religion as the two are often closely intermeshed; likewise, the ethnic group and the Muslim group overlap to a large extent, in terms of the populations concerned in our study. Nonetheless, the dedication of a separate section on the women's relationship to Islam and the Muslim group proves analytically valuable and rests on two main grounds; on the one hand, Islam encompasses dimensions which are left out of the ethnic group and, on the other hand, many of the women themselves establish a clear differentiation between the two entities. We shall now turn to the comparison between these parameters in Britain and France.

THE ETHNIC GROUP

The initial and immediate theatre of interaction for Muslim women is constituted by the family and the ethnic group. This interface is mediated by parents, men/husbands, in-laws, extended family and community. These are the agents which impact on the women's ability to study and take up employment. They are also influential in the women's capacity for individual and collective action in the civic and political spheres.

Parents and Immediate Family

Britain
On the whole the women in Britain highly valued their immediate family environment and almost none of those interviewed had broken links with their parents, barring very rare exceptions. The majority of the women displayed a strong emotional bond with their parents and tended to value their parents' and family's (often well-extended) support with respect to

education; most of the women had been allowed or encouraged to study by their parents. Differentiations were predicated on the educational level of parents and their milieu of origin: parents who were more educated, came from an urban middle-class background or had resided outside the Indian subcontinent for a long period of time were stronger advocates of girls' education. Adelmira (Birmingham), aged, 45, was born in an East African educated family who had promoted education, as did others of similar backgrounds. Nevertheless, although many of the women we met came from an educated home environment, several of those who had reached a high level of education also came from disadvantaged modest families of rural background; such as Leesha, whose father was working-class and illiterate in English and had allowed his two daughters to go to university away from home. Sometimes the family and in particular the mother were instrumental in enabling the women to pursue activities outside the home. For instance, 42 year old Reema (Birmingham), from a modest family of Azad Kashmiri origin, made it clear that she would not have been able to complete her studies (Bachelors and Masters in social work), if it had not been for her mother's support. Notwithstanding, the emotional and geographical closeness to parents did not entail unmitigated advantages. Sabreena (Birmingham), a 37-year-old graduate of a modest family from rural Azad Kashmir, held a high leadership position in politics. She recognised the positive side of living near her parents but added that it carried a cost as help was accompanied by criticisms and a judgement not so easy to ignore because of its emotional and cultural baggage.

Nonetheless, it was equally the case that parents could stand in the way of their daughters' aspirations. Limitations often related to the place of study (within the vicinity of home being favoured or imposed) and the choice of career. Jameela (Birmingham), aged 50, from a *Muhajir* family which fell victim to Partition in 1947, resented the unfairness of constraints which applied to her but had spared her brothers: she was barred from going to work for the Voluntary Services Overseas (VSO) and was steered to qualify as a maths teacher, while her brother was allowed to train as a medical doctor. Generally, fathers seemed to be more restrictive than mothers and almost invariably the role of the father was pivotal. 'My father was keen on his daughters' education' or 'my father did not object' were recurrent phrases. On other occasions, the ability to study was imputed by the women to the absence of their father, who died or divorced when they were young. As a case in point, Afiya (Birmingham), 40, well-educated and in a political leadership position, thought that the absence of her father, combined with the fact that her mother worked long hours in a factory, enabled her to do what she wanted in her choice of studies and other aspects of her life. It must be noted, however, that women in poor ethnic neighbourhoods and whose parents were from a rural background faced far greater obstacles in accessing education.

Among South Asian Muslim communities, parents considered that arranging a marriage for their daughter was a responsibility they had to deliver, although this did not apply to some other Muslim populations such as Bosnians, as testified by Lulu (Birmingham), aged 30, who had come to the UK in 1992 as a refugee. Among South Asian Muslims, the more customary practice is that parents actually choose the husband to be and, if in keeping with the tradition, the latter is sought from the ranks of the family among cousins or other relatives. This may entail bringing over to Britain a relative residing in the homeland. In the past, the bride customarily had no say in the matter and did not even meet her bridegroom before the wedding. Today, one growing practice among educated families is that parents choose a potential husband, while the daughter is asked her opinion and enjoys the chance to reject the option offered, possibly after meeting him a couple of times or receiving a description and a photo. On the whole, most of the women we interviewed conformed to this formula. This did not detract from the fact that, in other cases, two young people often meeting as students might autonomously wish to get married, the match being approved *a posteriori* by the respective families who 'organised' the arrangement subsequently. Leaving out refugee women from Bosnia, Iraqi Kurdistan and a student from Turkey in our sample, almost all the married women interviewed had had an arranged marriage. Depending on their age and social background, they had or had not been consulted but broadly did not disapprove of 'reasonably' arranged marriages. However, several mentioned they knew young girls mostly from poor families who had been sent to Pakistan/Bangladesh for a marriage forced upon them. Respondents who were in career advice posts kept encountering girls who were removed from school at 16 or at a younger age for that purpose. Shameem (London) indicated that a large number of her friends were subjected to a forced marriage. Strangely enough, although marriage partners had generally been chosen by parents, the latter were rarely blamed for the constraints subsequently imposed by husbands. What the women strongly opposed was the interference of the extended family and community, as seen below.

France
In France the women equally accorded a great deal of importance to parents and family and the majority of them testified to their good family relationship. Diana (Paris), who was 22 and from Mauritania, was quite representative when she unhesitatingly declared: 'The family is the most important thing'. For 42 year old Masara (Paris), born in France of Algerian parents, the family offered a valued comfort zone which acted as the guardian and vector of central 'values of warmth and hospitality', which her parents had imparted. Altogether, as in Britain, what stood out was the general picture of a negotiated relationship between daughters and parents, albeit with lighter family constraints in France. Diana (Paris) readily advocated the superiority of compromise over breaking up with the family, like Sadika (Paris) who was in favour of give and take which she felt allowed for 'respect towards parents' authority at the same time as a space of personal freedom'. Noticeably, the outcome of the negotiated compromise awarded a much greater choice and freedom in France than in Britain. Almost all the women recounted the parental support they enjoyed regarding education or taking up employment, education constituting an utmost priority among the vast majority of families. This was recurrent among the women we met, whatever their ethnic or social background. Sadika (Paris) explained how her parents never pressured her to find employment quickly but always encouraged the girls of the family to study.

As in Britain, mothers generally provided a supportive ally. In 28 year old Mounira's (Paris) family, of Turkish origin, the mother who had had a hard life played a central role in supporting her daughters' aspirations 'to stand on their own feet'. In fact, only a few women such as Safa (Paris), 44, of a Kabyle family, Ezina (Paris), born and raised in Guinea and Salima (Paris), 46, born in France of Algerian parents, specified that the mother had been a source of conflict and disagreement regarding their aspirations and life project (studies, employment, marriage, political engagement). For several of the respondents, the mother opposed the rest of the family, arranged to move out of a site where the extended community was overwhelming or divorced the father, all of which reduced potential constraints. As seen above, the latter scenario was less common in Britain but offered the same advantages.

Some of the comments evidenced a type of mother which we did not encounter in Britain so readily. These went further than simply supporting their daughters' studies and made a clear stance to promote their 'liberation'. Thirty year old Wahida (Fontenay-sous-Bois), whose grandparents had come from Algeria and whose father was a member of the Front de libération nationale (FLN), stated that her mother who went out to work transmitted the 'image of an independent woman' and had raised her into 'feminist values'. Indeed, the pattern of mothers who wished to 'liberate' their daughters and prompted them not to be dependent on a man seemed to be rather widespread as indicated by Farah (Paris), 40, born in France of Algerian parents who were divorced. What helped her and her friends was the fact that 'our mothers wanted to liberate us'; they always told us 'not to be dependent on a guy'. Another feature differentiates France and Britain regarding relationships with the family: in France there were more frequent cases of open challenge to parental control such as that of Keltoum (Paris), from Algeria, whose parents were divorced and who, like her sisters, 'did what she wanted' against her mother's wishes and more significantly did not feel bad about it.

The situation regarding fathers disclosed diverse scenarios. On the one hand, many of the women evidenced that their father supported their endeavours without putting pressure on them. To illustrate this first type, several women depicted fathers whose affection and support were appreciated. Twenty three year old Fatouma (Paris), born in France of Senegalese parents, enjoyed a rare relationship with her father whom she found 'affectionate, very close, even spiritually', and who backed her educational aspirations. Louisa (Paris), was able to benefit from an education whereby her father did not make any distinction between men and women, whether it applied to education, knowledge or political engagement. Contrary to the image perpetrated by French media, brothers did not seem to cause issues for the women we interviewed. Farah (Paris), who was 40 and born in Paris of Algerian parents, had an elder brother who played the role of her absent father and 'he always pushed us at school [...] he was a booster'. On the other hand, a few cases were quoted whereby the father demonstrated unmitigated control over his family. For 46 year old Salima (Paris), born in France of Algerian parents, the degree of paternal oppression experienced was such that living with her father was tantamount to tyranny. She was largely confined at home and was only able to escape because she became aware of her rights: 'he could not hide from me that I would reach majority at 18. I had learned from books that we live in a state of law, of equality'. She left home and later set up a community organisation and a bookshop. In another three cases, women had broken links with their family although confessing that it carried a painful emotional toll. Another problem raised was polygamy, which all the women interviewed vehemently condemned. Polygamous situations generally concerned sub-Saharan African families in France and were not encountered in Britain among our respondents. What rescued Keltoum (Paris) from an oppressive father who also imposed the cohabitation of several spouses was the fact that her mother eventually left her husband.

Generally, the women in France enjoyed a greater degree of freedom in most domains. For instance, in most cases, controversies did not arise if unmarried young women left their parents' home to settle on their own. Ryn (Paris) was not subjected to any family pressure when she moved out to live on her own in Paris. Lilly's (Paris) parents, of Kabyle background, appreciated the fact that their daughter's departure afforded them a less crowded home, and had accepted that she set up home and had a child with a non-Muslim partner—a scenario which was not very different from that of many non-Muslim French and British women, but one which would be radically more unacceptable among many Muslim families in Britain. A large number of the women in France also had marriages with non-Muslims, far more numerous than in Britain. In Masara's family (Paris) which had arrived in France in the 1960s, only one sibling married within the group, all the others lived with or were married to non-Muslim French people.

Nevertheless, a variety of parental reactions was experienced. Tina (Paris), from sub-Saharan Africa, evoked the 'delirious dream' of parents who expected their daughter to marry someone from their village of origin. She noted that some of the women successfully negotiated the matter whilst others complied with their parents' wishes. Siham (Saint-Denis), aged 46, born in France, whose Algerian parents had tried to impose a traditional marriage although to no avail, 'would rather have died'. However, apart from occasional instances of extreme pressure or coercion being applied, the question of marriage did not seem to provoke the same anxieties as in Britain. Where our respondents in France were concerned, the practice of parents choosing a spouse in the country of origin was found among families from sub-Saharan Africa but more rarely so among people from North Africa (who constitute the main component of Muslim populations in France). In contrast with their own position, several of the women talked about a different situation to theirs in the *cités* (disadvantaged neighbourhoods with a high concentration of ethnic minorities), where men and older brothers exercised greater control over young women.

Husbands, Men and In-Laws

Britain

The fundamental premise evidenced by most of the women was that they were partners in an unequal relationship with men and in particular with their husband. This is a predictable finding. It is what many women would say everywhere and feminists have been fighting against such inequality the world over. What is of interest to us are the modes and manifestations expressing this inequality, how they are distinctively felt by the women in our study, and to what extent this interferes with their autonomisation and engagement. Constraints imposed by some husbands applied to education, employment and political and civic engagement, either directly or indirectly. In most cases, decisions were men's prerogatives. Reema (Birmingham) was allowed by her husband to study for a degree as long as she took on the entire responsibility of the house, the children and her in-laws, without any help from him even at the time of her exams. Reema did not face a double burden but a triple one. Her husband was at the same time 'an enabler and an obstacle'. It was clear to many of our respondents that whatever activities they undertook outside the house had to be approved by their husband, so that the women found themselves weighing up to what extent they could 'push the limits', without going beyond what was 'acceptable to men folk' (Tahani, Birmingham). In some cases, husbands proved a complete obstacle to a respondent's life project. Tahani who had gained a First Class Honours degree was offered a sponsorship by a firm towards an accountancy course, a highly regarded qualification which she was keen to pursue, but which she could not take up because of her husband's opposition. Equally, there were examples of qualified women who had given up employment or political/civic activities outside the home in order to take care of elderly in-laws, on demand from their husband. Men could also constitute obstacles to women's initiative in the public realm as noted by Abida (Birmingham), a college student faced with the hostility of younger men: 'In the neighbourhoods and at school, boys were often seen attempting to control the girls…; younger men at sixth form college.' Several of the women indicted men as prime culprits where obstacles to outside engagement were concerned. Andala (Coventry) was confronted with such a conundrum when she was sent by her employer to advise a local organisation about how to make successful funding applications; the youth centre which had requested her visit eventually did not allow her to speak to the group because of her gender.

The case of domestic violence as the ultimate coercion preventing women from gaining autonomy was brought up by our respondents. This was a delicate issue and none of the women interviewed acknowledged that it existed in their family, although we knew from other sources that this was the case for two of them. It is worth reminding ourselves that domestic violence is not specific to the ethnic groups under study here but that it occurs across society regardless of 'race'/ethnicity and class. Disturbingly, some of the women felt that it was tolerated in their culture and that men implicitly knew this. In Adelmira's view, it was a question of ownership, the wife being considered the 'property' of the husband:

> In case of violence, I've actually been present when the man has done it... because he was asked, he turned round and said 'she's my wife, I can do whatever I want with her.' (Adelmira, Birmingham)

The reality is, nonetheless, multilayered. In the first place, a good number of women mentioned husbands who were supportive of their involvement in outside activities, including some heavy commitment to political activity. Some husbands actually encouraged their wives to do so. In addition, even in adverse situations the agenda seemed to be changing so that some women mustered the courage to go ahead, despite their husband's disapproval.

In-laws appeared as a recurrent theme when the women discussed potential obstacles to activities outside the home. This is also quite distinctive where Muslim women are concerned, whereas it is unlikely that the issue of in-laws would have been so salient among non-Muslim White women. This situation is brought about by the family structure among South Asian populations whereby the daughter, once married, becomes fully integrated into the husband's family, with reduced links to her own family. This situation was emotionally depicted by Reema (Birmingham): 'When I got married...I stopped having parents, I didn't have siblings, I didn't have any relatives.'

On the whole, in-laws were targeted as the prime cause of many of the women's problems at home and outside. It seemed to be an established truth that sharing a house with in-laws (in keeping with tradition) was fraught with difficulties, as forcefully stated by Adelmira (Birmingham). In a way, older women, namely, mothers-in-law, stood to gain by this custom and contributed to its continuance. In a traditional home, the daughter-in-law was expected to take on all the household chores as well as care of the children and elderly relatives (Zeinab, Birmingham) and none of her own interests or commitments seemed to justify any concession in this domain. Moreover, mothers-in-law, tilting the balance of power in favour of the husband, did not facilitate the day-to-day renegotiation of roles between husbands and wives, which constituted a central factor enabling the latter to engage in external activities (Tahani, Birmingham). The story recounted by several women was that their outside involvement was dependent upon meeting the expectations of the husband and in-laws, that the role of wife, mother and daughter-in-law was first fully carried out. In more traditional families, such trade-offs and accommodation were simply not conceivable (Zeinab, Birmingham). However, there is an increasing tension between the traditional pattern of social roles in the family and the economic contribution of the women. Several of the women interviewed went out to work and of these some were the main earner in their family. Although it was necessary for them to take up employment in order to maintain the family's material well-being, this was not always achieved without opposition. Being the sole breadwinner did not earn Zeinab (Birmingham) any 'recognition' from her family-in-law.

In a few cases, the family-in-law could prove supportive and, for example, helped to look after young children but this pattern was certainly not the most frequently quoted by the women interviewed. Moreover, the fact that traditionally any income coming into the household was deemed the family's possession undermined the potential increase in the women's autonomisation which may have been gained from being employed and generating resources. Hierarchies of power in the family did not relate much to economic power and in the case of older women, the weight of culture was so overbearing that some women had totally internalised it, 'Even to this day if I am earning, that is not my money. It is our money, it is family money' (Zeinab, Birmingham). Notwithstanding, this situation was less common among younger, educated women brought up in the UK.

France
The women in the UK laid most of the blame for obstacles to their outside activities at the feet of their in-laws, while their appreciation of their husband's role was more nuanced. Whereas in Britain, both gave rise to a good deal of debate, this was not the case in France, where only few comments were devoted to this issue. Several women stated that they enjoyed the non-interventionism or the assistance of their husband. Maya (Cergy-Pontoise), 33 years of age, well-educated, talked about having the

active backing of her husband and her own family for her engagement in the public sphere; they made available networks and financial support to enable her to further her endeavours. The rare exceptions to this scenario stand out dramatically. Nikia (Paris) who became the leader of a women's cultural organisation was threatened by her husband with being sent back to Algeria; he confiscated her French residence permit when she declared that she wanted to go out to work and, because she stood firm, took their child back to his country of origin after kidnapping him. But this kind of occurrence remained the exception.

Altogether, in France, problems were rarely mentioned regarding the family-in-law apart from relatively benign occurrences, such as the duty to join in prayers when visiting the home of in-laws (Rida, Paris). Husbands were almost invariably quoted as being either neutral vis-à-vis the women's activities outside home or supportive, which seemed to happen frequently.

Extended Family and Community

Britain
More so than the immediate family, the extended family and the community were blamed for creating obstacles in the path of the women's aspirations and initiatives. Several examples were quoted whereby the woman's father was criticised by the community when she was allowed to study at university, with older women and men predicting the deterioration of his daughter's behaviour. Both Reema's (Birmingham) husband and his parents had to withstand the pressure imposed by community members, along with catastrophic predictions about her future which found their way into her in-laws' home, when she expressed her wish to pursue higher studies. When it came to employment, similar issues were at stake. The wider community wielded its influence on the issue of women working outside the home, with questions fired about whom she was working with, doing what and where? Some parents connived with their daughter in an adaptation of the truth. Under scrutiny of the community, Leesha's parents (Birmingham) told everyone that she was a Maths teacher whereas she taught drama and acted as part of a drama troupe. Other outside activities, such as being involved in civic and political life, were also often badly looked upon by traditional sections of the community and certain spheres of activity were particularly limited. For instance, Sultana (Birmingham) gave up doing voluntary work with Alcoholics Anonymous on account of the community's disapproval.

The women identified a direct correlation between the density of community networks and limitations to their autonomisation. Constraints and controls where any kind of outside activity was concerned appeared to be tighter when living amidst a strong Pakistani/Bangladeshi community and, inversely, remained looser when living away from such a community neighbourhood. According to Martiza (Birmingham), what enabled her parents to abandon a traditional approach was the fact that they lived outside traditional South Asian communities. Andala (Coventry) told of her female cousin who lived in the tightly knit Pakistani community of Rochdale, and who was constantly told by her brother 'you can't do this; wear a headscarf', while she felt she 'could breathe' when she visited relatives in Coventry with its less densely concentrated ethnic neighbourhoods. One major problem was that of marriage which in the main constituted an extended family affair. The women commented at length on the implicit or explicit pressure which many young women had to endure so that they married within the extended family, the *biradari*. Some ominous threats were heard in relation to this question which Sultana (Birmingham) explained. While accepting the right of their parents to influence decisions on most questions, it was clear that the women interviewed opposed the encroachment of the wider community in their lives, drawing closer to a modern British family model according to which one may 'need to come to some agreement with the immediate family, but not in terms of the wider community' (Sultana, Birmingham). It is worth noting that the women shifted the blame that might fall upon parents and husband onto in-laws and the community. Keen to retain close links with their parents, the women were reluctant to incriminate them too much on account of the emotional cost involved; this was circumvented by indicting the community which, indeed, played a deleterious role regarding women's autonomisation. With respect to marital relationships, women who were paired up with a controlling husband found it easier to accuse his family; this rendered the situation more acceptable, since they were emotionally bound to their husband in a way which was not replicated with respect to in-laws. A cognitive dissonance was involved in order to permit the acceptance of compromises. In addition, obstacles to women's engagement do not only derive from external sources. Okin remarks that 'persons subjected to unjust conditions often adapt their preferences so as to conceal the injustices of their situation from themselves' (Okin 1999: 26). Several of the women in our study recognised that they themselves had contributed to the perpetuation of constraints and, in a way, 'connived' in their own predicament. While being conscious of it, Zeinab (Birmingham) recognised that 'that traditional role is still with me'. Moreover, many comments signalled women's lack of confidence and timidity as a contributary factor to men's dominating roles in organisations.

The weight of the community meant that taking up employment outside the home or any civic/political commitment was a hostage to fortune. Women who decided to do so were frequently exposed to ready criticisms. They had to make extra efforts in order to silence the view that they should stay at home. Sultana (Birmingham), who worked as a nurse while studying for a Masters degree, was also a member of a school board of governors, thus attending evening meetings which exposed her to pressures from the extended family. Another dimension came into play among populations of South Asian origin. The women had to pay particular attention to their behaviour and ensure that not only modesty but also evidence of it was preserved in every way: 'To be extra *izzat*...well, appear extra *izzat*' (Sultana, Birmingham). Indeed, the women were expected to uphold the family honour and for this reason disproportionately endured control by the extended family and community. The accusation of being a 'little trollop' (Adelmira, Birmingham) could be easily meted out and irreversibly damage the family's reputation. It is a well-established fact recalled by Van Bergen et al. that, in the domain of sexual and reproductive life, women are often pivotal guardians 'of the collectivity's identity and honour' (2009: 311). This in no way facilitated the women's ability to participate in political/civic life. For instance, being out late in the evening for meetings was likely to be frowned upon; mixing with men in a variety of activities could also attract objections. As noted by Tamir, the group's norms and interests were determined by elderly men who commonly endorse a rather orthodox point of view unfavourable to women's activity outside the community and even the home (1999: 48). These men also acted as gatekeepers to any opportunity for involvement in community activity. Patel remarks that women tend to act 'either within the parameters of permissible behaviour or if they transgress, they risk becoming pariah within their own community' (1997: 261). According to Sudbury the 'community' therefore becomes a contested political arena where Black and ethnic minority women risk asserting their right to self-determination in the face of considerable hostility, being accused of treason and of 'splitting the community' (1998: 73). Okin (1999) concludes that it might be difficult for older women who have lived by this code to challenge the status quo, all the more so as they may feel it is not in their interest to do so, given that their main experience of power is that exercised over their daughter-in-law. Even in the event of domestic violence, older women frequently blame the victim rather than the perpetrator: 'You often hear, even sometimes women saying "she must have deserved it" or "she got what she asked for" and really condoning those actions' (Sultana, Birmingham).

Younger women do not always buy into these cultural restrictions while, nonetheless, often complying with what is expected of them; that is, the weight of the moral community and their upbringing is such that they may continue to act accordingly. The constraints experienced by our respondents may be divided into two distinct strands. On the one hand, they shared the obstacles generally faced by women on account of their gender. On the other hand, they were caught in a pre-modern conceptualisation of the individual considered part and parcel of a community, a traditional view where women were contained in and subordinated to the collective. Nonetheless, despite a common baseline, the concrete situation of individuals created nuances related to levels of education, class and distance from immigration, whether first or second generation, from rural or urban background. Thus, a slow change is occurring with material change preceding cultural change. Moreover, when commenting on British society (as seen below in the section on Islam and the Muslim group) the women acknowledged the advantages of living in a society governed by multicultural policy, of which one cornerstone is a strong ethnic community.

France
As discussed in Chapter 3, France does not contain such tightly reconstituted communities among populations of Muslim background as Britain. In contrast with Britain, where almost all the women interviewed perceived that the community represented potential constraints to their activism, the French scenario was more varied and only a few instances were quoted whereby the extended community had presented obstacles to the capacity for action of our respondents. This was corroborated by a greater ability on the part of their mother's generation to take initiatives to neutralise or discard the possible influence of the extended group: through divorce, by moving into a new neighbourhood, by opposing the pressure and by taking up work.

In France, a significant number of women of sub-Saharan African origin progressed personally within community networks with several respondents describing such networks as homely. Tina (Paris), 19 years of age, of

Malian and Mauritanian parents, found herself comfortable in this environment and chose to interact socially with a group of persons of African origin. For Diana (Paris) of Mauritanian origin, conviviality developed as a result of geographical concentration so that girls found social interaction as much as boys did, in and around the tower blocks of the estates where they lived. Many women like Aman (Paris) who was from an Algerian family had not encountered any obstacles from family or community where their life projects and aspirations were concerned. In one significant case, community networks had functioned in a positive way. Wahida (Fontenay-sous-Bois), of Algerian background, active in an organisation dealing with domestic conflict and violence, bore testimony to the positive collaboration with leaders of African community organisations which contributed to the reduction of forced marriages among residents of African origin in Montreuil, a small town in the eastern suburbs of Paris.

Nonetheless, a small proportion of the women interviewed held a similar view to respondents in Britain on the advantages of living outside the ethno-religious community. Imoni (Paris) was grateful not to have grown up in a Muslim community, in a *cité*, so that she became open to a different vision instead of the traditional view limiting women's horizon to the home. Mounira (Paris), of Turkish background, noticed that when her family left their provincial home to live in Paris where community networks were denser, community pressure was tangible so that she and her mother started to wear a headscarf. Wahida (Fontenay-sous-Bois) linked her family's openness to diversity and marrying out with the fact that they did not live in the Algerian community. Safa (Paris) cited a situation comparable to ones discussed by some of the British respondents, whereby a large proportion of a Kabyle village settled in a Parisian *banlieue* kept a tight control on social behaviour and decided on everyone's life. Community and family members monitored dress codes, arranged marriages, jealously guarded girls' virginity and imposed related constraints. This had led her to break away from her family for many years and which had distressed her over years. Her own sister was almost 'driven mad' through family pressures, which had made her leave definitively. Although the vast majority of women interviewed had not suffered from much community interference, several of those who had lived within the community had to leave in order to gain their autonomy. This caused a family breakup for three of our respondents, two of whom repaired those links but only many years later.

Although most of the women interviewed stated that they had not faced community pressure, several pointed to the problematic situation of women growing up in the *cités* with a high concentration of people of immigrant family background. Almeda (Paris) explicitly pointed to the *cités* inhabited by people of Muslim background, where girls were the prime object of control, where their every move was known, and where eventually they ended up with a damaged reputation. This was confirmed by Najima (Saint-Fons), from a modest Tunisian family who practised as a solicitor in a *banlieue* and was the witness to recurrent incidents of violence, denunciation, restrictions on going out and the imposition of modest dress on the girls of the neighbourhood; Naima (Paris) concurred with this assessment of the *cités* where young men brought up in France were often those who exercised the greatest amount of pressure alongside older community 'guardians'.

In both France and Britain, Muslim women were often encouraged by the family to realise their aspirations, or they favoured a compromise, a give-and-take agreement. It also happened that some women stood firm and achieved their life project in the face of parents' or husband's opposition, while a few risked rupture in search of their autonomy, breaking links with their family and/or obtaining a divorce. Additional approaches were adopted to ensure the success of their life projects: some women circumvented the problem, for instance, by leading a 'double life' and conforming to all expectations when the family visited, while they ran their life as they wished at other times; or by postponing rather than refusing a marriage while they acquired higher qualifications and employment to strengthen their bargaining power. Another set of women seized upon arguments advanced within the family to defend their own viewpoint, for example, those who quoted Islam against ethnic traditions as examined below.

Islam and the Muslim Group

Muslim women's relationship to Islam and the Muslim group is complex and multifaceted. First, Islam, like other religions, is diverse and fragmented. It includes several schools and branches which are in constant flux according to differentiated trends and modes of implementation. The women in our study mostly belonged, respectively, in Britain and France, to Shafi and Maliki Sunni schools, while some followed *Tariqas* or were followers of Shi'ism. Second, not all the women interviewed practised or even believed in Islam. Rather than on theological aspects, we focus on the women's positioning vis-à-vis Islam and how this did or did not inform their life project.

Critique of Islam from Without in Britain and France

A notable discrepancy differentiates France from Britain regarding women who criticised Islam from the vantage point of a non-practising Muslim or a non-believer. While in France, a good number of the women rejected Islam, almost all of the women interviewed in Britain and in particular those of South Asian origin accepted some kind of link to Islam, whether as a cultural identity, a spiritual or religious connection. Antagonistic views of Islam were seldom encountered in Britain in the same way as atheism was a rare occurrence, the latter also being much less widespread among the British-majority population than in France. In France, a blanket rejection of Islam was voiced by several of the women from a philosophical and ideological stance, such as Marxism or atheism. In Britain, only two women did so, who were both communist refugees from Iran and Iraqi Kurdistan as well as one non-believer of Turkish origin, who upheld the Turkish secular heritage.

A radical critique of Islam was expressed from a gender standpoint. In Britain, only one woman, who was of Pakistani background and did not profess any religion, decried in Islam what she saw as an instrument of oppression against women, that is, the *hijab* that 'went against the fighting of our grandmothers' (Marjani, London). In France, many denounced Islam as an instrument of oppression against women, and condemned it for setting up obstacles to their autonomisation and participation in society. A comprehensive critique of Islam was formulated by two women who had suffered persecution and who had had to leave their country of origin as a consequence of the Front islamique du salut's (FIS) influence in Algeria. Lina, in her sixties, was of Algerian origin and an activist in the 1960s feminist movement. A well-educated woman, she embraced a radical stance against Islam, arguing that the subordinate position attributed to women was not only an add-on of some schools of Islam, but that it represented an intrinsic feature of the religion. The explanation she offered for its inherent 'inegalitarianism', was that it had been 'written by men for men' (Lina, Paris). Hayat (Paris), 30, whose communist father had been threatened by the FIS, was an atheist and found that she could not adhere to Islam in any way because of its treatment of women. This inequality constituted a decisive factor for a good number of women and is what made Natori (Paris), 32, an accountant of Tunisian parentage, detach herself from Islam: she 'did not like the place it accorded to women'. Some of the women's reactions revealed an unmitigated emotional hostility to Islam. Siham, 46, of Algerian parents, while claiming to be a cultural Muslim, rejected 'fundamentalism'. She was outraged by the ostentatious piety of some Muslim women, and incensed by their 'holier than thou' prejudices against those who did not practise. Irritated by their preaching and judgements, she used quite brutal language towards them (Siham, Saint-Denis). For Safa (Paris), 44, of Kabyle background, reclaiming Islam was simply tantamount to a regression which was detrimental to Muslim women who had struggled to achieve and maintain hard-won rights, thus echoing Marjani (London) in her appraisal of the religion. Farah (Paris), who was agnostic, was put off Islam because it had led women to accept men's physical or symbolic violence. Among several of our respondents, Islam thus elicited strong sentiments against what they perceived as unfair treatment of women. A few also called into question what can be labelled 'Islamic feminism', mostly denying that such a concept could exist, given the restrictions imposed on women by Islam (Natori, Paris). Some women affirmed a clear feminist commitment, which they identified as conflicting with Islam.

Although among the women who rejected Islam, some manifested a comprehensive opposition, it is evident that the main plank of the women's confrontational attitude to Islam stemmed from their stance on women's rights, which they deemed were undermined by it. Among those in France, a number of women who maintained their cultural heritage from Muslim-majority countries, while not adhering to the religion, put forward a claim to be 'cultural Muslims' and to be recognised as such.

Interrogating Islam from Within

Despite the Franco-British difference described above, the relationship of the women to Islam in France and Britain displayed a good deal of commonality, and uncovered a thread which cut across borders with regard to the vast majority of the Muslim women in Britain and all those who were believers in France. Rather than censuring Islam *per se*, they concentrated their criticisms on the way it had been interpreted and implemented; they challenged Muslims from within, from an Islamic standpoint. First, in both Britain and France, all the women unambiguously denounced the violent trends in Islam and organisations such as Al Qaeda. They asserted unambiguously that terrorism and suicide infringed Qur'anic prescriptions and ran absolutely counter to Islam, many of them echoing Nedira (Paris), a dentist from Morocco, who referred to a specific religious text to posit that Islam was a message of peace, and that suicide itself was forbidden in the Qur'an.

Britain
In Britain, the women opposed old and new prescriptive branches of Islam, whether in the form of *Deobandi, Wahhabi, Jamaat-e-Islami* or other similar political strands, particularly in so far as those branches supported the restriction of women's rights. They felt that Islam was being used to prevent discussion: 'when you say Islam—that is so authoritative...that you can't question it' (Ahlam, Birmingham). In Sadiqa's (Coventry) opinion, Islam had become obscured in such a way that its liberal traits had been buried under oppressive directives. What caused the women concern was the codification of Islam deriving from 'this more literal form of Islam coming through' (Tahira, Coventry). They detected a newly found zeal which seemed to pervade through Muslim communities in Britain, and several women objected to what they considered excesses and/or distortions. Women of different generations and background quoted multiple examples of what they judged went beyond the limits of acceptable norms and interfered with the minutiae of everyday life. Ahlam (Birmingham), originally from Punjab and in her fifties, was irritated by demands that 'you have to either prove it's *halal* or *haram*...there is no limit when you stop'. Sadiqa (Coventry), a Masters student, born in Britain, of Pakistani background, disagreed with the 'standard of what a proper Muslim is and should look like, and you have to cover your head and do different things'. Lulu (Birmingham), 35 years of age and a Bosnian refugee, was incensed at the insistence that she should wear a *hijab*, a measure imposed by the Birmingham Central Mosque in whose care Bosnian refugees had been placed.

The women felt that these prescriptions did not stop at concrete aspects of behaviour but that they also intervened in more fundamental domains, obstructing certain kinds of public engagement and a number of professional or leisure activities. Ahlam (Birmingham), who had qualified as an art teacher, a profession deemed perfectly respectable some years earlier among Muslims, was now being told by certain reformist schools of Islam that teaching an art curriculum was un-Islamic. All the women interviewed objected to Muslim groups which attempted to foist upon them measures such as gender segregation which they considered would restrict their access to many spheres of activity. For instance, Martiza (Birmingham) was concerned that these groups were too 'loud at the universities' where they enforced *inter alia* widespread gender segregation and Shula (London) was 'horrified' to discover that all the women sat at the back of her university's Islamic society meetings. Consequently, several of the female students we interviewed stopped attending or never joined an Islamic society on account of the intolerance exhibited. Effectively, this impeded their participation which was then rejected as potential engagement. Regarding the gender issue in Islam, their criticisms were wide-ranging: they ridiculed men's hypocrisy, objected to fundamental requirements which created inequality, condemned the discrediting and marginalising of women. They dismissed the argument that separation between men and women, on the pretext that the latter might incite a man to be 'tempted to sin', was necessary in the public domain and rejected the ideology which placed the onus of sexual temptation on women, turning the argument back against men. Tahira (Coventry), a Masters student of Pakistani background, turned on its head the accusation that women are responsible 'for what a bloke thinks', arguing on the contrary 'that's his thought then that he should be controlling'. Nabila (Coventry) very expressively illustrated this position: 'A man can look at a chair and see something sexual in it.' The women saw their position undermined in several ways, particularly by branches of Islam which curtailed their access to education. Ahlam (Birmingham) was incensed by the Taliban policy on girls' education. Each of the women developed her own version of what she believed was in keeping with good Muslim practice and acted accordingly. They all rejected the branches of Islam which placed obstacles in the path of their political action, such as demonstrating against the wars in Iraq and Afghanistan, and they confronted views which demonised the Western world. Ahlam (Birmingham) supported by Sultana (Birmingham) was adamant that she would take part in the British democratic process against groups such as Hizb ut-Tahrir which instructed Muslims not to take part in elections.

As a widely shared conclusion, Yasmin (Birmingham) advocated that Islam needed to adapt and compromise, that it should be open and flexible with the aim of constructing an Islam for Britain. It also led the women into an active search for religious sources, in order to elucidate the meaning behind the Qur'an.

France
In France a whole raft of criticisms were levelled at what the women considered erroneous interpretations and abusive implementations of Islam. Several of the women positioned themselves clearly against the varied pre-

scriptions they encountered which they estimated were recent developments, at least among Muslims in France. Many of the women opposed what they considered 'fundamentalist' interpretations of Islam, and Safia (Paris) stated her firm resolution never to associate with 'such people'. Ghufran (Paris), from a Turkish family, objected to what she called 'technical fact sheets', according to which Muslims were being told what was and was not allowed, thus stripping them of their humanity and transforming them into automatons. Fatouma (Paris), from a Sufi Senegalese family, also condemned the senseless practice of checking people's every action in everyday life in order to rank it as '*haram* or *halal*'.

The main reason behind the women's disapproval was what they considered the abuse of Islam by men who aimed to control women. For a good number of the women interviewed, contemporary, emerging schools of Islam were forging an instrument of oppression against women. Farah (Paris), a political activist from the Marche pour l'égalité period of the 1980s who was opposed to communitarianism, concluded that again 'men made rulings…and women paid the price'. For Aman (Paris), 34 years old, from Algeria and whose brother was killed by Islamists, the headscarf was a symbol of male domination, and 'fundamentalists' compelled women to wear a headscarf to further the patriarchal system. The full-face veil was a prime target of criticism by all, barring one follower of *Wahhabism*. Derifa (Paris), who declared herself 'profoundly Muslim', talked about the dire consequences of her anti-*niqab* stance which had prevented her from visiting Algeria, her country of origin, for fear of being persecuted and even kidnapped by extremist groups. As in Britain, the women objected to calls for separation between men and women in employment and other sectors of public life which in effect imposed restrictions on their participation in a number of activities and ventures. Keltoum (Paris), a follower of a *Tariqa*, fought against the separation of women and men which did not 'make sense [to her]'. Cantara (Paris), who took it for granted that the Qur'an treated women as equal to men, was exasperated when women accepted male domination. As in Britain, the women who did not conform to prescriptions were barred from taking part in certain community organisations and branches of the religion. Kadija (Livry-Gargan), a headscarf-wearing Muslim, signalled that community organisations and other groups generally did not tolerate any kind of divergence—if you wanted to work with the Union des organisations islamiques de France (UOIF) you had to go along with their ways completely. None of the women felt that they could adhere to the official body which represented

Islam in France, the Conseil français du culte musulman (CFCM). Radia (Paris) was unable to identify anything they had achieved on behalf of Muslims given that the organisation was fraught with power struggles and ethno-national divisions. Moreover, she pointed out that its leadership was composed of men only. Other features of Muslims' religious practice invited disapproval. Safia (Paris) decried the new 'invention' of leaving work to go and pray at a mosque, something which her grandfather, who was a member of a Muslim *Tariqa* and her father, a member of *ulema*, had never done. Makina (Paris) objected to the anachronism of an Islam followed literally which she estimated was detrimental to its image, and was also opposed to garments and behaviours which, while customary in other countries, were at odds with the here and now of French society.

From a Muslim standpoint, in both Britain and France, the women regarded the strands of political Islam, which some of them called 'fundamentalist', as an instrument of control clearly detrimental to women's rights. They deplored the negative image of Islam peddled by the media, which almost exclusively staged extremists and 'fundamentalists' in the public imaginary, and they proposed another kind of Islam adapted to their environment.

Islam and Ethnic Traditions, Islam a Tool of Emancipation

Britain

Although scholars recall that culture and religion are closely enmeshed, the vast majority of women in our British sample categorically expressed their refutation of what they called 'cultural Islam', which they characterised as ethnic traditions imbued with a patriarchal bias. They seized upon Islam as a tool of emancipation against the grip of what they identified as a traditional patriarchal environment. A call on Islamic guidelines has indeed become more prominent among young people of Muslim background, competing with and often superseding ethnic identification, a shift in emphasis noted by Abida (Birmingham), 18 years old, of an Iranian father: 'It's less tradition, it's more religion now.' What struck the women was the disproportionately large share of cultural traditions entangled in the kind of Islam they had learned to practise at home and in their communities. Husniya (Coventry), of Pakistani background, noted the overwhelming influence of culture on the religion, 'culture in my community is quite dominant in the religion'; while Tahira (Coventry), of Pakistani origin, articulated the necessary differentiation between culture and religion, 'For me there is Islam and cultural Islam'. Her vehemence revealed a strong disapproval of what she perceived as a cultural adulteration of Islam. The women scrutinised their customs and practices in the light of Islam, uncovering numerous disputable areas. For example, they generally did not blame Islam as an obstacle to more involvement outside home but pointed instead to tradition and community. They did not perceive that Islam restricted what women could and could not do, as stated by Sultana (Birmingham) of Kashmiri parents: 'I don't think that Islam actually limits what women can and cannot do. I find it's our culture which is a barrier.'

The women pitted themselves against a male ethnic interpretation of Islam, unfavourable to women, which was embraced by much of the Muslim community. Husniya (Coventry) expressed the group's feelings that this was not an acceptable representation of Islam, that young women in the group should certainly not acquiesce with 'men's view' about the way they should practise Islam. One very sensitive area was that of decisions regarding marriage. The women insisted that Islam stood in opposition to tradition, wherein arranged marriages were the norm, assorted with instances of forced marriages; this opinion cut across ethnic origins and generations. Indeed, the women enlisted against traditional approaches to marriage, the Islamic prescription that both the bride and bridegroom must fully agree to a marriage. Reema (Birmingham), 45 years old, of Azad Kashmiri parents, Adelmira, 50 years of age and Tahani, 30 years old, of East African Asian background, all of whom wore a headscarf testified to this, quoting the imam who 'will ask the girl…three times "Have you been forced?"'. This was not a benign distinction given the central influence husbands could have on their wives' ability to engage in the public domain, as seen in the previous section. Tahira (Coventry) also objected to the predominance of cultural tradition, such as the caste system, which contravened Islamic prescriptions. Another significant area of contention was the right to pursue an education which the women repeatedly quoted as being enshrined in the Qur'an, but which traditional practice frequently denied. The overwhelming duty to the extended family and in-laws was challenged in the name of Islam against tradition. Reema (Birmingham) drew a line between her duty to her husband and children, which in her view stemmed from her faith as a Muslim, while her responsibilities towards in-laws derived from what her culture took for granted. The question of money was a critical one in terms of power. The traditional outlook prescribed that money belonged to the family and not to the individual, so that a woman's earnings did not grant her more power within the family and vis-à-vis men or in-laws. This was not so where Islam was concerned, as Tahani (Birmingham) explained: 'Islamically, if a woman works, that money is hers.'

One could discern an emergent trend whereby Muslim women asserted the primacy of their Muslim identity, although this did not always prove an easy undertaking. Reema (Birmingham) did not relate to her Pakistani nationality/ethnicity of origin but chose to see herself as a British Muslim, fully aware that she was creating a new type of identification for herself, taking into her own hands how she chose to be guided in life. In the meantime, her family was unsettled by her identity claims which they construed as a threat to their traditions. Although Islam was becoming a pivotal instrument of challenge against traditions which the women perceived as a hindrance to the enjoyment of their rights and an obstacle to their autonomisation, they realised that brandishing Islamic arguments might not suffice, as signalled by Sultana (Birmingham): 'Just coming up with a religious argument is not necessarily going to change anything.' While the vast majority of women interviewed concentrated on challenging ethnic traditions, a few adopted a more radical stance such as Lulu (Birmingham) from Bosnia, who explained that the Qur'an was introduced for a specific society, in a particular historical context and therefore needed to evolve; several like her promoted a form of Islam adapted to Britain.

France
While in Britain, the vast majority of women emphasised the divergence between culture and religion with the aim of challenging male ethnic domination, in France the exegesis of Muslim practice derived from two distinct motivations: first, the combating of ethnic traditions; second, attaining a purer form of Islam divested of cultural interferences (examined below). In the first place, constraints attributed to tradition paralleled those outlined in Britain, the root of the problem being similarly identified by Mounira (Paris) who summarised it as 'male supremacy under the guise of religion'. Lutfiyah (Nanterre), of third generation North African background who wore a headscarf, blamed patriarchal structures and not Islam for practices such as forced marriages and female excision. Ezina (Paris) who had personally suffered a great deal from traditional practices in Guinea 'discovered truly what Islam is' thus feeling equipped to reject forced marriages, polygamy and female excision as non-Islamic. Gulcin (Paris) quoted Qur'anic guidelines to support a woman's right to work

and control her salary against traditions. Imoni (Paris), a practising Muslim who wore a headscarf, accused traditional male chauvinism of demands that women and men be separated in a medical environment. Several of the women categorically celebrated Islam as an instrument of emancipation. Kadija (Livry-Gargan) argued that it was Islam which gave her all her rights and her rightful place in life, in her family and in her relationship with her husband so that 'nothing justified that women should remain in the shadow of their husbands'. Natara (Paris) voiced powerful sentiments about Islam as a guarantor of her rights against potential encroachments by men: 'God gave me rights. Which man could take them away?'

Nuances related to the salience of issues differentiated France from Britain with arranged/forced marriages and constraints in education being raised more frequently in Britain, while female excision and polygamy were more common in France among people of sub-Saharan background. In both countries, Muslim women established a distinction between what pertained to ethnic traditions and an Islam unadulterated by cultural practices, although this was more prevalent in Britain. Their quest for gender equality led them to seek in the study of sacred texts a response to the constraints of patriarchy, so that Islam was construed as a tool of emancipation. For some of them, it signified an additional responsibility to pursue *ijtihad*.

Although, on the one hand, the women rejecting Islam altogether and, on the other hand, those reclaiming it from movements and interpretations of which they disapproved expressed what would seem to be divergent viewpoints, they shared a position which rested on a claim for gender equality. In other words, the women who rejected Islam for being an instrument of women's oppression subscribed to a rationale similar to that adopted by those who used Islam against patriarchal tradition or contested the 'man-led' interpretation of emerging political movements; all of the women upheld women's emancipation. A whole section of women thus found in Islam an answer to their life project and a response to male domination. They called on values against norms, Islamic values which they regarded as constituting a higher moral ground than traditional norms.

Individualised Islam, Bearer of Values and a Guide for Action

Britain
A debate developed among the women in our Sl focus groups between those who advocated a collective conception of Islam and who formed a minority position and the vast majority who professed a personal form of Islam. This

introduced the differentiation between private and public Islam, individual and community practice. The latter was represented, for example, by Abida (Birmingham), of English–Iranian parentage, who put forward a collective and community practice whereby one had 'to show Islam [and make it] visible' because she regarded it as a 'community religion'. This view was contested by most of the women such as Tahira (Coventry) on the basis that Islam was not 'a group thing, it is not collective, it is not communism, it is individual'. Lulu (Birmingham) also kept her Islam private and understood her religion as a totally personal affair, a moral and spiritual experience for which she did not feel accountable to anyone other than God: 'I believe that my religion is between me and God.'

The women revealed a number of contradictions between themselves and those they dismissed as 'the preachy type' (Tahira, Coventry). Among young women in particular, strong objections were levelled at what they considered to be simply normative Islam, often misconceived and imposed from without. The 'worthier than thou' attitude which they sometimes encountered was wholly disdained. Tahira (Coventry) took head on those who accused her of failing her religious duty because she danced: 'Who are you to tell me what is and is not Muslim?' For many of the young women who did not wear a headscarf, the respect it often commanded from the community, especially older women and men, was entirely unfounded and even unfair as they saw no relationship between pious and/or moral behaviour and the wearing of the headscarf. Some contended that wearing the material *hijab* was unnecessary because what counted was your own internalised modesty: 'modesty, *hijab* is inside of you' (Tahira, Coventry). Ahlam (Birmingham) made it explicit that one should not be fooled by appearances which could be paraded as good 'morals'. Similarly, Muslim television channels were seen to be taking advantage of naive women who were bombarded with recipes and guidance for life; the women in our SI focus groups accused such channels of manipulating women. Sadiqa (Coventry) pointed out that middle-aged women appeared to be especially vulnerable.

What was apparent in Britain, particularly among younger women, was that they claimed the right to develop their own understanding of Islam and did not accept prescriptions from anyone else, rejecting them unequivocally. Not only were the young women not bothered by comments from men or those they disparagingly called the '*hijabis*' ('self-righteous' headscarf-wearing women), but they were convinced that each individual was the only person qualified to decide whether or not her/

his Islam was understood and practised adequately. Nadeema, who ran a performing arts company and who sported body piercings, felt her faith deeply while she entirely defied the agenda followed by some emerging schools of Islam which forbade music. Her art was guided by a totally individualised form of Islam which she conceived as a framework for creation, 'Islam gives us parameters and within that we are free to create' (Nadeema, Coventry). This prevalent trend was summarised by the recurrent remark that Islam was 'such an individual thing' (Tahira Coventry), thus testifying to a kind of secularisation *à la britannique*. An additional group of women had taken initiatives to deepen their knowledge of Islam through their own efforts. Sadiqa (Coventry) recommended that the women should rely on their own resources and read sacred texts without 'an intermediate between them and God'. Ahlam (Birmingham) called on female initiatives to interpret the sacred text and advocated some kind of feminist *ijtihad*. Almost all the women promoted the right to elect one's form of practice. Several of the women wore a headscarf and a few also wore a long black coat while others did not display any distinctive sign of their religion. Regarding the full-face veil, they all agreed that it was not in any manner a requirement of Islam. Notwithstanding, they shared the view that any decision about Islamic dress should remain the woman's prerogative and be respected as such.[1] The SI focus groups we held comprised women from different schools and strands in Islam but one striking aspect was their willingness to accept differences. They opposed any sort of sectarian position.

Islam definitely provided the women with a moral guide and a framework for action, the moral dimension of Islam standing out as a feature which commanded complete unanimity amongst the women interviewed. They shared the aspiration to 'differentiate right from wrong', noting that young Muslims were particularly preoccupied with this question: 'our youth, all of them, boys and girls seem to be very much interested in promoting moral issues' (Adelmira, Birmingham). Some of the women prioritised what they called 'individual moral issues' (Adelmira) while others extended their responsibility as Muslims to wider questions and cited a 'humanitarian' duty (Sabreena, Birmingham). Islam was perceived as a guide for conduct which universalised rather than particularised attitudes and actions (Tahani, Birmingham). A recurrent comment presented Islam as a general moral standard. Jameela (Birmingham) followed the principles of Islam which 'exist in any religion'. For Rana (London), Islam meant 'responsibility to other people against injustices. It should be a broad church'. Manar's (Manchester) Islam was the benchmark allowing her to differentiate right from wrong. Bilkis (London) cited Islam as a moral guide according to which you 'should be judged by your deeds'. This moral/human responsibility was even extended to ecology, with some women quoting from the Qur'an about the need to live in harmony with nature and to care for the environment (Sultana, Birmingham). Besides the adherence to universal human values, it was stated that specific Islamic values also had to be preserved against some other moral codes which were widespread in Britain, for example, those pertaining to pre-marital sex, drugs and alcohol (Tahani, Birmingham).

Evidently, the women were seeking a way of carving out their own space within Islam and British society, refuting any suggestion that they would have to choose between the two (Ahlam, Birmingham). They also broadly objected to a demonisation of the West (Sultana, Birmingham). Muslim women were using their faith as a guide for action which brought together politics and morals.

France

As in Britain two positions were evident regarding the potential individual and collective dimensions of Islam. A few of the women promoted a collective responsibility. For example, Kadija (Livry-Gargan) held that it was not sufficient to nurture Islam in one's heart since it carried a collective duty to transmit a message, particularly when living in a non-Muslim context. Mahira (Paris) added a dimension pertaining to wider society, so that she combined her individual choice to practise according to her convictions with a collective responsibility to convey a good image of Islam for the sake of Muslim communities in France.

One can discern two approaches among women who advocated an individual mode. In the first place, a number of women manifested what amounts to a secularisation of their practice through an individualised form of Islam which was part of their life and justified what they wished to foster. Safa (Paris) practised her religion to fit in with her life in a way which did not constrain her. In her words she does what she calls the 'legal minimum' which is to conduct herself decently and not harm her body in any way—according to her, a principal teaching of the Qur'an. Rejecting any extraneous instructions, Ezina (Paris) felt perfectly comfortable in the practice of her religion which she felt did not inhibit her social interactions such as going out, dancing and so on. In brief, most of the women practised a kind of Islam which they considered tolerant and perfectly compatible with living their life without impediments.

Regarding the question of femininity in Islam, raised often by Muslims and non-Muslims, Maya (Cergy-Pontoise), a practising Muslim, saw no contradictions between her religion and her life as a woman. She felt that she could express her femininity in the way she practised Islam which provided a vehicle for her personal development. Ezina (Paris) summarised a common position whereby her faith and interpretation were 'no one else's business', since religion was a 'personal thing', interpreted by each in her own way. It is worth noting that the issue of the headscarf crystallised tensions between French society and Islam more so than in Britain. Those who were believers, as well as many cultural and 'political' Muslims, advocated that it should be solely the woman's choice, made independently of her family or majority society. A few specifically resented the argument put forward that wearing a headscarf unequivocally indicated a lack of freedom.

A second individual approach revealed a commitment towards a heightened knowledge of Islam for the sake of a better practice; that is, some women adopted an individualised conception of Islam which went further than a personal commitment in everyday life, and rested on a 'continuous search' (Keltoum, Paris). They considered it important to make up their own mind through learning, a quest which Rida (Paris) had turned into an active obligation. Some women pursued a spiritual route and had travelled to the site of *Tariqas* in order to deepen their grasp of spirituality (Fatouma, Paris). Many others extended efforts to seek knowledge in books, for example, Lilly (Paris) and Radia (Paris) who had examined Islam through different sources whether electronic, print, the family or mosque before she formulated her own opinion. Derifa (Paris) enjoined women to 'reappropriate' the sacred texts by 'go[ing] straight to sources'. Lilly considered that *ijtihad*, the exegesis of the sacred texts, was a necessity and constituted a Muslim duty. Nedira (Paris) went to such lengths to be better informed that she decided to undertake theological studies. She was representative of a nucleus of women who campaigned in favour of a better understanding of Islam among their family and community.

Leaving aside those who declared their atheism/agnosticism, Islam represented a guide in the conduct of their life for many of the respondents in France, whether they were followers of a private or publicly displayed Islam. Their comments duplicated those made by respondents in Britain. In the first place, Lutfiyah (Nanterre) stressed that internecine quarrels had no place in Islam and stressed the paramount value of respect for one another, which allowed for different schools of Islamic thought and practice: 'believing in God' was the key common trunk. Wahida (Fontenay-sous-Bois) reclaimed the spirituality of Islam and the shared values it carried which were essentially a guide to 'distinguish evil from good'. Many of the women shared Mounira's (Paris) view that Islam constituted the central inspiration behind their values. Bassema (Paris) looked upon Islam as a body of values and love while Najima (Saint-Fons) regarded Muslim philosophy as one of 'light and tolerance'. Sana (Paris) regretted that many young Muslims in France concentrated on appearances rather than the foundational values of Islam. In her view, form too often superseded content among the young women who wore a headscarf and the responsibility to be 'supportive and loving', 'not to hurt others' was neglected.

Over and above their attitudes towards Muslims, most of the women made a point of insisting on the duty of respect and tolerance to be extended to Muslims and non-Muslims alike (Lutfiyah, Nanterre). Nikia (Paris) took her conception of Islam a step further by adopting an ecumenical approach, whereby she equated 'rabbi, priest [and imam]'. What stood out in the women's discourse was the message of humanity and human values carried by Islam. Fatouma (Paris) chose to embrace her father's Sufi approach which rested on exchanges with and an acceptance of the whole of humanity. Shahina (Paris) defended above all human values which accorded others their full importance. Maya (Cergy-Pontoise) saw her humanity above all else as a Muslim, even above her feminity. Fatouma (Paris) stressed that Islam could not adopt a rigid posture but had to 'adapt to the theatre of each nation', because it demanded the capacity to 'live together' in harmony, without which religion lost its meaning. She remarked that one could find 'atheists closer to god than believers'. Imoni (Paris) underlined the universality of Islam which required that it could and had to be adapted to different contexts. And Maya (Cergy-Pontoise) concluded that Islam had the vocation to provide 'a tool for being a better human'.

In both countries, Islam and its religious dimension were perceived by many women as a marker according to which they could assemble and connect different facets of their identity. There were strong similarities between France and Britain in the treatment of Islam as a moral code, whether privately practised or publicly displayed. It was a guide for action in everyday life, vis-à-vis other Muslims and non-Muslims, through a commitment to human values. It also constituted a powerful motivation for engagement in civic and political life.

Our research reveals a diversity of positions regarding Islam among Muslim women. In the first instance, one category of women rejected a religious identification. This included four subcategories: women who held a philosophical stance opposed to religion such as atheists or Marxists; women whose main objections to Islam were based on grounds of gender equality; women who were not religious but wished to be recognised as cultural Muslims and reclaimed this cultural heritage and women who declared themselves as political Muslims. These women were active in a variety of initiatives across wider society and the ethnic group and remained unconnected to any religious reference, except when they opposed Islam or defended Muslims against religious discrimination. Second, a substantial number of women were religious, albeit with differentiated profiles. One type followed religion in a secularised manner, their Islam remaining private and individualised on the basis of a relationship between God and themselves. A second type seized upon Islam to challenge ethnic tradition. A third type pursued a personal spiritual quest. A fourth type searched for authenticity and may be subdivided into those who aimed to divest Islam of ethnic traditions and those who opposed the comprehensive prescriptions and technical instructions advocated by political reformist movements, both seeking an alternative insight to the prevalent one interpreted by men for men. A good number of women prioritised the ethical message in Islam and many emphasised its humanist spirit, through a double ethical and universalist dimension. In the main, religious women held Islam as a source of values and an ethical guide for their conduct and actions which played a significant role in making their public engagement and the issues they pursued meaningful. This engagement could be exercised in wider society and/or within the ethnic group and the Muslim arena, according to the opportunities available which in turn were governed by the legislative framework or male control.

Conclusion

For Muslim women in France and Britain the ethnic group acts both as an enabler and as an obstacle regarding the realisation of their life project and their participation in the public sphere. A number of factors influence the likelihood that women gain a greater measure of autonomy in connection with their family history and their origin on both sides of a dichotomy, the first one being usually less favourable and the second one more promising: a rural or urban origin, a recent arrival or a long-established residence in Europe, an extended family being present in France/Britain as opposed to a nuclear family, living within the ethnic community or apart from the community, and being raised by non-educated or educated parents. Generally, the longer the residence in Europe and the more generations which are brought up in the country of settlement, the more the women enjoyed a variety of opportunities. This is confirmed also in the case of South Asian women from East Africa whose family had left the Indian subcontinent as long ago as the end of the nineteenth century. Finally, parents' engagement in politics tends to have an impact on the women's outlook and on their capacity for action, hence also marking a difference between labour migrants and political refugees, the latter being more favourable to women's autonomisation and participation.

Our research broadly demonstrates that the women wanted to gain greater autonomy regarding their life project, whether it related to studying, employment, marriage or engagement in the public sphere. Notwithstanding, they manifested a strong emotional attachment to their parents and immediate family. In both countries, the relationship with parents generally demonstrated an understanding which rested on negotiation and compromise, although the compromise opened up a wider measure of opportunities and covered larger areas of life in France than in Britain, particularly with respect to marriage. This difference can be explained partly by the significance of the extended family and community which was more predominant in Britain, where it exercised greater control than in France.[2] On the whole, in both countries the women subscribed to a nuclear model of the family: in France the women's own modern version was already implemented in many cases (with a greater number of exceptions among families from sub-Saharan Africa); in Britain it constituted a goal and gradually evolved. Only a few of the women were driven to a breakup with their immediate family, such cases being more frequent in France than in Britain. Altogether, the women challenged restrictions placed upon their study, employment and political engagement projects imposed by the extended family and the community. They also deployed their efforts to further expand their autonomy, whenever necessary within the nuclear family, in interaction with their parents and their husband.

Regarding the women's position in relation to Islam, broadly speaking many similarities were noted between France and Britain. In the first place, the women denounced radical Islam and terrorism. Believers and non-believers alike unanimously voiced a total condemnation, the former emphasising that it transgressed the letter and the spirit of Islam. A number of non-believers indicted Islam, especially on grounds of gender inequality or on more fundamental philosophical grounds, and were to be found in greater numbers in France than in Britain. Turning specifically to women who were believers, many criticised Islam from within, from an Islamic viewpoint. On the one hand, they questioned the interpretation and implementation of many of the strands of contemporary Islam which they did not hesitate to defy. In both Britain and France, the women had arrived at an assessment of political reformist Islam as an instrument of control over people, with women bearing the brunt of the constraints. They rejected this control and its prescriptions so that only very few of them engaged with such movements. On the other hand, the women's critique of Islam also revolved around the distinction between what they called 'cultural Islam' and the Islam they embraced. They cast off the Islam which in their view was steeped in ethnic customs dressed up as Islamic injunctions, to espouse an Islam they deemed 'genuine', once divested of ethnic traditions. They seized upon Islam as a lever of emancipation against tradition and patriarchy, whether it related to the right to education, the banning of forced marriages, polygamy, female excision, the control of their earnings, gender segregation and so on. They stood for values against norms—religious values which they considered represented a higher moral ground than traditional norms. They bemoaned the fact that the gaining of those rights in practice should be so arduous, and that places of worship tended to remain in the grip of traditions fashioned by men. This critical position also enabled them to maintain a link with their family and origins while distancing themselves from oppressive traditions, so that some of the women found, in Islam, a solution to the complex negotiation between their origins and being part of majority Western society. Islam provided a response to an identity and a loyalty dilemma, thus acting as a vector of integration. It also enabled them to participate in wider society without breaking with their family and communities. In the same vein, other women who might not have been believers or did not practise Islam demanded the right to be recognised as cultural Muslims. Religion provided the women with a central channel for the dual task of remaining connected to the past while simultaneously preparing for the future and it acted as a guide for their conduct within European society in which they forged a future for themselves.

Generally, women who were believers promoted an individualised interpretation of their religion in both countries. They emphasised that they opted for and respected personal choice, whether that was to wear a *hijab* or not, whether or not to abide by any of the rituals and so on. They did not fail to disparage the artifice of visible symbols of Islam when this was not matched by a personal moral conduct. Their aspiration for gender rights and equality contributed to their researching sacred texts and arguments to challenge more 'fundamentalist' and/or traditional interpretations in order to attain greater autonomisation. Moreover, they argued that their capacity of analysis was enhanced through living in Europe where they were exposed to different visions of life and to better opportunities enabling them to undertake an exegesis of the texts. This drove some of them towards the quest for a female interpretation of Islam, in the tradition of *ijtihad*. The women in both countries undoubtedly adopted and promoted a more individualised approach and advanced Muslim values as a moral guide for their life. Against sectarian notions they embraced universal human values. Many of the women declared that Islam constituted for them a tool which allowed them to differentiate right from wrong in the conduct of their life and as a guide for action. What was paramount in their view was the moral message conveyed by Islam, a message of peace and tolerance which demanded respect for all Muslims and non-Muslims alike, prioritising the universal values and the humanitarian message that Islam carried.

Notes

1. The issue of Islamic dress is developed more fully in Chapter 8.
2. Most of the women we interviewed had not been brought up in the *cités*, where stronger community control was exercised.

CHAPTER 7

Majority Society and Women's Capacity of Action

INTRODUCTION

Although their immediate socialisation takes place within the family and the ethnic group, Muslim women are part and parcel of the society they inhabit and broadly consider themselves as such. However, their relationship to wider society displays complex features which disclose both positive and negative characteristics, according to French or British specificities. The first section of this chapter examines obstacles and facilitating factors presented by wider society to the women's autonomisation and capacity of action. The second part is dedicated to the parameters of action and the strategies adopted by Muslim women to access autonomy and pursue their respective projects.

MAJORITY SOCIETY: BRITAIN

Prejudice and Obstacles

In European society, populations of Muslim background are in the main also from Third World countries and, in Britain and France, mostly from former colonies. This heritage designates them as a potential target of racial discrimination. In Britain, they were first categorised and self-identified as 'Black', then as ethnic minorities and only later as Muslims (Joly 2012). In the first phase of settlement, they were not perceived as Muslims for several decades but were categorised on the basis of their 'skin

© The Author(s) 2017
D. Joly, K. Wadia, *Muslim Women and Power*, Gender and Politics, DOI 10.1057/978-1-137-48062-0_7

colour' and suffered from concomitant racial and ethnic discrimination, as quoted by several of the women. Jameela related how difficult it was for her family to buy a house in the late 1970s: as soon as potential sellers found out that they were of Pakistanis origin (i.e. non-White), they would declare that the house had been promised to another buyer. Meanwhile, Jameela (Birmingham) was also faced with discrimination in employment. All the women who had lived through that period were acutely aware of the disadvantage they had encountered. In the twenty-first century, enduring presumptions linked to their appearance also affected the women—for instance, it was inferred that they did not speak English, were uneducated and did not deserve the respectful treatment awarded to their White counterparts (Adelmira, Birmingham). Sultana (Birmingham) concluded that skin colour was still the predominant criterion superseding wealth, class and level of education.

Over and above racial discrimination, a new layer of prejudice is now intervening against Muslims qua Muslims. A term has been coined to express this novel social construction, Islamophobia. The women noted that your very name identified as Muslim could make you the target of discrimination (Ahlam, Birmingham). Moreover, a whole array of prejudices pertains to the supposed characteristics of a Muslim woman: several of the women cited events evidencing that their interlocutor expected them to be quiet and submissive, much to their surprise when they discovered that this was not the case. Another common prejudice related to Muslim women's social role as child bearers and carers. On her leaving hospital after giving birth Reema (Birmingham), a senior social worker and mother of two, was offended by the nurse's form of farewell, 'see you next year dear', exposing an assumption that she would produce a child every year. This image was compounded for women who wore the *hijab*, in the first place because it proclaimed to all that they were Muslim; secondly, because this code of dress was interpreted as a sign that they fully conformed to the stereotype attached to Muslim women. Adelmira (Birmingham) noticed the different way she was treated after she started wearing it, being addressed 'in one syllable words', a testimony to manifest expectations of a low level of education or a presumption that she was 'just off the plane' and an outsider.

There was a clear awareness among the women that their visibility as Muslims could be a handicap. In reality, it is not a matter of a simple addition but rather of a multiplication since the gender component aggravated the prejudice connected with Islam. Rabiya (London), a National Union of Students (NUS) officer in charge of Education, had found that she had to prove her worth a great deal more than others to convince students that she could represent them all. Undoubtedly, all these facets of prejudice hampered the women's chances of participation in the public realm on two main grounds. In the first place, it cast doubts on their capabilities and, secondly, it undermined their own confidence. To make matters worse, several of the women felt that hostility towards Muslims had drastically increased since 2001, even when it was not explicit (Sultana, Birmingham). Sabreena (Birmingham), British of Kashmiri origin, born and educated in Britain, was not left in any doubt about the enmity against her when she was spat at in the city centre of Birmingham shortly after the 9/11 events. In the realm of work, Afiya (Birmingham) quoted a friend who went to ten interviews wearing a *hijab* without success, and was offered the post on the two occasions when she had left it out. A Black non-Muslim member of the Birmingham Race Action Partnership (BRAP) summarised it as 'Faith is the new Black' (Claudette, Birmingham), referring to an earlier period when Black people were the prime target of acute racism.

Over and above prejudice, other kinds of obstacles hampered Muslim women's activism. One major issue was that of occasional *de facto* collusion between state institutions and community leaders, when women endeavoured to develop collective action. In effect, local and national governments have awarded community leaders, mostly first generation traditional males, greater powers to control their community and act as gatekeepers. Patel points out that the measure of autonomy accorded community leaders to govern their community strengthened their ability to control the family, women and children (1997: 263). For decades, the agencies of majority society have taken it for granted that the ethnic group was a homogeneous entity, thus ignoring the needs of subgroups such as women. Asian women were sometimes pressurised by police and housing officials to handle cases of domestic violence in a conciliatory way, which Sudbury explains by the fact that assumptions on Asian women's dependence were reinforced by consultation with community leaders (1998: 67). Sudbury cites a community organisation which ran a refuge for victims of domestic violence and was threatened with closure by an Asian councillor, if 'they continued encouraging women to leave violent homes' (Sudbury 1998: 75). Official recognition played a similar role regarding Muslim women's opportunities to act. Some women interviewed were concerned that the government emphasised collaboration with Muslim organisations which belonged to the more orthodox branches of Islam, dominated by male leaders and Islamic interpretations partial to men. The end result was a sidelining of what Afiya (Birmingham) called 'moderate Muslims', so that women without *hijab* felt intimidated to participate in those ventures.

The question of funding is a pivotal one. Social cohesion policy implemented after 2001 stipulated that groups providing specialist services to ethnic minorities would not benefit from government funding unless they developed a single generic service for all users in their catchment area. The issue was spectacularly illustrated by the Southall Black Sisters' situation whose local authority funding was withdrawn because they provided specialist services to Black and ethnic minority women. It was restored following a tribunal decision obtained with the support of the Equality and Human Rights Commission, but others were not to be so fortunate. Several of the women involved in community organisations mentioned the difficulty linked with this stipulation (Nadeema, Coventry). Another impediment encountered when applying for local authority funding was the concomitant red tape as testified by 46 year old Zakiya (Rotherham), a qualified woman born and educated in Britain, who founded a community organisation, in 1994, to offer support and protection to Muslim women who were victims of domestic violence. Finally, structural aspects of integration and immigration policy reinforced the dependence of women; for example, immigration laws which rendered the immigration status of a woman subordinate to that of her husband and left her at the mercy of his largesse in all aspects of her life.

Changes and Improvements

British society underwent significant changes regarding discrimination and ethnic relations between the 1950s and 2000 through strengthened legislation and policies to combat discrimination on criteria of race, colour, nationality, ethnic and national origin, as stipulated in the 1976 Race Relations Act (see details in Chapter 3), augmented with a religious criterion in the 2010 Equality Act. This societal evolution was reflected in the women's experience who remarked on improvements over the previous decades. It was illustrated by the contrasting school experiences between Reema, who was subjected to her teachers' dismissive attitude in the early 1980s, and Ulema (Birmingham), 15 years younger who was well-supported by her school to gain a place at university. The world of work appears to have progressed too, so that Ahlam's experience of discrimination in the 1970s was not matched by more recent events in Tahani's life (Birmingham).

As for Mumtaz (Birmingham) who was French of Algerian origin, she appreciated being able to work in a nursery wearing her *hijab*. This is not to say that prejudice did not occur and the women were aware of that possibility, but they stated clearly that it was not the norm any longer nor was it all-pervasive as used to be. According to Mumtaz (Birmingham), comparing her experience in France and Britain, it was a systemic matter, the British 'system' awarding greater protection to Muslims. Altogether, several of the women engaged in collective action have found support from White friends and non-Muslim activists on the Left, such as Rabiya (London), who studied journalism and obtained a position as Personal Assistant to an MP.

Multiculturalism and Opportunities

Many of the women positively evaluated British multicultural policy for building an environment which offered them 'choice', so that they could comfortably elect to keep their religion at the same time as being British and considered as such. Abida (Birmingham), a sixth form college student, summarised a widespread viewpoint among Muslim women, namely, that being British and Muslim were not exclusive of each other, a feature which they all celebrated: 'you can keep your identity and still be part of this society'. In terms of their personal improvement, the young women in our sociological intervention (SI) group took stock of what they had gained in Britain, such as a more open mind: this was a general feeling expressed by Akira (Coventry) and Husniyah (Coventry), a Social Work Masters student who testified to changes in her own views on homosexuality. Altogether, being exposed to mixed cultures was deemed a distinct advantage. Sultana (Birmingham) argued that involvement in different cultures made for more progressive mores. As a conclusion, the women stated that they squarely espoused mixing in British society and advocated against enclosure in one's ethnic group. The women felt they had gained a great deal from growing up and living in British society, which bestowed new prospects for women and girls. The chance of an education was a major benefit outlined by the women who also took stock of changes in the aspiration of Muslim women brought up in the UK, namely, that their world was not limited to marriage and family any longer but signified engaging with wider society (Adelmira, Birmingham). The women noted that British society opened doors which they otherwise might not access. Taking up employment, in particular, was perceived as a chance to seize additional life opportunities such as 'extra training, getting involved with unions' (Tahani, Birmingham). According to Sanye (Coventry) of Turkish background, it was the secularism of society which gave you the chance to achieve your goals.

The women gained support from varied quarters in British society. Leesha (Birmingham), from a modest family of rural Bangladeshi background, and whose father was illiterate, was able to study performing arts at university because her drama teacher convinced her parents to allow her to do so. She subsequently joined a performing troupe, found employment in a secondary school and engaged in wide range of activities in the public sphere. Zeinab (Birmingham), who arrived in the 1970s in a traditional family, found that support from wider society enabled her to secure a good position in the city council and to host a radio programme on the regional channel, while holding a leadership position in politics. She explained that she would not have had such a career in her country of origin because of gender discrimination: 'would Radio Pakistan give me a job? No'. Ahlam (Birmingham) pointed out that non-educated women were also able to take part in activities outside their home through government schemes in the inner city.

Moreover, certain public funding initiatives favoured Muslim women's participation since the presence of women on the steering committees of community organisations was a prerequisite to the award of a grant. In the realm of mainstream politics, the opportunities offered were evidenced by several of the women interviewed who had found support to run for councillor and MP positions within the ranks of the Respect Party and the Labour Party, and more rarely among other parties; some Muslim women held parliamentary seats and a good number had won local council seats such as Sabreena, 37 years of age and a local councillor and parliamentary candidate in Birmingham, and Manar, 26 years old and a solicitor and local councillor in Manchester.

9/11 and 7/7

The events of 9/11 and in particular 7/7 spread fear among Muslim communities and brought about repressive anti-terrorist laws (Kapoor 2013: 1029). Marjani (London) took stock of the backlash against Asians and Muslims caused by terrorist events in 2001 and 2005. In the same vein, Sabreena (Birmingham) noted the subduing of Muslim voices which hesitated to protest against the war in Afghanistan and Iraq 'because we were so desperate to fit in that we can't be seen with the trouble makers'. The 9/11 and 7/7 events generated suspicions and hostility towards Muslims, but also produced unintended consequences in terms of opportunities for Muslim women to participate in the public sphere. Indeed, the 9/11 events acted as a catalyst for Muslim women who were thus projected to the forefront; in the words of Sadiqa (Coventry), a Masters student in International Relations who had not paid much attention to Muslim issues before 9/11: 'I was given a role as a spokesperson'. Paradoxically, despite an adverse conjuncture whereby anti-Muslim prejudice had escalated and notwithstanding constraints placed on Muslim communities, Sabreena (Birmingham) rose to a leadership position largely through the support of White activists. In this instance, some sectors of British society acted against gender and ethnic stereotypes so that it 'created a reality' which gave Muslim women a central role in a movement where Muslim men would normally have been expected to dominate. The 7/7 London transport bombings further contributed to the widening of Muslim women's participation in the public domain. The fresh involvement of Muslim women in political activism prompted the government to develop policies which were designed to harness Muslim women's participation in the fight against terrorism, on the assumption that they could constitute a moderate element in their communities. This had the unintended effect of enabling some women's organisations to take their respective collective projects forward. Nadeema who founded a performing arts company, in 2004, involving Muslim women, thus gained recognition and funding whereas she had previously struggled to do so. This is even more marked in the case of Afiya (Birmingham), leader of a Muslim women's network, who remarked that before 7/7, 'the government were only engaging with Muslim men'. After the 7/7 events, she was recognised as a key interlocutor by the government, whose aim was to promote views they perceived would challenge traditional and 'extremist' Islamic views.

The women generally recognised that living in British society afforded them greater opportunities as women and they reiterated their will to participate. Lulu (Birmingham) stressed the importance of belonging to the society she lived in, while at the same time remembering where she came from. By way of a conclusion, Sabreena (Birmingham) emphasised her Britishness and rebuked people who might ask her to choose between being British and being Muslim. This was a firm stance expressed by the vast majority of the women interviewed.

Majority Society: France

Muslim women's attitudes and opinions about French society span over a wide spectrum which is indubitably more polarised than for their counterparts in Britain. In France, some of the women forcefully stated that French society rejected them or made it impossible to retain their identity as Muslims while being accepted as French. Moreover, several of the women who had not personally suffered from racial or religious discrimination, nonetheless, underlined the persistent prejudices against Muslims, Arabs and Blacks they had witnessed. On the other hand, a fair number of the women interviewed were perfectly comfortable in French society. A variety of nuances intervened along that spectrum. We now turn to the more positive perception of the women's interaction with French society.

A Positive Perception

A good number of women did not find that they encountered problems in France on account of their origins, and they felt good about their social environment. For instance, Imoni (Paris), a 20-year-old practising Muslim of Algerian parents who wore a *hijab*, counted mostly non-Muslim French people among her friends; and Salima (Paris), 46, of Algerian background, founder of a bookshop and a cultural centre, had 'not encountered xenophobia' in any of her employment positions. Several women emphasised the benefits they had gained from the structural and institutional contexts. Farah (Paris), 40, born in Paris of Algerian parents, did not hesitate to praise the French welfare state which permitted her to study, thanks to supportive grants, and she stated unequivocally: 'it is the French Republic that made me'. In addition, there were situations whereby a few women found in French institutions and civil society solid support against unbearable situations of oppression. Ezina, 22, born in Guinea and living in Paris, was contemplating suicide when she became aware of community and statutory organisations/agents which could help her, for instance, the social work service, Aide sociale à l'enfance (a statutory children's aid agency) and Voix d'elles rebelles (who provided help to women victims of violence) and local authority representatives. This launched her trajectory of engagement and she appreciated the support of both the local authority and the third sector when she set up a community organisation and wrote a book about her experience.

Other women gave examples of support from certain institutions; for example, in Paris, Lina, a 60-year-old of Algerian background, spoke of getting help from the Family Planning service which provided rent-free premises for her organisation which assisted irregular migrant women, those women who suffered domestic violence and whose children were taken away by their husband. Lutfiyah, from Nanterre, quoted her good relationship with the local authority which had agreed the purchase of premises towards a prayer hall and cultural activities. Besides those benefitting from local support, a few organisations received official recognition and assistance from the national government such as Ni Putes Ni Soumises whose president was co-opted to a ministerial post under Nicolas Sarkozy's presidency. In the realm of party politics, several women were able to pursue a political path thanks to the backing of mainstream politicians and party structures. Bassema (Paris), a Senator, was strongly assisted in her political career by a prominent male politician, and Najima (Saint-Fons, Lyon), encouraged by non-Muslim colleagues, became a councillor successively in two constituencies. Naja (Paris), an academic, was co-opted as adviser to the Minister for Family and Childhood, in the Jospin government in 2000.

A more informative overview begs the question as to who, among the women, and what amidst their organisations or projects, found favour with institutions. It is worth noticing that most of the organisations in receipt of support and enjoying a good relationship with institutions tended to be those which promoted secular social and educational projects. Nonetheless, negotiations and pragmatic accommodation about religious interests and headscarves occurred on the ground, as documented in other pieces of research (Bertossi 2016). Notwithstanding, although the public arena displays a haphazardly diversified attitude, our data disclose a hardening of public discourse and positions vis-à-vis Islam and its followers.

Exclusion

The positive testimonies forwarded by several of the women interviewed do not detract from the fact that the feeling of exclusion experienced by many remained a major issue. In the first place, all squarely negated the accusation often levelled at the populations concerned, that the latter were not prepared to integrate. Several women argued that French society itself was responsible for integration deficits, such as 34 year old Aman (Paris), of Algerian background, who identified ghettoisation and discrimination as prime exclusionary factors. One critical issue confronting the women was that they were frequently interrogated about their relationship to cultures of origin. France has often been charged with pursuing an assimilationist approach, predicated on a single identification to French culture matched with the discarding of one's parents' culture. Indeed, many of the women felt that being different in any way precluded acceptation as a member of the French collective. Asala (Mantes-la-Jolie) deplored the intolerance which marked out difference as a preclusive factor to Frenchness. Emani (Saint-Denis), 19, of Senegalese origin, found behind the term 'French' the naturalisation of a biological characteristic rather than a nationality, concluding that to have a Black skin at the same time as being French 'did not exist'. Negative images and stereotypes were recurrent themes raised by the women. Imoni (Paris), of Algerian origin, had personally been labelled 'riff raff', a common insult directed to North African people of the *banlieue*; suffice it to mention Nicolas Sarkozy's interjection about the 'racaille' when he visited the *banlieue* of Argenteuil on 26 October 2005. Furthermore, women suffered from compounded prejudices. For instance, Diana (Paris) denounced the prevalent image of Black women as uneducated persons confined to a cleaner's job. Radia (Paris) exposed the discrepancy between official version and practice, a discourse which peddled equality and fraternity whereas discrimination 'kept increasing'. More worryingly, one ran the risk of losing attributes of one's identity as a result of discrimination. Salima (Paris), organiser of a bookshop and cultural activities, was shocked by the predicament of a close family friend who was expressly asked to change his Arab name and surname by the company that wished to appoint him in a director's post.

Islam

Islam was earmarked as a major exclusionary factor. Louisa (Paris) sounded the alarm about a situation which *de facto* led to the exclusion of Muslims. There is evidence of a strong discrepancy between self-definition by many of the women (as French Muslims) and the frequent categorisation by wider society (of Muslim therefore not French), which foists on them a Procustes test to match the characteristics deriving from dominant ideas. Several declared that they were caught on the horns of an impossible dilemma if they were religious. Against prevalent ideas that Islam was incompatible with France, a notion corroborated by an opinion poll reported in *Le Figaro*

(7 November 2013), many Muslim women interviewed claimed a dual cultural base and stressed that it was an enrichment (Wahida, Fontenay-sous-Bois), a comment supported by data from previous research (Joly 2001). Derifa (Paris), a highly qualified author, who strongly felt both Muslim and French, denounced the 'presumption of foreignness' vis-à-vis Muslims on the part of French society. One pernicious outcome of the stigma attached to Islam was such that some of the women interiorised it, some of them striving not to 'be noticed' (Raja, Nanterre), others 'apologising' for their beliefs (Ghufran, Paris), which was symptomatic of the behaviour pertaining to a persecuted group. Similarly, Louisa (Paris) carefully hid her faith for fear that it could be detrimental to her career prospects in teaching. To make matters worse, the women noted the deleterious effect of the 9/11 events conjuring up terrorism as an attribute of Islam (Louisa, Paris) and particularly affecting Muslim women who wore a headscarf because their religious persuasion was open for all to see. Hamida (Mantes la Jolie) was the target of insults and threats in the street, people acting as though 'she had personally piloted the planes'.

Many women shared the sentiment that they were imprisoned in stereotypes. Several of them objected to the requirement to conform to a specific sexual mould in order to be accepted into the French national community, a theme that was documented through previous research. One researcher evidenced the categories imposing a choice between two dichotomous models: either Muslim women are considered as an incarnation of modernity and a vector of integration for their group of origin, in which case they must shed all attachment to family culture and practice, or they fit the image of native obscurantism in the best orientalist tradition (Guénif-Souilamas 2000: 94). One package includes reproducing tradition, maintaining links with the family, observing customs, adhering to a faith and preserving one's virginity. The alternative combination demands that they break with their family, denounce their culture and embrace modernity, pursue their education in opposition to customs, and are advocates of *laïcité* and claim their sexual liberation (Guénif-Souilamas 2000: 51). Despite changing circumstances, Barbara (1992: 18, 19) posits that Muslim women are locked into 'an orientalist stereotype' which commands that they be, at the same time, modern and fitting an orientalist imaginaire. Delphy refers to a double bind requiring that they should be the same as the majority population, while being portrayed as different by the latter (Delphy 2008: 149). Sexuality and sexual behaviour appeared to be the lynch pin in the eyes of their social environment in France. Louisa (Paris),

23, strongly opposed the injunction to choose between being 'integrated', 'liberated' and sexually rather promiscuous (at least sexually active outside marriage), or to match the presumption of submissiveness. She yet advocated a different model of modernity that would suit her.

Prejudices against Islam hindered Muslim women's societal participation and created increased difficulties for individual or collective action. Over and above issues of perception, structural constraints such as those concerning the wearing of a headscarf may act as a self-fulfilling prophecy with respect to the assumption that Muslim women are confined in the home. Indeed, the women who were barred from studies they may have wished to pursue might give up and resign themselves to getting married and raising children. As Imoni (Paris) stated, 'society did not offer any alternative'.

The Headscarf

Many spheres of employment are closed to headscarf-wearing women, namely, all public institutions and organisations delivering a public service. This situation can lead to the loss of a position if a woman decides to wear a headscarf, like Lutfiyah (Nanterre), who held a position of high responsibility in France Telecom and had to resign. Moreover, the promulgation of the law prohibiting the *hijab* in state educational establishments has generated a novel situation for women who wear it. This means that a number of young girls excluded from school on such grounds may not have access to the same quality of education as that open to their peers, and they are pretty much confined at home within narrow social circles. Altogether, prejudices appear to be reinforced as a result of the law and seem to have placed Muslim women under scrutiny.

At the same time, it was not guaranteed that wearing a headscarf in circumstances where it was not prohibited by law remained unproblematic. In higher educational establishments, where the 2004 law does not apply, it is not unusual for members of staff to demand that it be removed. This was Asala's (Mantes-la-Jolie) experience, a student at a prestigious selective higher education institution. Moreover, one significant development was that headscarf prohibition seemed to spread *de facto* from the public to the private sector. In the first place, the notion of 'public' was sometimes interpreted in the most extensive manner possible, beyond what reasonable logic would expect. For instance, in a private medical centre, the headscarf was not permitted 'on account of the patients' (Gulcin, Paris). This state of affairs had a forceful impact on Muslim women's capacity of action, with women who wore a headscarf being barred access to vast areas of the public space and institutions and beyond. Indeed, even charities sometimes closed the door to headscarf-wearing women, such as happened to one woman interviewed who volunteered to work for the Restos du Coeur (a national food bank charity). Similar incidents were reported in the media (*Le Monde* 11 November 2013).

There is an effective 'colonisation' of the private by the public space on the issue of the *hijab*. Kadija (Livry-Gargan), a *hijab*-wearing computer analyst, was incensed at the attitude of potential employers, which often changed in the space of time between the telephone interview and the face-to-face meeting; consequently she worked as a childminder. Intricate processes of interaction between majority society and Muslim women were illustrated by the headscarf. The headscarf might not in itself constitute an artefact of Islamness so that what mattered was the meaning of it, either as assumed by Muslim women or attributed by majority society: the religious rather than cultural dimension invoked by the woman who wore it or simply presumed by outsiders sufficed to demonise it (Ghufran, Paris). A power relation underpinned the significance of the headscarf which could entail acceptance or rejection by majority society. Discrimination was compounded by having to guard against the reading of one's mind or what was ascribed to it (cultural or religious), creating a big brother situation comparable to Orwell's 1984. Furthermore, several women argued that gendered discrimination followed from a distinctive sign not displayed by men (Kadija, Livry-Gargan). Raja (Nanterre) reached the conclusion that the state colluded in the very situation which it denounced, namely, the seclusion and submission of Muslim women.

Discrimination was also directed at what could be called a 'virtual' headscarf. Natara (Paris), who worked in education, was subjected to harassment by her head teacher when the latter came to know that she was a practising Muslim, although she did not display any visible signs of her religion. Accused of treason and contravening the good functioning of the school, she resigned. Comments and prejudices were extended to general clothing and diet. A mode of clothing or abstinence from alcohol could attract the same reaction as the headscarf and constituted a type of 'virtual' *hijab*.

Laïcité

Questions pertaining to French institutional structures and political culture generated an animated and mature debate among the women in our SI focus groups, a testament of the women's engagement with French society. The question of *laïcité* and related issues elicited a multifaceted heterogeneity of opinions. Several of the women supported the notion of a duty to abide by the French constitution. Imoni (Paris) asserted the obligation for Muslims to adapt and respect the law in the name of a 'tacit' contract between them and France. In the opinion of Sahar, 46, and Safa, 44, who were both Paris-based activists for women's autonomisation and who were not practising Muslims, *laïcité* constituted a protection for women against fundamentalism. Emani (Saint-Denis), aged 19, whose Senegalese father was a religious teacher (*marabout*), appreciated the neutrality guaranteed by *laïcité* which protected her religious practice against interference from outsiders and insiders. Mounira, a 28-year-old Parisian doctoral student of Turkish parents and a practising Muslim belonging to a *Tariqa*, held that the responsibility of the school was to impart values other than religious ones and stated that she would quite willingly remove her headscarf in an educational environment if she entered the teaching profession. Najima (Saint-Fons, Lyon), a barrister and a councillor of Tunisian background, also a follower of a spiritual branch of Islam, advocated the separation of the private and public spheres in keeping with *laïcité*.

Furthermore, the discussion on *laïcité* took the women further and deeper than the simple matter of agreeing or disagreeing with '*laïcité*' as a given. Many of them entered into an analysis of its meaning and impact: they discussed the text and the spirit of the 1905 law; they examined its interpretation and implementation and criticised the political instrumentalisation of it. It is worth noting that those who questioned and criticised it were not necessarily believers or practising Muslims. Layla, 33, born in France and a postgraduate student who was not a believer, deemed the law of 2004 against the headscarf at school a frank attack on *laïcité* which she held as guaranteeing the neutrality of the state vis-à-vis religions. In Rida's (Paris) view, religion was a private affair and the notion of *laïcité* won her approval but she did not deem that wearing a headscarf at school constituted a problem in terms of *laïcité*. Nedira (Paris), a dentist of Moroccan background who wore a headscarf, indicted what she called the interpretation of 'laïc extremists'. Keltoum (Paris), 40, of Algerian background, who called herself a 'private' Muslim, was personally opposed to the headscarf and would never wear one, but she was concerned that the rigid application of *laïcité* had largely fed and was being mirrored by an increasingly inflexible interpretation of Islam in France.

The range of opinions on *laïcité* did not follow a believer/non-believer divide. Indeed, more than half of the women who raised doubts on whether the legislation and implementation of *laïcité* was well-founded were not Muslim believers. Hiba (Paris), 30, of Algerian background and a leader of a political party, indicted *laïcité* for constituting an ideological weapon of the French state to stigmatise Muslims, reducing them to a situation comparable to colonisation. She held that racism against Arabs had turned into racism against Muslims, and *laïcité* constituted a tool of White male domination which disempowered Muslim women by confiscating their control over what they wished to wear under cover of liberating them. In her view, this 'unveiling' matched the orientalist tradition that made 'oriental women' sexually available to White males. Hiba also charged *laïcité* with using Muslim women as the Trojan horse of assimilation, to eliminate the cultures of formerly colonised people, in order to ensure the domination of the 'French one'. Naja (Paris), 40, of Algerian origin, an academic and an atheist, accused *laïcité* of 'essentialising' religion with its cortège of pernicious consequences. She advanced that it caused the depolitisation of Muslims and the stigmatisation of Islam, which in turn provoked group enclosure. Moreover, the belittling of Islam caused young Muslim men to increase control over Muslim women and hampered the emancipation of the latter. Najima (Saint Fons, Lyon) also deplored the deleterious effect of the 2004 law on the destiny of young Muslim women who, withdrawn from school, saw their opportunities reduced.

Many women quoted incidents which illustrated the way the hegemonic culture of contemporary *laïcité* had been well-strengthened by the 2004 law, and how it favoured its spreading to areas of the public and private domains where the legislation did not apply. Women who held leadership positions tended to fall on either side of a positional divide. A number were clearly favourable to *laïcité* even if some deplored the consequences of its strict application. This group might include atheists or practising Muslims; the latter generally followed a Sufi school of Islam and/or were what they called 'private Muslims'. Others who were very critical of *laïcité* included atheists who held political positions against racism and Islamophobia, as well as religious women who claimed a place for Islam in the public space.

Muslim Women and Action

This section is dedicated to Muslim women's capacity of action in the pursuit of their participation projects. It interrogates the parameters of engagement, namely, the mechanisms and factors which may lead to participation in the public domain and asks what are the sources of their political/civic interests. The section then traces the strategies adopted by the women to overcome obstacles and take advantage of enablers, so that they become capable of engaging in action according to the situational guidance offered by structural and cultural emergent properties. This includes presenting the main themes which motivate them.

Politics and the Parameters of Engagement

We established in previous chapters that traditional political science has often depicted the limited interest of women in politics. This view often endures although it was subsequently challenged by feminist scholars, partly through their redefinition of the field of politics (Chowdhury and Nelson 1994: 18; Githens et al. 1994: ix–xvi). To compound general assumptions about women and politics, widespread stereotypes of Muslim women as passive, submissive and thus outsiders to the political domain have continued to prevail as dominant ideas; the women themselves were not impervious to such a postulation. Indeed, when asked if they took an interest in and/or knew about politics, many of the women interviewed initially seemed to conform to the expectation that politics was a man's domain. As one of them exclaimed, 'My husband knows a lot about politics' (Adelmira, Birmingham). Another recurrent attitude is that of women who declared that they did 'not wish to get involved in politics', in the same breath describing their participation in civic organisations and/or institutions, such as Sultana (Birmingham) who 'left politics to the men' in her family, while she wielded a noticeable amount of influence on the management of a secondary school as a member of the board of governors.

Our research evidences Muslim women's interest in politics, straddling generations and ethnic or national origin, in both France and Britain. In the first place, almost all of them found that it was important to vote and went some way to refute the arguments of Muslims who promoted isolationism. The women were not impressed or taken in by politicians' conceitedness and 'lack of substance', talk about 'froth' (Sabreena,

Birmingham). Zeinab (Birmingham) derided and mocked the politicians she grilled on her radio programme, who were ill-prepared for her sharpness. Moreover, most of the women demonstrated an incontestable 'political' insight into political issues on the national and international level. Although Muslim women often hesitated to advance their viewpoint in public, this did not blunt their acumen. The best illustration of Muslim women's grasp of politics was supplied by Farah (Paris), who summarised what political engagement meant with a clarity surpassing that proposed by many: 'to be involved in the life of the city' (in the Greek 'polis' sense of the word).

Undoubtedly, many of the women expressed their interest and related their involvement in an impressive array of initiatives pertaining to the civic and political field, despite varied material and cultural obstacles being thrown in their path. This poses a question about the parameters and mechanisms which lie behind the women's engagement in action. In the first instance, it is worth characterising the kind of action undertaken. It is clear that their action does not lie in the realm of *habitus* (Bourdieu 1977: 95), since it is deliberately engaged in and reflected upon rather than routinely performed within accepted norms. Neither do those situations involve rational choice with a utilitarian objective, since most of this action is value-oriented drawing on *Weltrationalitat* (Weber 1978: 24, 25). In the main, their action was subjectively oriented in the pursuit of aspirations and concerns. The women encountered obstacles in structural and cultural frameworks, which impeded the pursuit of their concerns and the realisation of their projects within their immediate socialisation group (the family and the community) and within wider society. Amidst their ethnic group, many were facing a broadly patriarchal structure and assigned social roles which incorporated constraints. In wider society, racial discrimination, Islamophobia, social stratification, stereotypes about Muslim women, and general gender relations lined up another set of obstacles. Ideology and the women's own internalisation of difficulties completed this assortment. Although they were largely conscious of their environment and retained an interpretative freedom about their choice of action, awareness of objective realities was not sufficient to generate engagement. For this to give rise to action, it needs to acquire some significance for the women who must gain a heightened consciousness of the tensions that stand in the pursuit of their concerns and projects (Archer 2007: 17, 18), a motivation to overcome obstructions and a realisation that something can be done about it. We ground our findings about Muslim women's engagement in politics on the proposition that their action rests on the coming together of three parameters: an awareness of contradictions/tensions in the structural and cultural framework, an emotional commitment to concerns and issues and the confidence to engage in action oriented towards change.

An Awareness of Contradictions and Tensions in the Structural and Cultural Framework

One important parameter in the development of Muslim women's engagement is their awareness of tensions and contradictions in their environment. This is facilitated by their position as strangers, which stands them in good stead to grasp that the material and social reality surrounding them is not to be taken for granted but lends itself to questioning, because they are both insiders and outsiders in their immediate socialisation group and in wider society (Simmel 1964). *Ad minima*, their station as members of minority groups uncovers discrepancies, since they belong to an ethnic/racial minority whose roots have foreign origins, and to a religious minority with worldwide connections; they also live in a society with different characteristics to that of their minority reference groups. Previous research on young people of ethnic minority background revealed that they had a particularly sharp capacity of critical analysis about the structural and cultural framework shaping their life (Joly 2001). Muslim women are in the main at the interconnection of many tensions within their immediate socialisation group and in wider society, on account of their gender, their ethnicity, their religion and, in many cases, because they belong to socially disadvantaged strata in society. Although culture and ideology may have gone some way to mask these realities, the women displayed a sharp understanding of their social environment and of political discourse or manipulations.

Regarding relationships within the ethnic group, they deciphered with lucidity their disadvantage in relations of power within a patriarchal model. This held no mystery to the women who were not deceived by the cultural rationale imposing norms and rules, and they contested men's privileged position. Moreover, they appraised this model as tied to time and place, the society of origin, tradition and culture, well aware that it was fraught with tensions and undergoing modifications. Regarding Islam, many women exposed how Islam had been turned into an ideological instrument to better control women, while others remarked that living in a non-Muslim-majority country awarded a greater capacity to interrogate their own religion. The women also had a fair appreciation of the framework which informed their situation in wider society. They were acutely conscious of their group's potential disadvantages linked to 'race', religion and social strata. They evaluated the contradictions which traversed society and the political instrumentalisation turning ethnic minorities and Muslims into scapegoats. For example, they spent a good deal of time discussing the emergence of Islam, and the re-Islamisation taking place in France and Britain and provided the contours of an analysis which accounted for the resurgence of Islam in those countries. In their view, it stemmed from the discrimination and exclusion of Muslims which exacerbated a search for the recognition of their cultural and/or religious heritage. They also acknowledged that Islam met aspirations to conciliate multiple identities in dignity, and did not lose sight of the central role played by international events, namely, the backlash resulting from scenarios such as in 9/11 which had made them the target of exacerbated prejudice and hostility. In the main, the women attributed this re-Islamisation to the societal context and its cortège of rejection, exclusion, poverty, stigmatisation and the like. Several women in both countries related the choice of religious vestimentary codes as a response to foreign aggression against Muslim countries (Souhila, London; Sultana, Birmingham), the marginalisation of young people, ghettoes and humiliations (Natori, Paris; Salima, Paris). For some of the more politically active women like Hiba (Paris), reclaiming Islam did not include religious or cultural connotations but signified a political position against stigmatisation and exclusion, further strengthened by the state's position against Islamic dress in France. On the whole, most of the women (Aman, Paris) saw through dominant discourses and denounced the politics and even territorial issues hiding behind debates on religion, on the national as well as international plane. The women extended their critical analysis to many other questions and proved particularly perspicacious when it came to evaluating politicians' discourse and manipulation.

Emotional Commitment to Concerns and Issues

The women were not only able to rationally analyse their situation but the latter also generated a plethora of reasons conducive to an emotional and moral reaction against what they perceived as injustice worthy of intervention: those included issues of gender inequality, racial and religious discrimination, social disadvantage, human rights and general ethical questions.

Gender

In the first place, as *women* they suffered a general disadvantage in wider society. One vast area which incited an emotional reaction among most women interviewed was their condition as unequal to men in so many domains, a structural feature whatever the cultural or religious social milieu (Sultana, Birmingham). They also passionately contested constraints which derived from their cultural background, regarding access to education, employment and engagement in public spheres. These questions aroused impassioned responses such as Reema's (Birmingham) indignant refutation of her husband's smug pronouncement that he 'allowed' her to study; she claimed instead the unalloyed right to do so: 'aren't I a human being'. Education was indeed a central concern which motivated a good number of women in France and Britain to become active in initiatives to promote Muslim women's education. Another source of anxiety was the unwelcome pressure towards an early marriage inflicted on young women (Ulema, Birmingham). Even more sinister was the threat of gender-based violence which the women totally reviled. Those themes fuelled vehement condemnation from all the women interviewed, so much so that several had been prompted to engage in action to provide advice, support and hope contributing to or creating refuges for women victims of domestic violence. Zakiya (Rotherham), herself a victim of sexual abuse as a child, had founded an organisation that offered counselling and refuge accommodation to women. Ezina (Paris), who had endured extreme domestic violence, dedicated herself to helping women in a similar plight through a community organisation, and wrote a book to publicise her successful escape.

Ethnic and Racial Discrimination

Secondly, as *ethnic/racial minorities* Muslim women were likely to have faced some kind of prejudice and discrimination either personally or through family, acquaintances, the media and hearsay. In wider society, the discrepancy between discourse and practice sharpened dissatisfaction but also supplied ideals which could be deemed worth pursuing, such as the claim to the equal worth of human beings (in the Established Church), or the republican phraseology of French politicians. In France, the women decried the hypocrisy behind the slogan of 'Liberty, Equality and Fraternity' declaimed by politicians, while inequality reigned between nationals of different origins, well-evidenced by the unequal treatment and the 'misery of neighbourhoods inhabited by ethnic minorities' (Salima, Paris). Racism and racial discrimination remained well-entrenched in Europe, often augmented with lack of respect and humiliations. Consequently, any evocation of it instantly attracted the women's demonstrative condemnation. Moreover, unlike the sense of gender inequality which could be mitigated through family loyalty and emotional attachment, the wrong involved in racial inequality was perceived as irredeemable. In France, many of the older women had taken part in the mobilisation against racist crimes and for citizenship rights in the 1980s. In Britain, the 1970s had witnessed mass mobilisations against race discrimination and against racist immigration laws. In addition to racism and discrimination directed at non-White citizens, several of the women denounced certain immigration and integration policy and measures. Naima (Paris) was outraged at the arrest of an undocumented migrant in front of the nursery where he waited for his grandson, an experience which had motivated her involvement with Réseau Education Sans Frontières (RESF). The strong sense of wrong expressed by the women was testified by their engagement in a variety of actions to denounce racism: taking part in demonstrations, joining local organisations to redress racial disadvantage, voting, becoming active in mainstream political parties or in other organisations such as the Indigènes de la République.

Islam

Thirdly, Muslim women belonged to communities of *Muslim* background and they were plagued by a double handicap: on the one hand, traditional and political Islam frequently set up constraints on women; on the other hand, the latter were likely to suffer from the negative image of Islam on the national and international scene. The theme of Islam rarely failed to provoke emotional responses on the part of the women in our study from a great variety of vantage points. Islam *per se* elicited a vigorous refutation on the part of several non-believers, who read in Islam an intrinsic inequality between men and women and mobilised against such inequality. Those women made a point of avoiding any initiative to which the name of Islam was attached and engaged in secular spheres. Women who were believers expressed their indignation at modes and schools of Islam which interfered with their autonomisation in multiple aspects of their life. This entailed that Muslim women generally kept away from most mosques and traditional Muslim organisations, which in any case were mainly male preserves. It had induced the search for a different interpretation of Islam more suited to their life in Europe and their autonomisation. For most women who were believers, Islam constituted a lever for action in the shape of a strong moral driving force to act for the defence of human values, privately and in the public space.

Wider society's hostility to Islam regularly prompted the women's engagement. In Britain, the 9/11 and 7/7 events and the backlash against Muslims have converted many Muslim women into spokespersons for Islam. A good number have become active in the Stop-the-War campaign and protests in defence of their Muslim rights. In France, Muslim women have become the hostages of an anti-Islam systemic offensive, and numerous women interviewed were incensed by the numerous obstacles set in their path if they chose to adopt a particular dress code; so that they had taken steps to defend their religious rights, while at the same time asserting their citizenship rights.

Human Rights

The women's transnational networks and their international links supplied an additional potential basis for concerns. Their origins lay in the developing world and for many of them in former colonies where a national liberation struggle had taken place prior to independence. The population in most of those countries were in the grip of poverty and lacked basic resources, often compounded by undemocratic regimes or an Islamist terrorist menace. Although their preoccupation around racism and discrimination centred on France and Britain, many of the women accorded a good deal of importance to human rights across the world. In a few cases, the women or their family had been direct victims of human rights violations, which prompted them to become active in related initiatives. Furthermore, Muslim women partook of a religion, offshoots of which were considered either as a threat on the national plane or as the world's public enemy number one, and found their origins in countries where Islam was a majority religion and had been the target of military or other kind of intervention. One prime question related to the War on Terror, particularly among British women, undoubtedly because of Prime Minister Tony Blair's identification with Bush's military intervention in Afghanistan and Iraq. A good many of the women interviewed had demonstrated against the war in Iraq and were members of the Stop-the-War campaign. Other concerns included their indignation about Israel's treatment of Palestinians which they translated into participation in demonstrations and meetings in both Britain and France. Muslim countries themselves fell foul of the women's opinion, like Saudi Arabia with its multiple discriminations, or Pakistan for its treatment of women and those with disabilities.

Poverty and Social Inequality

Muslim women's sense of justice also related to socio-economic discrepancies and class contradictions. Indeed, many of these women belonged to disadvantaged strata since most of the population of Muslim background had joined the working class on arrival in Europe. This frequently led them to develop an identification with the socially disadvantaged across the board and to espouse causes linked to social justice. This was the case of Cantara (Paris) who was 'passionate about social justice', who had joined a neighbourhood organisation which provided social assistance, and Sabreena (Birmingham) who was 'shocked that 440 people in the world own half of the world's resources' and who had become a founding member of a party whose programme promoted social justice nationally and internationally. Altogether, the women expressed an absolute rejection of the *Zeitgeist* which they associated with money, neo-liberalism and individualism which negated any kind of solidarity. Most of the women clearly abhorred the prevalent doctrine of neo-liberalism and the undermining of the welfare state which together is seen to have dismantled the social fabric of British society. International natural disasters also motivated an upsurge of support and generosity on the part of many of the women in France and Britain who sent funds to Tsunami victims in Indonesia for instance.

Ethics

Altogether, it is indubitable that women of Muslim background who were interviewed had a heightened sentiment of what was right and wrong, just and unjust. Humanity was a paramount worth espoused by the women together with universal values, free from particularism. Much of the women's engagement was generated by their ethical sense, as illustrated by a selection of issues which have motivated their action as follows. Many women were active in the defence of general citizenship and social rights which included equal access to employment and labour rights, students' rights, the right to health care, the right to quality education for all and in particular for Muslim women, the promotion of Muslim women's opportunities for sport and cultural activities, the right to vote for long-term residents, opposition to caste-based inequality. Racial and religious discrimination in all domains mobilised many of the women, whether it be racism, Islamophobia, ethnic minority youth exclusion, Muslim women specific discrimination. The whole area of gender-related oppression within the ethnic group proffered another rallying concern for many of the women, which comprised domestic violence, forced marriage, excision, the ability to pursue an education, the ability to enter employment, male leaders/community control, women's isolation, the infantilisation of Muslim women. International matters inspired an interest in human rights, humanitarian questions, military aggression, terrorism, poverty and underdevelopment. The women engaged in a variety of initiatives to uphold these causes. They were carried by an enhanced sense of what they deemed unjust and ethically wrong, promoting solidarity against individualism and neo-liberalism, human universal values against the defence of specific interests. Those values provided the underpinning to their motivation for acting.

On one or several of the grounds examined above, the women developed an enhanced sense of disapproval, outrage or identification with a cause. This process could arise gradually or be the outcome of a catalysing incident which rendered tensions salient and uncovered their significance for the women. For instance, Sabreena awoke to the vulnerability of Muslims when she was aggressed in Birmingham city centre in the wake of 9/11. The assassination of Aman's (Paris) brother by Islamists in Algeria was a brutal wake-up call for action. The 2004 law on conspicuous religious symbols at school in France, Britain sending troops to Afghanistan and Iraq furnished strong grounds for protest and mobilisation. These concerns and commitments were often translated into participation in some form of action, in accordance with each person's sensitivity to specific issues at a particular point in time. Tensions that traversed their life were experienced differently by different individuals and the set of problems which emerged more prominently changed along the course of their life. This gave rise to a great diversity in the meaning and site of their engagement, one area of concern potentially yielding primacy to another, according to what was perceived as principal or secondary contradictions at particular points in their life.

Capacity to Engage in Action

The women's ability to engage in the public sphere is related to two elements: forming a vision that change is achievable and progressing their own capacity to act. Firstly, the apprehension that changes are conceivable is facilitated by the heterogeneity of experiences in their multilayered environment which points to the potentiality of alternative realities. Tensions and contradictions are numerous within each and across references groups, each of them in turn being fraught with cleavages of more or less antagonistic nature, so that claims for multiple societal projects can be advanced. This is actualised for the women by the necessity to negotiate living in tranches of environments which are predicated on disparate outlooks and require differentiated behaviours: the ethnic group and wider society, home and school, family and friends, home and work, tradition and Islam, countries of origin and Europe. Social relations outside immediate social circles may stand in contrast with the home and community environment, while ideas presenting an alternative reality challenge viewpoints which present it as immutable. Being acquainted with a variety of national theatres of action through the family or the diaspora in other countries also discloses a mosaic of variegated structural and cultural properties. Change can be envisaged as a material possibility, thanks to the consciousness of the anfractuosities and contradictions within systems and actors, the realisation that strengths versus weaknesses in the balance of power indicate avenues of action and the notion that transformation is attainable. In addition, serendipity intervenes when a change of circumstances occurs, which disrupts the routine and habitual state of things, supporting a belief that things are not static and can open unforeseen opportunities; for instance, migration, a move to a new neighbourhood, parents' divorce. By the same token, unfavourable alterations also point to previous better ways, particularly if they are sudden enough not to instil habituation.

Secondly, Muslim women must find ways of developing their own capacity of action. The latter draws on various possible sources which encompass resources of an external character in their environment, as well as subjective variables such as their determination and confidence in the capacity to act. One cornerstone of the edifice is the sentiment that they are justified in devoting time and energy to the public sphere, diverting it from motherhood and other family responsibilities. This process can be envisaged in terms of building blocks which enable the women to overcome obstacles and take advantage of facilitating factors, often through support available. The women are clear that education constitutes a pivotal instrument which equips them to engage in action in the public sphere, both in terms of access to knowledge and as a strong booster of confidence; moreover, it provides contacts and potential avenues for collective action. Many of the women interviewed had initially been introduced to public participation at university and sometimes at school. Employment outside home fulfils a similar role in terms of networks and openings for action, with the added advantage of accruing economic autonomy. This helps to loosen their dependence on family and/or husbands, both objectively because the women acquire their own resources and, subjectively as it validates a justification in taking their own decision. Our empirical data thus confirms the significance of education and employment, which has been noted repeatedly by scholars of gender and politics. Nonetheless, many obstacles potentially stand in the way of gaining access to quality education and employment, either from the family and community or from wider society. An even greater number of considerations need to be taken into account for the realisation of engagement in the public sphere. Obstacles have been analysed above in this book which broadly included family and community constraints, impediments pertaining to Islam and its interpretations, structural and cultural barriers from wider society. We shall now turn to the categories of factors which help women to engage in individual and/or collective action.

Individual Support

Support for the women's aspirations in their life project often comes from influential individuals. The latter can be located in the family such as a father, an uncle, a mother or a husband, sometimes an elder in the community who may extend moral and/or material support. It can also be found among other significant persons such as a doctor or a teacher, the latter being regularly mentioned by our respondents. For many women, education was the first building block which launched them into a job and participation projects. For instance, Najima's (Saint Fons, Lyon) confidence to read law was boosted by teachers' encouragement, and she then pursued a variety of political initiatives for equality of opportunity and against domestic violence. Where women have become active in party politics, on many occasions, they benefitted from the help of a prominent party member or a cluster of sympathetic members.

Environmental and Circumstantial Factors

A propitious social milieu unquestionably enhances the women's chances of engagement. The educational level of parents and their social status play a significant role in the women's capacity of action, awarding them social and cultural capital. Another significant enabler is the family's organisational and political experience, such as participation in a liberation movement, a political party, a trade union, a father who was a city councillor, a mother who was active in a feminist movement. In terms of family and community constraints, the women in both countries noted that their capacity to decide on individual and collective projects was heightened if they did not live in a dense community neighbourhood; for some women, the fact that their mother obtained a divorce was a decisive element in their greater autonomy. With respect to general resources, the social/territorial environment influenced what societal advantages they could draw upon. For instance, living away from the disadvantaged inner city and the *banlieue*, whether in a better area of the city or in smaller towns, reduced social and racial discrimination because it usually meant access to a better quality of education or to schools with a more auspicious social mix, favourable chances to gain employment, good socio-educational amenities, more access to culture and participation.

Legal and Structural Framework

The legal and structural framework together with institutions in majority society can provide significant assistance, as well as an outlet for women's action, thus palliating disadvantage. Welfare state agencies and material support constitute a valuable vector for the promotion of the women's life projects. Legislation and policies on race and religious discrimination have enabled some women to secure education, employment and participation in a number of public initiatives. Initiatives addressing victims of domestic violence have been facilitated by legal/policy instruments and institutional resources that helped some women to escape from it. On many occasions, it was reported that local government assisted with funding, premises and public recognition to women who were launching and running community organisations. Health and educational structures invited Muslim women as volunteers, for example, as parents' association representatives, members of school governing bodies, visitors in old people's homes and so on. Institutional structures such as the Défenseur des droits (an office of state responsible for defending citizens' rights) provided a resource women could draw upon.

Corporate Agents

One major facilitating factor for Muslim women's participation in politics is the existence of corporate agents (Archer 1995) which favour their concerns. Corporate agents appear in diverse forms including various political parties which welcome and seek out the participation of Muslim women, students organisations and trade unions which offer avenues of collective action. However, the bulk of participatory opportunities is supplied by civil society sites such as campaigns, NGOs and community organisations or associations. The staging of demonstrations to protest to defend a right or against an injustice attracted the participation of numerous women interviewed. The 'Marche pour l'égalité' and anti-racist law campaigns have involved a good number of women. The Stop-the-War campaign engaged numerous Muslim women in its actions, demonstrations and committees, many of which could boast a Muslim woman as regional/local secretary. In France, l'Ecole pour tous et pour toutes gathered a substantial number of Muslim women. The existence of numerous community organisations treating themes to which Muslim women were sensitive solicited a remarkable volume of participation. NGOs also gave participatory opportunities, like the Samaritans, the Ligue des Droits de l'Homme, the Citizens Advice Bureaux, Amnesty International, the Resto du Coeur, the Red Crescent.

Role Models

Finally, many women cite a central lever of action in the shape of role models and inspirational persons. For some of them it was a father who had fought in the liberation struggle in the homeland, a grandfather well-respected for his wisdom in the community, a mother who had joined a feminist movement. Encounters beyond immediate socialisation have completed or supplemented role models from inner circles. Individuals who have gained the respect and esteem of the women provided guidance such as a teacher, a work mate, a friend. Other women have found in public figures an encouragement to believe that engagement was possible: a political leader like Salma Yaqoob whose example was followed by many other young Muslim women; nationally known Muslim women in the media or in campaigns; on a local scale, a charismatic Muslim head teacher. All those components interconnect to enable and guide Muslim women to engage in civic and political activities on an impressive scale, as attested by our data. Small victories in autonomisation build confidence and add up to produce a virtuous circle towards an exponential progression. Furthermore, mobilising around a particular theme may be conducive to embracing other causes, and participation in one particular activity may be supplemented by other types of engagements.

A Typology of Strategies

Political and civic engagement is in no way a foregone conclusion or an easy path, even once the necessary parameters discussed above have come together. Myriad barriers first need to be overcome to realise one's engagement, so that the women chart an assortment of strategies in complex combinations to achieve their goal. There is a dynamic relationship between the character of the contradictions in place, the correlation of obstacles and enablers, the themes taken up, the objectives pursued, the modes of action and the choice of strategies. The women need to negotiate a variety of obstacles in their inner group, in wider society and among Muslim communities to pursue the causes to which they feel committed. Differentiated strategies are developed by the women in relation to the objective pursued and the zigzag of obstacles and enablers they encounter as per their bargaining powers and negotiating strengths (Archer 1995: 217). In practice, the women's action is implemented through making use of contradictions and evaluating the balance between obstacles and enablers in order to overcome the former while taking advantage of the latter, so that it becomes possible to engage in some form of political/ civic action. Although some arenas of action may lend themselves better to one strategy rather than another, most could be selected for any kind of situation. Moreover, it is not a matter of one single strategic avenue for one person, since the same person may adopt diverse manners of negotiating obstacles as a function of circumstances and of the specific objectives pursued. In the same way as personal matters are underpinned by political dimensions, the former frequently have a bearing on the balance of possibilities to engage in politics. For instance, we noted above that pursuing an education and entering employment not only formed assets in the ability to engage in civic and political participation but sometimes also constituted prerequisites to such an engagement, because it afforded a necessary measure of autonomisation and offered engagement opportunities. We shall now examine the repertoire of strategies enacted to pursue individual and collective life projects. Six main types of strategies have been identified which pertain to personal and public domains.

Confrontation

A confrontational approach is adopted when the contradictions are so antagonistic that no other path seems possible or when it is felt that confrontation will prove the most effective approach. It is also potentially the most risky and costly in personal terms. In a family situation, it implies a radical move such as breaking links with parents or divorcing a husband, which is the least frequent option chosen by the women in their personal environment because of its emotional cost. In the public sphere, it involves action such as taking part in prohibited demonstrations, helping to hide undocumented migrants, wearing a *burka* in a public space, in France, all of which involve infringing the law.

Cooperation

In some circumstances, no substantive contradiction bars the women from pursuing their project. The family may constitute an important source of values embedded in 'a cultural belief system' (Archer 1995: 211), favourable to the women's desire to undertake higher education and employment; their aspiration to get involved in politics can coincide with a family tradition and experience. Women whose values align with the politics of a particular party may find that the latter welcomes their participation; this may also apply to trade unions and other types of organisation which may be only too pleased to have women activists and members in their ranks.

Exit

The notion of exit does not exactly represent a strategy towards activism but it must be acknowledged. It stands in direct contrast with a confrontational approach and embodies situations where women abandon their project: they are resigned and withdraw, giving up outside engagement in the face of family opposition; emigrating to a Muslim-majority country because of hostility to one's religious practice, for example, leaving France for Britain to take up teaching while wearing a headscarf.

Lateral

Rather than frontally approaching obstacles, some women prefer to circumvent the latter, to attain their goal through a side step without losing sight of their objectives. For instance, rather than bluntly refusing an arranged marriage which would hamper their capacity of action, they may just postpone it and buy time to consolidate their autonomy and bargaining power. Women who were unwelcome in Muslim organisations controlled by men voted on their feet and created their own groups. In France, one frequent option chosen by women who wore a headscarf was to engage in community organisations since it was problematic to get involved in mainstream institutions and politics. To accommodate family and public responsibilities on a day-to-day level, solutions were devised through alternative modes of organising via telephone and the Internet.

Compromise

Compromise takes place a great deal in personal environments. For instance, women agreed on a husband proposed by parents against some measure of consultation. They fully took care of the home and children as a ticket to outside involvement. The privileging of compromise in the family is further enhanced by emotional attachment and the internalisation of some norms which some of them called alienation. In wider society, many women accepted to remove their headscarf in sectors where it caused a problem, as frequently happened in France.

Reversal

This strategy works from within the private and public framework. It turns the tables against the very system it is combatting, finding instruments and arguments in its own midst. One widespread undertaking among the women who wished to challenge ethnic traditions was to denounce them in the very name of Islam, to which all Muslim communities purportedly subscribed. In wider society, some women have argued in the name of ideals proclaimed by majority society and institutions: filing a court case against a state institution for discrimination, calling upon equality and *laïcité* in France on the grounds that both guaranteed freedom of conscience.

The strategies selected are influenced by the state of play and what the women evaluate as best destined to succeed. The mode of action chosen is also linked to the strategies deemed to obtain the best result possible, relative to the energy and cost involved.

Conclusion

In Britain the women took stock of a chronological evolution in the obstacles and opportunities presented by wider society. They registered the improvements that took place over the last three decades in terms of opportunities to study, work and engage in politics. They valued the anti-discrimination and multicultural policies which enabled them to pursue their life project, without the necessity of putting their religious beliefs and practices on the back burner. However, they took note of a more negative side to this situation, namely, the potential collusion between government institutions and traditional community leaders which could hamper their capacity of action. They noted continuing prejudices which portrayed Muslim women as passive and submissive, as well as the deleterious process undergone by the image of Islam in the aftermath of the 9/11 and 7/7 events, Muslims becoming the target of anti-terrorist legislation and policies with the resurgence of antagonism against Islam. Nonetheless, Britain's wars in Afghanistan and Iraq triggered an explosion of Muslim women's participation in the anti-war protest movement. This generated wider participation in a variety of spheres and channels such as mainstream politics, campaigns and community organisations, the latter being further assisted by government funding to combat terrorism.

In France, the chronology seems almost reversed to that of Britain. Many of the older women interviewed had been active in the social movement linked to the Marche pour l'égalité through the 1980s. The immediate upshot of this mass movement under Francois Mitterrand's government saw the expansion of engagement in public life among young men and women of Muslim background, with claims that were not of a religious but of a citizenship character. Muslim women's opportunities of engagement in French society have somewhat altered since then. Women who do not hold religious beliefs or who practise their religion privately may be able to pursue their projects and they sometimes consider *laïcité* as a protection. However, those who carry visible signs of their religious belief face countless obstacles in their access to studies, employment and their participation in civic and political life. One significant underpinning factor has been the legislation focused on Islam and dress code, whose impact was amplified by politicians' discourses and the media with their cortège of hostile communication regarding Muslims. This negativity vis-à-vis Islam spans over the whole political spectrum from extreme Right to extreme Left. Our interview data reveals Muslim women's perception of narrower opportunities in the public sphere, at least relative to their expectations.

Our research shows that Muslim women's capacity of action is well-substantiated. In the main, they possess a rational understanding about their life circumstances. They nurture concerns which underpin their aspirations for change through powerful commitments to values of gender, racial, religious and social equality, with a heightened sensitivity to humanitarian issues and the cause of human rights. Their motivation is strengthened by the growing confidence to drive their project to a successful outcome. Confidence remains their Achilles' heel but is bolstered by support and inspiration emanating from a variety of sources: significant individuals, circumstantial and environmental components, laws and structural frameworks, corporate agents and role models. Although some have opted for exit, most have negotiated obstacles and taken advantage of facilitating factors through a rich repertoire of strategies which span from confrontation to cooperation and include also compromise, lateral and reversal approaches.

CHAPTER 8

Islamic Dress, the War on Terror, Policing Muslim Women

INTRODUCTION

This chapter examines some of the issues of concern to the Muslim women with whom we spoke. Concern was expressed over several issues but not all can be examined in a single chapter. Therefore, we focus on issues of key importance, those which were most frequently broached in respondent interviews and sociological intervention (SI) focus group sessions and whose salience is emphasised by the attention paid to them in the public domain. Most important among the issues considered here is that of wearing Islamic dress in a Western context. We also reflect on the consequences of the War on Terror and the policing of Muslim women by Muslim men. Where the wearing of Islamic dress is concerned, both the British and French contexts are examined as the issue was raised repeatedly by respondents in both countries, whether or not they adhered to Islamic dress code. Inevitably it occupies the largest part of the discussion below. The War on Terror and its impact on women were raised by respondents in Britain. Very few women in France referred to it although had the interviews and group discussions taken place after the 2015 *Charlie Hebdo* and Paris multiple site attacks, a different order of issues may have emerged among respondents as France launched its own war against home-grown terrorism. The third issue mentioned, that of the control of Muslim women by Muslim men, was of considerable concern to the respondents in France. This chapter maps the views put forward by Muslim women on these issues while also considering their assessment of the impact of these issues. In doing so, it gives voice to the women as a counterpoint to the many opinions and assessments offered by those who enjoy authoritative and influential platforms in public life—politicians, newspaper editors, journalists, academics and also Muslim male 'community leaders'—but who have little understanding of Muslim women's real experiences and thinking. Caught up in what Heidi Mirza calls a 'collision of discourses' (2012: 121) Muslim women are rarely consulted about these issues when policy is formulated and are largely ignored when they raise a voice to oppose inequalities and injustices.

Issues of Concern to Women from Muslim Communities

Muslim women in Britain and France are subject to myriad inequalities and obstacles in common with the majority of women globally. These problems relate to issues of poverty created by lack of educational and employment opportunities; social exclusion resulting from discrimination within majority society based on gender, 'race'/ethnicity, faith on the one hand and prescribed gender roles within the family on the other hand; exclusion from political life and under-representation in elected assemblies. However, Muslim women face specific problems through an unfortunate conjuncture of factors: first, Muslim populations, and women in particular, constitute some of the most socio-economically disadvantaged and excluded communities in Europe; second, many women from Muslim communities, especially those living in extended family households, face culturally mandated constraints on their liberties, being assigned the role of the 'good' wife, mother, daughter/daughter-in-law and upholder of family honour—this is particularly the case among South Asian Muslim women in Britain who can become extremely isolated from majority society; third, Muslims have become a suspect community in the 9/11 era. In the Western public imaginary women, particularly the 'embodied' woman (the one who wears Islamic dress, the one subjected to genital mutilation, the one killed to restore her family's honour and so on), have come to symbolise what is seen as a barbaric religion. Thus, Muslim women are caught between being a visible symbol of a backward faith and being invisible through socio-economic and political exclusion. Such simultaneously visibilising and invisibilising processes mean that Muslim women face a set of issues and problems which do not confront other populations of women in the same way. Nevertheless, in common with issues faced by majority society women and by those from other minoritised communities, issues of concern to Muslim women can be categorised according to Marchbank's definition of 'women's interest issues' (2000: 19) as those which are not only addressed by policy and decision makers but also raised in order to challenge assumptions made by majority society about Muslim women and which therefore seek social transformation. We would argue that Muslims women's issues, as in the case of women's interest issues generally, are political and have ramifications for society in general rather than Muslim women alone.

Our interviews and focus group discussions, alongside the observation of events, revealed a fairly long list of issues facing women from Muslim communities in Britain and France. These are categorised and presented, though not in order of importance, in Tables 8.1, 8.2 and 8.3 under three headings: issues arising from and pertaining to Muslim women's presence in Western majority society, issues to do with the women's ethnic culture and community and those relating to Islam and Muslim communities.

Of the issues below some were cited more frequently by respondents in Britain than in France and vice versa. For example, among the issues relating to the women's ethno-cultural background, the burden of being a 'good' wife, mother, daughter/daughter-in-law and thus acquiescing to family demands at the expense of one's own personal freedom and development was far more of an issue for the women in Britain than in France. It was women in Britain, in education or employment, who most often spoke of the pressures of living 'a double life' between meeting the demands of their family and community and the expectations of their White

Table 8.1 Majority society

Islamic dress
Racism
Islamophobia
Discrimination in education
Discrimination in employment
Discrimination in public services—health and welfare
The impacts of the War on Terror
Negative media image of Islam and Muslim women
Political under-representation
Lack of consultation by policymakers

Table 8.2 Ethnic culture and communities

Islamic dress
Obligation to fulfil the role of 'good' mother/wife/daughter/daughter-in-law
Forced marriage
Family shame and honour
Lack of knowledge about sex and sexuality
Lack of personal independence
Low economic activity due to family role and expectations
Lack of personal independence
Living a 'double life'

Table 8.3 Islam and Muslims

Islamic dress
Young men policing young women's behaviour
Polygyny
Temporary marriage (*nikah*)
Extremists radicalising young people
Male misinterpretations of Islamic texts undermining women's rights
The right of Muslim women to offer more emancipatory interpretations of Qur'anic texts
Free mixing between women and men

student counterparts and work colleagues to participate in extracurricular activities or socialise after work. On the other hand, problems relating to marriage (polygyny in particular) were cited more often in France than in Britain although Muslim women in Britain were becoming concerned about the growing practice of temporary marriage (*nikah*) among young people which many saw as a licence for men to 'try out' several women, often at the same time, before discarding the women in whom they were no longer interested. And although forced marriage, which the respondents saw as an issue cutting across other ethno-religious communities, has figured on government policy agendas in Britain and France in the 2000s, respondents in both countries only raised it occasionally, stating that although they knew of it second-hand, particularly among more uneducated women, they had not experienced it directly. It is worth noting that arranged marriage was not seen as a problem because in principle it was a consensual affair and respondents in both countries agreed that as soon as any unwanted pressure was placed on either marriage partner, it was no longer a question of marriage by arrangement.

As far as issues related to majority society were concerned, more respondents in Britain than France expressed concern about the lack of Muslim women in political life and elected assemblies whereas the women in France spoke more extensively about discrimination in employment, education and public services. However, fears about rising racism and Islamophobia in the form of hate speech and acts were articulated across the board. Finally, there were also some differences in the issues prioritised where the area of Islam and Muslims was concerned, Thus, while the negative impact on women of masculine mis/interpretations of the Qur'an was discussed in almost equal measure by respondents in the two countries, the right and duty even of Muslim women to offer more emancipatory interpretations of Qur'anic texts was more fervently advocated in France where more women referred to the need to expose an authentic, non-masculine Islam and also to Islamic feminism. In addition, where the women in Britain frequently expressed alarm about young men in their communities becoming radicalised by extremists, in France, the issue of non/mixity between Muslim women and men was important.

We found that the issue of Islamic dress cut across the domains of majority society, ethnic culture and Islam. Thus, for many women, wearing some form of Islamic dress was part and parcel of being Muslim and expressing one's faith outwardly. For others, there was nothing Islamic about garments such as the headscarf, face veil and *burka* and it was argued that these were ethno-cultural artefacts imposed on women as a result of prescribed gender roles and relations within ethnic cultures. Islamic dress is an issue relating to Western majority society also because it is seen as a symbol of a backward religion in which women are second-class human subjects and hence of a faith which threatens to undermine liberal Western ideals.

The above provides a general tableau of issues raised by Muslim women, some more frequently and fervently than others. However, the most talked about issue emerging from the list above was that of Islamic dress (mainly the headscarf/*hijab*). Not a single interview or focus group meeting in either country passed without some discussion of it, even when it was not brought up by the researchers. Two other issues which were referred to frequently enough to warrant a separate mention here are the War on Terror and its consequences (in Britain) and the policing of women's behaviour by men (France). The latter encompassed issues of violence against women and while such issues were named by respondents (e.g. being forced into marriage, being physically and psychologically threatened into certain modes of behaviour, being physically barred from certain spaces), they were largely bunched under the label of controlling/policing women.

Islamic Dress

Much has been written, in English and French, about Muslim women, Islamic dress and its meanings—in history[1] and today—in Western society through an examination and analysis of the ideologies, opinions and actions of policy and political decision makers, lawyers, journalists, academics, religious experts and public intellectuals (see among many others Adrian 2015; Allwood and Wadia 2009; Bouamama 2004a, b; Bowen 2008; Bullock 2002; Fanon 1967; Gaspard and Khosrokhavar 1995; Hoodfar 1992; Kariapper 2009; Malik 2008; Meer et al. 2010; Stasi 2003; Rosenberger and Sauer 2012; Scott 2007; Winter 2008; Yegenoglu 1998). Few works are based on empirical research focusing on the testimonies of women who wear Islamic dress, those who wear it occasionally or outside work/school, those who have worn Islamic dress at some point in their life but no longer do so, or Muslim women whose close female relations and friends wear it. Among such texts are Naima Bouteldja's Open Society Foundation report on Muslim women who wear the face veil in France (2011), Part One of Eva Brem's edited collection which explores the experiences of face veil wearers in Europe (2014), Shirazi and Mishra's short work on young women who wear the face veil in Europe (2010), Dwyer on the construction of new identities by Muslim schoolgirls in Hertfordshire wearing the headscarf, Killian's work on Muslim immigrant women's attitudes towards the headscarf affair and Zerouala's small-scale study of women wearing the *hijab* in France (2015). What emerges from these writings is a wide-ranging response on the part of women from Muslim communities containing different and complex views about Islamic dress in contrast with dominant Western opinion which rests on a framework in which tolerance of women's Islamic dress is indicative of Western liberal thinking and practice but where the wearing of it demonstrates not just the backwardness of Islam and its oppression of women but also, in the post-9/11 era, the threat posed by Islam to Western society, its values and civilisation. In the section below, we consider what Muslim women have had to say about Islamic dress in its various forms and meaning.

Choice versus Imposition

The refutation of the view, prevalent in majority society, that Muslim women are largely forced to wear Islamic dress by their family or Muslim clerics constituted one of the strongest messages to come through in our interviews. The majority of our respondents who wore Islamic dress said that they chose to do so after thinking about it lengthily. As many explained, it was not a choice for the faint-hearted, knowing as they did about generally negative attitudes or outright hostility against Islamic dress in Western society but also because, in some cases, they were going against the wishes of family. Often the family of women who chose to wear Islamic dress were opposed to it for fear that the woman or girl concerned would face hostility and discrimination, especially after the events of 9/11, or because it jarred with their view of themselves as integrated in Western society. Thus Hamida (Paris) and other young women were told by their parents not to wear Islamic dress because they risked being attacked. Adelmira (Birmingham) told us that her husband was unhappy about her wearing the *hijab* because he felt awkward introducing her to his English clients and colleagues at business functions. Zakiya (Rotherham) spoke about her in-laws demanding that she stop wearing the *hijab* because she was wrecking their reputation: 'how dare you wear that. We are a modern family' they railed. All the respondents in Britain (whether headscarfed or not) and France (particularly those who wore the headscarf) believed that wearing Islamic dress was a matter of personal choice and individual conscience and not to be imposed on any woman or girl. None of the women felt that they had experienced pressure from family members to wear Islamic dress although some had been encouraged from an early age; for example:

> I started wearing the *hijab* when I was thirteen...My mum had put it on me for Sunday school when I was seven but I hated it. As I made more friends it got better. My sister wore *hijab* at nine because of me. (Tahani, Birmingham)

Zakiya had persuaded her pre-teen daughter to wear the *hijab* but said that once her daughter reached the age of 16, she refused to do so. This was not a problem for Zakiya, nor the fact that her daughter continues to wear Western dress.

However, some young women, particularly those who were members of university student societies or Muslim organisations, had faced peer pressure. Martiza, a university student, explained:

> Sometimes there is such a great deal of pressure, so many friends I have at university, they are only wearing *hijab* just because their friends do, from pressure. And for example, at the Islamic society in [name of university], I went there yesterday, and there were just women wearing *hijab*, and I just felt, like, you know, people were just looking down at me, not taking me seriously. (Martiza, Birmingham)

Similarly, Afiya, who was a member of a British Islamic organisation for a short time, told us that she wore the *hijab* for a few years after she started to attend the meetings of this organisation:

> The fact that most of the women who attended [name of organisation] events wore the *hijab* meant that I therefore formed the idea that I should wear one too, to show my commitment as a Muslim, though I now recognise an element of sheep mentality in my action. (Afiya, Birmingham)

Among the French respondents too, some spoke of arguments with peers about wearing Islamic dress. Keltoun, a practising Sufi and lawyer by profession, said that she had never worn any form of Islamic dress but that some of her friends and acquaintances did:

> I don't understand how a women can be submissive to a man; I couldn't tolerate that but that's my view because within my group opinions are divided. Some girls wear the veil although not many of them. All the same, discussions can be very heated. (Keltoun, Paris)

In France, peer pressure and bullying behaviour was also discussed in relation to young, macho men on large urban housing estates (*cités*) who harassed young women to the point that some of the latter decided to wear Islamic dress in order to be able to go about their daily business in peace.

While all the respondents who wore Islamic dress (the *hijab* in all cases) said they had chosen to wear it without pressure from their family, a few spoke very generally about girls and young women in traditional Muslim families being compelled to wear Islamic dress. This was more the case in Britain than in France where the generation of Muslim women who had migrated to France from North Africa and the Middle East had distanced themselves from religion and abandoned the traditional veiling practices of their mothers and grandmothers back home. In addition, anecdotal evidence from Muslim women's organisations in Britain suggests that many girls and young women who wear Islamic dress are 'conditioned' into doing so by their parents. Speaking on behalf of a leading national Muslim women's organisation in Britain, Feroza explained:

> From our experience speaking to girls at secondary schools, there is still an expectation of parents for daughters to dress 'respectably', particularly when attending family occasions where extended family may be present. How 'respectably' is translated and enforced often varies family to family. One particular Pathan girl had to wear the *jilbab* and headscarf to school from the age of 12 because 'all our girls do'. She came to accept this as her mode of dress. And even as an adult now would not dare to wear anything else even though she believes it is Islamically acceptable to do so. Girls who often believe it's their choice have been conditioned to think it. Have these girls ever been told 'wear whatever you want'? (Feroza, Birmingham)

Whatever the reasons behind the wearing of Islamic dress the decision to do so was not taken lightly. Similarly, a process of reflection had taken place among those who did not wear Islamic dress—or who wore it at certain times only—in order to feel secure about their standpoint in the face of detractors among their peers or elsewhere.

In Search of a Muslim Identity

Two distinct groups are identifiable within the category of women who may be seen to be searching for an Islamic identity: those for whom Islamic dress signified deep religious commitment and those for whom the visible demonstration of a Muslim identity was important in the 9/11 era. First, for some women the wearing of Islamic dress represented a clear religious commitment to Islam. They gave this commitment because their reading of Qur'anic texts had led them to conclude that Islam required a woman to cover her hair and body. Thus, for Imoni (Paris) it was a question of 'religious obligation' whereas for Hamida (Mantes-la-Jolie), who wore both the *hijab* and the *jilbab*, the covering of one's head and body was an order passed down from God. For both of them, and others who presented the same argument in favour of wearing Islamic dress, there was little if any room for alternative readings of the Qur'an on this issue:

> There are no other interpretations...about the obligation to wear the veil. Those who think the veil isn't required are 'Muslims by tradition'—they were brought up in a Muslim family without really understanding Islam... wearing the veil is written in black and white... (Imoni, Paris)

Such unequivocal assertions of faith, backed up by references to sacred texts, were frequently expressed by the respondents in France who wore Islamic dress. One respondent, Lutfiyah (Paris), remarked that hers was the generation educated in the West and that it was inevitable that her generation turned to Islamic texts for answers when Western knowledge had failed them; that once Islamic knowledge was consumed, wearing the veil, praying five times a day and so on was an inevitable development. In her study of Muslim women and the veil in France, Zerouala finds that the reason cited by all her respondents for wearing Islamic dress was that it was prescribed by Islam and that they had reached this view after undertaking considerable study of Islamic texts; that the wearing of Islamic dress was the crowning of an intellectual and spiritual journey into Islam which concretised their attachment to God and filled them with intense joy and a sense of autonomy (Zerouala 2015). Although some of our respondents in Britain also said they had started wearing Islamic dress as a means of visibly avowing their religious belonging and fidelity, their piety appeared to be inspired by a more pragmatic understanding of what being or becoming a good Muslim and human being entailed.

The second group in this category of women began to wear the *hijab* after the events of 9/11 as a way of standing up for themselves and Muslim communities which they believed were under attack by an all-powerful state. Many of these were young women and girls who not only felt ostracised by majority society but for whom the ethnic identity of their parents and grandparents was not enough to protect them or give them a sense of belonging in the 9/11 era. These children of a 'third culture'[2] sought refuge in Muslim-ness, an identity neither of majority society nor of their parents' generation. The link between the events of 9/11 (and in Britain those of 7/7) and an increase in the numbers of Muslim women and girls wearing Islamic dress was pointed out by several respondents:

> Things have changed, particularly since 9/11. People have recognised that it is not bad to show a commitment to religion. (Zakiya, Rotherham)

> The events of 7/7 made me want to show solidarity [by wearing the *hijab*]; the fact that I was becoming a Muslim leader meant that I needed to look the part and it made me feel more confident and more accepted in this role. (Afiya, Birmingham)

I think this sudden increase in the number of women wearing the veil is mainly due to the events of 9/11 which have had more of an impact than the *laïcité* law [of 2004]. Our religion was called into question, we were told 'your religion is crap, you're nothing but terrorists'. So people wanted to reaffirm their faith. (Wahida, Fontenay-sous-Bois)

Identification with Islam and Political Consciousness

There is little doubt that the increased identification with Islam went hand in hand with greater political awareness among Muslim women in the post-9/11 era and that the wearing of Islamic dress was not only a way of reaffirming and defending one's faith in a hostile environment but it was also a means of challenging or cocking a snook at the authorities and an antagonistic public. One respondent explained:

> When I was at school, nobody was wearing the hijab, but now, I went back recently to my old school, all the girls wear the hijab. Back in those days [before 9/11] when people saw a girl wearing the *hijab*, everybody used to think 'poor her, her parents must be very strict'…now it's almost a political statement for these girls to wear the *hijab*…Young Muslim girls want to show that they are proud to be Muslim. Since 9/11, Muslim people have been very much singled out as Muslim, it has been thrust upon them. (Indameera, London)

Another observed, 'We threw ourselves into it [wearing the headscarf] and frankly the headscarf controversies pushed us into making a more massive commitment because when you're excluded, frankly you wear it twice over' (Zarifa, Paris). On the other hand, Nabila (Coventry) who did not normally wear Islamic dress said that she would sometimes turn up wearing a headscarf in her university classes because she enjoyed provoking confusion among her student counterparts and lecturers, some of whom held stereotypical views about the submissiveness of Muslim women in a headscarf and it was one way of getting back at them.

Islamic Dress as Protection

Wearing Islamic dress as a protective device was frequently cited by the women with whom we spoke, although for many this was a secondary reason for adopting it. Thus Islamic dress was seen as a safeguard against the straying eyes of men and male sexual harassment, protection from conformity to Western norms of femininity and protection at times of psychological stress. Most women who cited the protective aspect of Islamic dress did so in relation to sexual objectification and harassment. For example, Yasmin (Birmingham), a university student, told us that she had started wearing the *hijab*, at first only at school because it was a way of dealing with 'immature boys' harassing her in class. However, she started to wear it full time when she left school as it spared her stress at university about what to wear each day in order to keep up with her peers. For Emani (Paris) who wore Western clothes but hoped one day to wear the *hijab*, not only did the veil offer protection against harassment by young men, but she felt it actually commanded respect: 'when young men see a woman wearing the veil, they can't do anything'. Naima (Paris) who also wore Western dress said she understood why young women who lived in the inner city housing estates of Paris covered themselves. She believed they deliberately made themselves unattractive, wearing formless clothing, to avoid sexist taunts from groups of young men. However, some like Zafira (Paris), who called herself a Muslim feminist, put forward a more thought-out, political position:

> It's really about a life principle where a woman isn't reduced to her body…I no longer want to see ads with naked women, plunging cleavages at work, or that our relations with men, with our bosses must be flirtatious…I'm fed up of being reduced to a piece of flesh, I'm not bothered about a bit of leg or hair which is uncovered, it's the meaning I attach to it that's important.

There were also women who wore Islamic dress to hide away from the world during periods of trauma. Shaza (Birmingham) told her story of wearing the *hijab*:

> When my husband passed away I wore the *hijab*. My heart was broken, I had no place to go, I didn't want to see anyone…In Islam you have a four months, ten days period after the loss of your husband when you can't see any man except [your] brother, father, son. But…you have 101 per cent permission to go to work and earn money to support your children. Because I couldn't stop working, I wore the *hijab* to protect myself. I wore it for about 5 months. I felt comfortable in it…All my sisters and cousins were telling me I was stupid, I shouldn't do it. I said that I was comfortable in it and that when I wasn't comfortable in it anymore, I would take it off…after five months I said 'that's it Shaza, this is not you'.

Maya (Paris) also felt that Islamic dress could constitute a temporary refuge for girls as they grew up: 'the veil can be experienced as...a protection during adolescence when girls are undergoing psychological development and which can be removed once they are adult'. The idea that the veil offers women protection from the male gaze, from sexual harassment and from the world while they are undergoing a difficult period in their life also emerges in Zerouala's study (2015).

Islamic Dress as a Means of Self-Assertion

A small number of respondents spoke about Islamic dress giving them control over their own body and hence constituting a means of self-assertion. For Zakiya, it added an extra weapon in her feminist armoury in that she was telling people loudly and proudly—including her ex-husband and in-laws—that she would dress as she pleased, in line with 'her politics'. For Rida (Paris), on the other hand, the veil was a means of fighting for the right of women to not be objectified and manipulated:

> Wearing the veil is not about subjugation, it's about valuing yourself and being able to choose how to handle yourself without being used as a medium of exchange. Today women are used to tap into all sorts of urges from buying a car to buying a sandwich...

While the idea of the veil as a means of women's self-assertion and empowerment is invoked also by Zerouala's respondents and has been debated extensively elsewhere (Bunting 2001; Haddad 2007; Ruby 2006), it did not form a large part of the narrative of our respondents.

Voices Against the Veil

Among our respondents in Britain and France who did not wear Islamic dress, the majority supported the right of Muslim girls and women to dress as they pleased. Moreover, in France, most respondents, including those who accepted the principle of *laïcité*, disagreed with the law of 2004 which effectively prohibits schoolgirls from attending school unless they remove their headscarf. While there were a number of respondents in France who were diametrically opposed to Islamic dress, one young woman (Keltoun, Paris), who belonged to a Sufi *tariqa* and was married to a French convert to Islam, expressed her opposition as outright revulsion for women who wore Islamic dress, particularly those who chose full face and head coverings:

> Personally, they get on my nerves, I can't stand them, I can't stand looking at women who wear the burka, but that's me and I'd never say it publicly because Islam is so stigmatised that I'd watch what I say in public but they really infuriate me and I feel like saying 'go lock yourselves away, stay at home'.

Respondents in both countries put forward arguments against the wearing of Islamic dress; these are presented below.

Islam Does Not Require Women to Cover up; Male-Dominated Culture Does

One of the main arguments put forward against the wearing of Islamic dress was that it was not a prescription of Islam. Those who held this view argued that Qur'anic scriptures on modest dress which applied to both women and men had been deliberately misinterpreted over centuries, by men, and that the only religious obligations were the five pillars of Islam. A common concern was that Islamic dress was fast becoming established as the sixth pillar of Islam, by those professing religious expertise, as a means of controlling women. Amane (Paris), echoing the feelings of other respondents, argued:

> [It is] the fundamentalists who require women to wear the veil because it suits their agenda, it's political, because they want male domination, a patriarchal system, it suits them...they have a strategy for society. The headscarf is a way of isolating women and subjecting them to men's laws.

Natori (Paris) argued that it was not even the actual garment which bothered her but the context of male-dominated culture in which the women who wore Islamic dress made that choice. She said she knew of girls and young women who submitted themselves to male authority like sheep rather than understanding what the Qur'an said about Islamic dress.

Young Women Are Undoing the Struggles of Previous Generations of Muslim Women

Some respondents' rejection of Islamic dress was based on women's past struggles against covering up. Thus, Marjani (Coventry) questioned how young Pakistani women could cover themselves up knowing that their mothers and grandmothers had fought for their right to go out, work and mix, uncovered, in the same spaces as men. Souhila (London), who helps run a North African women's centre, also recounted witnessing the transformation of girls of Moroccan origin, born and bred in London, who had suddenly opted for the veil when it did not belong to their culture. She wondered how they came to take an identity which was so foreign to their mothers and grandmothers. Souhila and others put the '*hijab* turn' of the younger generation down to 'Muslim obscurantism linked with Wahhabism…a formalistic and de-spiritualised form of Islam' (Keltoun, Paris).

Religious Commitment Should Be Private, Not Publicly Paraded
The argument that one's commitment to Islam did not require public demonstration through the wearing of Islamic dress was also advanced by several women. Some felt that Muslims were becoming too concerned by outward appearances: 'wearing the *hijab* doesn't make you a good Muslim, you're judged on your deeds, not based on whether you wear the *hijab* or not' (Bilkis, London). Others were critical of the fact that by becoming obsessed with public manifestations of their faith, Muslims were becoming increasingly judgemental about women who did not wear Islamic dress and separating 'good hijabis' from the apparently bad 'non-hijabis' (Afiya, Birmingham) and that this had real discriminatory effects on women. For example, Shadia (Birmingham) who stood as a local council election candidate for the Respect Party told the story of the opposing Labour Party candidate who instructed Muslim voters not to vote for her because she did not wear the *hijab* and was therefore untrustworthy. Janna (London) was also critical of attitudes within Muslim circles which dictated that women who did not wear the *hijab* were not to be taken seriously. In France also it was reported that women often faced hostility from veil-wearing women for not wearing Islamic dress. Randa (Marseille) told us: 'These girls tell you "you're not Muslim" and I say "what's my Islam got to do with you?…I don't have to wear a scarf on my head…" These girls, either you're like them or you're not Muslim.'

Simply a Fashion?
Some respondents felt that the *hijab* was merely a fashion to be followed. Tabasam (Bradford) decried the many Muslim women she knew who wore the *hijab* with tight-fitting tops and jeans hence contradicting their supposed religious commitment, while Fatima (Paris) confirmed a similar

trend in France, 'Usually you wear the veil because you're religious but over the last few years many young women have made it into a fashion statement'. And Tahira (Coventry) referred to '*hijab* fashionistas' like her sister who:

> hung around with this artsy crowd and they were going to start some Islamic thing and she actually wore like a headscarf for a few days until my mum was like 'get it off. Get it off, don't wear it just for the sake of wearing it'. But you get the ones that they wear it with pretty pins on it…

You Do Not Cover up in a Secular Country
In France, a number of respondents voiced their refusal of Islamic dress on the grounds that 'it's normal not to wear it [the veil] in France because we live in a secular country' (Naima, Paris). Sadika (Paris) also admitted that she did not agree with girls wearing the headscarf in school which represented a secular space. Moreover, the argument in favour of maintaining a secular space by disallowing the wearing of Islamic dress was often linked with being able to mix with others of a different culture and with facilitating the integration of young Muslim women in French society.

Wearing Islamic Dress and Its Consequences

Apart from media reports, the everyday consequences for women who wear Islamic dress in a Western context have been recorded by only a small number of authors including Bouteldja who draws comparisons between the French and British contexts (2014) and Chakraborti and Zempi who mainly consider the British context (2015). These authors focus on the impacts on women who wear the face veil or *niqab* only, presumably because the latter is publicly perceived as the greater challenge to Western ideals of freedom and democracy while the *hijab* is the more tolerated, though not always accepted, form of Islamic dress in the West. These authors paint a dismal picture of the consequences of wearing the face veil in France and Britain although, according to Bouteldja, face veil wearers in France have been subjected to more severe negative impacts than their counterparts in Britain. She argues that the harshness of the French public debates on the face veil which drew a consensus across politico-ideological lines, placing even traditional enemies—feminists and male state elites—on the same side, to support a law banning it, led to an utter disregard for the 'physical and moral well-being of those who wore the veil' (2014: 116) and hence to 'a climate in which abuse was more frequent than in the UK' (Ibid.: 160). But, as Chakraborti and Zempi demonstrate, the British media, political class and public are not innocent when it comes to placing face-veiled Muslim women in a situation of insecurity and isolation through their misrecognition and misrepresentation over a period of time. Below we consider some of the consequences faced by Muslim women who wear Islamic dress. Except for one woman wearing the face veil, our respondent samples in both countries included women who wore the headscarf.

In line with Bouteldja's findings, our study revealed that the greatest negative consequences of wearing the headscarf or *hijab* were felt by Muslim women in France. The more pragmatic attitudes of political elites, the media and public intellectuals in Britain have meant that the *hijab* is largely accepted as the preferred dress of many Muslim women and girls who wear it in the workplace, in schools and colleges, elected assemblies and even as participants in sports. This acceptance of the *hijab* is illustrated by the fact that even in traditionally male-dominated public institutions such as the fire and police services, the introduction of uniforms incorporating the *hijab* for Muslim women was seen as one way to increase gender, ethnic and religious diversity in the workforce.

While our respondents in Britain had much to say about Islamic dress generally, few spoke of the negative consequences of wearing the *hijab* on a day-to-day basis. Those who wore the *hijab* did so unhindered although most acknowledged that Islamophobia formed the wallpaper of their life which sharpened in focus each time Islamic terrorist events occurred. Thus, as a Muslim made visible by her *hijab*, Sabreena (Birmingham) was spat at, in public, after the events of 9/11 while others reported being called 'towel head' (Husniya, Coventry) among other names or had their headscarf tugged at in the street (Rabiya, London), following the 7/7 London transport bombings. While the women who wore the *hijab* led a relatively unharassed life, many feared they could face discrimination because of it:

> I have gone to an interview wearing *hijab* and thinking 'look at the other boys and girls who are there, I have no chance. I'm qualified, but I have a feeling that this is going to let me down'. On this occasion it didn't because I had an open-minded person in front of me. Brilliant! But on occasions you find that maybe they don't want you in front of customers…in certain places, because you're not quite the right image. (Tahani, Birmingham)

In France, numerous barriers (including legal ones) are raised against wearing the *hijab* freely and we gathered innumerable accounts of the negative impacts on respondents' daily life. As it is impossible to recount even a small proportion of these stories, we have summarised respondents' experiences under three main headings: education, employment, immigration and nationality.

Education
Most respondents who wore the *hijab* spoke of the 2004 law against the wearing of conspicuous religious symbols acting as a brake on their freedom of religious expression either when they had been schoolgirls or subsequently as school teachers. The majority removed their headscarf with misgiving but a few spoke of friends finding it so difficult that they eventually left their job. Several respondents pointed out that the 2004 law had so emboldened school and university teachers and authorities that rules were often invented. For example, despite the fact that it was perfectly legal to wear the *hijab* at university, we were told of lecturers not allowing students to attend their classes wearing the *hijab*. One respondent told the story of a friend whose research grant was stopped after two years because she refused to comply with the demand made by her research director that she stop wearing the *hijab* (Zafira, Paris). Yet another reported being refused service in the university canteen because she was wearing a headscarf: 'I stand in the queue with my friend and there was the canteen supervisor who was at the till that day. She comes running over and says "excuse me miss, you must remove your headscarf…you're in a public institution, the French Republic"…so I left and ate outside on my own' (Annisa, Paris). Many such cases led to stand-offs with students losing unless they were prepared to make an official stand and follow through complaints procedures.

Employment
A government circular of 13 April 2007 stipulated that any public servant who demonstrated his or her religious belief through the wearing of conspicuous religious symbols was in breach of his/her contractual obligations. This set the scene for the banning of the headscarf in French public sector institutions and consequently impacted negatively on headscarfed women providing a public service—this message came through clearly among respondents. Moreover, respondents also told us that private employers were equally quick to make rules against the wearing of the

headscarf because of the overwhelming public consensus against Islamic dress. Thus we were told that many women, especially those working for large companies which had an image to protect, who would normally wear the *hijab* were compelled by their bosses to remove it. Others spoke of it simply being easier to remove the headscarf in order to avoid assumptions being made about them or being labelled as extremists or troublemakers. Finally, some respondents spoke of not getting jobs as a headscarfed woman, 'You send in your CV, you talk to them on the phone, everything's fine but the minute they see your face it's as if you're a moron. And that's really shocking' (Soundous, Livry-Gargan).

Immigration and Nationality
The consequences of wearing Islamic dress on immigration and nationality status were also raised. Respondents' testimonies chime with instances reported in the media of the authorities placing barriers in the way of people seeking French nationality. For example, in 2008, a French court denied citizenship to a Moroccan woman on the grounds that her 'radical practice of Islam'—wearing the *burka*—conflicted with French values (Chrisafis 2008). Online discussions (bladi.net 2006) also reveal the difficulties women wearing Islamic dress can face when sorting out their immigration and/or nationality papers. One headscarfed respondent, Soundous (Livry-Gargan), told her story of obtaining French nationality, a relatively straightforward process until she was called to the sub-prefecture to complete the remaining formalities. When she got to the sub-prefecture she was in a long queue of women, of whom many wore the headscarf. As each headscarfed woman was called in, she removed her headscarf because people had been previously told that religious symbols were forbidden in the offices of a secular state. When it came to Soundous's turn she went in with her headscarf on. When asked to remove it, she refused arguing that nowhere in any documentation did it state one had to remove one's headscarf in order to obtain French nationality. In the end, after being sent away, subsequently complaining and being recalled, she obtained her French nationality, content that she had not given in to the whims of petty bureaucrats:

> I'm proud I stood my ground…I don't understand the logic. You accept me, you tell me I'm French and then you humiliate me in front of people… And in the end I was summoned 10 days later and it only took five minutes [to get the approved papers] and no-one asked me to remove my headscarf.

The experiences recounted above show that in France women and girls wearing the headscarf ran the risk of exclusion from important spheres of life either due to legal restrictions such as the 2004 law banning conspicuous religious symbols in schools or simply because someone in authority decided that the headscarf was not permissible in what they considered a secular space. In Britain, the headscarf is largely accepted in public life but against a constant presence of Islamophobia and racism, women who wear it (and other forms of Islamic dress) remain fearful of a time in the future when they could become the target of active state discrimination in education, employment and other domains.

The War on Terror—Britain

In September 2001, Prime Minister Blair announced that Britain was 'at war with terrorism' (BBC 2001). While the global war on terrorism included the Afghanistan and Iraq wars among other global operations, Britain's own War on Terror was launched after 2001 and reinforced after the London bombings of 2005 with a series of hard measures contained in terrorism legislation[3] and soft security measures aimed at building trust among Muslims, based on the idea that 'communities defeat terrorism' (Spalek and McDonald 2011). Hard security measures have included increased police stop-and-search of those profiled as Muslims, heavy-handed policing at international borders leading to travel disruptions for Muslims, pre-charge and pre-trial detentions, surveillance and covert intelligence gathering, control orders and Terrorism Prevention and Investigation Measures (TPIMs[4]), proscription of groups deemed extremist by the government and so on. Soft security measures, particularly after 2005, when young British Muslim men turned into suicide bombers wreaking over 50 deaths and countless injuries, saw the initiation of the Prevent (Preventing Violent Extremism—PVE) strand of Britain's counter-terrorism strategy in which Muslim women and young people were targeted as resistants to terrorism and bridge-builders between Muslims and majority British society. The training of these resistants-cum-bridge-builders would take place through state funding of educational programmes against radicalisation and various women's empowerment projects.

The impact on Muslim women of the War on Terror in all its aspects has not been documented extensively. However, some accounts are worth noting, among them Victoria Brittain's *Shadow Lives: The Forgotten Women of the War on Terror* (2013) and Surinder Guru's (2012) piece on the effects of the hard measures of the War on Terror on women and their children in families of those suspected of terrorism or charged with having carried out acts of terror. These effects range from shock at the knowledge that a family member is or could be involved in terrorism to being shunned by family, friends and neighbours, subsequent isolation from the community, compounded by harassment, a sense of guilt and trauma. Where the engagement by the state of Muslim women as resistants to terrorism and as bridge-builders is concerned, a number of works are worth mentioning, including Allen and Guru (2012), Rashid (2014), McDonald (2012). They consider Muslim women's involvement in the National Muslim Women's Advisory Group (NMWAG) established by the government in 2007 and in other Prevent projects supposedly aimed at integrating Muslim communities in Britain and hence resisting terrorism. Below, we summarise our findings in respect of the impact of the War on Terror although the women with whom we spoke did not refer to it as that.

In the Glare of Unwanted Attention

After 9/11, for the first time, almost all our respondents experienced a deep uneasiness about their presence in Britain. The events of 9/11, and subsequently those of London 7/7, made them visible outside their home and family in a way they had not experienced before. For women who wore Islamic dress the feeling of exposure was greater and they feared for their safety. Whether at work, college, out shopping or at the school gates with their children Muslim women felt scrutinised and on trial by people. They found themselves having to explain to people they had known over years that they did not support Al Qaeda or the London 7/7 bombers. They were having to coach their children about what to say at school when friends, or sometimes even teachers, asked what they thought about terrorism. For those living in the areas where the 7/7 bombers or terrorist suspects came from, it was even more difficult. One respondent spoke of the difficulty in going about one's daily business in the Leeds area of Beeston, home to three of the 7/7 bombers. Reliving her time in Leeds, she said, 'the whole world's media was in Leeds to film where the bombers came from' (Rabiya, London). Others living in areas with large Muslim populations told similar stories of police raids at the homes of people they knew directly or indirectly. Almost all the respondents had male relatives or friends who had been stopped and searched or detained at a UK airport. One young woman, a leader of a Muslim LGBT organisation, told of her experience of being stopped with male colleagues at a London mainline station on their return from France and being questioned by police about alleged links with Islamic extremists suspected of planning terrorist acts. Commenting wryly on the policemen's lack of perception, she said: 'we in [name of LGBT organisation] would be the last to know if such plans were on the way; extremists would kill us well before they kill other Britons' (Indameera, London).

Also, for the first time, some of the women directly experienced hate speech and acts in public areas. While always aware of the racism in British society, they had felt relatively protected from its worst effects in their close-knit families and hitherto largely ignored communities. For many, racism and hate crime happened to others but now they felt they were a potential target on any given day. For many, reporting incidents to the police was not an option. Tabasam (Bradford), a victim of hate speech, said she knew of Muslim taxi drivers and others who had been attacked in the wake of the 9/11 events but that none had gone to the police in whom they had little faith. Moreover, young women like herself were reluctant to let information about being attacked get back to their parents for fear of being questioned about why and with whom they were out at a certain time and so on.

The War on Terror as an Instigator to Public Involvement and Engagement with the State

One of the unanticipated consequences of the War on Terror was the increased involvement in civic and political life which Muslim women including several of our respondents came to enjoy. Their involvement came about in three main ways: fired by concern or anger and through their own individual initiative, they felt a need or duty to do something to reverse negative public perceptions of Muslim communities or counter the attacks and prejudices that Muslims faced in the aftermath of the 9/11 and 7/7 events; they were already active in civic and political life and were consequently approached by political organisations anxious to be seen as diverse and inclusive; or they entered public life through government programmes to engage Muslim women as a means of countering Islamic terrorism—for example, the 'Muslim women talk' campaign launched in August 2005 as the start of a dialogue between Muslim women and government after the 7/7 London bombings, the creation of the NMWAG and the Prevent programme which saw the emergence of various Muslim women's organisations.

A number of women decided individually that they had to do something to reverse the negative effects of the War on Terror. Thus Tabasam (Bradford), a teacher, started extracurricular citizenship classes at her school for Muslim pupils in the hope that this would reduce their alienation from majority British society. She claimed that whereas Britain had provided opportunities in education and political engagement and also important human rights to her, younger Muslims were alienated from civic and political life and felt they had few if any rights. She believed that learning about the social and political institutions of British society would ultimately improve their relationship with Britain. Rabiya (London), at University at the time of the 7/7 London bombings and involved in student politics, offered mediation between Muslim students and the university authorities. She believed she became an essential 'point of call for lots of people' and that she contributed to the prevention of a backlash against Muslim students at the university. In the case of another two respondents, the War on Terror sowed a desire to join British counter-terrorism agencies. Tahira (Coventry) wanted to get into counter-terrorism not only to combat extremist violence but also to change the way state agencies dealt with it—for example, she was horrified by their complete disregard for human rights. Almeera (Coventry) actually applied to MI5 but failed to get past her interview. Almeera's motives centred on stopping groups using religion for their own political ends: 'I hate these people; it's not fair on people who peacefully believe in religion, it's not fair on people like me and my brothers who are Muslim but don't really practice and are discriminated against.' Other respondents, already active in civic and political life, were approached by political parties. Thus, Almeera was approached by Young Labour to join the party and was seen as a potential local election candidate while Shula (London) was courted by the Conservative Party and ended up running its women's Muslim group.

Finally, several women became involved in government counter-terror programmes following the 7/7 London bombings. Some were approached as individuals while others formed part of new or existing organisations which benefitted from Prevent funding. Bilkis (London), a head teacher, was one such individual asked by Tony Blair to be part of a group to advise government on understanding and stemming disaffection among young British Muslims. Bilkis accepted the invitation in order to tell government 'not to marginalise the majority of law-abiding, good Muslim people because when Islam and terrorism become linked, it makes people feel society is not caring for them'. Indameera (London) and Farhat (Glasgow), both leaders of Muslim women's organisations, accepted engagement with the state and thus benefitted from funding made available through the Prevent programme even though Farhat had misgivings about using funds which 'linked Islam and terrorism' and because she argued 'women can't stop terrorism'. Indameera also recognised that while the War on Terror had impacted negatively on Muslims, it had, nevertheless, placed them in a position where 'in terms of funding we have tended to receive more money than other similar groups'. This uncomfortable position was acknowledged by many Muslim women's organisations which were often accused by other Muslims of signing up to a snoopers' charter drawn up by the state.

Policing Women's Behaviour—France

Many of our respondents expressed enormous concern about the emergence and consolidation, since the early 2000s, of groups of young Muslim men, largely of Maghrebi origin on urban housing estates (*cités*), who had taken it upon themselves, as they became increasingly influenced by a hyper-masculine interpretation of Islam, to police the morals and social/sexual behaviour of young women. Accordingly, young women who rebelled, whether against Islamic dress or against what was deemed appropriate behaviour for Muslim women, had to be brought under control by *les grands frères*.[5] This issue was raised by women's organisations shortly after the events of 9/11. In 2002, the organisation Ni putes ni soumises was founded by Fadela Amara to fight what she saw as the increasing degradation of gender relations into violence, in a context of socio-economic deprivation, particularly in urban areas which were home to large populations of Muslim and migrant background.[6] Ni putes ni soumises promised to shatter the silence surrounding male violence and the policing of women in Muslim communities (Amara 2004). Individual testimonies about the violent policing of women by men also fed concerns about the security and freedom of young Muslim women. For example, in her firsthand account, *Dans l'enfer des tournantes* (2003), Samira Bellil revealed the nature of gang rapes of young women carried out perhaps because the women had spoken with a young man in what was seen as a flirtatious manner or had gone out clubbing with friends—in other words, had 'misbehaved'. Others have blogged about being punished by *les grands frères* for not dressing modestly, going out and having fun or for having a sexual relationship (Menusier 2008).

While none of our respondents had been victims of such violent policing, several had lived or worked in disadvantaged Muslim communities and had moved away from those neighbourhoods precisely to escape a world where women's whereabouts and actions were constantly monitored and reputations broken at the drop of a hat:

> ...girls can't go out because of their father or brother...these girls who live in the *cité* where everyone knows everything about everyone else, everyone's keeping tabs on everyone—you only have to be seen once with such and such a person or doing something out of the ordinary and you get known as a not very nice girl and that goes round the estate, there goes your reputation... (Radia, Paris)

Farah, Natori, Keltoun and Safa (all from Paris) had moved away from neighbourhoods they described as 'closed in'. Farah argued that growing up and staying in one place all your life necessarily placed you in a relation with other groups jostling for power. Thus, young Muslim men who are so watched and controlled by the police became 'guards' and in turn policed young women. She believed that by moving away from the *cité* where she was born and brought up, she had escaped the oppressive chain of groups and hence control by young men. The others also spoke of being able to breathe and enjoy freedom from the scrutiny of neighbours and control of *les grands frères*.

While the respondents who raised the issue of men policing women utterly condemned the violence of the young men who claimed to be the guardians of morality, they pointed out that these represented only a minority of Muslim men and, moreover, that violence against women took place in all social strata and ethnic groups of French society. They also said they could see how these young men got into this situation, laying at least part of the blame on French society. There was a consensus among respondents that while young men were being led to radical variants of Islam by extremist imams and scholars, this path was made easier for them by recurrent government policies of social and economic neglect which saw rising unemployment, the deterioration of education provision and social services and ultimately the pushing of young people, particularly boys and young men of Black and ethnic Muslim background, into the margins of society. The convergence of poverty, exclusion and radical Islam as an apparent cure-all had led some young men to set themselves up as *petits caïds* who believed they had the right to control women through violence.

Our respondents' analysis of the entrapment of young Muslim women in cycles of male control was multilayered and consisted of explanations which took into account the socio-economic situation of the women as well as the psychological aspects of their relations with family and others in the *cités*. For some respondents, the main reason as to why young Muslim women became prey to violent control was that they were failed by French society. Their disadvantage and inevitable lack of success, particularly in education, led to a sense of despair and loss of confidence—an 'imprisonment in what was familiar, an inability to move towards the unfamiliar' (Farah, Paris). According to Sahar (Saint Denis), this then reproduced timeworn patterns of 'dropping out of school, having babies early—lots of them and—[being stuck] in the housing estates'. Soundous (Paris) who worked on neighbourhood projects with such women testified to their sense of resignation to a particular fate and unwillingness, at least initially, to try out new experiences or be responsible for any neighbourhood project tasks. For other respondents, the fact of being caught between cultures—that of their parents and that of French society—provided a reason as to why young Muslim women had turned increasingly towards religion, sometimes using that as a reason to give up on their own agency and consequently become compliant with the demands made by *les grands frères*. Lina (Paris) echoed others' thinking when she claimed:

> French Muslim girls born in France have the opportunity to have a twin culture, that of their parents, at home, and that which they learn outside [in French society]. But at some point in their life, instead of seeing this twin culture as an advantage, they find themselves caught in between—they don't know which foot to put forward—outside it's friends, boyfriends, dates and sex but at home they come up against taboos...They lose their bearings and so religion becomes an explanation for all the taboos they face; religion becomes a cover.

For Randa (Marseille) and Wahida (Fontenay-sous-Bois), increased religiosity among Muslim girls and women explained why some of them became susceptible to violent control by young men in the *cités*. One strategy deployed by young women to acquire a degree of independence and power in their neighbourhood was to align themselves with young men. Diana, a young Muslim woman of Mauritanian origin and inhabitant of a low-rise estate in Paris, who dropped out of school and had a history of petty crime, decided early in her teens to become one of the boys not only because she found the girls tedious but because it also afforded her protection. Natori (Paris) spoke of pious Muslim women who colluded in policing other young women. She mentioned women she knew from school who had continued to keep a check on her and felt free to judge her years after she had moved away from her old neighbourhood:

> Last year I saw some of them and they said 'you're 30, unmarried, no kids, you're renting with people, you're not working! Come with us to the mosque…you're sinning, a stray sheep who needs to get back to her religion'.

Thus being a tough girl/woman and one of the boys or being a 'good' Muslim woman who helped control others served young women as useful strategies in gaining a space where male control could be circumvented and they could operate with relative independence.

Conclusion

This chapter demonstrates that Muslim women are interested in a range of issues pertaining to the political, economic, social and cultural–religious domains. It counters prevalent public perceptions that they are uninterested in what happens beyond their doorstep. Not only are women from Muslim communities concerned by a number of different issues but they are eager and able to provide as insightful an analysis of themselves as politicians and other specialists who dominate public platforms. In articulating their views, they appear undaunted by dominant opinions in majority society and their own communities. Therefore, they offer a different and direct voice about matters affecting them most. This chapter presents the issues over which concern was expressed and examines in greater depth issues which were raised repeatedly in our discussions. Thus, where the wearing of Islamic dress in a Western context is concerned, we were compelled to look beyond the idea that, on the one hand, head and face coverings are a requirement in Islam and, on the other hand, that they signify women's oppression in Islam which is how they are frequently presented in Western media and public discourses. Second, in considering the impact of the War on Terror on Muslim women in Britain, not only were we offered insights into the effects of hard counter-terrorism measures on respondents' daily life, we were also informed about the unexpected opportunities for public engagement which emerged through counter-terrorism/extremism programmes and about the discomfort and contradictions respondents experienced in engaging with the British state. Finally, our respondents in France discussed the violent control exerted by Muslim men over young Muslim women in disadvantaged urban neighbourhoods, providing an insider analysis of factors influencing the degradation of gender relations. These issues are political—they relate to gender, race/ethnic rights and the right to practice one's faith and have been the subject of public and parliamentary debate and law making. They are also the object of study in political science and sociology, having been highlighted by feminist social scientists. The issues of Islamic dress, salient in both countries, and that of the War on Terror and its impacts in Britain address relations of power between Muslim women and the state on the one hand and between Muslim women and majority civil society on the other hand. The issue of violence and control within deprived ethnic/Muslim communities in France relates not only to private *versus* public spaces for women and the gendered power relations which arise from that division but also to state policy which determines the distribution of resources and the accumulation of economic, social and cultural capital among such communities. In raising and acting upon these issues through their participation in civic and political arenas, women from Muslim communities are going to the root of struggles for gender, race and faith equality and in doing so are acting as agents of societal change. This chapter constitutes one of the few sources which give voice to women from Muslim communities in Britain and France.

Notes

1. There is a postcolonial literature on women and Islamic dress which traces contemporary Western thinking to nineteenth-century orientalism and critiques the prolific literature produced by colonialists which depicted the veil as a symbol of the oppression of colonised women who could only be emancipated as part of the West's civilising mission (Fanon 1967; Hoodfar 1992; Yegenoglu 1998).
2. The notion of 'third culture children' developed by Pollock and Van Reken (2009) refers to children—and adults—born and raised in a culture not of their parents and who do not feel entirely part of the culture of the country in which they are born/brought up.
3. Since 2001 a panoply of laws has been added to the Terrorism Act of 2000, including the Anti-Terrorism, Crime and Security Act

2001, the Prevention of Terrorism Act 2005, the Terrorism Act 2006, the Counter-Terrorism Act 2008 and most recently the Counter-Terrorism and Security Act 2015.
4. TPIMs may be placed on terror suspects who cannot be charged or deported due to lack of evidence. TPIMs may last for two years or longer if new suspicions of involvement in terrorist activity arise. TPIMs include electronic tagging, regular reporting by terror suspects to the police, the obligation to remain at a permanent UK address without recourse to temporary movement, supervised use of mobile telephones and the Internet.
5. *Les grands frères* refers to young men—bound together by non-familial social ties—who gain power in socially deprived urban housing estates. 'Good' *grands frères* often assume a mediating role in social conflicts which occur in these areas while 'bad' *grands frères* may be involved in crime. Either way, according to Duret (1998: 9), *les grands frères* are able to gamble with the lives of young residents in their neighbourhoods in games of personal power. They are also referred to as *petits caïds*—petty gang leaders.
6. Amara and her associates were provoked to act by the brutal murder of 17-year-old Sohane Benziane who was burned alive because her boyfriend and his gang did not accept her rebellious behaviour.

CHAPTER 9

Conclusion

Our research evidences the aspirations and engagement of Muslim women in public life against presumptions to the contrary. Thus, it is at variance with prevailing prejudices about Muslim women's passivity and lack of interest in civic and political life. Moreover, the women under study here display inventive modes of participation and strategies in order to negotiate the numerous obstacles thrown in the path towards their autonomisation, in an environment fraught with constraints emanating from their own communities and majority society.

Our investigation of Muslim populations in Britain and France reveals that women comprise almost half of the seven million plus Muslims in both countries. It provides an understanding of this population of women through an examination of both countries' migration histories—with the arrival of the first large cohorts of Muslim women in the 1970s and the emergence of subsequent generations of daughters—and also through the construction of a socio-demographic portrait based on population characteristics, educational experience and attainment and economic activity, from available data disaggregated by gender, ethnic/national origin and religious affiliation (Britain only). The portrait which emerges is that of a young and multi-ethnic population concentrated in Paris, London and other major conurbations. Moreover, the majority are positioned at the bottom of the socio-economic pyramid. This knowledge forms an important backdrop for an understanding of not only how Muslim women live and move between different areas of social and political life but also of the barriers and facilitators they encounter in staking a claim in British and French society. Nevertheless, this picture of Muslim women is necessarily subjective for it relies on often imperfect counting methods used by population statisticians and scholars. Recognising this deficiency, our study elucidates the French universalist and British multiculturalist frameworks which determine whether and how Muslims should be counted and understood.

In France and Britain, most Muslims trace their roots to ex-colonies although more recently arrived groups from the Muslim world have joined them. Muslims have thus been written into a historical relationship with the country of their settlement which has influenced their capacity to participate in civic and political life. First, racism and discrimination have governed the interaction between the receiving countries and these populations. Another shaping factor was their access to full political rights which, as Commonwealth subjects, they enjoyed immediately upon their settlement in Britain while in France their status as foreigners/*étrangers* denied them such rights. Moreover, Muslims faced a differentiated approach towards immigrants in the two countries. In Britain there developed a multicultural/multifaith policy according recognition to ethnic and religious communities in contrast with France where republican assimilationism, reinforced by a rigid interpretation of *laïcité*, prevented such recognition. However, anti-Muslim hostility and prejudice hit both countries as Islam emerged internationally and nationally due to the events of 9/11, 7/7 and the Afghanistan and Iraq wars. Subsequently, populations previously identified as Arab in France and Pakistani or Bangladeshi in Britain became Muslim in public discourse and policies. Islam which came to represent Otherness was also constructed as an existential threat: through the War on Terror in Britain and women's Islamic dress in France. Restrictive legislation and policies bore down on Muslims in both countries, undermining their efforts to make a place for themselves in Britain and France and multiplying obstacles to their political and civic participation. However, state policy has also spurred Muslim women to enter the public arena, for instance, through their participation in anti-war campaigns in Britain, their mobilisation against the 2004 law which effectively targeted the headscarf in French schools and their involvement in community organisations. Additionally, Muslim women's engagement in politics and civic life has been influenced by their relationship with majority women's movements and the extent to which their issues are included in feminist agendas and demands made of the state to improve women's lives.

Historically, mainstream feminism has failed to include Muslim women's issues in the struggle for women's rights. At worst it is accused by Muslim women of collusion with the state in introducing legislation impacting negatively on them, while at best majority feminists have remained silent. In France, most feminists supported the law of 2004, banning conspicuous religious symbols in schools but which really targeted the Muslim headscarf, and that of 2010 which prohibits the face veil in public. In Britain, the women's movement is criticised for not lending clear support to Muslim women and recognising the damaging effects of racism and Islamophobia on them. White British feminists have been reproached for not wanting to touch 'cultural' or religious issues (such as female excision or freedom to wear the face veil) affecting minoritised and Muslim women and leaving them entirely to Black and ethnic minority feminism. Notwithstanding recent tentative alliances between younger Western and Muslim activists, the absence of sure support from majority feminism, compounded by the refusal of many mainstream feminists to recognise that feminism may be combined with Islamic belief, has led Muslim women to organise and campaign separately or within Black and ethnic minority feminism.

Our respondents assessed the obstacles and facilitators they encountered in three significant spheres: the ethnic group, majority society and Islam/the Muslim group. The sphere (ethnic group) where their primary socialisation took place was perceived by them as an ambivalent source of restrictions and support. The family and community offered a familiar and protective environment in a new, sometimes hostile majority society while also limiting the women's capacity for action. Generally the women valued their closeness to the immediate family upon whom they often called for emotional or logistical help despite the possibility of eliciting responses which could thwart their aspirations. Conversely, the extended family and community were considered a source of impediment to their autonomisation. The women blamed them for restrictions and norms grounded in patriarchal traditions where women were duty-bound to the men and elders in the group while being subordinated to the collective. This view was more prevalent in Britain than in France owing to the greater weight of the ethnic community there. Generally the women completely rejected any authority claimed by the community, invariably led by older men, to interfere in their plans—whether to pursue education, undertake employment or become involved in civic and political life.

Islam and Muslims have become the hostages of geopolitical and societal tensions in France and Britain. The spotlighting of Islam nationally and internationally has inflicted increased prejudice and constraints on Muslims while Islam has been constructed as public enemy number one following the events of 9/11 and those of 7/7.[1] This has crystallised around two major themes, namely, the securitisation of Islam in Britain and that of national identity in France. The legislative and cultural counterpart to the War on Terror in Britain has been the onslaught on women's Islamic dress in France with the full force of the state being deployed, although both questions arise in the two countries with a differentiated emphasis. Consequently, Muslim women suffer from multiple disadvantages, on racial and religious grounds, on gender grounds generally but also because of specific stereotypes to which they are subject. In Britain, the War on Terror made Muslims a target of intensified prejudice and hostility, generating widespread Islamophobia. Nevertheless, while denouncing the state offensive and public hostility towards Muslims, the vast majority of our respondents identified with Britain, as British Muslims, as they acknowledged the advantages of living in a multicultural/multifaith policy context, which allowed them to maintain their faith and belonging to Britain. In France, the events of 9/11 constituted less of a landmark and were superseded by the debate over women's Islamic dress, thus placing Muslim women in the front line of anti-Islam legislation and all-pervasive antagonism. Many women denounced the ideology behind a reinterpreted *laïcité* and its instrumentalisation by politicians who were arraigned for the predicament faced by Muslim women. Certainly, the latter found that it raised difficulties if they wished to identify as French and Muslim at the same time and hindered their engagement in the public sphere if they displayed visible markers of their faith. However, some of the respondents adopted a secular/*laïc* outlook on the grounds that it prevented Muslim and non-Muslim encroachment into their life. In both Britain and France, the women analysed the worsening of their situation as Muslims but also acknowledged that they had received support from some sectors of majority society in the realisation of their personal and collective projects. While majority society presented our respondents with challenges and constraints arising from prejudice, discrimination and legislation, it was also able to offer them tools of autonomisation.

Muslim women have had to steer through complex interconnections between their cultural and religious groups and wider society. They have had to negotiate the zigzag of facilitators and obstacles within the private sphere of family and the public spaces of community and Western society with various intersecting disadvantages arising from the interaction between these domains; for instance, restrictions based on gender relations within traditional communities could be reinforced by wider society's stereotypes of Muslim women. In Britain, respondents denounced governments and political parties for excluding Muslim women from policymaking as, historically, state-recognised interlocutors had been older Muslim men who by virtue of their position in local mosques, businesses or voluntary organisations claimed to speak for all Muslims. In France, legislation such as that prohibiting the headscarf in the public sector entailed comparable restrictions as it barred Muslim women who wore Islamic dress from employment and engagement in state institutions and services. On the other hand, majority society also assisted the women in their autonomisation. For instance, progressive legislation, public or third sector services could offer Muslim women protection in several areas—domestic violence, forced marriage and so on. The women's capacity for action rested on their being able to take advantage of facilitators while neutralising obstacles arising from oppressive cultural norms or majority society discriminatory practices.

Furthermore, engagement in civic and political life depends on variables which pertain not only to structural features but also to subjective considerations. Our empirical research allowed us to trace the parameters of Muslim women's action. One feature revealed by our research was the women's self-reflexivity and capacity to examine their situation critically. Many demonstrated a rational understanding of their environment by identifying the contradictions and tensions in the structural–cultural framework they submitted to analysis. This was favoured by the societal references they could make to their or their parents' country of origin, their links to a world religion within a minority situation and the society wherein they lived. Thus they were well-placed to recognise and remove the wool pulled over their eyes by custom and ideology. The second variable was their emotional commitment to certain issues and problems which prompted them into action. This commitment was heightened by their personal experiences of gender, ethnic/'race' discrimination, hostility to their religion and their links to the developing world where human rights violations and military aggressions occurred in conditions of poverty and social inequality. Finally, a more fragile component underpinning their engagement was confidence in themselves to take action. This was wrought by a combination of four elements we identified. First, many women found *individual support* for their projects among influential people in their immediate family; or a well-established Muslim/ethnic community or majority society member, for example, a doctor, teacher, *imam*. *Environmental and circumstantial factors* also played a significant role, for example, the cultural and social capital or experience of political activism possessed by one's parents or access to decent public services and educational opportunities. The *legal and structural framework* (progressive gender policies and legislation supported by well-resourced welfare bodies, local government, etc.) could offer support through the reduction of socio-economic disadvantages. The existence of 'corporate agents' (Archer 1995)—trade unions or cooperatives organisations—promoting collective interests, including those of minoritised women, represented an important catalyst for activism and action. Finally, many women cited *role models and inspirational persons* as a central lever of action. Such confidence boosters, leading to small victories in autonomisation, fed into a virtuous cycle often resulting in an exponential increase in political and civic engagement. Furthermore, political mobilisation around a specific issue could lead to activism in other areas while one type of participation could lead to another and expand one's repertoire of action.

Evaluating the balance between favourable and adverse factors the women elaborated strategies to pursue their participation in public and advance their life projects. This collection of strategies comprised six main types which operated in various combinations: *confrontation*, often when contradictions were so antagonistic that no other option was feasible; *cooperation*, either with the family or with majority society institutions when the latter parties' schemes coincided with the women's aspirations and plans; *compromise*, where a give-and-take approach satisfied respondents and those with whom they interacted; a *lateral* approach which entailed sidestepping obstacles rather than tackling them head on; a *reversal* approach which involved appropriating the opponents' arguments and tools in order to challenge them. Finally, some respondents adopted an *exit* strategy, renouncing their aspirations and plans. Of these strategies, none was deployed exclusively by any particular individual, in any particular situation. They were used in combination or succession according to circumstances, the power relations at play and what was deemed most likely to succeed. The chosen mode of action was also linked to the best-judged strategy and expected result relative to the personal cost involved.

Turning to Islam and the Muslim group, we found that it was important in terms of both Muslim women's identification and their engagement in the public sphere. Besides, their relationship to Islam was expressed in relation to the societal and institutional frameworks in Britain and

France. Islam and the Muslim group displayed multifaceted characteristics, whether they hindered action or constituted a tool of autonomisation and catalyst for action. Their position vis-à-vis Islam also influenced respondents' modes of action, where they participated and the issues they pursued. Islam elicited diverse responses from Muslim women.

First, the women who rejected a religious identification (more so in France than in Britain) listed four different reasons. Some women articulated complete opposition to Islam because they held an atheist or Marxian worldview. This led them to join organisations and campaigns in majority society to either confront Islam or challenge discrimination affecting Muslims. Other women adopted a confrontational attitude to Islam arguing that it eschewed equality between women and men altogether, that women should be subservient to men. Women in this category were most likely to join feminist organisations. Yet other women were not religious but wished to be recognised as 'cultural Muslims'; they faced the double conundrum of asserting this cultural heritage independently of the religious group while spurning a religious labelling by majority society. Lastly, some women declared themselves 'political Muslims', defending the rights of Muslims against all forms of discrimination. The latter were often active in majority society and the ethnic group, in initiatives which were unconnected to religion, except when they opposed Islam or defended Muslims against religious discrimination.

Second, a significant number of women were religious and identified with Islam; in Britain they comprised the majority of our informants. Here again they spanned a diversity of types. One type followed religion in a secularised manner, their Islam remaining private and individualised—a relationship between God and themselves—in common with followers of other religions in Europe. This group did not allow outside interference with their practice and decisions to participate in the public domain. A second type seized upon Islam as an instrument to contest traditional practices. They searched Islamic texts for arguments to support their autonomy and reclaim their right to participate in education, employment, political and civic life against established groups they accused of promoting masculine interpretations of Islam aimed at controlling women. A third type pursued a personal, spiritual quest to attain a better understanding of their religion; many of them followed Sufi strands of Islam. A fourth type searched for authenticity and developed into two different but interconnected directions: those who aimed to divest Islam of ethnic traditions and those who opposed the all-embracing prescriptions presented by political reformist movements, both seeking alternative insights to the prevalent masculine ones. Rather than censuring Islam *per se*, religious women focused their critique on established interpretations and implementation. They challenged Muslims from within, from an Islamic standpoint. A substantial number of Muslim women discovered in Islam a response to male domination and a means to develop their life projects. They called on Islamic values against cultural norms, believing that the former possessed greater moral worth than the latter.

Despite nuances differentiating the two countries, the relationship of the respondents to Islam in France and Britain displayed much commonality with Islam acting as an important compass for their action in public life. For most of the Muslim women in Britain and all those who were believers in France, Islam represented a powerful motivator of engagement, linking politics and ethics. It was held up as a source of values, an ethical guide for the conduct of their actions, and it played a significant role in the meaning of their engagement and the causes they embraced. Many women also emphasised its humanist vocation, through a twin ethical–universalist dimension. In both France and Britain, whether privately or publicly expressed, Islam was adopted as a moral code and guide for action in everyday life towards both Muslims and non-Muslims, through a commitment to human values. The women could perform their activism in majority society or within the ethnic or Muslim group, according to the opportunities available, though conditioned by the legislative framework and male control, respectively. Clearly, these women were staking a claim to their place in Islam and majority society, refuting any suggestion that they should choose between the two. Muslim women were using their faith as a guide which connected politics with morals. In both countries, Islam and its religious dimension were perceived by many women as an experience which could assemble and connect different facets of their identity. Muslim women steered their action within a complex social fabric, across the three spheres of reference: the ethnic group, the Islam/Muslim group and majority society. The inner workings of each provided them with opportunities but also threw up contradictions which incited them to act. Consequently, a syncretism of action emerged from the interaction between the three spheres with obstacles and facilitators within each influencing the issues mobilising Muslim women and their modes of action.

Our study of Muslim women's engagement in politics also led us to re-examine the definition of politics and the areas of activity covered. This re-examination underpins our typology of Muslim women's activism. Four main areas were identified: formal institutional politics; street politics; everyday politics and public service and community politics. Within this spectrum, in both countries, the most common forms of participation among Muslim women are voting and action in community organisations. Conversely, Muslim women were least likely to be involved in formal institutional politics which explains their low presence in political parties, elected assemblies and political executives, and more so in France than in Britain. In terms of other forms of participation, Muslim women in France were more present in street politics, strike action, political discussions and petitioning while in Britain they registered higher levels of volunteering and involvement in charity campaigns. This difference correlates with the political cultures of the two countries—conflictual in France and consensual in Britain—and reflects majority society modes of action. A paradox revealed by our research is that while many respondents stated they knew or understood little about politics, they often advanced an articulate analysis of national and international events. The participation of respondents in both countries was staged through complex interconnections involving their ethno-religious communities, international Islam and majority society. Many displayed a sharp awareness of their social and political environment, including national and international contexts and consequently produced sophisticated analyses of their own political thinking and engagement. Moreover, while we could have inferred that Muslim women's scarce presence in formal institutional politics implied a lack of interest in the *res publica*, they demonstrated a determination to take action through community organisations.

Until the late 1990s, Muslim women's participation was related to their/their parents' country of origin, mobilisation against racism and discrimination in majority society and/or patriarchy within their own communities. In France this was delayed because of the 'foreigner'/*étranger* status of many immigrants who therefore lacked any political rights, unlike Commonwealth immigrants in Britain, and because they were legally barred from founding associations until 1981. The 2000s saw an expansion of Muslim women's organisations. In Britain, this can be explained by the mobilisation against Islamophobia, Muslim women's demands to be heard by the authorities, independently of men, and by the state's attempts to co-opt their support for counter-terrorism programmes by offering funds for existing and new organisations. In France, the dire lack of funding constituted a huge barrier against the advancement of Muslim women's organisations. However, the 2004 'headscarf law', the rampant Islamophobia fuelled by the Front National and the anti-Muslim discourses of politicians provoked Muslim women into action. Their organisations provided social welfare, legal and other services according to their members'/clients' needs. Moreover, some developed variants of Islamic feminism and a critique of established Islam while also confronting French feminist responses to racism and Islamophobia. Both countries witnessed the growth of Muslim women organisations fulfilling important social and educational functions among disadvantaged populations. The issues championed by Muslim women and which figure on the agenda of their community organisations revolve around social justice and care, nationally and internationally; gender inequality, ethnic/racial discrimination and Islamophobia; poverty, social inequality and human rights. Those who professed their faith affirmed that their involvement was geared towards making a difference for the better; that it was their Islamic duty to advance social justice and care. Such aims unquestionably pertain to the domain of politics while their attainment lends itself to collective political and civic action. Thus we argue for a broad conceptualisation of 'doing politics' which includes not just institutional and timeworn unconventional forms of politics but also activities in the civic sphere, undertaken by third sector organisations and informal groups.

Finally, our study shows that Muslim women are concerned by a range of socio-economic and political questions and problems. Among these we highlight three—that of Islamic dress, the impacts of the War on Terror and the policing of young women by men—because these were most frequently raised by respondents in our discussions with them. Our examination of these issues through the lens of Muslim women confirmed their interest in public life and their capacity not just to understand and analyse the specificities of Muslim women's situation in two major Western countries, but also to communicate that insider understanding. Thus, they compelled us to look beyond the simplistic argument that head and face coverings are a requirement in Islam or that they signify Islam's oppression of women and led us to consider other meanings. In considering the impact of the War on Terror in Britain, not only did we gain insights into the effects of 'hard' counter-terrorism measures on respondents' daily lives, but we also learned of the opportunities for public engagement which Muslim women encountered through participation in 'soft' counter-terrorism programmes and of the contradictions they experienced in engaging with the state. Finally, the respondents in France presented an analysis, without fear or favour, of factors contributing to the playing out of gender relations in certain Muslim neighbourhoods where men exercised violent control over young Muslim women. In all cases, the insights and analyses presented ran counter to the assumptions made about Muslim women which prevail in majority society.

What is the future for women from Muslim communities and their participation in political and civic life? Part of their story will be tied with that of women generally, and women's participation in parties, elections, local politics, elected assemblies, civic organisations, street politics and so on. While there has been a lessening of the participation gender gap, women continue to lack resources—time, money, support networks, political skills and experience—and face barriers such as those deriving from the type of electoral and party systems in place or working conditions within legislatures which block or restrict their access to decision-influencing/making sites. Additionally, Muslim women's particular positioning within and at the intersection of majority society, their ethnic group and Islam and the development of this emplacement will determine their future participation in public life.

Muslim women account for about 3.4 million or half of all Muslims in Britain and France. The majority live in some of the most deprived communities where they are often economically dependent on family, bound by duty to be 'good' wives/mothers/daughters and where male community elders are the preferred interlocutors of political/civic authorities. Consequently, their lack of financial, time and network resources will impact severely on their capacity for political and civic action and accumulating political experience and skills. Nevertheless, Muslim women are contesting patriarchal community norms about their appropriate family/community roles, the authority of male elders to speak on their behalf and their own leadership capabilities. Moreover, many are using opportunities provided by majority society and their interpretation of Islam as the provider of women's rights to facilitate their participation in public life. These once-started challenges will continue to run and multiply. Finally, although majority society has provided Muslim women with certain tools for their autonomisation, barriers arising from racism, Islamophobia and the reluctant accommodation of Muslims will resist their progress. But while political elites continue to restrict the place of Muslims in French and British society, Muslims are received favourably by seven in ten adults in both countries (Stokes 2015).

Note

1. The 2015 terrorist attacks in France took place after our fieldwork was completed and are too recent to be incorporated in our analysis.

References

Abbas, T. (Ed.). (2005). *Muslim Britain: Communities under pressure*. London: Zed Books.

Adler, R. P., & Goggin, J. (2005). What do we mean by "civic engagement'? *Journal of Transformative Education, 3*(3), 236–253.

Adrian, M. (2015). *Religious freedom at risk: The EU, French schools and why the veil was banned*. Heidelberg, New York, London: Springer.

AFP (2010) (Agence France Presse). (2010). Entre 5 et 6 millions de musulmans en France. *Le Point*, 28 June. Retrieved July 12, from http://www.lepoint.fr/politique/entre-5-et-6-millions-de-musulmans-en-france-28-06-2010-471071_20.php

Afshar, H. (1998). Strategies of resistance among the Muslim minority in West Yorkshire: Impact on women. In N. Charles & H. Hintjens (Eds.), *Gender, ethnicity and political ideologies* (pp. 107–126). London: Routledge.

Afshar, H., Aitken, R., & Franks, M. (2005). "Feminisms', Islamophobia and identities. *Political Studies, 53*(2), 262–283.

Ahmad, F. (2001). Modern traditions? British Muslim women and academic achievement. *Gender and Education, 13*(2), 137–152.

Ahmad, F., Lissenburg, S., & Modood, T. (2012). South Asian women and employment in Britain: Diversity and social change. In E. Spaan, F. Hillmann, & T. Van Naerssen (Eds.), *Asian migrants and European labour markets* (pp. 115–137). London: Routledge.

Akbarzadeh, S., & Roose, J. M. (2011). Muslims, multiculturalism and the question of the silent majority. *Journal of Muslim Minority Affairs, 31*(3), 309–325.

Akhtar, J. (1996). *Pakistanis in Britain in the 1990s and beyond*. Birmingham: Pakistani Forum.

Akhtar, P. (2012). British Muslims and local democracy: After Bradford. *openDemocracy*, 20 April. Retrieved May 20, 2015, from https://www.opendemocracy.net/idea/parveen-akhtar/british-muslims-and-local-democracy-after-bradford

Akhtar, P. (2015). The paradox of patronage politics. Biradari, representation and political participation amongst British Pakistanis. In T. Peace (Ed.), *Muslims and political participation in Britain* (pp. 15–31). London: Routledge.

Ali, Z. (2012). Des musulmanes en France: féminisme islamique et nouvelles formes de l'engagement pieux. *Religioscope*, 19 September. Retrieved September 14, 2015, from http://religion.info

Alibhai-Brown, Y. (2015). As a Muslim women, I see the veil as a rejection of progressive values. *The Guardian*, 20 March. Retrieved January 20, 2016, from http://www.theguardian.com/commentisfree/2015/mar/20/muslim-woman-veil-hijab

Allen, S. (1998). Identity: Feminist perspectives on "race', ethnicity and nationality. In N. Charles & H. Hintjens (Eds.), *Gender, ethnicity and political ideologies* (pp. 46–64). London: Routledge.

Allen, C., & Guru, S. (2012). Between political fad and political empowerment: A critical evaluation of the National Muslim Women's Advisory Group (MWMAG) and Governmental processes of engaging women. *Sociological Research Online*, *17*(3). Retrieved May 10, 2014, from http://www.socresonline.org.uk/17/3/17.html

Allen, C., Isakjee, A., & Ogtem, O. (2013). *Maybe we are hated. The experience and impact of anti-Muslim hate on British Muslim women (Report)*. Birmingham: University of Birmingham Institute of Applied Social Studies.

Allwood, G. (1998). *French feminisms: Gender and violence in contemporary theory*. London: UCL Press.

Allwood, G., & Wadia, K. (2000). *Women and politics in France 1958–2000*. London: Routledge.

Allwood, G., & Wadia, K. (2001). Gender and class in Britain and France. *Journal of European Area Studies*, *9*(2), 163–189.

Allwood, G., & Wadia, K. (2002). Feminism: National and international perspectives. *Modern & Contemporary France*, *10*(2), 211–223.

Allwood, G., & Wadia, K. (2004). Improving women's representation in France and India. *Canadian Journal of Political Science*, *37*(2), 107–126.

Allwood, G., & Wadia, K. (2009). *Gender and policy in France*. Basingstoke: Palgrave Macmillan.

Allwood, G., & Wadia, K. (2010). *Refugee women in Britain and France*. Manchester: Manchester University Press.

Amar, N. (2001). Les jeunes femmes issues de l'immigration sont-elles victimes de discrimination ? *La lettre des Amis de la Médina*, *11*, 22–24.

Amara, F. (2004). *Ni putes, ni soumises*. Paris: Éditions La Découverte.

Amiraux, V. (2002). The situation of Muslims in France. In *Monitoring the EU accession process: Minority protection* (pp. 101–103). Budapest: Open Society Institute.

Amiraux, V. (2003a). Discours voilé sur les musulmanes en Europe: comment les musulmans sont-ils devenus des musulmanes? *Social Compass, 50*(1), 85–96.

Amiraux, V. (2003b). The perception of political Islam in Europe after September 11: Changing paradigm or changing actors. In A. Karam (Ed.), *Transnational political Islam*. London: Pluto Press.

Amiraux, V. (2012). *Muslims in Paris (At home in Europe project)*. New York: Open Society Foundations.

Amiraux, V., & Simon, P. (2006). There are no minorities here: Cultures of scholarship and public debate on immigrants and integration in France. *International Journal of Comparative Sociology, 47*(3–4), 191–215.

Amnesty International. (2012). *Choice and prejudice: Discrimination against Muslims in Europe*. London: Amnesty International Ltd.

Amos, V., & Parmar, P. (1984). Challenging imperial feminism. *Feminist Review, 17*, 3–19.

Andall, J. (Ed.). (2003). *Gender and ethnicity in contemporary Europe*. Oxford: Berg.

Andezian, S. (1983). Pratiques féminines de l'Islam en France. *Archives des Sciences Sociales des Religions, 55*, 53–66.

Anwar, M. (2012). *Race and politics: Ethnic minorities and the British political system*. London and New York: Routledge.

Anwar, M., & Shah, F. (2000). Muslim women and experiences of discrimination in Britain. In J. Blaschke (Ed.), *Multi-level discrimination of Muslim women in Europe* (pp. 203–248). Berlin: Parabolis.

APPG (All-Party Parliamentary Group) on Race and Community. (2012). *Ethnic minority female employment: Black, Pakistani, Bangladeshi heritage women (first report of session 2012–2013)*. London: Runneymede Trust.

Archer, M. (2007). *Making our way through the world*. Cambridge: Cambridge University Press.

Archer, M. (1995). *Realist social theory: The morphogenetic approach*. Cambridge: Cambridge University Press.

Audit Commission. (2008). *Preventing extremism. Learning and development exercise*. London: Audit Commission/HMIC. Retrieved August 24, 2015, http://www.justiceinspectorates.gov.uk/hmic/media/preventing-violent-extremism-learning-and-development-exercise-20080930.pdf

Aziz, R. (1992). Feminism and the challenge of racism: Deviance or difference? In H. Crowley & S. Himmelweit (Eds.), *Knowing women: Feminism and knowledge* (pp. 291–305). Cambridge: Polity Press.

Ba, A. H. (2014). Femmes africaines immigrées responsables d'association face aux enjeux de citoyenneté et de développement: entre mimétisme et innovation en Île de France et dans le Nord-Pas-de-Calais. *Espace Populations Sociétés*. Retrieved October 4, 2015, from http://eps.revues.org/5891

Bagguley, P., & Hussain, Y. (2007). *The role of higher education in providing ppportunities for South Asian women*. Bristol: Policy Press (for Joseph Rowntree Foundation).
Ball, W., & Beckford, J. (1997). Religion, education and city politics: A case study of community mobilisation. In N. Jewson & S. MacGregor (Eds.), *Transforming cities. Contested governance and new spatial divisions* (pp. 193–204). London: Routledge.
Ballard, R. (1996). Negotiating race and ethnicity: Exploring the implications of the 1991 census. *Patterns of Prejudice, 30*(3), 3–33.
Bano, S. (2012). *Muslim women in Shari'ah councils: Transcending the boundaries of community and law*. Basingstoke: Palgrave Macmillan.
Barbara, A. (1992). Représentation de la femme musulmane par les non musulmans. *Migrations Sociétés, 4*(19), 11–22.
Barry, B. (2001). The muddles of multiculturalism. *New Left Review, 8,* 49–71.
Baston, L. (2012). *The Bradford earthquake*. Liverpool: Democratic Audit.
Baubérot, J. (1997). *La morale laïque contre l'ordre moral*. Paris: Seuil.
Baubérot, J. (2000). *Histoire de la laïcité*. Paris: PUF.
Baubérot, J. (2004). *La laïcité en question*. Paris: IFRI.
Baumard, M. (2015). François Hollande estime inutiles les statistiques ethniques. *Le Monde*, 5 February. Retrieved May 20, 2015, from http://www.lemonde.fr/societe/article/2015/02/05/francois-hollande-estime-inutiles-les--statistiques-ethniques_4571106_3224.html
BBC News. (2001). Britain "at war with terrorism'. *BBC News*, 16 September. Retrieved October 20, 2015, from http://news.bbc.co.uk/1/hi/uk_politics/1545411.stm
BBC News. (2006). "Remove full veils' urges Straw. *BBC News*, 6 October. Retrieved June 12, 2015, from http://news.bbc.co.uk/1/hi/uk/5411954.stm
Beauchemin, C., Hamel, C., & Simon, P. (Eds.) (2010). *Trajectoires et origines: enquête sur la diversité des populations en France* (Collection Documents du travail). Paris: INSEE/INED. Retrieved May 20, 2015, from https://www.ined.fr/fichier/s_rubrique/19558/dt168_teo.fr.pdf
Beckford, J. (2003). *Social theory and religion*. Cambridge: Cambridge University Press.
Beckford, J., & Gilliat, S. (1998). *Religion in prison, 'equal rites' in a multi-faith society*. Cambridge: Cambridge University Press.
Beckford, J., & Joly, D. (2006). "Race' relations and discrimination in prison: The case of Muslims in France and in Britain. *International Journal of Immigrant and Refugee Studies, 4*(2), 1–30.
Beckford, J., Joly, D., & Khosrokhavar, F. (2005). *Muslims in prison: Challenge and change in Britain and France*. Basingstoke: Palgrave Macmillan.
Belhadj, M. (1998). *Une révolution tranquille: stratégies professionnelles et dynamique familiale d'un groupe de femmes françaises d'origine algérienne*, PhD thesis. Paris: École des Hautes Études en Sciences Sociales.

Bell, D. S. (2000). *Presidential power in fifth republic France*. Oxford: Berg.
Belli, A. (2013). Limits and potentialities of the Italian and British political systems through the lens of Muslim women in politics. In J. Nielsen (Ed.), *Muslim political participation in Europe*. Edinburgh: Edinburgh University Press.
Bellil, S. (2003). *Dans l'enfer des tournantes*. Paris: Éditions Denoël.
Bengtsson, H., Weale, S., & Brooks, L. (2015). Record numbers of female and minority-ethnic MPs in new House of Commons. *The Guardian*, 8 May. Retrieved May 14, 2015, from http://www.theguardian.com/politics/2015/may/08/record-numbers-female-minority-ethnic-mps-commons
Benyon, J., & Solomos, J. (Eds.). (1987). *The roots of urban unrest*. Oxford: Pergamon.
Bernard, P., & Weill, N. (1998). Une virulente polémique sur les données "ethniques" divise les démographes. *Le Monde*, 6 November. Retrieved May 20, 2015, from http://www.lemonde.fr/archives/article/1998/11/06/une-virulente-polemique-sur-les-donnees-ethniques-divise-les-demographes_3698118_1819218.html?xtmc=une_virulente_polemique_sur_les_donnees_ethniques_divise_les_demographes&xtcr=3.
Bertossi, C. (2016). *La citoyenneté à la française. Valeurs et réalités*. Paris: Editions CNRS.
Bertossi, C. (2001). *Les frontières de la citoyenneté en Europe: nationalité, résidence, appartenance*. Paris: L'Harmattan.
Bertossi, C. (2004). Politics and policies of French citizenship, ethnic minorities and the European agenda. In P. Ruspini & A. Gorny (Eds.), *Migration in the new Europe: East-west revisited* (pp. 109–129). Basingstoke: Palgrave Macmillan.
Bhimji, F. (2012). *British Asian Muslim women. Multiple spatialities and cosmopolitanism*. Basingstoke: Palgrave Macmillan.
Bindel, J. (2013). Why are my fellow feminists shamefully silent over the tyranny of the veil, asks Julie Bindel. *Mail Online*, 17 September. Retrieved June 12, 2015, from http://www.dailymail.co.uk/debate/article-2424073/Why-fellow-feminists-shamefully-silent-tyranny-veil-asks-JULIE-BINDEL.html
Bladi.net. (2006). Refus de nationalité parce que hijab. *Bladi.net Forums*, 15 December. Retrieved October 20, 2015, from http://www.bladi.info/threads/refus-nationalite-hijab.85955/page-4
Boepflug, F., Dunand, F., & Willaime, J.-P. (1996). *Pour une mémoire des religions*. Paris: La Découverte.
Booth, H. (1985). Which "ethnic question'?: The development of questions identifying ethnic origin in official statistics. *The Sociological Review*, 33(2), 254–274.
Bouamama, S. (2004a). Ethnicisation et construction idéologique d'un bouc émissaire. In C. Nordmann (Ed.), *Le Foulard islamique en question*. Paris: Éditions Amsterdam.
Bouamama, S. (2004b). *L'affaire du foulard islamique: la production d'un racisme respectable*. Paris: Geai Bleu Éditions.
Bouchier, D. (1983). *The feminist challenge: The movement for women's liberation in Britain and the USA*. London: Macmillan.

Bourdieu, P. (1977). *Outline of a theory of practice.* Cambridge: Cambridge University Press.
Bourne, J. (1983). Towards an anti-racist feminism. *Race & Class, 25*(1), 1–22.
Bourque, S., & Grossholtz, J. (1974). Politics an unnatural practice: Political science looks at female participation. *Politics and Society, 4*(2), 225–266.
Bouteldja, N. (2011). *Why 32 Muslim women wear the full-face veil in France.* London, New York, Budapest: Open Society Foundations.
Bouteldja, N. (2014). France vs. England. In E. Brem (Ed.), *The experiences of face veil wearers in Europe and the law* (pp. 115–160). Cambridge: Cambridge University Press.
Bouvier, G. (2012). *Vue d'ensemble. Les descendants d'immigrés plus nombreux que les immigrés: une position française originale en Europe.* Paris: INSEE. Retrieved May 2, 2015, from http://www.insee.fr/fr/ffc/docs_ffc/ref/IMMFRA12_b_VE_posfra.pdf
Bouyarden, S. (2013). Political participation of European Muslims in France and the United Kingdom. In J. Nielsen (Ed.), *Muslim political participation in Europe* (pp. 102–128). Edinburgh: Edinburgh University Press.
Bowen, J. R. (2004). Pluralism and normativity in French Islamic reasoning. In R. Hefner (Ed.), *Remaking Muslim Politics* (pp. 326–346). Princeton, NJ: Princeton University Press.
Bowen, J. R. (2008). *Why the French don't like headscarves: Islam, the state and public space.* Princeton, NJ: Princeton University Press.
Bowen, J. R. (2009). *Can Islam be French?: Pluralism and pragmatism in a secularist state.* Princeton, NJ: Princeton University Press.
Boyd, R. (n.d.). Race, place and class: Who's speaking for who? British Library Spare Rib archives (theme: Representation and identity). Retrieved January 12, 2016, from http://www.bl.uk/spare-rib/articles/race-place-and-class-whos-speaking-for-who
Boyer, A. (1998). *L'Islam en France.* Paris: Presses Universitaires de France.
Brah, A. (2001). 'Race', and 'Culture' in the gendering of labour markets: Young South Asian women and the British labout market (WLUML Dossier 23–34). Retrieved May 10, 2014, from http://www.wluml.org/sites/wluml.org/files/import/english/pubs/pdf/dossier23-24/D23-24.pdf
Brem, E. (Ed.). (2014). *The experiences of face veil wearers in Europe and the law.* Cambridge: Cambridge University Press.
Brittain, V. (2013). *Shadow lives: The forgotten women of the War on Terror.* London: Pluto Press.
Brouard, S., & Tiberj, V. (2005). *Français comme les autres: enquête sur les citoyens d'origine maghrébine, africaine et turque.* Paris: Presses de la Fondation Nationale de Sciences Politiques.
Brouard, S., & Tiberj, V. (2007). L'incorporation politique "à la française': modèles explicatifs des alignements politiques des Français d'origine maghrébine, africaine et turque. *Migrations Société, 19*(113), 127–148.

Brown, K. (2008). The promise and perils of women's participation in UK mosques: The impact of securitisation agendas on identity, gender and community. *British Journal of Politics and International Relations, 10*(3), 472–491.

Bryan, B., Dadsie, S., & Scafe, S. (1985). *The heart of the race: Black women's lives in Britain*. London: Virago Press.

Buaras, E. A. (2014). 277 Muslim councillors elected. *The Muslim News*. Retrieved January 24, 2016, from http://muslimnews.co.uk/newspaper/home-news/277-muslim-councillors-elected/

Budgeon, S. (2011). *Third wave feminism and the politics of gender in late modernity*. Basingstoke: Palgrave Macmillan.

Bullock, K. (2002). *Rethinking Muslim women and the veil*. London: ITT.

Bunting, M. (2001). Can Islam liberate women? *The Guardian*, 8 December. Retrieved June 20, 2015, from http://www.theguardian.com/education/2001/dec/08/socialsciences.highereducation

Burlet, S., & Reid, H. (1998). A gendered uprising: Political representation and minority ethnic communities. *Ethnic and Racial Studies, 21*(2), 270–287.

Burns, N., Schlozman, K., & Verba, S. (2001). *The private roots of public action: Gender, equality and political participation*. Cambridge, MA: Harvard University Press.

Camus, E. (2013). Voile intégral: une loi difficilement applicable. *Le Monde*, 2 April. Retrieved August 25, 2015, from http://www.lemonde.fr/societe/article/2013/08/02/voile-islamique-une-loi-difficilement-applicable_3455937_3224.html

Candappa, M., & Joly, D. (1994). *Local authorities, ethnic minorities and 'pluralist integration' (Monographs in ethnic relations)*. Coventry: CRER, University of Warwick.

Cantle, T. (2001). *Community cohesion: A report of the independent review team*. London: Home Office.

Carby, H. (1997). White women listen! Black feminism and the boundaries of sisterhood. In H. S. Mirza (Ed.), *Black British feminism: A reader* (pp. 45–92). London and New York: Routledge.

Carsed. (2009). *Le retour de la race: contre les statistiques ethniques*. La Tour d'Aigues: Editions de l'Aube.

Cesari, J. (1998). *Musulmans et républicains. Les jeunes, l'Islam et la France*. Bruxelles: Complexe.

CEVIPOF-Ministère de l'Intérieur. (2007). *Enquête post électorale présidentielle 2007*. Paris: CEVIPOF (Centre d'études de la vie politique française).

Châabane, N. (2008). Diversité des mouvements de "femmes dans l'immigration'. *Les Cahiers du CEDREF, 16*, 231–250.

Chaïb, S. (2004). Femmes, migrations et marché du travail en France. *Les Cahiers du Cedref, 12*, 211–237.

Chaïb, S. (2006). Femmes immigrées et emploi: le bas de l'échelle pour propriété? In P. Cours-Salies & S. Le Lay (Eds.), *Le bas de l'échelle. La construction sociale des situations subalternes*. Paris: Eres.

Chakraborti, N., & Zempi, I. (2015). They make us feel like we're a virus': The multiple impacts of Islamohobic hostility towards Muslim women. *International Journal for Crime, Justice and Social Democracy*, 4(3), 44–56.

Charles, N., & Hintjens, H. (Eds.). (1998). *Gender, ethnicity and political ideologies*. London: Routledge.

Charles, N., & Wadia, K. (2014). *UK Feminista: Young women's feminist activism*. Coventry: MYPLACE. Retrieved August 12, 2015, from http://www.fp7-myplace.eu/documents/D7_1/Cluster%204%20Gender%20and%20Minority%20Rights%20movemnts/MYPLACE_7.1REPORT_UW_%20UKFeminista%20(UK).pdf

Cheruvallil-Contractor, S. (2012). *Muslim Women in Britain: De-mystifying the Muslimah*. London: Routledge.

Chirac, J. (2003). *Discours relatif au respect du principe de laïcité dans la république*. Commission Nationale du Débat public. Retrieved August 25, 2015, from http://www2.cndp.fr/laicite/pdf/chirac.pdf

Chowdhury, N., & Nelson, B. (Eds.). (1994). *Women and politics worldwide*. New Haven/London: Yale University Press.

Chrisafis, A. (2008). France rejects Muslim woman over radical practice of Islam. *The Guardian*, 12 July. Retrieved October 20, 2015, from http://www.theguardian.com/world/2008/jul/12/france.islam

Christy, C. (1994). Trends in sex differences in political participation: A comparative perspective. In M. Githens, P. Norris, & J. Lovenduski (Eds.), *Different roles, different voices: Women and politics in the United States and Europe* (pp. 27–37). New York: Harper Collins.

Cissé, M. (1997). *The sans-papiers: The new movement of asylum seekers and immigrants without papers in France–A woman draws the first lessons'*. London: Crossroads.

Claystone. (2014). *The right to choose: Things you should know about the face-veil debate*. London: Claystone. Retrieved June 12, 2015, from http://www.claystone.org.uk/wp-content/uploads/2014/02/ClaystoneReport_FaceVeil.pdf

CNCDH (Commission nationale consultative des droits de l'homme). (1993). *La lutte contre le racisme et la xénophobie: exclusions et droits de l'homme*. Paris: Documentation Française.

CNHI (Cité/musée nationale de l'histoire de l'immigration). (n.d.). De 1945 à 1975 (L'Histoire de l'immigration), CNHI. Retrieved May 5, 2015, from http://www.histoire-immigration.fr/dix-themes-pour-connaitre-deux-siecles-d-histoire-de-l-immigration/emigrer/de-1945-a-1975

Cochrane, K. (2013). *All the rebel women: The rise of the fourth wave of feminism*. London: Guardian Books.

CoDE (Centre on Dynamics of Ethnicity). (2012). More segregation or more mixing? *Dynamics of Diversity: Evidence from the 2011 Census Series*, December. Retrieved May 20, 2015, from http://www.ethnicity.ac.uk/medialibrary/briefingsupdated/more-segregation-or-more-mixing.pdf

Cohen, C. (2015). Almost 100 years on from winning the vote, women shun the polling booths. *The Telegraph*, 9 January. Retrieved June 2, 2015, from http://www.telegraph.co.uk/women/womens-politics/11333915/British-women-general-election-voters-shun-the-polling-booths.html

Collins, P. H. (1990). *Black feminist thought: Knowledge, consciousness, and the politics of empowerment*. New York: Routledge.

Combahee River Collective. (1979). A black feminist statement. In Z. R. Eisenstein (Ed.), *Capitalist patriarchy and the case for socialist feminism*. New York: Monthly Review Press.

Comedd. (2010). *Inégalités et discriminations: rapport pour un usage critique et responsable de l'outil statistique?*, 3 February. Retrieved May 15, 2015, from http://www.ladocumentationfrancaise.fr/var/storage/rapports-publics/104000077.pdf

Commission on British Muslims and Islamophobia. (1997). *Islamophobia: A challenge for us all*. London: Runnymede Trust.

Conseil d'État. (2008). Conseil d'État, 2ème et 7ème sous-sections réunies, 27/06/2008, 286798. *Legifrance*. Retrieved August 25, 2015, from http://www.legifrance.gouv.fr/affichJuriAdmin.do?idTexte=CETATEXT000019081211

Coote, A., & Campbell, B. (1987). *Sweet freedom: The struggle for women's liberation*. Oxford: Wiley-Blackwell.

Couvreur, G. (1998). *Musulmans de France: diversité, mutations et perspectives del'islam français*. Paris: Éditions de l'Atelier/Éditions Ouvrières.

CRAN (Conseil Représentatif des Associations Noires). (2012). Enquête exclusif du CRAN et Banlieue citoyenne sur les législatives et la diversité, 24 June 2013. Retrieved May 14, 2015, from http://www.le-cran.fr/document-cran-associations-noires-de-france/60-les-legislatives-et-la-diversite-enquete-exclusive-du-cran-et-banlieue-citoyenne.pdf

CRAN. (2014). *Parité et diversité: maires & adjoint.e.s*. Paris: CRAN.

Crenshaw, K. (1989). Demarginalizing the intersection of race and sex: A black feminist critique of antidiscrimination doctrine, feminist theory and antiracist politics. *Chicago Legal Forum, 1*, 139–167.

Cross, M., Johnson, M., & Cox, B. (1988). *Black welfare and local government: Section 11 and social services departments*. Coventry: CRER, University of Warwick.

Dargent, C. (2011). Les électorats sociologiques: le votedes musulmans. *Les Notes du CEVIPOF*, December. Retrieved August 20, 2015, from http://www.cevipof.com/rtefiles/File/AtlasEl3/NoteDARGENT.pdf

Davis, S., & Cooke, V. (2002). *Why do Black women organise? A comparative analysis of Black women's voluntary sector organisations in Britain and their relationship with the state*. London: Policy Studies Institute/Joseph Rowntree Foundation.

DCLG (Department of Communities and Local Government). (2009). *The Pakistani Muslim community in England*. London: Communities and Local Government Publications.

DCLG (Department of Communities and Local Government). (2010). *Cohesion delivery framework 2010 overview*. London: DCLG.

Deakin, N. (1965). *Colour and the British electorate: Six case studies*. London: Pall Mall Press.

Delphy, C. (2008). *Classer, dominer. Qui sont les 'autres'?* Paris: La Fabrique.

Delphy, C. (2005). Race, caste et genre en France. In J. Bidet (Ed.), *Guerre impériale, guerre sociale* (pp. 163–175). Paris: PUF.

Delphy, C. (2015). *Separate and dominate: Feminism and racism after the War on Terror*. London: Verso.

Delphy, C. (2004). Une affaire française. In C. Nordmann (Ed.), *Le foulard islamique en questions* (pp. 64–72). Paris: Editions Amsterdam.

Denham, J. (2001). *Building cohesive communities (Report of the Ministerial Group on Public Order and Community Cohesion)*. London: Home Office.

Denni, B. (2011). Intérêt pour la politique et pour la campagne électorale à l'automne 2011. *Programme TriÉlec 2012*, 18 November. Retrieved August 12, 2015, from https://sites.google.com/a/iepg.fr/trielec/resultats-analyses/enquetes-pre-electorales/vague-2---octobre-2011/interetpourlapolitiqueetpourlacampagneelectoraleal%E2%80%99automne2011

Dubet, F. (1999). Où en est la méthode de l'intervention sociologique? Research seminar, Centre d'analyse et d'Intervention sociologiques (CADIS), Paris, 6 January.

Dubet, F. (1994). *Sociologie de l'expérience*. Paris: Seuil.

Dubet, F., & Wieviorka, M. (1996). Touraine and the method of sociological intervention. In J. Clark & M. Diani (Eds.), *Alain Touraine* (pp. 55–75). London: Falmer Press.

Duret, P. (1998). *Anthropologie de la fraternité dans les cités*. Paris: Presses Universitaires de France.

Dwyer, C. (1999). Veiled meanings: Young British Muslim women and the negotiation of differences [1]. *Gender, Place & Culture: A Journal of Feminist Geography*, 6(1), 5–26.

Dwyer, C., & Shah, B. (2009). Rethinking the identities of young British Pakistani Muslim women: Educational experiences and aspirations. In P. Hopkins & R. Gale (Eds.), *Muslims in Britain: Race, place and identities* (pp. 55–73). Edinburgh: Edinburgh University Press.

Dyke, A. H., & James, L. (2009). *Immigrant, Muslim, female: Triple paralysis?* London: Quilliam Foundation.

ECRI. (2011). *Annual report on ECRI's activities covering the period from 1 January to 31 December 2010.* Strasburg: ECRI. Retrieved May 12, 2015, from https://www.coe.int/t/dghl/monitoring/ecri/activities/Annual_Reports/Annual%20Report%202010.pdf

ECU. (Equality Challenge Unit). (2013). *Equality in higher education: Statistical report 2013 Part 2: Students.* London: ECU.

EOC. (Equal Opportunities Commission). (2007). *Key statistics. Moving on up? Bangladeshi, Pakistani and Black Caribbean women and work.* Manchester: EOC.

Evans, E. (2015). *The politics of third wave feminisms: Neoliberalism, intersectionality and the state in Britain.* Basingstoke: Palgrave Macmillan.

Fanon, F. (1967). Algeria unveiled. In *A dying colonialism* (pp. 35–63). New York: Grove Press.

FASILD. (2004). *Femmes d'origine étrangère: travail, accès a l'emploi, discriminations de genre.* Paris: La Documentation Français.

Fawcett Society. (2006, December 14). *The veil, feminism and Muslim women: A debate.* Retrieved August 14, 2015, from http://www.mwnuk.co.uk/go_files/files/veil%20debate.pdf

Fawcett Society. (2009). *Poverty pathways: Ethnic minority women's livelihoods.* London: Fawcett Society.

Felouzis, G., Liot, F., & Perroton, J. (2005). *L'apartheid scolaire–enquête sur la ségrégation ethnique dans les collèges.* Paris: Éditions du Seuil.

Fenton, S. (2003). *Ethnicity.* Cambridge: Polity Press.

Fieldhouse, E., & Cutts, D. (2007). *Electoral participation of South Asian communities in England and Wales.* York: Joesph Rowntree Foundation.

Flint, J. (2010). Faith and housing in England: Promoting community cohesion or contributing to urban segregation? *Journal of Ethnic and Migration Studies, 36*(2), 257–274.

Ford, R., & Grove-White, R. (2015). *Migrant voters in the 2015 general election.* London: CoDE, University of Manchester and Migrants Rights Network.

Fournier, L. (2008). Le "féminisme musulman' en Europe de l'ouest: le cas du réseau féminin de Présence Musulmane. *AMNIS,* 1 September. Retrieved September 15, 2015, from http://amnis.revues.org/593; doi:10.4000/amnis.593

Fourquet, J. (2012). Le vote des musulmans à l'élection présidentielle. *IFOP Focus,* July. Retrieved August 20, 2015, from http://www.ifop.com/media/pressdocument/599-1-document_file.pdf

France Inter. (2014). Les engagés: les nouvelles formes de militantisme. France Inter radio programme, broadcast 7 January. Retrieved August 14, 2015, from http://www.franceinter.fr/emission-service-public-les-engages-les-nouvelles-formes-de-militantisme

Franceschet, S. (2005). *Women and politics in Chile.* Boulder, CO: Lynne Rienner.

Fredette, J. (2014). *Constructing Muslims in France: Discourse, public identity, and the politics of citizenship.* Philadelphia: Temple University Press.
Garcia, A. (1994). The development of Chicana feminist discourse, 1970–1980. In M. Githens, P. Norris, & J. Lovenduski (Eds.), *Different roles, different voices: Women and politics in the United States and Europe* (pp. 190–195). New York: Harper Collins.
Gaspard, F. (1996). De l'invisibilité des migrantes et de leurs filles à leur instrumentalisation. *Migrants-Formation, 105,* 15–30.
Gaspard, F., & Khosrokhavar, F. (1994). La problématique de l'exclusion. De la relation des garçons et des filles de culture musulmane dans les quartiers défavorisés. *Revue Française des Affaires Sociales, 2,* 3–26.
Gaspard, F., & Khosrokhavar, F. (1995). *Le foulard et la République.* Paris: La Découverte.
Gelb, J. (1986). Feminism in Britain: Politics without the power? In D. Dahlerup (Ed.), *The new women's movement.* London: Sage.
Gelb, J. (1989). *Feminism and politics: A comparative perspective.* Berkeley: University of California Press.
Gémie, S. (2010). *French Muslims: New voices in contemporary France.* Cardiff: University of Wales Press.
German, L. (2007). *Material girls: Women, men and work.* London: Bookmarks.
GHK. (2010a). *Study on volunteering in the European Union: Country report France.* London: GHK-ICF. Retrieved August 24, 2015, from http://ec.europa.eu/citizenship/pdf/national_report_fr_en.pdf
GHK. (2010b). *Study on volunteering in the European Union: Country report United Kingdom.* London: GHK-ICF. Retrieved August 24, 2015, from http://ec.europa.eu/citizenship/pdf/national_report_uk_en.pdf
Gibbon, G. (2012). Biradari, Ed Miliband and Bradford. *Channel 4 News,* 30 March. Retrieved May 20, 2015, from http://blogs.channel4.com/gary-gibbon-on-politics/biradari-ed-miliband-and-bradford/18712.
Gilby, N., Ormston, R., Parfrement, J., & Payne, C. (2011). *Amplifying the voice of Muslim students: Findings from literature review.* London: Department for Business Innovation and Skills.
Gilroy, P. (1993). *Small acts, thoughts on the politics of black cultures.* London: Serpent's Tail.
Githens, M., Lovenduski, J., & Norris, P. (Eds.). (1994). *Different roles, different voices.* New York: Harper Collins.
Goot, M., & Reid, E. (1984). Women: If not apolitical then conservative. In J. Siltanen & M. Stanworth (Eds.), *Women and the public sphere.* London: Hutchinson.
Gorce, B. (2013). François Hollande définit la laïcité comme "un principe et de liberté et de cohésion'. *La Croix,* 8 April. Retrieved August 25, 2015, from http://www.la-croix.com/Actualite/France/Francois-Hollande-definit-la-

laicite-comme-un-principe-et-de-liberte-et-de-cohesion-2013-04-08-930279
GREC (Groupement de recherches, d'échanges et de communication). (1990). *Femmes, Immigré. Quelles chances pour quelles insertions sociales et professionnelles?* Paris: GREC.
Guénif-Souilamas, N. (2000). *Des 'beurettes' aux descendants d'immigrants nord-africains.* Paris: Grasset.
Guru, S. (2012). Reflections on research: Families affected by counter-terrorism in the UK. *Journal of International Social Work, 55*(5), 689–703.
Haddad, Y. (2005). The study of women in Islam and the West: A select bibliography. *Hawwa, 3*(1), 111–157.
Haddad, Y. (2007). The post-9/11 hijab as icon. *Sociology of Religion, 68*(3), 253–267.
Hall, S., Critcher, C., Jefferson, T., Clarke, J., & Roberts, B. (1978). *Policing the crisis: Mugging, the state and law and order.* London and Basingstoke: MacMillan Press Ltd.
Hall, S., & Du Gay, P. (1996). *Questions of cultural identity.* London: Sage.
Hansard Society. (2009). *Audit of political engagement 6: The 2009 report.* London: Hansard Society.
Hansard Society. (2010). *Audit of political engagement 7: The 2010 report.* London: Hansard Society.
Hansard Society. (2015). *Audit of political engagement 12: The 2015 report.* London: Hansard Society.
Hassini, M. (1997). *L'école, une chance pour les filles de parents maghrébins.* Paris: L'Harmattan.
Haut Conseil à l'Intégration. (2000). *L'islam dans la République.* Paris: La Documentation Française.
Haw, K. (1998). *Educating Muslim girls: Shifting discourses.* Buckingham: Open University Press.
Haynes, J. (1998). *Religion in global politics.* London: Longman.
Heath, A., Fisher, S., Rosenblatt, G., Sanders, D., & Sobolewska, M. (2013). *The political integration of ethnic minorities in Britain.* Oxford: Oxford University Press.
Heath, A., & Martin, J. (2013). Can religious affiliation explain "ethnic' inequalities in the labour market? *Ethnic and Racial Studies, 36*(6), 1005–1027.
Hernes, H. M. (1984). The role of women in voluntary associations and organisations. In *The situation of women in the political process in Europe Part 3.* Strasbourg: Council of Europe.
Home Office. (2001). *Building cohesive communities: A report of the ministerial group on public order and community cohesion.* London: Home Office.
Hoodfar, H. (1992). The veil in their minds and on our heads: The persistence of colonial images of Muslim women. *Resources for Feminist Research, 22*(3/4), 5–18.

Hopkins, N., & Greenwood, R. M. (2013). Hijab, visibility and the performance of identity. *European Journal of Social Psychology, 43*, 438–447.
House of Commons. (1976). *Commonwealth immigration to the United Kingdom from the 1950s to 1975: A survey of statistical sources (Library Research Paper, 56)*. London: HMSO.
House of Lords. (2006). Judgments–R (on the application of Begum (by her litigation friend, Rahman)) (Respondent) v. Headteacher and Governors of Denbigh High School (Appellants). *UKHL, 15.* http://www.publications.parliament.uk/pa/ld200506/ldjudgmt/jd060322/begum-1.htm
Howard, E. (2014). How "clickitivism' had changed the face of political campaigns. *The Guardian,* 24 September. Retrieved August 14, 2015, from http://www.theguardian.com/society/2014/sep/24/clicktivism-changed-political-campaigns-38-degrees-change
Huntington, S. (1993). The clash of civilisations. *Foreign Affairs,* Summer 1993.
Hussain, S. (2008). Becoming visible. In S. Hussain (Ed.), *Muslims on the map: A national survey of social trends.* London: I. B. Tauris.
IFOP. (2011). *L'Analyse: 1989–2011. Enquête sur l'implantation et l'évolution de l'islam en France.* Paris: IFOP (for *La Croix*). Retrieved May 20, 2015, from http://www.ifop.com/media/pressdocument/343-1-document_file.pdf
ILO (International Labour Organisation). (1974). Social policy: The uniting of families. *Migrant Workers* (Report VII/1 of the International Labour Conference, 59th Session), 27–32. Retrieved May 20, 2015, from http://staging.ilo.org/public/libdoc/conventions/Technical_Conventions/Convention_no._143/143_English/73B09_350.pdf
INED. (2013). Flux d'immigration par sexe et âge en 2013. Retrieved June 2, 2015, from http://www.ined.fr/fr/tout-savoir-population/chiffres/france/flux-immigration/sexe-age/
INSEE. (2005). Enquêtes annuelles de recensement 2004 et 2005. Retrieved June 2, 2015, from http://www.insee.fr/fr/mobile/etudes/document.asp?reg_id=0&ref_id=ip1098#inter3
INSEE. (2008). L'activité des immigrés en 2007. *Insee Première,* October. Retrieved May 20, 2015, from http://www.insee.fr/fr/ffc/ipweb/ip1212/ip1212.pdf
INSEE. (2012). *Immigrés et descendants d'immigrés en France.* Paris: INSEE.
INSEE. (2015). Population totale par sexe et âge au 1er janvier 2015 par tranche d'âges. Retrieved May 20, 2015, from www.insee.fr/fr/themes/detail.asp?ref_id=bilan-demo&reg_id=0&page=donnees-detaillees/bilan-demo/pop_age2.htm
Ipsos-Mori. (2014). Perceptions are not reality: Things the world gets wrong, 29 October. Retrieved May 20, 2015, from https://www.ipsos-mori.com/researchpublications/researcharchive/3466/Perceptions-are-not-reality-Things-the-world-gets-wrong.aspx

Jacobson, J. (1997). Religion and ethnicity: Dual and alternative sources of identity among young British Pakistanis. *Ethnic and Racial Studies, 20*(2), 238–256.

Janmohamed, S. (2013). Calling all feminists: Get over the veil debate, focus on real problems. *Aljazeera*, 25 September. Retrieved June 12, 2015, from http://www.aljazeera.com/indepth/opinion/2013/09/calling-all-feminists-get-over-veil-debate-focus-real-problems-201392573343242621.html

Jawad, H., & Benn, T. (2003). *Muslim women in the United Kingdom and beyond: Experiences and images.* Leiden: Brill.

Jepperson, R. L. (2002). Political modernities: Disentangling two underlying dimensions of institutional differentiation. *Sociological Theory, 20*(1), 61–83.

Johnston, C. P. (1994). Feminists and the gender gap. In M. Githens, P. Norris, & J. Lovenduski (Eds.), *Different roles, different voices: Women and politics in the United States and Europe* (pp. 51–60). New York: Harper Collins.

Joly, D. (1989). *Ethnic minorities and education: The interaction between Muslims and schools in Birmingham, (Muslims in Europe Research Papers in Ethnic Relations 41).* Coventry: Centre for Research in Ethnic Relations.

Joly, D. (1991). *The French communist party and the Algerian war.* Oxford: MacMillan.

Joly, D. (1995). *Britannia's crescent: Making a place for Muslims in British society.* Aldershot: Avebury.

Joly, D. (2001). *Blacks and britannity.* Aldershot: Ashgate.

Joly, D. (2007). *L'Émeute.* Paris: Denoel.

Joly, D. (2012). Race, ethnicity and religion: Emerging policies in Britain. *Patterns of Prejudice, 46*(5), 467–485.

Joly, D. (2016). Women from Muslim communities: Autonomy and capacity of action. *Sociology,* advance online publication. doi:10.1177/0038038515621677

Joly, D., & Imtiaz, K. (2002). Muslims and citizenship in the United Kingdom. In R. Leveau, K. Mohsen-Finan, & C. W. de Wenden (Eds.), *New European identity and citizenship* (pp. 117–133). Aldershot: Avebury.

Joly, D., & Wadia, K. (2012). Dossier musulmanes et féministes en Grande-Bretagne. *Hommes et Migrations, 1299,* 4–96.

Jones, S. H., O'Toole, T., DeHanas, D. N., Modood, T., & Meer, N. (2014). Muslim women's experiences of involvement in UK governance (Public spirit project: 'Has UK policy succeeded in "empowering" Muslim women?'). Retrieved May 10, 2014, from http://www.publicspirit.org.uk/muslim-womens-experiences-of-involvement-in-uk-governance/

Josephides, S. (1992). *Towards a history of the Indian Worker's Association (Research Papers in Ethnic Relations).* Coventry: CRER, University of Warwick.

Journet, N. (2011). Michèle Tribalat: une démographe qui dérange. *Sciences Humaines* (Newsletter). Retrieved May 15, 2015, from http://www.scienceshumaines.com/michele-tribalat-une-demographe-qui-derange_fr_25561.html

Kabeer, N. (2001). Reflections on the measurement of women's empowerment. In B. Sevefjord & B. Olsson (Eds.), *Discussing women's empowerment: Theory*

and practice (pp. 17–57). Swedish International Development Agency: Stockholm.
Kandiyoti, D. (Ed.). (1991). *Women, Islam and the state*. Philadelphia: Temple University Press.
Kapoor, N. (2013). The advancement of racial neoliberalism in Britain. *Ethnic and Racial Studies, 36*(6), 1028–1046.
Kariapper, A. S. (2009). *Walking a tightrope: Women and veiling in the United Kingdom*. London: Women Living Under Muslim Laws.
Keaton, T. D. (2006). *Muslim girls and the other France*. Bloomington, IN: Indiana University Press.
Keslassy, E. (2010). Quelle place pour les minorités visibles? *Note Institut Montaigne*. Retrieved January 24, 2016, from http://www.institutmontaigne.org/res/files/publications/regionales_minorites_visibles.pdf
Keslassy, E. (2012). 2 % de députés issus des minorités visibles: bien mais peut mieux faire! *Le Nouvel Observateur*, 19 June. Retrieved May 14, 2015, from http://leplus.nouvelobs.com/contribution/573797-2-de-deputes-issus-des-minorites-visibles-bien-mais-peut-mieux-faire.html
Khattab, N. (2009). Ethno-religious background as a determinant of educational and occupational attainment in Britain. *Sociology, 43*(2), 304–322.
Khattab, N., Johnston, R., & Manley, D. (2015). All in it together? Ethnoreligious labour-market penalties and the post-2008 recession in the UK. *Environment and Planning A, 47*(4), 977–995.
Khattab, N., Johnston, R., Modood, T., & Sirkeci, I. (2011). Economic activity in the South Asian population in Britain: The impact of ethnicity, religion and class. *Ethnic and Racial Studies, 34*(9), 1466–1481.
Khosrokhavar, F. (1996). L'universel abstrait, le politique et la construction de l'islamisme comme forme d'altérité. In M. Wieviorka (Ed.), *Une société fragmentée?* (pp. 113–151). Paris: La Découverte.
Khosrokhavar, F. (2000). L'islam des jeunes Musulmans: sur l'exclusion dans la société française contemporaine. *Comprendre, 1*, 81–97.
Killian, C. (2003). The other side of the veil: North African women in France respond to the headscarf affair. *Gender and Society, 17*(4), 567–590.
Killian, C. (2006). *North African women in France*. Stanford, CA: Stanford University Press.
Kivisto, P. (2007). Rethinking the relationship between ethnicity and religion. In J. Beckford & N. J. Demerath (Eds.), *The Sage handbook of the sociology of religion* (pp. 1202–1239). London: Sage.
Klausen, J. (2005). *Islamic challenge: Politics and religion in western Europe*. Oxford: Oxford University Press.
Knott, K., & Khokher, S. (1993). Religious and ethnic identity among young Muslim women in Bradford. *New Community, 19*(4), 593–610.

Knowles, C., & Mercer, S. (1992). Feminisms and antiracisms: An exploration of the political possibilities. In J. Donald & A. Rattansi (Eds.), *'Race', culture and différence* (pp. 104–125). London: Sage.

Kocturk, T. (1992). *A matter of honour: Experiences of Turkish women immigrants.* London: Zed Books.

Kofman, E., Phizacklea, A., Raghuram, P., & Sales, R. (2000). *Gender and international migration in Europe* (pp. 163–191). London and New York: Routledge.

Kofman, E., & Sales, R. (1994). Towards fortress Europe? In M. Githens, P. Norris, & J. Lovenduski (Eds.), *Different roles, different voices: Women and politics in the United States and Europe* (pp. 196–200). New York: Harper Collins.

Koşulu, D. (2013). The Alevi quest in Europe through the redefinition of the Alevi movement: Recognition and political participation; A case study of the FUAF in France. In J. Nielsen (Ed.), *Muslim political participation in Europe* (pp. 255–276). Edinburgh: Edinburgh University Press.

Krolokke, C., & Sorensen, A. S. (2006). *Gender communication theories and analyses: From silence to performance.* London: Sage.

Kundnani, A. (2002). The death of multiculturalism. *Race & Class, 43*(4), 67–72.

Kundnani, A. (2009). *Spooked: How not to prevent violent extremism.* London: Institute of Race Relations. Retrieved May 10, 2015, from http://www.irr.org.uk/pdf2/spooked.pdf

Kymlicka, W. (1999). Liberal complacencies. In S. Moller Okin (Ed.), *Is multiculturalism bad for women?* (pp. 31–34). Princeton, NJ: Princeton University Press.

Lapeyronnie, D. (1993). *L'individu et les minorités: la France et la Grande-Bretagne face à leurs immigrés.* Paris: Presses Universitaires de France.

Lapping, B. (1970). *The Labour government 1964–70.* London: Penguin.

Laurence, J., & Vaïsse, J. (2006). *Integrating Islam: Political and religious challenges in contemporary France.* Washington: Brookings Institution Press.

Layton-Henry, Z. (1984). *The politics of immigration.* Oxford: Blackwell.

Layton-Henry, Z., & Studlar, D. (1985). The electoral participation of Black and Asian Britons: Integration or alienation. *Parliamentary Affairs, 38*(3), 307–318.

Lazaridis, G., & Wadia, K. (Eds.). (2015). *The securitisation of migration in the EU: Debates since 9/11.* Basingstoke: Palgrave Macmillan.

LDA (London Development Agency). (2010). *Valuing family, valuing work: British Muslim women and the labour market.* London: LDA.

LDH Toulon. (2003). Les harkis, qui étaient-ils? LDH (Ligue des droits de l'homme) Toulon. Retrieved October 20, 2015, from http://ldh-toulon.net/les-harkis-qui-etaient-ils.html

Le Bars, S. (2013). La religion musulmane fait l'objet d'un profond rejet de la part des Français. *Le Monde,* 24 January. Retrieved August 25, 2015, from http://

www.lemonde.fr/societe/article/2013/01/24/la-religion-musulmane-fait-l--objet-d-un-profond-rejet-de-la-part-des-francais_1821698_3224.html#XG6b6L0rVTy7sPvZ.99
Le Bras, H. (1998). *Le démon des origines. Démographie et extrême droite*. Paris: Éditions de l'Aube.
Le Lohe, M. J. (1975). Participation in elections by Asians in Bradford. In I. Crewe (Ed.), *The politics of race*. London: Croom Helm.
Le Lohe, M. J. (1984). *Ethnic minority participation in local elections*. Bradford: University of Bradford Press.
Le Lohe, M. J. (1990). The Asian vote in a Northern city. In H. Goldbourne (Ed.), *Black politics in Britain*. London: Gower.
Le Monde. (2005). Selon les RG, les émeutes en banlieue n'étaient pas le fait de bandes organisées. *Le Monde*, 7 December. Retrieved August 25, 2015, from http://www.lemonde.fr/societe/article/2005/12/07/selon-les-rg-les-emeutes-en-banlieue-n-etaient-pas-le-fait-de-bandes-organisees_718347_3224.html
Le Monde. (2009). Selon les services de la police nationale, 367 femmes portent la burqa en France. *Le Monde*, 29 July. Retrieved August 25, 2015, from http://www.lemonde.fr/a-la-une/article/2009/07/29/selon-les-services-de-la-police-nationale-367-femmes-portent-la-burqa-en-france_1223749_3208.html
Le Monde. (2015). Fillon réclame la fin du "tabou' des statistiques ethniques. *Le Monde*, 20 September. Retrieved September 29, 2015, from http://www.lemonde.fr/immigration-et-diversite/article/2015/09/20/fillon-reclame-la-fin-du-tabou-des-statistiques-ethniques_4764167_1654200.html
Lesselier, C. (Ed.) (2000). *Femmes étrangeres et immigrées en France* (Proceedings of conference organised by Le Comité de suivi des lois sur l'immigration). Retrieved November 25, 2005, from http://maisondesfemmes.free.fr/rajfire/analyses/1.pdf
Lesselier, C. (2006). Aux origines des mouvements de femmes de l'immigration, Conference Histoire, genre et migrations', Paris, 1–2 March. Retrieved October 12, 2015, from http://barthes.ens.fr/clio/dos/genre/com/lesselier.pdf
Leveau, R. (2002). Islam in France. In S. T. Hunter (Ed.), *Islam: Europe's second religion* (pp. 3–29). London: Praefer.
Lewis, P. (1997). Arenas of ethnic negotiation: Cooperation and conflict in Bradford. In T. Modood & P. Werbner (Eds.), *The politics of multiculturalism in the new Europe: Racism, identity and community*. London and New York: Zed Books.
Lewis, P. (2002). *Islamic Britain: Religion, politics and identity among British Muslims*. London: I. B. Tauris.
Lloyd, C. (1997). Struggling for rights: African women and the "sans papiers' movement in France. *Refuge*, 16(4), 31–34.
Lloyd, C. (2003). Women migrants and political activism in France. In J. Andall (Ed.), *Gender and ethnicity in contemporary Europe* (pp. 97–116). Oxford: Berg.

Long, J. (2012). *Anti-porn: The resurgence of anti-pornography feminism*. London: Zed Books.
Lovenduski, J. (1986). *Women and European politics*. Brighton: Wheatsheaf.
Lovenduski, J., & Hills, J. (Eds.). (1981). *The politics of the second electorate: Women and public participation*. London: Routledge and Kegan Paul.
Lovenduski, J., & Norris, P. (Eds.). (1996). *Women in politics*. Oxford and New York: Oxford University Press.
Macey, M. (1999). Class, gender and religious influences on changing patterns of Pakistani Muslim male violence in Bradford. *Ethnic and Racial Studies, 22*(5), 845–866.
Mackay, F. (2015). *Radical feminism: Feminist activism in movement*. Basingstoke: Palgrave Macmillan.
Malik, M. (2008). Complex equality: Muslim women and the "headscarf". *Droit et Société, 68*, 127–152.
Manier, M. (2007). Genre et identités ethniques: la construction de la figure sociale de la "femme musulmane' dans les associations d'insertion et les dispositifs d'intégration des populations issues de l'immigration, conference on 'Classe, ethnicité, genre …: les mobilisations au piège de la fragmentation identitaire?', 8–9 March 2007. Retrieved August 2, 2015, from http://www.crape.univ-rennes1.fr/documents/colloque_ethnicite/comm_MANIER.pdf
Marchbank, J. (2000). *Women, power and policy: Comparative studies of childcare*. London: Routledge.
Martinez, L. (2000). *The Algerian civil war, 1990–1998*. London: Hurst & Co.
Mas, M. (2003). Nicolas Sarkozy contre le foulard islamique. *RFI*, 21 April. Retrieved August 25, 2015, from http://www1.rfi.fr/actufr/articles/040/article_21545.asp
Massoumi, N. (2015). *Muslim women, social movements and the 'war on terror'*. Basingstoke: Palgrave Macmillan.
Maumoon, D. (1999). Islamism and gender activism: Muslim women's quest for autonomy. *Journal of Muslim Minority Affairs, 19*(2), 269–283.
Maynard, M. (1994). "Race', gender and the concept of "difference' in feminist thought. In H. Afshar & M. Maynard (Eds.), *The dynamics of 'race' and gender: Some feminist interventions* (pp. 9–25). London: Taylor & Francis.
McAndrew, M. (2006). The hijab controversies in western public schools: Contrasting conceptions of ethnicity and ethnic relations. In H. Moghissi (Ed.), *Muslim diaspora: Gender, culture, identity* (pp. 51–166). Abingdon, Oxford and New York: Routledge.
McDonald, L. Z. (2012). Gender within a counter-terrorism context. In B. Spalek (Ed.), *Counter-terrorism: Community-based approaches to preventing terror crime* (pp. 100–118). Basingstoke: Palgrave Macmillan.
Meer, N., Dwyer, C., & Modood, T. (2010). Embodying nationhood? Conceptions of British national identity, citizenship, and gender in the 'Veil Affair'. *The Sociological Review, 58*(1), 84–111.

Mélis, C. (2003). Nanas-Beurs, Voix d'Elles-Rebelles et Voix de Femmes. Des associations au carrefour des droits des femmes et d'une redéfintion de la citoyenneté. *Revue Européenne des Migrations Internationales, 19*(1), 81–100.

MEND. (2010). Jack Straw apologises for his anti-niqab comments at ENGAGE hustings in Blackburn. *MEND*, 26 April. Retrieved June 12, 2015, from http://mend.org.uk/jack-straw-apologises-for-his-anti-niqab-comments-at-engage-hustings-in-blackburn/

Menegaux, C. (2011). Guéant: la hausse du nombre de musulmans pose de problème. *Le Figaro*, 5 April. Retrieved June 12, 2015, from http://www.lefigaro.fr/politique/2011/04/04/01002-20110404ARTFIG00660-gueant-la-hausse-du-nombre-de-musulmans-pose-probleme.php

Menusier, A. (2008). Quand les "grands frères sont un calvaire'. *Bondy Blog/ Libération*, 12 June. Retrieved October 20, 2015, from http://bondyblog.liberation.fr/200806120002/quand-les-grands-freres-sont-un-calvaire/#.VxeqcNQrJnI

Merckling, O. (2002). L'emploi des femmes étrangères et issues de l'immigration. *Hommes et migrations, 1239*, 100–111.

Merckling, O. (2011). *Femmes de l'immigration dans le travail precaire*. Paris: L'Harmattan.

Merckling, O. (2012). *Parcours professionnels de femmes immigrées et de filles d'immigrés*. Paris: L'Harmattan.

Meurs, D., & Pailhé, A. (2008). Descendantes d'immigrés en France: une double vulnérabilité sur le marché du travail? *Travail, Genre et Sociétés, 20*(2), 87–107.

Miles, R., & Phizacklea, A. (1984). *White man's country: Racism in British politics*. London: Pluto Press.

Mirza, H. S. (1992). *Young, female and black*. London: Routledge.

Mirza, H. S. (Ed.). (1997). *Black British feminism*. London: Routledge.

Mirza, H. S. (2012). Multiculturalism and the gender gap: The visibility and invisibility of Muslim women in Britain. In W. Ahmad & Z. Sardar (Eds.), *Muslims in Britain: Making social and political space* (pp. 120–138). Abingdon, Oxford and New York: Routledge.

Modood, T. (2004). Capitals, ethnic identity and educational qualifications. *Cultural Trends, 13*(2), 87–105.

Modood, T. (2003). Muslims and the politics of difference. *The Political Quarterly, 74*(s1), 110–115.

Modood, T. (2007). *Multiculturalism*. Cambridge: Polity Press.

Modood, T., Beishon, S., & Virdee, S. (1994). *Changing ethnic identities*. London: Policy Studies Institute.

Modood, T., & Khattab, N. (2015). Explaining ethnic differences: Can ethnic minority strategies reduce the effects of ethnic penalties? *Sociology* (online first), 12 May, advance online publication. doi:10.1177/0038038515575858

Moghadam, V. M., & Senftova, L. (2005). Mesurer l'autonomisation des femmes: participation et droits dans les domaines civil, politique, sociale, économique et culturel. *Revue Internationale des Sciences Sociales, 2*(184), 423–449.

Moller Okin, S. (Ed.). (1999). *Is multiculturalism bad for women?* Princeton, NJ: Princeton University Press.

MORI Social Research Institute. (2004). *Audit of political engagement.* Retrieved November 25, 2015, from http://www.auditofpoliticalengagement.org/media/reports/Audit-of-Political-Engagement-1-2004.pdf

Mortimore, R., & Kaur-Ballaghan, K. (2006). Ethnic minority voters and non-voters at the 2005 British general election, PSA/EPOP conference, University of Nottingham, September. Retrieved June 29, 2015, from https://www.ipsos-mori.com/Assets/Docs/Archive/Publications/ethnic-minority-voters-and-non-voters.pdf

Mounir, H. (2003). Quand les femmes maghrébines remettent en question la place des hommes. *Hommes et migrations, 1245*, 102–111.

Muslim Council of Britain (MCB). (2015). *British Muslims in numbers.* London: MCB.

Mustafa, A. (2015). *Identity and political participation among young British Muslims: Believing and belonging.* Basingstoke: Palgrave Macmillan.

Muxel, A. (1988). Les attitudes socio-politiques des jeunes issus de l'immigration maghrébine en région parisiènne. *Revue Française de Sciences Politiques, 21*(6), 925–940.

Naili, H. (2014). Muslims say French feminism shuts them out. *We.News,* 3 November. Retrieved February 2, 2016, from http://womensenews.tumblr.com/post/101676015786/muslims-say-french-feminism-shuts-them-out

Nielsen, J. (1992). *Islams, Muslims and British local and central government, CSIC Papers Europe.* Birmingham: Centre for the Study of Islam and Christian-Muslim Relations.

Nielsen, J. (1997). Muslims in Europe: History revisited as a way forward? *Islam and Christian Muslim Relations, 8*(2), 135–287.

Nielsen, J. (1999). *Towards a European Islam.* Basingstoke: Palgrave Macmillan.

Nigaud, K., & Ripoll, F. (2004). Femmes magrébines dans la ville. In S. Denéfle (Ed.), *Femmes et villes* (pp. 489–499). Tours: PUFR.

NISRA (Northern Ireland Statistics and Research Agency). (2015). Religion: KS211NI. Retrieved August 2, 2015, from http://www.ninis2.nisra.gov.uk/public/PivotGrid.aspx?ds=6657&lh=74&yn=2011&sk=136&sn=Census%202011&yearfilter=2037

Noden, P., Shiner, M., & Modood, T. (2014). University offer rates for candidates from different ethnic categories. *Oxford Review of Education, 40*(3), 349–369.

Noiriel, G. (2007). *Immigration, antisémitisme et racisme (XIXe–XXe siècle). Discours publics, humiliations privées.* Paris: Fayard.

NOMIS. (2015a). Country of birth by religion by sex. Census 2011 table finder. Retrieved August 12, 2015, from https://www.nomisweb.co.uk/census/2011/data_finder

NOMIS. (2015b). Ethnic group by religion. Census 2011 table finder. Retrieved August 12, 2015, from https://www.nomisweb.co.uk/census/2011/data_finder

NOMIS. (2015c). Religion by sex by age. Census 2011 table finder. Retrieved August 12, 2015, from https://www.nomisweb.co.uk/census/2011/data_finder

NOMIS. (2015d). Economic activity by religion by sex by age. Retrieved August 12, 2015, from https://www.nomisweb.co.uk/census/2011/data_finder

NOMIS. (2015e). Highest level of qualification by religion. Retrieved August 20, 2015, from https://www.nomisweb.co.uk/census/2011/data_finder.

Nordmann, C. (2004). *Le Foulard islamique en questions*. Paris: Éditions Amsterdam.

Norris, P. (1991). Gender differences in political participation in Britain: Traditional, radical and revisionist models. *Government and Opposition, 26*(1), 56–74.

Norris, P. (1993). Conclusions: Comparing legislative recruitment. In J. Lovenduski & P. Norris (Eds.), *Gender and party politics*. London, Thousand Oaks and New Delhi: Sage.

Norris, P., & Lovenduski, J. (1995). *Political recruitment: Gender, race, and class in the British parliament*. New York: Cambridge University Press.

Norris, P., Lovenduski, J., & Campbell, R. (2004). *Gender and political participation*. London: Electoral Commission.

Observatoire des Inégalités. (2012). Plus de députés issus de l'immigration en 2012, 20 June. Retrieved May 14, 2015, from http://www.inegalites.fr/spip.php?page=breve&id_breve=863&id_rubrique=28&id_mot=25&id_groupe=17

OBV (Operation Black Vote). (2013). *Power of the black vote in 2015: The changing face of England & Wales*. London: OBV.

ONS (Office of National Statistics). (2004). *Focus on religion*. Retrieved May 20, 2015, from http://www.ons.gov.uk/ons/publications/re-reference-tables.html?edition=tcm%3A77-50856

ONS. (2012). *Ethnicity and national identity in England and Wales 2011*. Retrieved May 2, 2015, from http://www.ons.gov.uk/ons/dcp171776_290558.pdf

ONS. (2013). Full story: What does the census tell us about religion in 2011? Retrieved May 2, 2015, from http://www.ons.gov.uk/ons/dcp171776_310454.pdf

Osman, S., & Arati. (1983). Editorial. *Spare Rib, 127*, 3.

Owen, D. W. (1995). *Ethnic minorities in Great Britain: Patterns of population change, 1981–1991*. (1991 Census Statistical Paper 1). Coventry: Centre for Research in Ethnic Relations/University of Warwick.

Parekh, B. (1990). *The social logic of pluralism*. London: Commission for Racial Equality.
Parekh, B. (2000). *Rethinking multiculturalism, cultural diversity and political theory*. Basingstoke: Palgrave MacMillan.
Parmar, P. (1982). *Gender, race and class: Asian women in resistance*. London: Hutchinson.
Parvez, Z. F. (2013). Representing "Islam of the *banlieues*': Class and political participation among Muslims in France. In J. Nielsen (Ed.), *Muslim political participation in Europe* (pp. 190–213). Edinburgh: Edinburgh University Press.
Patel, P. (1997). Third wave feminism and black women's activism. In H. S. Mirza (Ed.), *Black British feminism* (pp. 255–268). London: Routledge.
Pateman, C. (1988). *The disorder of women: Democracy, feminism and political theory*. Cambridge: Polity Press.
Patterson, S. (1968). *Immigrants in industry*. London: Oxford University Press.
Peace, T. (2013). Muslims and electoral politics in Britain: The case of the Respect party. In J. Nielsen (Ed.), *Muslim political participation in Europe* (pp. 299–321). Edinburgh: Edinburgh University Press.
Peace, T. (2015a). *European social movements and Muslim activism: Another world but with whom?* Basingstoke and New York: Palgrave Macmillan.
Peace, T. (Ed.). (2015b). *Muslims and political participation in Britain*. London: Routledge.
Peach, C. (2006). Muslims in the 2001 census of England and Wales: Gender and economic activity. *Ethnic and Racial Studies, 29*(4), 629–655.
Peach, C., & Vertovec, S. (Eds.). (1997). *Islam in Europe: The politics of religion and community*. Basingstoke: Palgrave Macmillan.
Phillips, A. (1993). *Democracy and difference*. Oxford: Polity Press.
Pickerden, A. (2010). Muslim women in higher education: New sites of lifelong learning. *International Journal of Lifelong Learning, 21*(1), 37–43.
Pidd, H. (2012). How women won it for George Galloway. *The Guardian*, 4 April. Retrieved May 20, 2015, from http://www.theguardian.com/politics/2012/apr/04/how-women-won-it-for-galloway
Pinto, D. (2004). La France et les quatre religions. *Esprit, 302*(2), 78–88.
Platt, L. (2005). *Migration and social mobility: The life chances of Britain's minority ethnic communities*. York: Joseph Rowntree Foundation.
Poli, A. (2005). *L'expérience vécue du racisme et des discriminations raciales en France. De la condamnation morale à la prise en charge de la subjectivité des victimes*, unpublished PhD thesis. Paris: École des Hautes Études en Sciences Sociales.
Pollock, D., & Van Reken, R. (2009). *Third culture kids: The experience of growing up among worlds*. Boston: Nicholas Brealy.
Pottier, C. (1993). La fabrication sociale de médiateurs culturels: le cas de jeunes filles d'origine maghrébine. *Revue Européenne des Migrations Internationales, 9*(3), 177–190.

Poulat, E. (1987). *Liberté, laïcité, la guerre des deux Frances et le principe de la modernité*. Paris: Cerf/Cujas.

Purdham, K., Fieldhouse, E., Kalra, V., & Russell, A. (2002). *Voter engagement among black and minority ethnic communities*. London: Electoral Commission.

Quiminal, C. (2000). The associative movement of African women and new forms of citizenship. In J. Freedman & C. Tarr (Eds.), *Women, immigration and identities in France*. Oxford: Berg.

Qureshi, I. (2012, April 3). Where are the Muslim women in Bradford politics? *The Culture Vulture*. Retrieved May 20, 2015, from https://theculturevulture.co.uk/blog/speakerscorner/where-are-the-muslim-women-in-bradford-politics/

Ramzanoglu, C. (1989). *Feminism and the contradictions of oppression*. London: Routledge.

Randall, V. (1987). *Women and politics: An international perspective* (2nd ed.). Basingstoke: Palgrave Macmillan.

Randall, V. (1994). Feminism and political analysis. In M. Githens, P. Norris, & J. Lovenduski (Eds.), *Different roles, different voices: Women and politics in the United States and Europe* (pp. 4–16). New York: Harper Collins.

Randall, V., & Lovenduski, J. (1993). *Contemporary feminist politics: Women and power in Britain*. Oxford: Oxford University Press.

Rashid, N. (2013). Giving the silent majority a voice. In N. Rashid (Ed.), *Veiled threats: Producing the Muslim woman in public and policy discourse in the UK*, PhD thesis, Department of Sociology, London School of Economics (pp. 127–162).

Rashid, N. (2014). Giving the silent majority a stronger voice? Initiatives to empower Muslim women as part of the UK's "War on Terror'. *Ethnic and Racial Studies, 37*(4), 598–604.

Ray, K. (2003). Constituting "Asian women': Political representation, identity politics and local discourse of participation. *Ethnic and Racial Studies, 26*(5), 854–878.

Reitz, J., Breton, R., & Phan, M. (2008). *Multiculturalism and social cohesion : Potentials and challenges of diversity*. New York: Springer.

Rex, J. (1973). *Race colonialism and the city*. London: Routledge and Kegan Paul.

Rex, J. (1988). *The Ghetto and the underclass: Essays on race and social policy*. Aldershot: Avebury.

Rex, J. (1995). Multiculturalism in Europe and North America. *Nations and Nationalism, 1*(2), 243–259.

Rex, J., Joly, D., & Wilpert, C. (Eds.). (1987). *Immigrant associations in Europe*. Aldershot: Gower Press.

Rex, J., & Tomlinson, S. (1979). *Colonial immigrants in a British city*. London: Routledge and Kegan Paul.

Richard, J.-L. (1999). Comment votent les jeunes français issus de l'immigration. *Ville-École-Intégration, 118*, 119–134.

Roald, A. S. (2001). *Women in Islam: The western experience.* London: Routledge.
Rochefort, F. (2002). Foulard, genre et laïcité en 1989. *Vingtième Siècle, 75,* 145–156.
Rosenberger, S., & Sauer, B. (2012). *Politics, religion and gender: Framing and regulating the veil.* Abingdon, Oxford and New York: Routledge.
Roucaute, D. (2015). Quatre questions sur les statistiqes ethniques. *Le Monde,* 6 May. Retrieved May 15, 2015, from http://www.lemonde.fr/les-decodeurs/article/2015/05/06/quatre-questions-sur-les-statistiques--ethniques_4628874_4355770.html
Rowbotham, S. (1977). *Hidden from history* (3rd ed.). London: Pluto Press.
Roy, O. (Ed.). (2005). *La laïcite face à l'Islam.* Paris: Stock.
Ruby, T. (2006). Listening to the voices of hijab. *Women's Studies International Forum, 29,* 54–66.
Runnymede Trust. (2000). *The future of multi-ethnic Britain (Parekh Report).* London: Profile Books.
Ryan, L. (2011). Muslim women negotiating collective stigmatization: "We're just normal people'. *Sociology, 45*(6), 1045–1060.
Salway, S. (2007). Economic activity among UK Bangladeshi and Pakistani women in the 1990s: Evidence for continuity or change in the family resources survey. *Journal of Ethnic and Migration Studies, 33*(5), 825–847.
Sanders, D., Clarke, S., Stewart, M., & Whiteley, P. (2005). *The 2005 general election in Great Britain.* London: Electoral Commission.
Sanghera, G., & Thapar-Björkert, S. (2007). "Because I am Pakistani ... and I am Muslim ... I am political'–Gendering political radicalism: Young femininities in Bradford. In T. Abbas (Ed.), *Islamic political radicalisms in a European perspective* (pp. 173–191). Edinburgh: Edinburgh University Press.
Scotland's Census. (2012). Religion, Scotland, 2001 and 2011. Retrieved August 2, 2015, from http://www.scotlandscensus.gov.uk/documents/censusresults/release2a/rel2asbtable7.pdf
Scott, J. (2007). *The politics of the veil.* Princeton, NJ and Oxford: Princeton University Press.
Shadid, W. A. R., & Van Koningsveld, P. S. (Eds.). (1996). *Political participation and identities of Muslims in non-Muslim countries.* Kampen, Netherlands: Kok Pharos.
Sherif, J. (2011). A census chronicle: Reflections on the campaign for a religion question in the 2001 Census for England and Wales. *Journal of Beliefs and Values, 32*(1), 1–18.
Shirazi, F., & Mishra, S. (2010). Young Muslim women on the face veil (niqab): A tool of resistance in Europe but rejected in the United States. *International Journal of Cultural Studies, 13*(1), 43–62.
Siddiqui, H. (2000). Black women's activism: Coming of age? *Feminist Review, 64,* 83–96.

Siddiqui, A. D., Shahid, A. R., & Barkati, J. B. (2005). Why Muslims should vote for a Labour government. *The Guardian*, 19 April. Retrieved August 25, 2015, from http://www.theguardian.com/politics/2005/apr/19/election2005.labour.

Simmel, G. (1964). *The sociology of Georg Simmel*. New York: The Free Press.

Simpson, L., Gavalas, V., & Finney, N. (2008). Population dynamics in ethnically diverse towns: The long-term implications of immigration. *Urban Studies*, 45(1), 160–183.

Sivanandan, A. (2006). Britain's shame: From multiculturalism to nativism. *IRR News*, 22 May. Retrieved August 14, 2006, from www.Irr.Org.Uk/2006/May/Ha000024.Html

Smith, B. (Ed.). (1983). *Home girls: A black feminist anthology*. New York: Kitchen Table/Women of Colour Press.

Smith, J. (2006). Murder is always wrong, and has nothing to do with faith. *Independent*, 7 November. Retrieved June 12, 2015, from http://www.independent.co.uk/voices/commentators/joan-smith/joan-smith-murder-is-always-wrong-and-has-nothing-to-do-with-faith-2127305.html

Solomos, J. (1986). *Riots, urban protest and social policy: The interplay of reform and social control (Research Paper in Ethnic Relations)*. Coventry: CRER, University of Warwick.

Son, T. L., & Riegert, A. (2015). *Mixité sociale et scolaire et ségrégation inter- et intra-établissement dans les collèges et lycées français*. Paris: Conseil National d'Evaluation du Système Scolaire. Retrieved August 25, 2015, from http://www.cafepedagogique.net/lexpresso/Documents/docsjoints/cnescosegreg.pdf

Spalek, B., & McDonald, L. Z. (2011). *Conflict with and between communities: Exploring the role of communities in helping to defeat and/or endorse terrorism and the interface with policing efforts to counter terrorism*. Birmingham: University of Birmingham/AHRC. Retrieved October 20, 2015, from http://www.ahrc.ac.uk/documents/project-reports-and-reviews/connected-communities/exploring-the-role-of-communities-in-helping-to-defeat-and-or-endorse-terrorism-and-the-interface-with-policing-efforts-to-counter-terrorism/

Springer, K. (Ed.). (1999). *Still lifting, still climbing*. New York and London: New York University Press.

Stasi, B. (2003). *Rapport de la commission de réflexion sur l'application du principe de laïcité dans la République*. Paris: La Documentation Française.

Stokes, B. (2015). Anti-minority sentiment not rising. *Faith in European project reviving*, PewResearch Centre, 2 June. Retrieved October 20, 2015, from http://www.pewglobal.org/2015/06/02/chapter-3-anti-minority-sentiment-not-rising/

Sudbury, J. (1998). *Other kinds of dreams*. London: Routledge.

Sudbury, J. (2001). (Re)constructing multiracial blackness: Women's activism, difference and collective identity in Britain. *Ethnic and Racial Studies*, 24(1), 29–49.

Takhar, S. (2003). South Asian women and the question of political organization. In N. Puwar & P. Raghuram (Eds.), *South Asian women in the diaspora* (pp. 215–226). Oxford: Berg.

Takhar, S. (2007). Expanding the boundaries of political activism. *Contemporary Politics, 13*(2), 123–137.

Takhar, S. (2011). The construction of political agency: South Asian women and political activism. *Community Development, 46*(3), 341–350.

Takhar, S. (2013a). Conceptualising the uneasy relationship of religion to political agency. In S. Takhar (Ed.), *Gender, ethnicity and political agency: South Asian women organising* (pp. 158–196). London: Routledge.

Takhar, S. (2013b). *Gender, ethnicity and political agency: South Asian women organising*. London: Routledge.

Tamir, Y. (1999). Siding with the underdogs. In S. Moller Okin (Ed.), *Is multiculturalism bad for women?* (pp. 47–52). Princeton, NJ: Princeton University Press.

Tang-Nain, G. (1994). Black women, sexism and racism, black or anti-racist feminism? In M. Githens, P. Norris, & J. Lovenduski (Eds.), *Different roles, different voices: Women and politics in the United States and Europe* (pp. 214–228). New York: Harper Collins.

Taylor, C. (1994). The politics of recognition. In A. Guttmann (Ed.), *Multiculturalism and 'the politics of recognition': An essay* (pp. 25–73). Princeton, NJ: Princeton University Press.

Tersigni, S. (2008). Jalons pour une lecture imbriquée du genre et du religieux dans le champ des migrations et des relations interethniques en France. *Les Cahiers du CEDREF, 16*, 251–273.

The Guardian. (2005a). Full text: The Prime Minister' statement on anti-terror measures. *The Guardian*, 5 August. Retrieved August 25, 2015, from http://www.theguardian.com/politics/2005/aug/05/uksecurity.terrorism1

The Guardian. (2005b). Why Muslims should vote for a Labour government. *The Guardian*, 19 April. Retrieved August 15, 2015, from http://www.theguardian.com/politics/2005/apr/19/election2005.labour

Thiara, R. K. (2003a). Difference, collective action and women's groups: South Asian women in Britain. In M. B. Cohen & A. Mullender (Eds.), *Gender and group work*. London: Routledge.

Thiara, R. K. (2003b). South Asian women and collective action in Britain. In J. Andall (Ed.), *Gender and ethnicity in contemporary Europe* (pp. 79–96). Oxford: Berg.

Thomlinson, N. (2016). *Race, ethnicity and the women's movement in England: 1968–1993*. Basingstoke: Palgrave Macmillan.

Tietze, N. (2001). European forms of imaging "the golden age of Islam': A comparison of religiosity among young Muslims in French and German public spheres. In J. Rüsen (Ed.), *Kulturwissenschaftliches Institut: Jahrbuch 2000/2001* (pp. 67–91). Kulturwissenschaftliches Institut im Wissenschaftszentrum NRW: Essen.

Timera, M. (2004). Islam et renégociation des rapports de genre en contexte migratoire. In I. Taboada-Leonetti (Ed.), *Les femmes et l'islam: entre modernité et intégrisme*. Paris: L'Harmattan.
Touati, Z. (2012). Travail des maghrébines en France: spécificités et freins. *Sociologies*. Retrieved August 2, 2015, from http://sociologies.revues.org/4028
Touraine, A. (1965). *Sociologie de l'action*. Paris: Seuil.
Touraine, A. (1973). *Production de la société*. Paris: Seuil.
Touraine, A. (1978). *La voix et le regard*. Paris: Seuil.
Touraine, A. (2013). *La fin des sociétés*. Paris: Seuil.
Touraine, A. (2015). *Nous, sujets humains*. Paris: Seuil.
Touraine, A., Wieviorka, M., & Dubet, F. (1984). *Le mouvement ouvrier*. Paris: Fayard.
TPA (Tax Payers' Alliance). (2009). Council spending uncovered II: No 5 the Prevent strategy. Retrieved May 10, 2015, from http://old.taxpayersalliance.com/prevent.pdf
Tribalat, M. (1995). *Faire face*. Paris: La Découverte.
Tribalat, M. (1998). A propos de "l'impossible descendance étrangère" d'Hervé Le Bras. Réponse de Michèle Tribalat. *Population, 53*(3), 655–656.
Tribalat, M. (2004). Le nombre de musulmans en France: qu'en sait-on? In Y. C. Zarka, S. Taussig, & C. Fleury (Eds.), *L'Islam en France* (pp. 21–32). Paris: PUF.
Tribalat, M. (2007). Les enjeux de la connaissance statistique des populations musulmanes ou d'origine musulmane. In H.-O. Luthe, M.-T. Urvoy, & G. Gobillot (Eds.), *Pluralisme religieux: quelle âme pour l'Europe?* Paris: Éditions de Paris.
Tribalat, M. (2011). Dynamique démographique des musulmans de France. *Commentaire, 4*(136), 971–980.
Tribalat, M. (2013). *Assimilation, la fin du modèle français* (ebook). Paris: Télégraphe/Editions du Toucan. Retrieved August 2, 2015, from http://www.amazon.co.uk/reader/2810005532/ref=rdr_sb_li_hist_1&state=01111
Tyrer, D., & Ahmad, F. (2006). *Muslim women and higher education: Identities, experiences and prospects* (Liverpool John Moores University and European Social Fund Report). Retrieved May 10, 2014, from http://www.educacionenvalores.org/IMG/pdf/muslimwomen.pdf
University of Bristol. (2015). Muslim women much more likely to be unemployed than white Christian women. *University of Bristol News* (press release), 15 April. Retrieved June 2, 2015, from http://www.bristol.ac.uk/news/2015/april/muslim-women-and-employment.html
Vaillancourt, J. G. (1991). Mouvement ouvrier et nouveaux mouvements sociaux: l'approche d'Alain Touraine. *Cahiers de recherche sociologique, 7*, 213–222.
Van Bergen, D., Saharso, S., Smit, J. H., & Van Balkom, A. (2009). Suicidal behavior of young immigrants in the Netherlands: Can we use Durkheim's concept of "fatalistic' suicide to explain their high incidence of attempted suicide? *Ethnic and Racial Studies, 32*(2), 297–311.

Van Poperin, A. (2004). *Gender, Islam and public participation: A case of Muslim women in Bradford*, MPhil thesis, Department of Peace Studies, University of Bradford.
Van Reekum, R., Duyvendak, J. W., & Bertossi, C. (Eds.). (2012). National models of integration and the crisis of multiculturalism: A critical comparative perspective. *Patterns of Prejudice, 46*(5), 417–426.
Vassberg, L. M. (1997). Immigration maghrébine en France; l'intégration des femmes. *The French Review, 70*(5), 710–720.
Verba, S., Schlozman, K. L., & Brady, H. (1995). *Voice and equality: Civic voluntarism in American politics*. Cambridge, MA: Harvard University Press.
Verbrunt, G. (1980). *L'intégration par l'autonomie. La CFDT, l'église catholique, la FASTI face aux revendications d'autonomie*. Paris: CIEMM.
Wadia, K. (1999). France: From unwilling host to bellicose gatekeeper. In M. Cole & G. Dale (Eds.), *The European Union and migrant labour* (pp. 171–202). Oxford: Berg.
Wadia, K. (2004). United Kingdom: Challenges posed by refugee women to the existing reception infrastructure. In N. Schlenzka, L. Sommo, K. Wadia, & G. Campani (Eds.), *Refugee women–Hoping for a better future* (pp. 299–358). Berlin: Edition Parabolis.
Wadia, K. (1993). Women and the events of May 1968. In K. Reader (with K. Wadia), *The May 1968 events in France: Reproductions and interpretations* (pp. 148–166). London: Macmillan Press Ltd.
Wadia, K. (2015). Women from Muslim communities in Britain: Political and civic activism in the 9/11 era. In T. Peace (Ed.), *Muslims and political participation in Britain*. London: Routledge.
Wadia, K., & Allwood, G. (2012). The crisis of multiculturalism in Britain. In M. Labelle, J. Couture, & F. Remiggi (Eds.), *La communauté politique en question. Regards croisés sur l'immigration, la diversité et la citoyenneté* (pp. 97–119). Québec: Presses de l'Université du Québec.
Wakim, N., & Le Cœur, P. (2007). Vincent Geisser: "Vote musulman ou vote maghrébin, des constructions imaginaires'. *Le Monde*, 1 March. Retrieved August 20, 2015, from http://www.lemonde.fr/societe/chat/2007/02/28/vincent-geisser-vote-musulman-ou-vote-maghrebin-des-constructions-imaginaires_877096_3224.html
Walker, N. (1994). What we know about women voters in Britain, France and West Germany. In M. Githens, P. Norris, & J. Lovenduski (Eds.), *Different roles, different voices: Women and politics in the United States and Europe* (pp. 61–70). New York: Harper Collins.
Ward, I. (2006). Shabina Begum and the headscarf girls. *Journal of Gender Studies, 15*(2), 119–131.
Waylen, G. (1998). Women's activism, authoritarianism and democratization in Chile. In N. Charles & H. Hintjens (Eds.), *Gender, ethnicity and political ideologies* (pp. 146–167). London: Routledge.

Weber, M. (1978). *Economy and society* (Vol. 1). Berkeley and Los Angeles: University of California Press.
Werbner, P. (1996). Public spaces, political voices: Gender, feminism and aspects of British Muslim participation in the public sphere. In W. A. R. Shadid & P. S. Van Koningsveld (Eds.), *Political participation and identities of Muslims in non-Muslim states* (pp. 53–70). Kampen, Netherlands: Kok Pharos.
Wieviorka, M. (2015). *Retour au sens.* Paris: Robert Laffont.
Wilkinson, M. L. N. (2015). *A fresh look at Islam in a multi-faith world: A philosophy for success through education.* Abingdon, Oxfordshire: Routledge.
Willaime, J.-P. (2004). *Europe et religions. Les enjeux du XXIe siècle.* Paris: Fayard.
Williamson, M., & Khiabany, G. (2010). UK: The veil and the politics of race. *Race & Class, 52*(2), 85–96.
Wilson, A. (1975). Racism sexism. *Spare Rib, 41*, 8. Retrieved February 12, 2016, from https://data.journalarchives.jisc.ac.uk/britishlibrary/sparerib/view?pubId=P523_344_Issue41PDFP523_344_Issue41_0008_15pdf&terms=Amrit%20Wilson&brandedSearch
Wilson, B. R. (1995). Religious toleration, pluralism and privatization. *Kirchliche Zeitgeschichte, 8*(1), 99–116.
Wilson, A. (2006). *Dreams, questions, struggles: South Asian women in Britain.* London: Pluto Press.
Wilson, E., & Weir, E. (1986). *Hidden agendas: Theory, politics, and experience in the women's movement.* London: Tavistock.
Winter, B. (2008). *Hijab & the republic: Uncovering the French headscarf debate.* Syracuse, NY: Syracuse University Press.
Wintour, P. (2011). David Cameron tells Muslim Britain: Stop tolerating extremists. *The Guardian*, 5 February. Retrieved August 25, 2015, from http://www.theguardian.com/politics/2011/feb/05/david-cameron-muslim-extremism
Withol de Wenden, C. (1988). *Les immigrés et la politique.* Paris: Presses de la FNSP.
Wood, J., & Cracknell, R. (2015). *Ethnic minorities in politics, government and public life.* Standard Note SN/SG/1156. London: House of Commons Library.
Yaqoob, S. (2005). Interviewed by Joly, D. 26 January.
Yaqoob, S. (2006). So much for the sisterhood. *The Guardian*, 13 October. Retrieved June 12, 2015, from http://www.theguardian.com/commentisfree/2006/oct/13/whathappenedtosisterhood1
Yaqoob, S. (2008). Muslim women and war on terror. *Feminist Review, 88*, 150–161.
Yegenoglu, M. (1998). *Colonial fantasies: Towards a feminist reading of orientalism.* Cambridge: Cambridge University Press.

Yuval-Davis, N. (1998). Beyond differences: Women, empowerment and coalition politics. In N. Charles & H. Hintjens (Eds.), *Gender, ethnicity and political ideologies* (pp. 168–189). London: Routledge.

Zerouala, F. (2015). *Des voix derrière le voile*. Paris: Première Parallèle.

Zia, A. S. (2009). The reinvention of feminism in Pakistan. *Feminist Review, 91*, 29–46.

Zubaida, S. (2003). Islam in Europe. *Critical Quarterly, 45*(1–2), 88–98.

Zukin, C., Keeter, S., Andolina, M., Jenkins, K., & Delli Carpini, M. X. (2006). *A new engagement? Political participation, civic life and the changing American citizen*. Oxford/New York: Oxford University Press.

Index

A
Afghanistan: British intervention, 18, 57, 218, 220, 228
Afshar, H., 32, 42
age profile: Muslims
  Britain, 96, 97, 99
  France, 103
  women, 261
Aide sociale à l'enfance, 204
Algeria
  French citizenship, 19–20n7
  Front Islamique du Salut (FIS), 179
Algerians. *See also* Maghrebis
  legal status: France, 59, 93, 119n11
  migration to France, 93–94, 119n10
Algerian War, 60, 61, 63, 83n12, 94
Al Houda, 156
Ali, Zahra, 11
Alibhai-Brown, Yasmin, 79
Allen, C., 251
All Faiths for One Race (AFFOR), 147
All Pakistan Women's Association, 147
Allwood, Gill, 29

Al Qaeda, 180
Amara, Fadela, 130, 161n1, 161n3, 254
Amina Muslim Women's Resource Centre, 151
Amiraux, V., 42
An-Nisa societies, 148
anti-racism, 217, 220, 224, 270
  Britain, 50, 152
  France: *mouvement beur*, 61, 148
Anti-Terrorism Crime and Security Act (2001), 57, 258n3
Apna Haq, 151
Arab-Berbers, 8, 20n8
Archer, M., 4, 15
art
  Islam, 181
  projects, 153
  teaching deemed un-Islamic, 181
Asian Muslims: arranged marriages, 166
assimilationism: France, 61, 206, 211, 262

Note: Page numbers followed by "n" refer to notes.

'associational' model of society, 48, 51 France, 59
Association de solidarité avec les femmes algériennes démocratiques (ASFAD), 150
Association des travailleurs marocains en France, 147
associations, membership of, 33
asylum seekers
 Britain, 93
 political participation, 6
atheism, 179, 191
Audit of political engagement (IPSOS-MORI), 10, 128, 129, 139
autonomisation, 11, 20n11
Avaz, 147

B
Baby Loup affair, 64
Badran, Margot, 43
Ball, W., 30
Bangladeshis
 education, 112
 employment, 105, 108, 114
 political participation, 134–5, 135, 161n6
Bangladesh Women's Association, 147
Banlieues. See cités
Barelvis, 37
Barnet Muslim Women's Network, 153
Baubérot, J., 63, 66
Beckford, J., 30
Bellil, Samira, 254
Benziane, Sohane, 259n6
Bindel, Julie, 79
biradari, 35
biradari politics: Britain, 136, 137, 160
Birmingham
 discrimination, 198–199
 focus group, 11–13

birth, country of: Muslims: Britain, 96-8
black British feminism, 75—77, 80
Blair, Tony, 55, 57, 218, 250, 253
Bosnians, 166, 181
Bouamama, Saïd, 74
Bourne, Jenny, 75
Bousquet, Marie Laure, 74
Bouteldja, Houria, 73
Bouteldja, Naima, 236, 246–7
Bradford
 male aggression, 39
 Muslim voting patterns, 134–5, 136, 137
 riots (2001), 35
Brem, Eva, 236
Britain and France: as comparative research locations, 7–9
British Campaign to Stop Immigration, 135
British Humanist Association (BHA), 88
British Nationality Act (1948), 119n7
Brittain, Victoria, 250
Brixton riots, 148, 162n11
brothers: impact on women's participation in civic and political life: France, 168, 169
Brouard, S., 142
Burns, N., 126

C
Cameron, David, 58
Cantle report, 83n6
Casanova, José, 53
Caseneuve, Bernard, 68
caste, 40, 185
Catholic Church: France, 63, 66
census: Britain, 86–7, 93, 106, 118n1
 (1991), 9, 53, 86–7
 (2001), 9, 56, 87–8, 104, 108
 (2011), 95–100, 108–9, 110

censuses: France, 8, 88, 91, 100, 101
Chakraborti, N., 246–7
change, possibility of: motivator for action, 221
Chevènement Act (1998), 95
Chile: women's political participation, 29
Chirac, Jacques, 62, 64, 66
Chouder, Ismahane, 74
Chowdhury, N., 4
Christy, Carol A, 29
church and state
　Britain, 53, 54
　France. *See* laïcité
cités, 169, 178, 196n2, 238, 254–7
citizenship. *See* nationality and immigration status
civic and political engagement: strategies, 225–7, 229, 266
civic engagement. *See also* community organisations: Muslim women; political participation
　Muslim women's capacity for, 221–2, 265–6, 271
　relationship to politics, 126–7, 270
clan based voting, 136–7, 145, 160
'clash of civilisations', 38
class
　education: France, 116–7
　patriarchy and, 39
Cochrane, Kira, 79
cohesion, social/community, promotion of: Britain, 56, 83n6, 200. *See also* Prevent programme (PVE)
Collectif contre l'islamaphobie en France, 64
Collectif d'associations pour le droit de l'avortement et à la contraception, 72
Collectif des féministes indigènes, 73
Collectif des musulmans de France, 73
Collectif féministes pour l'égalité (CFPE), 73, 82, 144, 157

Collectif national pour les droit des femmes, 72, 74
Collectif une école pour tout-e-s (CEPT), 73, 144, 157. *See also* École pour tous et pour toutes
collective agency, organisation of: Jepperson's typology, 48
Comité pour la mesure et l'évaluation de la diversité (Comedd), 90
Commission against Racism and Intolerance, 89
Commission alternative de réflexion sur les statistiques ethniques et les discriminations (Carsed), 90
Commission for Racial Equality (CRE), 50, 83n5
Commission nationale de l'informatique et des libertés (CNIL), 9, 90, 101, 118n2
Commission on British Muslims and Islamophobia, 57
Commission on Integration and Cohesion, 56
Commissions départementales d'accès à la citoyenneté (CODAC), 68, 84n16
Commonwealth Immigrants Act (1962), 119n8
Commonwealth subjects: legal status, 49–50
communalism: France, 61–2, 64, 81
Communist Party (France), 133
communitarianism, 73, 183
community cohesion, promotion of: Britain, 56, 83n6. *See also* Prevent programme (PVE)
community: impact on women's participation in civic and political life, 263
　Britain, 173–6
　France, 176–8
community leaders
　as interlocutors, 51, 232, 265, 271

community organisations: Muslim women, 145–50, 151, 159–60, 217, 227, 269
  Britain, 148, 150–1, 152–5, 200, 202, 203, 269
  France, 148–9, 150, 155–9, 204, 205, 269
community politics: Muslim women, 129–30
community religion, Islam as, 187–8, 190
compromise: political and civic engagement strategy, 227, 266
confidence to take action: Muslim women, 175, 199, 221–2, 224–5, 229, 256, 265–6
confrontation: political and civic engagement strategy, 226, 266
Conseil de réflection sur l'Islam en France (CORIF), 67
Conseil français du culte musulman (CFCM), 31, 67, 68–9, 183–4
Conservative Party, 155, 253
constitution, French, duty to abide by, 210
contraception, 70, 72
cooperation: political and civic engagement strategy, 226, 266
corporate agents: facilitation of political participation, 224, 266
Counter-Terrorism Act (2008), 259n3
Counter-Terrorism and Security Act (2015), 259n3
counter-terrorism: Muslim women's engagement, 153, 203, 252–3, 269, 270–1. *See also* Prevent programme (PVE); War on Terror
Coventry: focus group, 12, 13
creativity: Islam, 189
Crenshaw, Kimberle, 46n1
Crignon, Monique, 73
Croix, La, 100, 103, 104

cultural emergent properties (CEPs), 26, 27
cultural feminism, 42
cultural framework: awareness of contradictions and tensions, 214–15
cultural Islam, 184, 185, 195
cultural Muslims, 3, 180, 193, 195, 267
cultural traditions and Islam. *See* Islam, cultural traditions and
Cutts, D., 138

D
dance, 188, 190
Dans l'enfer des tournantes (Bellil), 254
data, availability of, 9
Dati, Rachida, 160n1
decentralisation: ethnic relations: Britain, 51–3
Défenseur des droits, 223
Delphy, Christine, 72, 73, 207
demand and supply: women and politics, 23–4
demonstrations: Muslim women, 130, 132, 217, 224
Deobandis, 37
detention periods: Britain, 57
difference, French attitudes to, 206
disasters, international: motivator for action, 219
discrimination, 80–1, 215, 223, 235, 262, 265
  Britain, 152, 197–9, 200–1; census, 86
  ethnic and racial: motivator for action, 216–17, 220
  France, 69–70, 84n16, 89–90, 117, 141, 204–11
  resurgence of Islam and, 215

divorce, 43, 176, 178
  right to, 43
domestic violence, 36, 171, 176, 177, 223, 265
  Britain, 77, 171–2, 176, 199, 200, 214, 216
  France, 205, 216, 223
Dot-Pouillard, Nicolas, 72
dress, Islamic, 231, 235, 236–50, 257, 258
  Britain, 77–80, 189
  choice *vs.* imposition, 237–9
  consequences of wearing, 246–50
  division, cause of, 245
  fashion, 245–6
  France, 33, 178, 215, 228, 254, 262, 263, 264, 265 (*see also* face veil: France; headscarf: France)
  Islam, not prescribed by, 244
  Muslim identity, 239–41
  opposition to from majority society, 246–50
  opposition to from Muslim women, 243–5
  political consciousness, 241, 243
  postcolonial literature, 258n1
  protection, 241–3
  retrograde, 243–5
  secular country, in, 246
  self-assertion, 243
Duret, P., 259n5
Duverger, Maurice, 28
Dwyer, C., 236

E
earnings: family's possession, 172, 186
Ebaugh, Rose, 38
École des hautes études en sciences sociales, 4
École pour tous et pour toutes, 224
ecumenicalism, 192

education
  arena of contestation: Britain, 54
  motivator for action, 216, 222, 223
  Muslim women, 216; Britain, 111–14, 182, 201; France, 114–17, 255
  parents' attitude to; Britain, 164–6, 202; France, 167
  women's right to: Qur'an, 185
Education Reform Act (1988), 38, 54
elections: Muslims: Britain, 55
electoral participation. *See* political participation; vote, right to; voting
Elele, 149
emergence, 25–26
emotional commitment to concerns and issues, 215–20, 265
employment, 43, 164, 178. *See also* labour market: Muslim women
  Britain, 170, 172, 173, 175, 198, 202
  France, 183, 248–9
  motivator for action, 222
  opportunities. *See* labour market: Muslim women; Britain, 91–2, 93, 105, 108–11, 114, 202; France, 93–4, 106–8, 115, 167, 204, 208, 209
empowerment: Islamic dress, 243
English Defence League (EDL), 58
environment: motivator for action, 223, 266
equality. *See also* gender inequality
  feminism, 31, 42–5, 69, 82, 155, 267
  France, 69–74, 67, 71, 73, 149, 205–6, 216–17, 227
  Islam, 40, 187, 193, 195, 196, 217, 267 (*see also* gender inequality, Islam); Britain, 55, 155, 181–2; France, 48, 179, 183
Equality Act (2010), 58, 83n4, 200

Equality and Human Rights
  Commission, 200
Equality Challenge Unit (ECU), 114
Equal Opportunities Commission
  (EOC), 105
essentialism, 28, 35
  Black feminism, 77
ethics: motivator for action, 219–20
ethnic groups, 30–1, 33–6, 98–100.
  See also community
  impact on women's participation in
    civic and political life, 163–4,
    193
ethnicity and religion, 30–1, 36–8
  young women, 40
ethnic question: census: Britain, 86–7,
  88, 93
ethno-religious communities, 30, 38,
  73, 177, 234, 269
Étude de l'histoire familiale (EHF), 101
European Monitoring Centre on
  Racism and Xenophobia
  (EUMC), 118n4
European Union (EU)
  funding programmes, 149
  migration to Britain: women, 97
excision, female: France, 187
exclusion: Muslim women: France,
  205–11
exit: political and civic engagement
  strategy, 226, 266
extended family: impact on women's
  participation in civic and political
  life, 263
  Britain, 173–6, 185, 194
  France, 178, 194
'external protection': ethnic groups, 163

F
Fabbiano, Giulia, 4
face veil, 235, 236, 246–7. *See also*
  dress, Islamic

Britain, 77–80, 84n23, 189, 235,
  263
France, 32, 65, 68, 81, 83n13,
  161n3, 183, 263
families: attitudes to Islamic dress,
  237, 243
family
  ambivalent role, 43
  impact on women's participation in
    civic and political life, 163,
    193–4, 222, 223, 224, 226, 263,
    265–6, 271; Britain, 164–6,
    170–2; France, 167–9, 172–3
family, extended: impact on women's
  participation in civic and political
  life
  Britain, 173–6, 185–6, 194
  France, 176–8
family responsibilities, 233, 271
  unemployment and, 110–11
fathers
  attitude to children's education:
    Britain, 165
  impact on women's participation in
    civic and political life: France,
    168–9
Fatima Women's Network, 153
Fawcett Society, 79, 105
Fédération des associations de
  solidarité avec les travailleurs
  immigrés (FASTI), 147
feminism
  Britain, 74–80
  community organisations; Britain,
    155; France, 156, 270
  conceptual approach, 23–5
  critiques of Islam, 179–80, 263
  France, 69–74
  Islamic (*see* Islamic feminism)
  legacy feminism, 71–2, 73
  Muslim women and, 82, 263, 267;
    Britain, 77–80, 263
  Western, 69–80, 82, 84n17, 156, 263

Femmes aujourd'hui, 156–7
Femmes françaises et musulmanes engagées (FFME), 144, 156–7
Femmes maghrébines en action, 149
Femmes marocaines de France, 147
Fête de l'Humanité, 133
Fieldhouse, E., 138
Figaro, Le, 206–7
focus groups, 11–15
  Britain, 11–14
  France, 14–15
Fonds d'aide et de soutien pour l'intégration et la lutte contre les discriminations (FASILD), 106, 149–50
food banks: Britain, 126
France and Britain: as comparative research locations, 7–9
French Muslim: self-definition, 206
French Revolution, 61
Front Islamique du Salut (FIS), 3, 64, 84n20, 179
Front National (FN), 59, 68, 88, 118n3, 140, 158, 270
fundamentalism, 38. *See also* radicalisation
  laïcité and, 210
  legacy feminist attitudes, 72
  opposition to, 41, 179–80, 183, 184, 196, 244
  public opinion: France, 65
funding, state: organisations
  Britain, 200
  France, 155, 269–70
fundraising events: Muslim women, 130

G
Galloway, George, 136, 137
Garcia, Alma, 43
Gaspard, F., 41

gender
  critique of Islam, 179–80, 193, 195
  Muslim population: statistics: France, 102–3
gender inequality, 31, 34–6, 39, 196. *See also* men; patriarchy
  Islam, 217–18, 232–3
  motivator for action, 216, 220
gender roles: Muslim feminist views, 43–4
gender segregation, 181–2, 183, 187
genital mutilation, 36
geographical distribution: Muslims
  Britain, 98–9
  France, 103–4
German, Lindsey, 79
ghettoisation, enforced: France, 67, 205–6, 215
Gilby, Nicholas, 113
Githens, M., 29
grands frères, les, 254–7, 259n5
Groupe d'études et de luttes contre les discriminations (GELD), 68
Groupe femmes algériennes, 147
Groupement de recherches, d'échanges et de communication, 106
Groupe d'information et de soutien aux travailleurs immigrés (GISTI), 147
Guardian, The, 137
Guénif-Souilamas, Nacira, 33, 207
Guru, Surinder, 250, 251

H
habitus, 213
Hall, Stuart, 57
harkis, 20n8, 94, 119n12
hate speech: Britain, 235, 252
Hattersley, Roy, 54
Haut Conseil à l'Intégration, 66

Haynes, J., 53–4
headscarf (*hijab*), 196, 235. *See also* dress, Islamic
  Britain, 179, 181, 188–9, 198, 199, 200, 201, 247
  discrimination linked to, 32; Britain, 199; France, 208–9
  France, 48, 64–5, 83n13, 84n19, 191, 192, 241, 247–50, 265 (*see also* schools: France: headscarf); community organisations, 227; community pressure, 177, 183; feminist views, 149, 157
higher education: France: headscarf, 208
hijab. *See* headscarf (*hijab*)
Hizb ut-Tahrir, 182
Hollande, François, 63, 64–5, 91, 130–1, 141
homosexuality, views on, 201
'honour', family, 34, 36, 39, 41, 42, 175, 232
  headscarf, 41
housing associations, 147, 162n10
humanism: Islam, 192–3, 268
human rights: motivator for action, 218–19, 253
Huntington, S., 38
husbands: impact on women's participation in civic and political life, 194
  Britain, 170–2, 173, 178, 185, 200
  France, 172–3, 178

I
identity, cultural
  Britain, 179
  France, 54, 85, 89
identity, national: France, 61–6, 264
identity, sense of, 26, 27, 40

Islam, 151, 192, 195, 239–41;
  Britain, 41, 49, 54–5, 179, 186, 201, 245; France, 73, 204
IFOP, 100, 103, 104
ijtihad, 38, 187, 189, 191, 196
Imkaan, 151
Immigration Act (1971), 82n1
immigration and nationality status: France. *See* nationality and immigration status: France
immigration policy: France, 58–60, 269
independence movements: women's participation, 6
Indigènes de la République, 73, 217
industrial disputes: feminists: Britain, 76
inequality, gender. *See* gender inequality
inequality, social: motivator for action, 219
Information Technology and Civil Liberties Act (1978), 88
in-laws: impact on women's participation in civic and political life, 171–3, 174, 185
Inspire, 153
Institut national de la statistique et des études économiques, L' (INSEE), 90, 101, 106, 119n13, 119n14, 143
Institut national d'études démographiques (INED), 90, 101, 143
integration
  France, 205–6
  relation to: Muslim women and social imaginary, 33
  'internal restrictions': ethnic groups, 163
international solidarity: organisations, 148

intersectionality, 46n1
IPSOS-MORI, 10, 65
Iranian and Kurdish Women's Rights Organisation (IKWRO), 150
Iraq: British intervention, 18, 32, 38, 55, 56–7, 218, 220, 228, 262
Islam
   cultural traditions and, 193, 195, 267–8; Britain, 184–6; France, 186–7
   driver of politics, 3
   exclusionary factor: France, 206–8
   feminisation of question: France, 64
   moral code, 189–90, 192–3, 196, 268
   motivator for action, 217–18, 268
   Muslim women's criticisms of interpretations: 179–81, 194–5, 214, 227, 235, 244, 267–8; Britain, 181–2, 184–6; France, 182–4, 186–7
   non-practising women, 3, 179–80, 193, 267
   private and public, 192, 196; Britain, 187–90; France, 190–3
   religious mobilisation: Britain, 38, 53–4
   resource for women, 40–5, 184–7, 189–93, 195–6, 267–8
   schools of, 178, 191–2
   universalism, 38, 40–1, 44, 189, 193, 268
   women's organisations, 151; Britain, 152–5; France, 155–9
   women's participation in civic and political life, impact on, 164, 178–96, 267–8, 269
   women's rights, 181–7
Islamic classes, 42
Islamic dress. *See* dress, Islamic
Islamic feminism, 42–5, 84n17, 235
   Britain, 82, 155
   France, 73–4, 180, 235, 270

Islamic organisations, male dominated, 153–4
Islamic Society of Britain (ISB), 153
Islamophobia, 33, 82, 133, 198, 213, 235, 271. *See also* prejudice, anti-Muslim
   Britain, 32, 38, 55, 57, 81, 199, 263, 264; Commission on British Muslims and Islamophobia, 57; electoral participation, impact on, 135–6; headscarf, 247, 249, 250; Jack Straw, 78; women's organisation, 57, 82, 152, 156, 270
   France, 64, 141, 207, 211, 270
Israel: treatment of Palestine, 218–19

J
Jacobson, J., 40
Jamaat-e-Islami, 37, 181
Jenkins, Roy, 50
Jepperson, R. L., 48, 59
Jeunes musulmanes sportives de France, 156
job offers: North Africans, 68
Joly, Danièle: research background, 4
Joxe, Pierre, 67

K
Kandiyoti, Deniz, 5
Keslassy, E., 83n9
Khattab, Nabil, 105, 111
Khokher, S., 41
Khosrokhavar, F., 41
Killian, C., 236
Kivisto, P., 30
Knott, K., 41
Knowles, C., 77
Kymlicka, W., 163

L

labour market: Muslim women. *See also* employment, opportunities
    Britain, 104–6, 108–11
    France, 105–8, 110, 111
Labour Party, 52, 56–7, 134, 135, 137–8, 202, 245, 253
laïcisme, 63
laïcité, 31, 48, 62–6, 81, 227, 228, 262, 264
    discrimination and, 209–11
    feminist attitudes, 71, 72–3, 74
    fundamentalism and, 210
    law (1905), 62, 66, 155, 210
    state funding of religious groups, 155
language: fluency, 112
learning: Islam, 191
Le Bourget Muslim fair, 133
Le Bras, Hervé, 88, 89, 90
Leeds: post-7/7 bombings, 251
legacy feminism, 71–2, 73
legal and structural framework: motivator for action, 223
legislation, 223, 262, 263, 264–5, 266, 268
    Britain, 49–51, 54, 200, 250 (*see also specific legislation*)
    France, 59–60, 64, 66, 68 (*see also specific legislation*)
Le Lohe, M. J., 134–5
Le Pen, Jean Marie, 158
liberalism, 32
liberty of conscience, 63, 66, 67
Ligue française de la femme musulmane (LFFM), 144, 156
Local Government Act (1966), 82n3
local government, community organisations and: Britain, 148, 223
Loi de securité quotidienne, 157
Loi informatique et libertés, 118n2

Loi pour la securité intérieure (2003), 158
London Development Agency (LDA), 105, 114

M

Macey, M., 35, 39
Maghrebis. *See also* Algerians
    education, 115
    employment, 107–8
    migration, 93–5
    political participation, 142, 149, 150
male, Muslim: standard model, 1
Marchbank, J., 233
Marche pour l'égalité et contre le racisme, 61, 224, 228
marginalisation: Muslim women, 1–2, 23, 35
Markazi Jamiat-al-e-Hadith, 37
marriage
    arranged, 36, 178, 227, 234; Britain, 166, 185–6, 187
    extended families, 174
    forced, 36, 195, 220, 234, 265; Britain, 132, 150–1, 166, 185–6; France, 149, 169, 177, 186–7
    France, 169, 194, 233
    pressure for early, 216
    temporary: Britain, 234 (*see also nikah*)
Marxism: rejection of Islam, 179, 193, 267
Maumoon, D., 42–3
McAndrew, M., 28
McDonald, L. Z., 251
media: hostility to Muslims, 57, 216
men. *See also* patriarchy
    ethnic interpretation of Islam, 184, 185, 186, 244

impact on women's participation in civic and political life, 213, 263, 268; Britain, 165–6, 170–1, 175, 181–2, 199; France, 168–9, 183
young: self-appointed moral guardians: France, 254–7, 271
Mercer, S., 77
migration: Muslims
  to Britain, 91–3, 95, 117–18; women and families, 92, 93, 95
  to France, 93–5, 117–18; women and families, 95
Ministère des Droits des femmes (MWR), 70–1, 149
minorités visibles, 83n9
Mirza, Heidi, 232
Mishra, S., 236
modesty, 36, 43, 175, 178, 188, 244, 254. See also dress, Islamic; headscarf
money: family's possession, 172, 185–6
moral code: Islam, 189–90, 192–3, 196, 268
moral panics, 57, 81
mosques, 37, 54, 67, 184
  women's involvement, 44, 217–18
mothers: impact on women's participation in civic and political life, 223, 224
  Britain, 165
  France, 167–8
mouvement beur, 148–9
Mouvement contre le racisme et pour l'amitié entre les peuples (MRAP), 147
Mouvement de libération des femmes (MLF), 69–72
Mouvement pour la liberté de l'avortement de la contraception (MLAC), 70

Mouvement pour le planning familial, 72
multiculturalism, 40, 44
  Britain, 7, 31, 34, 55, 118, 176, 262, 264; community, idealisation of, 35; establishment of policy, 50, 51, 52; face veil and, 78; feminism, 79; forms of political participation and civic engagement, 160; interpretations, 52; local authorities, 52; men as representatives, 36; opportunities for women, 201–2, 228; opposition to, 57–8; riots and, 55–6; stereotyping, 32
'Muslim'
  emergence as category, 47; Britain, 49, 53; France: variations in definition, 100
Muslim brotherhood: France, 37
Muslim Council of Britain (MCB), 56–7
Muslim feminism. *See* Islamic feminism
Muslim group: impact on women's participation in civic and political life, 163–4
Muslim Liaison Committee (Birmingham), 54
Muslim organisations: pressure over Islamic dress, 237–8
Muslims
  communalism: France, 62, 64, 81
  demographic profile; Britain, 95–100; France, 100–4
  migration; to Britain, 91–3, 95, 117–18; to France, 93–5, 117–18
  perceived as threat; Britain, 31–2, 55–6, 57–8; France, 31–2, 62, 64–6, 67–8

Muslim Teachers' Association, 152
Muslim women
  between cultures, 240, 256
  demographic profile, 104–18;
    Britain, 95–6, 97–8, 99–100
  disregarded, 1–2, 23
  feminism and (*see* feminism, Muslim women and; Islamic feminism)
  stereotyping, 105, 198
Muslim Women's Advisory Council, 153
Muslim Women's Association, 153
Muslim Women's Council, 153
Muslim Women's Network, 153, 155
Muslim Women's Sports Foundation, 153

N
Nain, Gemma Tang, 43
nanas beurs, Les, 149, 150
national identity, *laïcité* and, 65–6
Nationality and Commonwealth Act (1948), 49
nationality and immigration status
  Britain, 37, 47, 49, 59, 119n8
  France, 19–20n7, 47, 59, 140, 141, 269; headscarf, 249–50
Nationality Code (France), 59–60
National Muslim Women's Advisory Group (NMWAG), 251, 252
Ndimbeul, 156
Nelson, B., 4
neo-liberalism, 7, 55
  Britain, 51
  rejection of, 219, 220
  religion and, 53
neo-republican feminism, 72–3
New Commonwealth immigrants: rights, 49, 130
New Commonwealth immigration, 50, 82n3, 91, 92, 119n7
  census, 86

NGOs, 224. *See also* specific organisations
nikah, 234
Ni putes ni soumises, 72, 150, 205, 254
niqab. *See* face veil
Norris, Pippa, 126
North African Islam: France, 37
North Africans: job offers, 68
nuclear family, preference for, 194

O
Observatoire de la laïcité, 65
Observatoire des discriminations, 68
Office for National Statistics (ONS), 87
Office National d'Immigration (ONI), 58–9, 93
Okin, S. Moller, 174
Open Society Foundation, 142–3, 236
organisation, collective. *See also* community organisations: Muslim women
  immigrants; Britain, 49; France, 60–1, 269
  Muslims; Britain, 53–5; France: women: voting, 144
Organisation of Women of African and Asian Descent (OWAAD), 147
orientalism
  laïcité, 211
  stereotyping of Muslim women, 207
Otherness, 61, 81, 262

P
Pakistan: human rights issues, 219
Pakistani Forum, 32
Pakistanis
  demographics, 95–6, 98, 119n9
  education, 32, 112

employment, 108, 114
migration to Britain, 91–2
political participation, 135, 161n6
Pakistan Welfare Association, 147
Palestine, 24, 151, 157, 218–9
parents: impact on women's participation in civic and political life, 194, 223, 269
Britain, 164–6, 173, 174
France, 167–9
Paris
attacks (2015), 1, 19n1, 64, 68, 157, 231
focus groups, 14
parole aux négresses, La (Thiam), 70
Pasqua, Charles, 59
Patel, P., 175, 199
patriarchy, 34–5, 39, 75, 163, 213, 214, 269, 271. *See also* gender inequality; men
class and, 39
cultural Islam, 184, 186
dress, 79, 183, 244
ethnic groups, 163
family, 42, 263
Islamic tools against, 42, 184, 187, 195
stereotyping, 32
Penny, Laurie, 79
people emergent properties (PEPs), 26, 27
petits caïds, 255, 259n5
Pidd, Helen, 137
Poli, Alexandra, 4
police
France: aggression, 158
Britain: harassment, 51, 250, 251–2
political and civic engagement: strategies, 225–7, 229, 266
political consciousness: Islamic dress, 241–3
political institutions

ethnic minority under-representation: France, 60–1, 68
Muslim under-representation: Britain, 55
political Islam, 37–8, 184, 217
political Muslims, 191, 193, 267
political participation. *See also* civic engagement; voting
definition, 4
feminist studies, 125
Muslim women, 127–45, 201–3, 212–29, 235, 252–4, 268–71; cultural politics, 132–3; digital politics, 132, 133; literature, 123–4; political parties, 130–1, 202, 205, 222, 224, 226, 269; typology, 129–33
women, 29–30
political struggles: women's histories, 24–5
politics
Muslim women's knowledge and interest, 128–9
women's participation: marginalisation, 23–5, 29, 44
Pollock, D., 258n2
polygamy: France, 67, 168–9, 186, 187
polygyny, 234
post-colonial women's organisations, 147
poverty: motivator for action, 219
Powell, Enoch, 134–5
power, unequal relations of, 28, 34, 45
gender, 31, 34–6, 39, 44, 45
prejudice, anti-Muslim, 38, 215, 216, 262, 263–4. *See also* discrimination; Islamophobia
Britain, 32–3, 57–8, 81, 198–9, 203, 228, 252–3
France, 33, 67, 201, 204, 206, 208, 209
Présence Musulmane, 156–7

Prevention of Terrorism Act (2005), 57, 258–9n3
Prevent programme (PVE), 18, 56, 77, 80, 154–5, 250, 251, 252, 253–4
  cuts, 58, 162n12
private and public space
  headscarf ban, 208–9, 248–9
  laïcité, 210, 211
  violence and control, 258
'private Muslims', 210–11, 267
Prochoix, 72
property entitlement, 43
protest, 125, 224
  Britain, 38, 54, 202–3, 218, 220, 228
  France, 61, 143–4
public and private space. *See* private and public space
public opinion: Islam: France, 65
public service work: headscarf: France, 208
public spaces: law against concealment of face, 7, 32, 65, 68, 77, 84n14, 208–9, 226

Q
Qur'an, 182, 186, 190
  dress, 239, 244
  ecology, 190
  gender, 42, 155, 183, 185, 186–7, 235
  reformist movements, 37
  social justice and equality, 155
  suicide and terrorism, opposition to, 180–1

R
Race Relations Act (RRA, 1976), 50, 51, 83n4, 200
race relations: Britain: history, 50–5. *See also* Islamophobia; prejudice, anti-Muslim: Britain

racial harassment: police: Britain, 51, 250, 251–2
racism, 80–1, 82, 262, 271. *See also* anti-racism
  Britain, 82n2, 252; census, 86
  feminism; Britain, 75, 82; France, 69–74, 82, 269–70
  France, 68, 211; lack of legislation, 60
  against Muslims, 31–2, 42, 235
  sexism and: France, 149
radicalisation, 44, 67, 154, 235, 250, 255. *See also* fundamentalism; Prevent programme (PVE)
Ramadan, Tariq, 156–7
rape, gang: France, 254
Rashid, N., 251
realist sociology, 4, 25–6
reformist movements, Islamic, 37–8, 181, 193, 195, 267–8
refugees: political participation, 6
refuges: abused women: Britain, 148, 216
religion. *See also* Islam
  British and French attitudes, 8–9
  criterion of discrimination, 50
  ethnicity and (*see* ethnicity and religion)
  migration and, 36–8
  state and, 31–2
religiosity, increased: France, 256–7
religious affiliation: statistics, 104
  Britain, 86–8, 93, 105, 119n9
  France, 100–1, 102–3
Religious Affiliation Sub-Group (RAG), 87–8
religious symbols in schools, law against. *See* schools, France: headscarf
Republican Party (France), 119n6
republican universalism: France, 7, 131, 150
research
  aims and scope, 5–9
  methodology, 9–15

Réseau Education Sans Frontières, 217
residence, length of: impact on women's participation in civic and political life, 194
residence permit, ten-year: France, 61
Respect Party, 136, 202, 245
Restos du Coeur, 209
reversal: political and civic engagement strategy, 227, 266
Rex, J., 34
Richard, J-L., 140, 141–2
rights: Muslims: Britain and France, 47, 262
riots
   Britain, 51, 55–6, 82n2, 135–6, 138, 148, 162n11; Bradford (2001), 35
   France (2005), 67–9, 89–90, 141, 158
Rochdale: by-election (1972), 135
role models: motivators for action, 224–5, 266
Roy, O., 63, 66
Rushdie, Salman, 38, 54

S
Safra Project, 153
Sahel, immigrants from: education, 115
Sarkozy, Nicolas, 61, 89–90, 130–1, 143–4, 145, 206
Satanic Verses (Rushdie), 38, 55, 56
Saudi Arabia: human rights issues, 219
Scarman enquiry, 148
Schlozman, K., 126
schools
   Britain; citizenship classes, 253; headscarves, 239, 241, 247; Pakistani girls, 32
   France: headscarf, 7, 32, 63, 64, 65, 77, 208–11, 246, 248, 249; feminist positions, 71–4, 149, 262; opposition to law, 38, 157, 211, 220, 243, 248
Sebag, Yadiz, 90
secularised Muslims, 3, 159, 189, 190, 193
secularism
   Britain, 202
   France (*see laïcité*)
self-identification: Muslims: community organisations, 52
sexes, mixing of, 43
sexism
   racism and: France, 149
   women's organisations: France, 158
sexual difference: women's organisations, 153
sexuality and sexual behaviour: Muslim women: France, 207–8
sexual objectification: Islamic dress, 241–3
sexual temptation, 182
Shadow lives (Brittain), 250–1
Shi'a/Sunni division, 37
Shirazi, F., 236
skin colour: discrimination: Britain, 197–8
Smith, Joan, 78–9
social action, theory of, 11, 26–7
   Muslim women, 27–8, 45–6
social cohesion, promotion of: Britain, 56, 83n6, 200. *See also* Prevent programme (PVE)
Socialist Party (France), 72, 131
social services: France, 204–5
'societal model': collective authority: Britain, 48
society
   majority; France, Muslim women's views on, 204–11; support for Muslim women, 212–25
   organisation of: Jepperson's typology, 48

socio-economic status: Muslim
  women, 261, 270
  Britain, 105, 108–11
  France, 105–8, 110, 111
Sociological Intervention (SI), 4, 11,
  14–15, 26–7
solidarity
  ethnic group, 34
  feminism, 61, 79, 80
  international, 148, 150
  Islam, 44, 240–1
  against neoliberalism and
    individualism, 219, 220
Southall Black Sisters, 76, 147, 200
South Asians: Britain, 37, 83n6
  education, 113
  employment, 108–9, 120n16
  migration to, 37, 91, 119n8
  political participation, 135, 136,
    138
  women: industrial disputes, 76
Southwark Muslim Women's
  Association, 148
Spare Rib, 75–6, 77
sports projects, 152–3
Stasi Commission, 64–6
state and religion, 31. *See also* church
  and state; *laïcité*
statistics, ethnic: France, 9, 88–91,
  118n4–19n6
  Muslims, 100–8, 110, 111
'statist model': collective authority:
  France, 48
stereotyping of Muslims, 31
  women, 5, 32, 212, 213, 264–5;
    Britain, 32, 105, 198, 203,
    228, 241; France, 206, 207
Stop the War, 57, 130, 218, 224
strategies: political and civic
  engagement, 225–7, 229, 266
Straw, Jack, 78

street politics: Muslim women, 130,
  224, 269
strikes
  Britain, 50, 76, 130
  France, 62, 130, 143–4, 269
structural emergent properties (SEPs),
  26, 27
structural framework: awareness of
  contradictions and tensions,
  213–15, 265
structure and agency, 26
students
  mediation service for Muslim, 253
  peer pressure over Islamic dress,
    237–8
  stereotyping Muslim women, 198–9
subjectivation, 27
Sudbury, J., 175, 199
Sufism, 37, 192, 211, 267
suicide, 180–1
Sunni/Shi'a division, 37
supply and demand: women and
  politics, 23–4

T
taboos, religion and, 256
Taliban: girls' education, 182
Tariqas, 191
Tax Payers' Alliance, 155
television channels, Muslim, 188
terrorism, 31–2, 180–1, 194–5, 203,
  218. *See also* counter-terrorism
  Britain, 47–8, 57–8, 81, 228, 250–4
    (*see also* Prevent programme
    (PVE); War on Terror)
  family members, 6, 250–1
  France, 47, 48, 64, 81, 207, 231
    (*see also* Paris: attacks (2015))
  Islamic dress, 78, 79, 207, 240–1,
    247

Terrorism Act (2000), 258–9n3
Terrorism Act (2001), 58
Terrorism Act (2006), 57, 258–9n3
Terrorism Prevention and Investigation Measures (TPIMs), 250, 259n4
Thatcher, Margaret, 51
Thiam, Awa, 70
'third culture', 240, 258n2
Tiberj, V., 142
Tietze, N., 41
Time Bank programme, 149–50
Tomlinson, S., 34
Touraine, Alain, 4, 11, 26–8
trade unions, 147, 223, 224, 226, 266
  recognition: Britain, 50
Trajectoire et origines géographiques (TeO), 90, 101–3, 104, 143
Tribalat, Michèle, 88–9, 100, 101, 102, 118n3, 143
Turks
  education, 116
  employment, 107, 111
  political participation, 143, 149

U
Ulfah Arts, 153
'underclass,' Muslims as, 49
unemployment
  ethnic minorities, 104
  Britain; immigrant women, 108–11; Muslims, 35, 114; Pakistani and Bangladeshi graduates, 114; women, 105
  France; immigrant women, 106–8
Union des Organisations Islamiques de France, 145, 183
Union of Muslim Organisations, 88
Union pour un Mouvement Populaire (UMP), 67, 131

universalism
  Islam, 38, 40–1, 44, 189, 193, 268
  women, 40–1, 44, 160, 219
universities: Muslim students: Britain, 113

V
Vallaud-Belkacem, Najat, 130–1, 160–1n1
Van Bergen, D., 175
Van Reken, R., 258n2
veil, full face. *See* headscarf
Verba, S., 126
violence
  domestic (*see* domestic violence)
  against women, 180; Britain, 39; France, 254–7, 258, 271; organisations opposing, 149, 150
Voix de femmes, 150
Voix d'elles rebelles, 144, 150, 204
voluntary organisations, 125, 126, 146, 159, 209, 269
vote, right to: France, 59, 61, 134, 140–1, 142–3, 144–5
voting
  immigrants: Britain, 52
  Muslims, 56–7; Britain, 83n7, 134–6, 161n6; France, 139–40, 141–5
  Muslim women, 127, 129, 159–60, 212, 269; Britain, 129–30, 136–9, 182; France, 129–30, 140, 142, 143–5
  un-Islamic, 138–9
  young people, 144; Britain, 136, 137, 138; France, 141–2, 143–4
VPF residence card, 94–5

W

Wadia, Khursheed, 29
  research background, 4
Wahhabism, 183, 245
War on Terror. *See also* counter-terrorism: Muslim women's engagement
  Britain, 18, 57, 77, 81, 218, 235, 250–4, 257–8, 264, 270 (*see also* Prevent programme (PVE); terrorism); electoral participation, 135–6; feminists, 80; Otherness, 262
  France, 64, 231
Waylen, G., 29
welfare state, undermining of: Britain, 51, 219
Weltrationalitat, 213
West, demonisation of the, 182, 190
White feminism, 75–7, 79–80, 82, 84n22
Wieviorka, M., 11, 27
Willaime, J.-P., 63
Wilson, Amrit, 76
Wingz, 153
women from Muslim communities: definition, 2–3, 19n3

women's liberation movement (WLM):
  Britain, 74–7, 78, 82. *See also* feminism
women's organisations, Islamic. *See* Islam, women's organisations
women's resource centres, Asian:
  Britain, 148, 151
women's rights
  Islam, 181–6
  organisations, 146–59

Y

Yade, Rama, 130–1, 160–1n1
Yang, Helen, 38
Yaqoob, Salma, 137–8, 224
Yuval-Davis, N., 32, 35

Z

Zempi, I., 246, 247
Zerouala, F., 236, 240, 243
Zia, A. S., 44
Zubaida, S., 40–1, 42, 43, 44
Zukin, C., 125

The manufacturer's authorised representative in the EU is Springer Nature Customer Service Centre GmbH, Europaplatz 3, 69115 Heidelberg, Germany. If you have any concerns regarding our products, please contact ProductSafety@springernature.com

Printed and bound by CPI Group (UK) Ltd, Croydon, CR0 4YY

23/03/2026

02076662-0012